THE OXFORD SHAKESPEARE

General Editor · Stanley Wells

The Oxford Shakespeare offers new and authoritative editions of Shakespeare's plays in which the early printings have been scrupulously re-examined and interpreted. An introductory essay provides all relevant background information together with an appraisal of critical views and of the play's effects in performance. The detailed commentaries pay particular attention to language and staging. Reprints of sources, music for songs, genealogical tables, maps, etc. are included where necessary; many of the volumes are illustrated, and all contain an index.

T. W. CRAIK, the editor of *The Merry Wives of Windsor* in the Oxford Shakespeare, is Emeritus Professor of English in the University of Durham. He is the author of *The Tudor Interlude*, has edited plays by Marlowe and Massinger for The New Mermaids, a selection of Elizabethan tragedies for Everyman's Library, and Beaumont and Fletcher's *Maid's Tragedy* for The Revels Plays, and was joint editor of *Twelfth Night* for The Arden Shakespeare.

THE OXFORD SHAKESPEARE

Currently available in paperback

The rest of the plays are forthcoming

OXFORD WORLD'S CLASSICS

WILLIAM SHAKESPEARE

The Merry Wives of Windsor

Edited by
T. W. CRAIK

OXFORD
UNIVERSITY PRESS

OXFORD
UNIVERSITY PRESS

Great Clarendon Street, Oxford OX2 6DP

Oxford University Press is a department of the University of Oxford.
It furthers the University's objective of excellence in research, scholarship,
and education by publishing worldwide in

Oxford New York

Athens Auckland Bangkok Bogotá Buenos Aires Calcutta
Cape Town Chennai Dar es Salaam Delhi Florence Hong Kong Istanbul
Karachi Kuala Lumpur Madrid Melbourne Mexico City Mumbai
Nairobi Paris São Paulo Singapore Taipei Tokyo Toronto Warsaw

with associated companies in Berlin Ibadan

Oxford is a registered trade mark of Oxford University Press
in the UK and in certain other countries

First published 1990 as an Oxford University Press paperback
and simultaneously in a hardback edition
First published as a World's Classics paperback 1994
Reissued as an Oxford World's Classics paperback 1998
Reissued 2008

British Library Cataloguing in Publication Data

Data available

Library of Congress Cataloging in Publication Data

Shakespeare, William, 1564–1616.
The merry wives of Windsor / edited by T. W. Craik.
(Oxford World's classics)
Includes index.
I. Craik, T. W. (Thomas Wallace). II. Title. III. Series:
Shakespeare, William, 1564–1616. Works. 1982.
PR2826.A2C7   1989   822.3'3—dc19   88-29363

ISBN 978–0–19–953682–5

6

Printed in Great Britain by
Clays Ltd, St Ives plc

PREFACE

I AM grateful to Stanley Wells for his careful scrutiny of this edition in draft form, and for his acute and constructive criticism of it. I thank too his colleagues Gary Taylor and John Jowett for letting me see unpublished material of theirs. My debt to previous editors and commentators, whether or not I have agreed with their views, will be evident. The University of Durham granted me a term's study leave in order to complete the edition.

T. W. CRAIK

CONTENTS

LIST OF ILLUSTRATIONS

INTRODUCTION

Shakespeare's Garter Play: The Occasion and the Date of The Merry Wives of Windsor

TOPICAL allusion has been sought in many places in Shakespeare's plays, but the seekers' findings have generally met with a sceptical reception. Some indisputable topical allusions there are, notably the hope in the Chorus to Act Five of *Henry V* that Essex may return in triumph from his campaign in Ireland (5.0.29–34); and it is widely agreed that the lines in *Macbeth* (4.3.141–60) celebrating Edward the Confessor's power of curing scrofula by his touch, though their substance is found in Holinshed and though they are appropriate in their context, are a compliment to James I, who likewise touched sufferers from the 'king's evil'.[1] In the final scene of *The Merry Wives of Windsor* there occurs (in the Folio of 1623) a passage more directly complimentary to the monarch than the lines in *Macbeth* and as specific, in its allusions to the royal seat of Windsor Castle and to the Order of the Garter, as the Essex passage in *Henry V*:

> About, about!
> Search Windsor Castle, elves, within and out.
> Strew good luck, oafs, on every sacred room,
> That it may stand till the perpetual doom
> In state as wholesome as in state 'tis fit,
> Worthy the owner and the owner it.
> The several chairs of order look you scour
> With juice of balm and every precious flower.
> Each fair instalment, coat, and several crest,
> With loyal blazon, evermore be blest!
> And nightly meadow-fairies, look you sing,
> Like to the Garter's compass, in a ring.
> Th'expressure that it bears, green let it be,
> More fertile-fresh than all the field to see;
> And *Honi soit qui mal y pense* write
> In em'rald tufts, flowers purple, blue, and white,
> Like sapphire, pearl, and rich embroidery,
> Buckled below fair knighthood's bending knee.
> Fairies use flowers for their charactery.

[1] See, e.g., the note by K. Muir (ed.), *Macbeth* (The Arden Shakespeare, 1951).

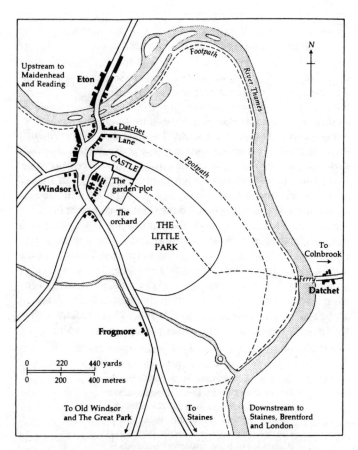

1. Sketch-map of Windsor and district (after Irving/Marshall; based on Christopher Saxton's map of Berkshire (1576) and John Norden's map of Windsor Castle and environs (1607), both reproduced in Green)

A feature of this passage is its superfluousness to the dramatic situation, in which Falstaff's third assignation with Mistress Ford (and, as it happens, with Mistress Page too) is interrupted by a troop of pretended fairies in Windsor Park, who proceed to pinch him for his lechery. All that is required are some lines to bring the fairies in and to explain their presence at Herne's Oak, the place of the assignation, and these are provided in the earlier speeches of the Fairy Queen, Hobgoblin, and Sir Hugh Evans, and in the Fairy

Queen's three lines that immediately follow the quoted ones. The complimentary passage is usually omitted when the play is performed, and there is not a trace of it in the first published text of the play, the 'bad' Quarto of 1602, where some obviously non-Shakespearian lines about brokers and serjeants replace it. Everything points to its having been intended to stand out from its context, to draw attention to itself, as a topical compliment.

The natural inference is that the occasion on which *The Merry Wives of Windsor* was first performed was in some way connected with the Order of the Garter. This inference was drawn in 1790 by Edmond Malone, but it was not until 1931 that Leslie Hotson produced good reasons for connecting the play with a particular occasion, the Garter Feast of 23 April 1597.[1]

One of the five newly elected Knights of the Order of the Garter on that occasion was George Carey, second Baron Hunsdon. In July 1596, at the age of 49, he had succeeded his father Henry Carey both as Baron Hunsdon and as the patron of the company of players to which Shakespeare belonged and which was called the Lord Chamberlain's Men, the first Baron Hunsdon having been appointed Lord Chamberlain of the Household in 1583. On Henry Carey's death the office of Lord Chamberlain passed briefly to William Brooke, Baron Cobham, who himself died on the night of 5–6 March 1597. On 17 April George Carey was appointed Lord Chamberlain, an office which court rumour had predicted for him since mid-February.[2] He had been nominated for election to the Order of the Garter every year from 1593 to 1596; there had been no elections made in the three years 1594–6, but Elizabeth I had promised that there would be elections in 1597; his recently deceased father had himself been a Knight of the Garter (and had nominated his son in 1594). All these factors virtually ensured that he would be elected in 1597, especially as he was one of the Queen's favourite cousins. If he is assumed to have been aware in February 1597 that he was likely to become the next Lord Chamberlain and also to receive the Garter, he would have enough time to commission an appropriate play from Shakespeare, to be performed on St George's Day, 23 April, at the Garter Feast, probably in the evening after supper, as his special contribution to the festivities.

---

[1] Hotson, pp. 111–22. For full references for works cited repeatedly in the Commentary and Introduction, see pp. 68–72.

[2] Green, pp. 58–9. The information in this and the following paragraph is from Green.

The Garter Feast was held annually, whether there were to be any elections or not, and occupied three days, the first being the day of arrival and the third the day of departure. It was customarily held at one of the royal palaces in the London area; in 1597 it was held at Whitehall Palace in Westminster. If there were any elections, the new Knights of the Order were installed at St George's Chapel, Windsor, in the following month (on 24 May in 1597). The Queen, however, had discontinued her presence at installations since 1567, and appointed special commissioners to conduct them. Extant documents show that only seven Knights of the Garter attended the 1597 installation at Windsor, the three commissioners and the four newly elected Knights who were being installed in person. In contrast, all twenty-four Knights of the Order (in addition to the Sovereign) were expected to attend the Garter Feast, and only under special circumstances could they be excused. A first performance of *The Merry Wives of Windsor* at the installation can therefore be ruled out, and so can a first performance between the Garter Feast and the installation, for immediately after the Feast the Knights were free to disperse.

The inference that the first performance was at the Garter Feast is supported by the fact that, in the lines previously quoted, the fairies are ordered to clean and perfume 'the several chairs of order'; this implies that the installation is still to come. The title-page of the Quarto, which carries the words 'As it hath bene diuers times Acted by the right Honorable my Lord Chamberlaines seruants. Both before her Maiestie, and else-where', provides further support. So also, though of a flimsier kind, does the tradition that the play was written at the Queen's command. This tradition is first found in John Dennis's dedication of his adaptation of the play, under the title *The Comical Gallant*, in 1702, where he states that she 'commanded it to be finished in fourteen days; and was afterwards, as tradition tells us, very well pleased at the representation'.[1] In 1709 Nicholas Rowe mentions the royal command but not the fourteen days; he adds the information that the Queen 'was so well pleased with that admirable character of *Falstaff*, in the two parts of *Henry the Fourth*, that she commanded him to continue it for one play more, and to shew

---

[1] John Dennis, *The Comical Gallant* (1702), A2. In the prologue he repeats that 'Shakespeare's Play in fourteen days was writ', but in a letter he says that Shakespeare wrote it 'in ten days' (John Dennis, *Original Letters*, 1721, ii. 232).

him in love'.[1] Rowe's version looks like invention superimposed on Dennis's version in order to provide the Queen with a motive for her command, for if that motive had been part of a tradition that reached Dennis it is unlikely that he would have omitted it. Dennis's own version too may be invention, though not necessarily his own; if he got the story from Dryden, who may have got it from Davenant,[2] either of them may have invented it. Whether or not the statement on the Quarto's title-page was known to whoever started the tradition of the royal command, the evident compliment about Windsor Castle ('Worthy the owner and the owner it') would have been enough to give a lead to speculation. Therefore, though we are not compelled to reject the tradition, either in its separate forms or in its conflated one, we are by no means compelled to accept it as a true account of the play's origin. Those who do accept it can easily accommodate it to the strong probability that it was Hunsdon who commissioned the play.[3]

One other topical aspect of the play requires mention. At the Garter Feast of 1597 a German nobleman, Frederick, Duke of Württemberg, was elected Knight of the Garter *in absentia*. This was the culmination of a series of requests by him beginning in August 1592, when, as Count Mömpelgard, he visited England for a month. His persistence, especially shown in March 1595 when he sent an envoy to London to remind the Queen of her alleged promise of the Garter and to lobby important noblemen on his behalf, had made him notorious. In 1596 he was nominated for election, but no elections took place. His election in 1597, however, was firmly expected, especially as England's trading relations with the German lands were deteriorating (by January 1598 merchants from the Hanse towns were ejected from England by royal proclamation), and it was in England's interest to secure the friendship of as many German princes as possible. Accordingly there is every reason to connect his election *in absentia* with the references, in the episode involving the stealing of the Host's horses, to three Germans and to a German

[1] Rowe, i, pp. viii–ix.

[2] This was suggested by Malone, i/2. 190 n.

[3] His players acted at court on 26 and 27 Dec. 1596, 1 and 6 Jan. 1597, and 6 and 8 Feb. 1597 (Chambers, *Elizabethan Stage*, iv. 165). They may have performed *1 Henry IV*, and the Queen may thereupon have told Hunsdon that she would like to see a comedy devoted to Falstaff.

duke who is alleged to be coming to the English court. The puzzled Host asks Bardolph, or asks himself, 'What duke should that be comes so secretly? I hear not of him in the court', and, after the stealing of the horses, Caius announces to him, 'it is tell-a me dat you make grand preparation for a duke de Jarmany. By my trot', dere is no duke that the court is know to come.' These look like topical references to the Duke of Württemberg's election, introduced to amuse the original audience as well as to provide a plausible context for the revengeful trick played by Evans and Caius on the Host for having made them look foolish at their abortive duel.[1] But there is no reason to suggest that the horse-stealing episode reflects any scandalous conduct on the part of the Duke or his followers, or to relate it to an incident in 1596 when the visiting Governor of Dieppe was involved in a quarrel at Gravesend for allegedly commandeering two horses belonging to inn-guests as substitutes for post-horses, or to seek in the Host's self-reassuring phrase 'Germans are honest men' an allusion either to the current trade-dispute or to the activities of a Württemberg cloth-merchant called Stamler, who in 1595 had pretended to be acting on the Duke's behalf in purchasing cloth and thereby tried to export it from England without paying export duty.[2]

Besides these convincingly topical allusions—to the forthcoming installation ceremony of the Garter at Windsor Castle and to the election of the absent German Duke—other more doubtful allusions have been sought, sometimes, though not always, in an attempt to show that there is personal satire in the play. The dozen white luces in the family coat of arms of which Shallow boasts in the opening scene have long been associated with the three silver luces (pike) in the coat of arms of the Lucy family, and also, since the early eighteenth century, with the tradition that Shakespeare was forced to leave Stratford for London because he had stolen deer from a park owned by Sir Thomas Lucy of Charlecote nearby.[3] This tradition seems to be an invented one,

---

[1] The Quarto's curious phrase 'three sorts of cosen garmombles', corresponding to Evans's 'three Cozen-Iermans' in the Folio, may have been derived from the Duke's other title, Count Mömpelgard. See Commentary, 4.5.72.

[2] These theories, and their originators' arguments, are reviewed in more detail by Bullough, ii. 11–16, Green, pp. 121–76, Oliver, pp. xlvi–xlix, and Roberts, pp. 10–11, 13, 27–30, 37–8.

[3] The tradition is independently recorded by Richard Davies before 1708 and by Rowe 1709. Their slightly differing accounts are reprinted by Oliver, pp. l–li.

2. The arms of the Lucy family: *Gules, semée of cross crosslets or, three luces haurient argent* (On a red field strewn with golden crosses each having a gold cross-piece through each arm, three silver pike placed perpendicularly)

for Sir Thomas Lucy, who died in 1600, had no park in Warwickshire, only a rabbit-warren.[1] Like the story of the Queen's command it may have originated in the play itself, where Shallow accuses Falstaff of killing his deer. Admittedly nothing more is said about either the luces or the deer-killing after the first scene, a fact which can be interpreted as showing that a couple of satirical allusions have been dragged in. On the other hand one can argue that Falstaff's deer-killing is just a convenient way of introducing Shallow (and hence Slender, Anne Page's ridiculous suitor) into the play, and that Shallow's luces are just a convenient way of exhibiting Evans's unconscious humour. On balance it seems unlikely that Shakespeare is indulging in either revengeful or capricious mockery of Sir Thomas Lucy in particular or of the Lucy family in general. This is not to suggest that he would be unaware of the Lucy arms: on the contrary, Shallow's white luces can hardly have had any other origin. But the luce/louse joke looks like a schoolboy's pun, which Shakespeare may have remembered from his schooldays in Stratford, where the Lucy arms would be a familiar sight, and which he introduced into this play for a purely comic purpose.

The silver luces of the Lucy arms also figure in Leslie Hotson's argument that Shallow is a satire upon William Gardiner, one of the justices of the peace in Surrey, who lived at Bermondsey near Southwark and died in November 1597 aged 66, and that Slender is a satire upon Gardiner's stepson William Wayte.

[1] Mark Eccles, *Shakespeare in Warwickshire* (Madison, Wis., 1961), p. 73.

During Michaelmas term 1596 (October/November) writs were taken out, first by Francis Langley, the owner of the Swan theatre, against Gardiner and Wayte, and then by Wayte against Shakespeare, Langley, and Dorothy Soer and Anne Lee (neither of whom has been identified). These writs obliged the parties complained of to swear to keep the peace on pain of forfeiting a specified sum of money. At the same time Gardiner had pending three lawsuits against Langley for slandering him with perjury, to which Langley replied with the defence of justification; these suits were never brought to trial. Hotson further discovered that in a suit of 1591 (not involving the other parties to the 1596 dispute) Gardiner was described as 'a justice of the peace' and Wayte as 'a certain loose person of no reckoning or value, being wholly under the rule and commandment of the said Gardiner'. Gardiner's coat of arms was a griffin passant, but by his first marriage to the widow Frances Wayte, whose maiden name was Frances Lucy, he was entitled to bear the Lucy arms side by side with his own. Hotson's discoveries are of great interest (particularly in their suggestion that in 1596 Shakespeare may have been living near the Swan and his company may have been performing there), but his conclusions that the unimportant Wayte is portrayed as Slender and the powerful and acquisitive Gardiner is portrayed as Shallow do not carry conviction. That Gardiner was a justice, and so was Shallow, and that he owned a park, and so did Shallow, is no proof of identity or even of 'sympathy';[1] that in common with all the other justices of Surrey and Middlesex he received instructions from the Privy Council (in July 1597, later than the date that Hotson assigns to the play) to close down the playhouses in and around London does not make him an enemy of the theatre and therefore marked down for theatrical satire; and that he seems to have been both litigious and rapacious makes him more like Massinger's Sir Giles Overreach than Shakespeare's Gloucestershire justice.[2]

---

[1] See 2.1.7–9. Oliver (p. l) calls Gardiner's park, acquired in 1592, 'a deer park', but Hotson (pp. 97–9) does not.

[2] Hotson makes two other points. In 1556 Gardiner was fined 3s. 4d. for making an affray and drawing blood on one William Beeston; this Hotson compares to Shallow's boast of 'monstrous skill in old-time sword-play' (p. 96). Shallow's part in urging Slender's courtship, and Slender's remark that heaven may decrease the married couple's love for each other, are related by Hotson to Wayte's first marriage. Gardiner's opponent in the lawsuit of 1591 alleged that he

A quite different topical aspect, sympathetic and not satirical, is proposed by G. R. Hibbard, who finds the Anne Page story paralleled in the impoverished young nobleman Lord Compton's marriage to the daughter of the rich city alderman Sir John Spencer, who rejected another of his daughter's suitors, the elderly alderman Anthony Ratcliffe, and approved a third, the son of Sir Arthur Heningham. Despite Spencer's opposition the marriage took place in April 1599, not before the father had been committed to prison for contempt of court and concealing his daughter, and had had her removed from his custody for beating and ill-treating her; rumour had it that Compton stole her away in a basket after disguising himself as a baker's boy. The vivid details of this story, however, both the factual and the rumoured ones, work against Hibbard's claim that Shakespeare based his plot upon it, with Caius in Ratcliffe's role and Slender in young Heningham's: the only mildly interesting resemblance between the real-life story and the play is the social and economic one, for three suitors (one of them old) are a typical ingredient of intrigue comedy, as in *The Taming of the Shrew*, and many a person is smuggled away in a container in popular comic tales. This is not strong enough to base an argument on.[1]

Two attempts have been made to connect the occasion of *The Merry Wives of Windsor* with the Cobham family, one member of which, William Brooke, seventh Baron Cobham, has been mentioned as being Lord Chamberlain between the first and second Barons Hunsdon. As is well known, the character in *1 Henry IV* now named Sir John Falstaff was originally called Sir John Oldcastle. Before *2 Henry IV* was performed the name had been changed, and the probable occasion of the change was the Christmas holidays of 1596–7, when, as already stated,[2] Lord Hunsdon's men acted at court, where Baron Cobham was Lord Chamberlain. The historical Sir John Oldcastle had married the

conspired with a young heiress's guardian to marry her to Wayte as a means of ultimately securing her property to his own children, and that she did not long survive the loss of her goods and lands by this marriage. She had died in 1590, the year before the lawsuit (pp. 100–3)—and seven years before the probable date of the play.

[1] Hibbard, pp. 38–42. Bullough, ii. 26–44, prints two narratives in which persons are carried out of houses in containers; neither of these closely resembles the buck-basket incident.

[2] See p. 5, n. 3, and p. 3.

widowed Lady Cobham and had been known as Lord Cobham, and the present Cobhams were no doubt offended by his presentation in *1 Henry IV*.[1] Whether it was the Lord Chamberlain or his son Henry Brooke, who inherited the Cobham title in March 1597, who caused the change of name is unknown, but it is a fact that the eighth Baron Cobham was jestingly called Sir John Falstaff in letters written from court in February 1598 and July 1599.[2]

Upon this foundation of fact and probability Alice-Lyle Scoufos has raised a fantastic pile of conjecture, which as far as *The Merry Wives of Windsor* is concerned relates both to interpretation (which will be mentioned later) and to occasion (which must be mentioned now). She maintains that the play was 'written in 1599 between 23 April, when Henry Brooke, eighth Lord Cobham, was elected as a new knight of the Garter, and 6 June when he was installed at Windsor'. According to her theory, the Queen directly commissioned a play showing Falstaff in love, its purpose being to probe a recent piece of court gossip connecting Lord Cobham with Margaret Ratcliffe, one of the Queen's maids of honour. She believes that Ford's speech in the final scene, triumphing over Falstaff and using 'Master Brook' five times in the vocative, was addressed directly to Lord Cobham at the first performance, 'at Windsor Castle on 6 June 1599'. But it is beyond belief that Elizabeth, whose strong point was diplomacy, should have contrived to insult one of her nobles on the very day when he was receiving an honour; and since she was not present at the installation (a fact which Scoufos ignores) she would not have been able to observe, as Hamlet was later to do, the effectiveness of a play as a conscience-catcher.[3]

Gary Taylor, who accepts the generally agreed date of 23 April 1597 for the first performance, also finds provocative intent in the choice of Brook as Ford's false name. For him, however, the provocation was offered by Shakespeare and his company, triumphing in the fact that though they had to change Oldcastle to

---

[1] See Gary Taylor, 'The Fortunes of Oldcastle', *Shakespeare Survey 38* (Cambridge, 1985), pp. 85–100.

[2] Alice-Lyle Scoufos, *Shakespeare's Typological Satire* (Athens, Ohio, 1979), pp. 202–3, quotes the letters.

[3] Scoufos, pp. 199–212. She also attempts to connect the courtship of Anne Page with the question of who would marry Arabella Stuart, a possible claimant to the English crown after Elizabeth's death.

Falstaff in the previous Lord Chamberlain's time, the new Lord Chamberlain was their own patron Lord Hunsdon.[1] Why and when the name Brooke (as it is given in the Quarto) was changed to Broome (as it is given in the Folio) will be discussed later in comparing the two texts.

The Merry Wives of Windsor, with Falstaff as its central character, is evidently a by-product of the English history plays which Shakespeare was also writing in the later 1590s. Its precise relationship to them, however, has often been the subject of argument. That Falstaff (originally called Oldcastle) first appeared in *1 Henry IV* is beyond doubt. The question is whether *The Merry Wives of Windsor* was written before, between, or after the other two plays in the series, or even during the writing of one of them.

1 Henry IV is agreed to have been written in time to be performed during the winter season of 1596–7; *Henry V* can be precisely dated between March and September 1599 because of the Essex reference in the Chorus to Act Five; *2 Henry IV* must have come between them, but its date is uncertain.[2]

Being a by-product and not a part of the sequence, *The Merry Wives of Windsor* is under no obligation to conform to the chronology of the three related history plays, and in fact stands outside it. In *2 Henry IV* Falstaff renews his acquaintance with Shallow after the lapse of many years; at the end of the play he is rejected by the new king; the action is continuous. But in *The Merry Wives of Windsor* there is no suggestion that he has been rejected; his lawless behaviour in Shallow's deer-park, and his fear that he would be mocked 'if it should come to the ear of the court' how he had been treated on his two visits to Mistress Ford's house, imply the contrary. Fenton is regarded as an unsuitable son-in-law by Page both because he is not rich and because 'he kept company with the wild Prince and Poins'; Page's use of the past tense suggests rather that the Prince has left his wildness than that Fenton has left the Prince, and therefore implies that at this point in the play Henry V is on the throne. The obvious purpose of the passage, however, is to make vivid Page's objections to Fenton, not to establish the date of the action. Mistress

---

[1] Gary Taylor, 'William Shakespeare, Richard James, and the House of Cobham', *RES*, NS 38 (1987), 334–54.

[2] A. R. Humphreys, edn. of *2 Henry IV* (The Arden Shakespeare, 1966), p. xvi, places it early in 1597; Oliver, p. liv, places it late in 1598.

Quickly's circumstances in *The Merry Wives of Windsor*, where she is Dr Caius's housekeeper, is unmarried, and has to introduce herself to Falstaff, are quite different from those in *1* and *2 Henry IV*, where she is the married (in *2 Henry IV* widowed) hostess of a London tavern and has known Falstaff for nearly thirty years. Pistol, whose first encounter makes a disagreeable impression on Mistress Quickly in *2 Henry IV*, has married her in *Henry V*, and in *The Merry Wives of Windsor* concludes that she is a 'punk' whom he may obtain as his 'prize'. Clearly Shakespeare has no purpose of giving his characters self-consistent life-histories, such as the characters in sequences of novels by Trollope and Galsworthy have, and therefore no ready-made chronology of composition can be obtained from the facts, such as they are, presented in each play. Even if the characters' life-histories were self-consistent, this chronology need not reflect the order of composition. It is legitimate, of course, to argue that the order of composition can be deduced from Shakespeare's own creative process: for example, Pistol's pursuit of Mistress Quickly, without marriage in mind, in *The Merry Wives of Windsor*, may have disposed Shakespeare to make him her husband in *Henry V*. But such deduction is necessarily a matter of personal opinion.[1]

There is one matter of fact which has a significant bearing on the relationship between *2 Henry IV* and *The Merry Wives of Windsor*. At some stage during the writing of *2 Henry IV* Shakespeare changed his mind about Shallow's county of residence. When Falstaff is recruiting soldiers on his way to fight the rebels in Yorkshire, and calls at Shallow's for the purpose, Shallow is introduced talking to Silence and asking him about livestock prices at Stamford fair (3.2). The implication is that he lives somewhere in the East Midlands, near the Great North Road on which Falstaff would naturally be travelling.[2] The first statement that Shallow lives in Gloucestershire comes after the campaign (4.2), when Falstaff asks Prince John's permission to go through Gloucestershire on his return, and presently tells Bar-

[1] See Green, pp. 177–92; Hibbard, pp. 48–9; Oliver, p. lii; Roberts, pp. 45–7, on the relationship between *Merry Wives* and the history plays.

[2] Humphreys (ed.), *2 Henry IV*, Appendix IV. To his point about Stamford fair it may be added that in Shallow's London reminiscences 'Will Squeal, a Cotswold man' (*2 Henry IV*, 3.2.19–20) is mentioned, along with a man from Staffordshire, as being among his companions. This implies that Shallow himself does not come from the Cotswold area, i.e. Gloucestershire.

dolph, 'I'll through Gloucestershire, and there will I visit Master Robert Shallow, Esquire.' As Oliver suggests, Shakespeare may have moved Shallow to Gloucestershire for *The Merry Wives of Windsor* because it is nearer (within fifty miles, whereas Shallow's original home would be about twice that distance away), and then stuck to this change when completing *2 Henry IV*. This implies that he interrupted his writing of *2 Henry IV* somewhere between 3.2 and 4.2 (the intervening scene, 4.1, deals with the collapse of the rebellion) in order to write the specially commissioned *Merry Wives of Windsor*, an implication consistent with the theory that he composed it for the Garter Feast of 1597.[1] Work that has been done on the vocabulary of *The Merry Wives of Windsor* helps to reinforce this conclusion, since it has a few words and phrases in common with *2 Henry IV* and with no other play of Shakespeare's, and a significantly higher percentage of shared vocabulary with that play than with any of the others.[2]

Shakespeare's English Comedy: The Substance and the Dramatic Structure of the Play

The Merry Wives of Windsor is unique among Shakespeare's comedies in being set in England, rather than in Ephesus, Athens, France, Italy, Illyria, or ancient Britain. This English setting—a very local one, with its allusions to Windsor, Eton, Frogmore, and Datchet—goes to confirm the play's connection both with the Garter Feast and with the English history plays. Its social world is that of the Gloucestershire scenes of *2 Henry IV*, where there are no kings or dukes, and none of the characters is above the rank of a knight. The incidents in which its central character, Falstaff, is discomfited recall the spirit of the Gadshill robbery episode in *1 Henry IV*. Everything points to Shakespeare's having intended to write a comedy of which the material should be his English

[1] Oliver, p. lv. The suggestion that Shakespeare interrupted his writing of *2 Henry IV* at 4.3 was originally made by H. N. Paul (in the New Variorum Shakespeare *1 Henry IV*, ed. S. B. Hemingway, Philadelphia and London, 1936, p. 355), without reference to Shallow's county's being moved to Gloucestershire. Perhaps Falstaff's decision to 'ride all night' from Shallow's to London for Henry V's coronation (*2 Henry IV*, 5.3.130–1) helped Shakespeare decide to keep the change. The mention in *2 Henry IV* 5.1.21 of Hinckley fair should, however, be noted: Hinckley is much nearer to Stamford than to Gloucester.

[2] Oliver, p. lv. Eliot Slater, 'Word Links with *The Merry Wives*', *N & Q* 220 (1975), 169–71.

histories with the history left out. Falstaff, already a more important figure in the histories than his subsidiary role required him to be, was now to have a whole play to himself.

For this new Falstaff play Shakespeare needed a plot, a plot involving a succession of comic discomfitures from which Falstaff would emerge defeated but irrepressible, as he had done from the Gadshill robbery. On the face of it, it is not likely that any ready-made plot would serve his purpose, and so it is not surprising that no source for the play as a whole has been found. (That a lost play called *The Jealous Comedy*, performed by the Lord Chamberlain's Men in 1593, was the source is the merest conjecture.)[1] Shakespeare, then, may be assumed to have invented his own plot, drawing upon his memory for suitable incidental material, as he remembered Chaucer's *Knight's Tale* when inventing the plot of *A Midsummer Night's Dream*. The most substantial piece of material of this sort is a story from a collection of *novelle*, Ser Giovanni Fiorentino's *Il pecorone*.[2] In this story a student asks a professor to teach him the art of love (that is, of seduction), and duly applies the teaching and reports his progress to the professor; suspecting that the woman is his own wife (as she is), the professor follows the student to the house, but does not find him because the wife has hidden him under a heap of damp washing; next day the student reports his adventure to the professor, who consequently stabs the heap of washing the next time he follows the student to the house; the student, of course, has escaped in a different way, and the professor is treated as a madman by his wife's brothers, whom he has caused to witness his search. Though there are major differences (chiefly that in the *novella* adultery takes place), there are striking resemblances. The lover's confiding in the husband, the concealment under the washing, and the husband's assault on the washing upon the second occasion, all suggest that Shakespeare knew this story, particularly because another story in *Il pecorone* is agreed to be the source of the main plot (the bond, the wife disguised as a lawyer, and the business of the ring) of *The Merchant of Venice*, which he probably wrote in 1596 or 1597. No other proposed source for elements of

---

[1] Oliver, p. lx, reviews the arguments that have been brought forward to support this theory.

[2] Bullough, ii. 19–26, gives a translation of this story (*Il pecorone* (1558), Giornata I, Novella II).

the play comes anywhere near so close as this, which may be taken to be the point from which Shakespeare's plot grew.[1]

Ser Giovanni's *novella* is a simple comedy of ironic situation, satisfying enough within its conventional limits but strictly limited in characters and in incidents.[2] It would not in itself make a play. Shakespeare seizes on its situational irony and develops round this a humorous comedy of character. He also substitutes for the amoral sexual opportunism of the original a quite different moral spirit, in which 'wives may be merry and yet honest too', and in which not only is Falstaff's lechery frustrated but also Ford's jealousy is cured—yet all this without sententious moralizing or undue seriousness. One method by which the mood of the whole play is kept light and cheerful is the multiplying of the dramatic interest. Though Falstaff's first two discomfitures take place at Ford's house and turn upon his attempts to seduce Mistress Ford, the facts that he has also written a love-letter to Mistress Page, that the two women have compared their letters, that Ford and Page have both been told of his intentions by his discarded hangers-on, that Falstaff has been (as he thinks) independently engaged by the supposed Brook to seduce Mistress Ford, and that Ford has Page and two or three eccentrics in tow when he searches his house for Falstaff, all go to confirm that there are to be no unpleasantly lifelike treatments of sexual misconduct or of marital jealousy.

Along with this filling-out of his main plot Shakespeare introduces two subsidiary actions. In the first of these, Page's daughter is courted by three suitors, two of them ridiculous, and is won by Fenton, the young gentleman whom she favours, while her two unwelcome suitors (the respective choices of her father and

[1] Leo Salingar, *Shakespeare and the Traditions of Comedy* (Cambridge, 1974), pp. 231–2, suggests that the play originated in Plautus' *Braggart Soldier* (*Miles Gloriosus*), in which 'the boaster, inordinately vain about his sexual charm, ... is lured into an intrigue with a married woman (a pretended married woman in Plautus), steals into his neighbour's house, is soundly thrashed and is terrified into avowing his fault'.

[2] Its denouement is that the student, going to the university as usual next day, learns that the professor is mad and confined to his house. When he pays a sympathetic call, with other students, he recognizes with astonishment that his visits were to the professor's wife, but conceals his surprise and in his turn addresses the professor with commiseration. The professor bids him go away, for he has learned only too well at his teacher's expense. The wife hastily declares that the professor's words are just part of his madness, and the student leaves Bologna and returns home.

mother) are ludicrously disappointed, in the final scene. The second subsidiary action centres upon one of Anne Page's two ridiculous suitors, Dr Caius the French physician, and the Welsh parson of the town, Sir Hugh Evans; the former challenges the latter to a duel for intervening to forward Slender's courtship of Anne, the Host of the Garter Inn frustrates the duel by appointing them contrary places, and they combine to revenge themselves on him by arranging for some pretended Germans to run away with his horses. Their revengeful trick is so lightly sketched in that several critics have supposed one or more scenes to have been lost, but there is no necessity for more than a sketch of this very minor element in the plot. Its usefulness, apart from further filling out the play with the humours of Caius, Evans, and the Host, is that it adds the Host to the number of those who suffer reverses in the latter part of it—Page and Slender, Mistress Page and Caius. It is important that Falstaff should not be the only loser.

Shakespeare gives most of the principal characters more than one function in the play's multiple action. Mistress Page, for instance, is both Mistress Ford's confidante and an intriguer on behalf of Caius in his suit to her daughter Anne; Page intrigues on behalf of Slender and is also a foil to the jealous Ford; Mistress Quickly, besides being Caius's housekeeper, acts as go-between in Mistress Ford's dealings with Falstaff; Caius and Evans, besides being absurd would-be duellists, are reasonable spectators of Ford's searches of his house, and Caius is also a suitor and Evans a pedant who conducts a Latin lesson; the Host, in addition to his involvement in the duel and in the duellists' revenge, is an assistant in Fenton's elopement with Anne Page.

It is typical of Shakespeare's method, which the following discussion will explore, to have more than one action afoot in a comedy. The opening scene proclaims the breadth of interest, in event and character, that we are to be offered. The first three persons on stage—Justice Shallow, his nephew Slender, and Sir Hugh Evans—are a trio of notable eccentrics, and presently they are confronted with an equally eccentric quartet in Falstaff and his hangers-on, Bardolph, Pistol, and Nim. The only normal people—Page and his wife, their daughter, and Mistress Ford—are outnumbered, and provide a scale by which the abnormality of the others can be measured. Shallow's complaint against Falstaff, which gives the scene and the play their kick-start, is never heard of again, and the chief business set going is the wooing of Anne Page by (or rather, on behalf of) Slender, which is carried on in the second scene when Sir Hugh sends Slender's servant Simple with a letter to Mistress Quickly asking her to use her influence with Anne. Only then, in Scene 3, do we reach the beginning of the main action, with Falstaff proposing to make Mistress Ford and Mistress Page his East and West Indies, cashiering Pistol and Nim for refusing to deliver his love-letters, and thereby motivating their betrayal of his scheme to Ford and Page. Among Shakespeare's artful touches in these first three scenes Falstaff's one speech to Mistress Ford is to be noted:

Mistress Ford, by my troth, you are very well met. By your leave, good mistress.

Even if general kissing breaks out after the next line, when Page says, 'Wife, bid these gentlemen welcome', Falstaff's speech and kiss have made their dramatic point, with their conscious gallantry; consequently his announcement of his scheme in Scene 3, though it has all the impact of novelty, has continuity too. We may also notice that Falstaff has already parted with his third follower, Bardolph, to the Host—in whose employment he will be dramatically useful later—before he breaks with the other two and gives both letters to his page Robin (another minor character who will have his uses: 'And Falstaff's boy with her!').[1]

Ford, who grinds out the line just quoted, does not appear until well into the first scene of Act 2. In the mean time, true to Shakespeare's usual method of alternating action, Sir Hugh's letter is delivered to Mistress Quickly, and her employer Dr Caius discovers the messenger, becomes incensed at Sir Hugh's meddling on behalf of a rival suitor, and sends him a challenge. The French doctor is obviously the Welsh parson's equivalent in the play's gallery of eccentrics, though not so obviously as if they were themselves rival suitors, which would be too obvious a device for Shakespeare. Before the scene is over, Fenton—Anne's third suitor, and so evidently the successful one that there is no need,

---

[1] The order in which Shakespeare worked out his plot cannot, of course, be known; but it seems probable, assuming that the play precedes *Henry V* and that Nim makes his first appearance here, that he was created because Shakespeare needed two characters, each with a distinctive mannerism of speech, to warn Ford and Page simultaneously—a much better situation than if Pistol warned them both, either simultaneously or consecutively.

here or later, to spend more than the minimal time in establishing the fact—also appears. Then, in the first scene of Act 2, the main plot is greatly developed: Mistress Page and Mistress Ford compare their letters, Ford and Page are informed of Falstaff's scheme by Pistol and Nim, Mistress Quickly is engaged by the wives as a messenger to Falstaff, and Ford arranges with the Host that he shall be introduced to Falstaff under the assumed name of Brook.

Shakespeare's skill in dramatic construction is so easy that it is the easiest thing in the world to ignore it. In this scene the arrival of the Host, whom Caius has appointed umpire in his duel with Sir Hugh, with Shallow at his heels, allows Ford to come to his arrangement with the former while the latter talks to Page about the duel. And this dialogue with Page allows Shallow to vent his opinions on modern swordsmen and to reflect with satisfaction on his own feats of former days:

'Tis the heart, Master Page; 'tis here, 'tis here. I have seen the time, with my long sword, I would have made you four tall fellows skip like rats.

This is a good instance of how, in this play as in others, Shakespeare gives his scenes room to breathe. Then, with the exits of the Host, Shallow, and Page, Ford is left on stage to reinforce our knowledge of his intention to visit Falstaff in disguise in a very short soliloquy.

Of course, we are eager to see him put his plan in practice, and the sight of Falstaff browbeating a crestfallen Pistol is our assurance that Ford is even now on his way. But first Mistress Quickly must arrive and appoint Falstaff's assignation for next morning. The result is that Ford's arrival finds Falstaff in a hubristic mood of self-gratulation:

Sayst thou so, old Jack? Go thy ways. I'll make more of thy old body than I have done. Will they yet look after thee? Wilt thou, after the expense of so much money, be now a gainer? Good body, I thank thee. Let them say 'tis grossly done, so it be fairly done, no matter.[1]

---

[1] This is the fat Falstaff's equivalent of the deformed Richard's soliloquy after successfully wooing Lady Anne:

> Upon my life, she finds, although I cannot,
> Myself to be a marv'lous proper man.
> I'll be at charges for a looking-glass,
> And entertain a score or two of tailors
> To study fashions to adorn my body. (*Richard III*, 1.3.240–4)

Both speakers adopt an ironical tone, but whereas Richard is under no illusion about his looks, Falstaff really does feel complacency.

Master Brook offers Falstaff money for seducing Ford's wife. The oddity of this proposal from one who declares himself in love with her is not lost on Falstaff, so Master Brook has to justify it. The dialogue is conducted, at some length, with great politeness on both sides, which throws into strong relief the contrast in style when Falstaff begins to talk of Ford, 'the jealous rascally knave her husband'. Every change is rung on the abusive terms—'poor cuckoldly knave', 'jealous wittolly knave', 'cuckoldly rogue'— and Falstaff's exuberant invention supplies new ones like 'mechanical salt-butter rogue'. This serves to work Ford up to the explosive fury of his soliloquy—a long one this time—with which he ends the scene.

The next two scenes show Caius and Evans respectively waiting for their opponents, the Host having appointed them contrary places. These are leisurely scenes—plenty of breathing-room here—and are almost wholly displays of humorous character. Their only consequence, at a long interval, is the stealing of the Host's horses by the pretended Germans.

By the middle of Act 3 we return to the main action with the buck-basket scene, out of which Shakespeare gets full comic value. Especially worth noting, in this scene of so much activity, is the point of rest, when the buck-basket has left by one of the doors (of Shakespeare's stage) on its way to Datchet Mead and the Thames, and Ford and his neighbours have left by the other door to search the upstairs rooms of the house. Mistress Ford and Mistress Page have the whole stage to themselves, and their remarks make sure that the audience has got the comedy in the right moral focus:

MISTRESS PAGE Is there not a double excellency in this?
MISTRESS FORD I know not which pleases me better—that my husband is
    deceived, or Sir John.

What is doubly excellent about this exchange is its combination of moral rightness and artistic rightness: its neat summing-up of the moral situation springs naturally from the symmetry of the stage action. On the occasion of Falstaff's second assignation (4.2) the different stage situation allows a different form of moral comment, when Falstaff has fled upstairs to disguise himself, Mistress Ford has gone to summon the servants to carry the buck-basket, and Mistress Page remains on stage to speak the moral couplets that refer to the play's title:

> We'll leave a proof, by that which we will do,
> Wives may be merry and yet honest too.
> We do not act that often jest and laugh;
> 'Tis old but true: 'Still swine eats all the draff.'

Falstaff's three unsuccessful assignations are the chief structural feature of the play, and perhaps no other of Shakespeare's comedies so thoroughly exploits the pleasures of variety-within-repetition. Johnson has a somewhat discontented editorial comment on 'I spied a great peard under her muffler' (4.2.179–80):

As the second stratagem, by which *Falstaff* escapes, is much the grosser of the two, I wish it had been practised first. It is very unlikely that *Ford* having been so deceived before, and knowing that he had been deceived, would suffer him to escape in so slight a disguise.

But he overlooks the fact that by being practised second this stratagem permits the reappearance of the buck-basket, for the sake of which we willingly turn a blind eye to the alleged improbability.

In the Herne's Oak scene (5.5), the third of Falstaff's assignations, every reader and every spectator must be struck by the way in which this domestic comedy turns fantastical. There is a much greater shift here than at the end of *As You Like It* when Rosalind, as Ganymede, undertakes to bring Orlando his true Rosalind by magic, and is then led in, in her own person, by one representing Hymen the marriage-god. *As You Like It* has already developed a lyrical romantic mood bordering on the fantastic: it needs only a touch to steer it to this mythological tableau. Many critics have felt that the last scene of *The Merry Wives of Windsor* is produced not by a touch in the right direction but by a wrench in the wrong one. Falstaff frightened of fairies is more than they can endure.

It must be admitted that Falstaff is the last person one would expect to believe in fairies, and that he would not easily be persuaded to come to Herne's Oak at midnight wearing a pair of antlers. Still, Shakespeare himself cannot have been unaware of the implausibility of these things, so it is worth trying to understand his purpose in ending *The Merry Wives of Windsor* in this way.

In the last movement of the play he evidently has two objects in view. The first is to finish off the main plot with the third assignation and Falstaff's final and public discomfiture. The second is to finish off the minor plot with Anne Page's marriage to Master Fenton. This minor plot has hitherto been kept alive rather than developed; it is less a plot than an existing situation. But it has provided one strategically placed scene (3.4) that has brought together Fenton and Anne, Slender and Shallow, Page and Mistress Page, and Mistress Quickly, and has emphasized that Fenton is Anne's own choice, Slender is her father's choice, and Caius is her mother's choice. Much of that scene is in blank verse—not, of course, anything said by Slender, Shallow, or Mistress Quickly—and blank verse, in Shakespearian comedy, is often a gesture towards romance. No more than a gesture here: a touch of *Romeo and Juliet* would be quite out of keeping. Nevertheless, the blank verse in this scene (the first scene in which it appears in any quantity and with other than burlesque intention) points forward to the next blank verse scene (4.4), between Page, Ford, Mistress Page, Mistress Ford, and Evans. Of these only Sir Hugh is confined to prose throughout the scene. Ford, who opens it, uses blank verse to express his wholehearted conversion from jealousy:

> Pardon me, wife. Henceforth do what thou wilt.
> I rather will suspect the sun with cold
> Than thee with wantonness. Now doth thy honour stand,
> In him that was of late an heretic,
> As firm as faith.

Page, here as always the reasonable man, approves of Ford's sentiments but cuts short his expression of them and gets down to business:

> But let our plot go forward. Let our wives
> Yet once again, to make us public sport,
> Appoint a meeting with this old fat fellow,
> Where we may take him and disgrace him for it.

FORD
There is no better way than that they spoke of.

PAGE How, to send him word they'll meet him in the Park at midnight?
Fie, fie, he'll never come.

EVANS You say he has been thrown in the rivers, and has been grievously peaten as an old 'oman. Methinks there should be terrors in him, that he should not come. Methinks his flesh is punished; he shall have no desires.

PAGE So think I too.

MISTRESS FORD
> Devise but how you'll use him when he comes,
> And let us two devise to bring him thither.

MISTRESS PAGE
> There is an old tale goes that Herne the Hunter,
> Sometime a keeper here in Windsor Forest,
> Doth all the winter-time, at still midnight,
> Walk round about an oak, with great ragg'd horns ...

The dialogue has been quoted at some length to show how Shakespeare anticipates the charge of implausibility by letting Page and Evans voice it in prose, and then meets it with Mistress Ford's confident verse reply, which he follows with Mistress Page's speech reminding them of the legend of Herne the Hunter. As this speech runs on, we yield ourselves to the stream:

> Nan Page my daughter, and my little son,
> And three or four more of their growth we'll dress
> Like urchins, oafs, and fairies, green and white,
> With rounds of waxen tapers on their heads ...

This is not a matter of convincing us that what will happen is true to life but of persuading us to suspend our disbelief for the sake of enjoying what will happen.

Shakespeare might still have some difficulty in persuading us to do this if the whole scene were devoted to the planning of Falstaff's discomfiture. But the fairy disguise has started a train of thought in Page's mind: hearing that Anne is to be the queen of the fairies, 'Finely attirèd in a robe of white', he says

> That silk will I go buy. (*Aside*) And in that time
> Shall Master Slender steal my Nan away
> And marry her at Eton.

A few lines later, left alone on the stage, his wife determines that Dr Caius shall have her daughter. The minor plot thus comes right to the foreground, and it is kept there in the next scene, where Fenton (again in verse) confides to the Host that he and Anne mean to elope while Slender and Caius are diversely obeying her parents' different instructions. The effect of this sudden concentration on the marriage of Anne Page is to deflect our attention from the improbability of the device against Falstaff, who, when we next see him, is already persuaded to the assignation, not in process of being persuaded to it.

Shakespeare has a further object besides finishing off his two plots and combining them; he uses the denouement as a vehicle for his compliments to the Queen, to Windsor Castle, and to the Order of the Garter. By setting the last scene in a wood—whether in the Little Park or in the Great Park (Windsor Forest) is left vague[1]—he removes the action further from the commonplace houses, inns, streets, and fields in which it has been taking place. *The Merry Wives of Windsor* and *A Midsummer Night's Dream* are as different from each other as any two of his comedies, but there can be no doubt that his earlier fairy play was in his mind when he was planning the end of this one. Perhaps the original connection was his remembering the compliment to the Queen as the 'fair vestal thronèd by the west' which he had worked into Oberon's speech about the magic flower (*Dream*, 2.1.158). In neither play has the Fairy Queen an allegorical, or even allusive, reference to Elizabeth, the Faerie Queene of Spenser's poem, but it would have been impossible to compliment the Queen in the 1590s without having Spenser's immense tribute in mind. Shakespeare's fairies are nothing like the inhabitants of Spenser's Faerie Land, but belong to the popular tradition of playful, mischievous, and punitive immortals who live in the country and sometimes enter mortals' houses. In making them pinch Falstaff he may have remembered Lyly's complimentary court comedy of 1588, *Endymion* (where Elizabeth is allegorically portrayed as Cynthia), in which they pinch Corsites.[2] Of course it can never have crossed his mind to bring real fairies into *The Merry Wives of*

---

[1] The wives propose to send Falstaff word that 'they'll meet him in the Park at midnight' (4.4.16–17). Herne the Hunter is said to have been 'Sometime a keeper here in Windsor Forest' (4.4.26). After making a fool of Falstaff the conspirators will 'mock him home to Windsor' (4.4.62). Falstaff says to Ford (as Brook), 'Be you in the Park about midnight, at Herne's Oak, and you shall see wonders' (5.1.9–10). Page, Shallow, and Slender go to 'couch i'th' Castle ditch' till they see the lights carried by the fairies (5.2.1–2), which suggests that the assignation will be in the Little Park adjoining the Castle. Mistress Page bids Caius 'Go before into the Park. We two must go together' (5.3.3–4: implying that she and Mistress Page will also go there). Falstaff calls himself 'a Windsor stag, and the fattest, I think, i'th' forest' (5.5.12–13). Mistress Page says that Falstaff's horns 'Become the forest better than the town' (5.5.107). The tradition that identified an oak in the Little Park as Herne's Oak (Green, p. 18) probably arose from the play's popularity and is unreliable as evidence either of the location of 5.5 or of the antiquity of the Herne story. More than one tree has been so identified (Roberts, p. 149 n. 59).

[2] Bullough, ii. 55–8. In *Endymion*, as in Shakespeare's play, the pinching is accompanied by a song in trochaic metre.

Windsor as he had done in *A Midsummer Night's Dream*; these fairies are William Page and other children of Windsor. Yet in the Fairy Queen's speech the lines in which she invokes an everlasting blessing on Windsor Castle are in the elevated tone in which Theseus's palace is blessed at the end of *A Midsummer Night's Dream*. There is undeniable incongruity here, but anyone who regards the incongruity as a fault is out of tune with the spirit of this final scene. For Shakespeare's original court audience the unexpected complimentary flourish would be a delightful surprise, and even now that the play's occasion is far in the past his ingenuity can still delight us.

There is incongruity of a different kind in Falstaff's interjection, after Sir Hugh's line 'But stay! I smell a man of middle earth',

Heavens defend me from that Welsh fairy, lest he transform me to a piece of cheese!

The incongruity lies in Falstaff's joke—for a joke it undeniably is—at the expense of one of the fairies while he is in awe of them collectively:

> They are fairies; he that speaks to them shall die.
> I'll wink and couch; no man their works must eye.

In that speech he is subdued to the couplets of the surrounding verse, but his prose interjection (like 'Rebellion lay in his way, and he found it', interjected into the serious blank-verse altercation between the King and Worcester before the battle of Shrewsbury)[1] shows him in his usual irreverent and irrepressible mood. It is one of Shakespeare's surest artistic touches. It provides us with an escape from the conclusion that Falstaff is filled with craven terror, while at the same time it does not go so far in the other direction as to suggest that he is only pretending to be afraid.[2]

The success of the final scene depends on the maintaining of a delicate balance. The sudden development of the Anne Page plot, as has been said, predisposes us to accept Falstaff's comic tormenting by the fairies. In this final scene the elopement of

---

[1] *1 Henry IV*, 5.1.28.

[2] In a review of the Royal Shakespeare Company's 1955 production (*Bolton Evening News*, 15 July 1955) it was noted that it received not only the usual laughter but 'even some applause, as if it were extempore'.

Anne with Fenton, and the carrying-off by Slender and Caius of boys whom they mistake for Anne, acts as a distraction from his plight, which might seem too moralistically presented if it demanded our whole attention. It also provides excellent theatre, especially when, as we anticipate, Slender and Caius return to complain—each in his characteristic style—of how they have been deceived. And it distributes the discomfiture, which is not allowed all to fall on Falstaff's head; Page and his wife, as well as Slender and Caius, whom they respectively favoured, have missed their aim. The return of Fenton and Anne, whom Page and his wife finally congratulate upon their marriage, makes the play end as a comedy of forgiveness and reconciliation and not as one of retribution and satirical exposure. Ford, of course, must have his speech of triumph at Falstaff's expense, and reclaim the money that he paid over as Master Brook. This speech occurs when everyone is uniting to denounce Falstaff, before the reappearance of Slender, Caius, Fenton, and Anne. But at the very end, it is Ford who presses Mistress Page's invitation on Falstaff ('Let it be so, Sir John'),[1] and his final couplet,

> To Master Brook you yet shall hold your word,
> For he tonight shall lie with Mistress Ford,

is best taken as his happy afterthought, and as a joke which Falstaff can share.

Interpretations, Critical and Theatrical, of the Play

The Merry Wives of Windsor has always been a popular play in the theatre.[2] Though it has undergone the vicissitudes of theatrical taste—interpolated songs, omitted and rearranged scenes, and

[1] On the punctuation of Ford's final speech see Commentary, 5.5.236.
[2] There are accounts of its stage history in Irving/Marshall, pp. 190–2, NCS, pp. 135–8, Oliver, pp. ix–xiii, and Shattuck, pp. 20–38, as well as references to it in such general works as C. B. Hogan, *Shakespeare in the Theatre, 1701–1800* (Oxford, 1952, 1957) and G. C. D. Odell, *Shakespeare from Betterton to Irving* (New York, 1920): Odell (pp. 80–1) summarizes the plot-structure of Dennis's adaptation *The Comical Gallant* (see p. 4). Two unpublished dissertations are devoted to it: George David Glenn, 'The Merry Wives of Windsor on the Nineteenth Century Stage', University of Illinois (Ph.D.), 1969, and Peter Lindsay Evans, 'The Stage History of *The Merry Wives of Windsor*, 1874–1933', University of London (M.Phil.), 1981. The existence of operas based on the play also testifies to its popularity. Those by Salieri (1799) and Balfe (1838) have dropped out of the
[*cont. on p. 26*].

the like—it has never been regarded as essentially unsuitable for performance, as *Measure for Measure* and *Cymbeline* have for different reasons sometimes been regarded. The one attempt to remodel it completely for the altered taste of the time, John Dennis's *The Comical Gallant* (1702), failed to dislodge it. Undoubtedly its theatrical popularity is chiefly due to its robust and easily followed plot, its situations of broad comedy with a large amount of physical action, its gallery of humorous character-sketches, its everyday domestic atmosphere and local colour, and its uncomplicated moral assumptions and conclusions. Audiences like the play because it entertains them, actors because it gives them plenty of parts in which to shine.

In the seventeenth and eighteenth centuries literary critics also liked it. Johnson, whose judgement is representative, commended particularly the uniting of the two dramatic actions in the final scene.[1] The decline in its reputation among literary critics can be traced back to the Romantic period, when Shakespeare's plays began to be seen not only as separate works of art but also, and more importantly, as evidence of his many-sided mind and creative imagination. *The Merry Wives of Windsor*, being a domestic comedy almost wholly in prose, obviously gave the reader less of such evidence than *The Tempest*. Other factors also contributed to the gradual decline of critical interest in it. The growth of knowledge about Shakespeare's artistic development,

repertoire, though Salieri's has recently been recorded (Hungaroton HCD 12789-91, 1985) and broadcast by the BBC (16 Oct. 1986). Nicolai's (1849) follows Shakespeare's plot closely, except that in the final scene Fluth (Ford), impersonating Herne, superintends Falstaff's tormenting, while Caius and Spär-lich (Slender) mistake each other for their bride. Verdi's *Falstaff* (1893) adapts it freely. The libretto, by Boito, is a good vehicle for Verdi's music, but Charles Osborne (*The Complete Operas of Verdi*, 1969, repr. 1973, pp. 477–8) is extravagant in declaring it a great improvement on Shakespeare's 'ploddingly repetitive pot-boiler'. As drama the divergences are always to Shakespeare's advantage. Boito makes Ford empty the buck-basket *before* Falstaff gets into it, and incongruously incorporates parts of Falstaff's *soliloquy* on honour from *1 Henry IV* into his *harangue* to Pistol and Bardolph for refusing to carry his letters to the wives. By making Nannetta the daughter of the Fords instead of the Pages, and omitting Page altogether, Boito seriously reduces the plot's double interest, and by giving Caius in the opening scene the complaining speeches both of Shallow and of Slender (who are also omitted, as is Evans) he creates an implausible character. Vaughan Williams's *Sir John in Love* (1929) reverts to Shakespeare's plot, omitting only the 'fat woman of Brentford' episode, and introduces English folk-tunes and lyrics from the Elizabethan poets to create an appropriate sense of the period.

[1] In his note on 5.5.170.

as it could be deduced from the chronology of his plays, led critics to concentrate upon the romantic and the transcendental in his comedies; in a prospect that led the eye to *Twelfth Night* and beyond that to *The Winter's Tale* and *The Tempest*, it was not to be expected that *The Merry Wives of Windsor* would be a conspicuous landmark. The preoccupation with the Falstaff of the *Henry IV* plays, and particularly with his rejection, led to a neglect of the Falstaff of *The Merry Wives of Windsor*, in which he is removed from Prince Henry and from the serious historical drama with which he has so original a relationship. The belief that because *The Merry Wives of Windsor* was first printed in 1602 it must have been written at about that time, following *Henry V*, in which Falstaff's death is reported, and reviving him to play an ignoble part in a comedy which its bourgeois setting and physical action rendered liable to be belittled as a farce, further depressed the play's reputation, as did the inference that if Shakespeare had written it in obedience to the Queen's command his heart could not have been wholly in the work.[1]

There have been signs in recent years of a reappraisal. The consensus of the majority of scholars that *The Merry Wives of Windsor* was written for the Garter Feast of 23 April 1597, though it cannot be proved that it was, has weakened the conviction that Shakespeare reluctantly or cynically reanimated the dead Falstaff. The study of Shakespeare's plays as works for the stage, especially for the Elizabethan and Jacobean stage, has improved our appreciation of his dramatic technique. There have been books on Shakespeare's use of the traditions of comedy, especially the classical and Italian comedies of intrigue; on his dramatic exploitation of the advantages which the audience and some of the characters enjoy over other characters in respect of their awareness of the true situation; on the artistry of Shakespeare's prose; and on citizen comedy in the age of Shakespeare.[2] In all these books *The Merry Wives of Windsor* receives serious attention and approval. A review of the criticism of Shakespeare's earlier comedies between 1953 and 1982

---

[1] Roberts, pp. 61–118 and elsewhere, provides a detailed history of the criticism of the play.

[2] Salingar (see p. 15 n. 1); Bertrand Evans, *Shakespeare's Comedies* (Oxford, 1960); Brian Vickers, *The Artistry of Shakespeare's Prose* (1968); Alexander Leggatt, *Citizen Comedy in the Age of Shakespeare* (Toronto, 1973).

contains the statement that *The Merry Wives of Windsor* is 'full of problems that can attract the attention of critics interested in the treatment of underlying ideologies in Shakespeare's drama', such as exploitation and jealousy in marriage, women both as commodities and as moral arbiters, and the motivations produced by one's social position and economic aims.[1] Another group of critics are specially interested in comedy as a social ritual with deep and ancient roots: for them the antlered Falstaff, tormented and derided by the inhabitants of Windsor, is the *pharmakos* or scapegoat, whose expulsion restores the health of the society; or he is the centre of an ancient celebration of the defeat of winter.[2] By other interpreters he is seen as the antithesis of a worthy Garter Knight, his various discomfitures related to the degradation ceremony in which an expelled Knight's heraldic achievements were thrown down from his stall in St George's Chapel and kicked into the castle ditch; in addition one of them sees his experiences as an 'evasively symbolic' dramatization of all the satire on the Cobhams, from Sir John Oldcastle onwards, which she finds widespread in Shakespeare's history plays and his Windsor comedy.[3]

While it is pleasing to see so much critical interest aroused by the play, it will probably be admitted—by all but those critics who, at least in theory, refuse to admit the superiority of any interpretation over any other—that not all these interpretations can be equally sustained by its text, or apply equally to the whole of it. It will also probably be admitted—except by the exponents of the interpretations that least square with it—that the interpretation most likely to be true is the one that takes most account of the literal sense of the action and dialogue, since this is what is mainly conveyed to the audience in the theatre, assuming that the text of Shakespeare's comedy is played in unadulterated form. In discussing the interpretation of the play, therefore, it is

---

[1] R. S. White, 'Criticism of the Comedies up to *The Merchant of Venice*, 1953–82', *Shakespeare Survey* 37 (Cambridge, 1984), 1–11 (quotation from pp. 7–8).

[2] Northrop Frye, *Anatomy of Criticism* (Princeton, N.J., 1957); Roberts. See pp. 44–7.

[3] Scoufos (see p. 10 n. 2). Jan Lawson Hinely, 'Comic Scapegoats and the Falstaff of *The Merry Wives of Windsor*', *Shakespeare Studies*, 15 (1982), 37–54, sees Falstaff as a scapegoat for Windsor in general and also for the Garter Knights in particular.

desirable to bear in mind simultaneously what has been or might be written about it and how it has been or might be performed. This method will appear less systematic than a review of criticism followed by a review of performance, but it may be a more useful method in the long run.

Most people, when asked what they recall of *The Merry Wives of Windsor*, think first of Falstaff's misadventures, particularly in the buck-basket; his disguise as Herne the Hunter is usually recalled next, together with the doings of Anne Page and her three suitors in the same scene; his disguise as Mother Pratt the fat woman of Brentford is often forgotten, though Ford's emptying of the buck-basket on this second occasion is always remembered, and is usually mentioned in the same breath as Falstaff's first misadventure. These two buck-basket incidents display two of the play's most memorable characteristics, comic physical activity and situational irony.

The fullest analysis of situational irony in this and Shakespeare's other comedies has been made by Bertrand Evans.[1] His concisely written account of *The Merry Wives of Windsor* extends to some twenty pages, designed to show exactly what advantage in knowledge of the true situation some characters have over others and on what occasions, and how Shakespeare directs our attention to this by dramatic means. No attempt will be made to reproduce it here, but some of his general observations will be stated, and some of his particular instances re-examined.

One of his observations is fundamental to the right understanding of the play. The numerous intrigues and deceptions practised by the characters upon each other are not calculated to arouse complex or conflicting emotions in the audience. Good humour and mirth are what they arouse. Falstaff's villainy—to dignify it with an inappropriate name—is ridiculous, and so is Ford's passionate jealousy; despite Falstaff's complacency and Ford's threats, there is no danger that Mistress Ford will be either seduced or physically illtreated. Falstaff's plan is no sooner launched than it is shipwrecked twice over, first by the wives' virtuous indignation and immediately afterwards by Pistol's and Nim's revelations to Ford and Page; Ford's politic disguise as

---

[1] Bertrand Evans, pp. 98–117.

Brook, while it gives him an advantage over Falstaff in their interviews, exposes him to the hearing of Falstaff's abuse of the 'cuckoldly knave' Mistress Ford's husband, and exposes him also to his wife's indignation and his neighbours' astonishment when he confidently makes fruitless searches for the seducer. It is appropriate, therefore, that Falstaff should be the most deceived as to the true state of affairs, and that Ford should be the next most deceived; Ford is more deceived than Page because, unlike Page, he mistrusts his wife and supposes her to be encouraging Falstaff when she makes assignations with him, whereas Page trusts his wife, gives no further thought to Nim's warning, and knows nothing about the assignations. It should be added, however, that when, having emptied the buck-basket of the last of its contents, Ford speaks the hilariously obvious and anti-climactic line

Well, he's not here I seek for,

and Page rejoins (whether in pity or exasperation is for the actor to decide)

No, nor nowhere else but in your brain,

Page is wrong, for Falstaff is at that moment upstairs being dressed in women's clothes. That he is wrong is not in any way a point against him, but it is a detail which adds to the audience's pleasure; we are placed in a position of superior awareness shared only by Mistress Ford (for Mistress Page is dressing Falstaff upstairs). Since Ford now turns to Page and his other friends and asks them to help him search his house again, Mistress Ford can (if she wishes, and is capable of doing it without exaggeration) quickly register her special knowledge of the true situation.

Considering how numerous are its intrigues and deceptions, *The Merry Wives of Windsor* makes very little use of the 'aside' speech.[1] It is therefore largely left to the audience to appreciate the ironies inherent in the situations. Bertrand Evans writes particularly interestingly about the two scenes in which first Falstaff, then Mistress Page, and finally Ford and his neighbours,

---

[1] One of the few, Mistress Page's beginning 'Doctors doubt that', in the final scene (5.5.173), is effective precisely because it exposes to the audience the error of her own belief at the very moment when she is commenting on the error of her husband's.

arrive at Ford's house. He draws attention, on the first occasion (3.3), to the immediately preceding scene, which lets us know that Ford is actually approaching, whereas the wives, knowing nothing of his approach or of his disguise as Brook which has given him notice of Falstaff's visit, merely intend to frighten Falstaff by pretending that he is approaching. On the second occasion (4.2) he maintains that the audience itself is over-reached: that we believe the situation to be exactly as before, whereas it turns out that this time Mistress Page knew that Ford was coming, and was telling the literal truth when, speaking louder in order that Falstaff should overhear her, she told Mistress Ford of this. Though Evans is right in concluding that this fore-knowledge of Ford's approach allows the wives to play the buck-basket trick on him, it is hard to see any dramatic advantage in Mistress Page's being better informed than the audience sup-posed, and he gets into difficulties by asking, and attempting to explain, how it came about: she may, he says, have seen Ford and the rest coming while she was hearing William's Latin examination. At a snail's pace? This is one of those situations, not uncommon in Shakespeare, where what matters is dramatic effectiveness, not verisimilitude or factual consistency. When frightening Falstaff is in question, Ford can be 'Hard by, at street end'; then, after the buck-basket has been firmly rejected by Falstaff as a hiding-place, and all other hiding-places have been enumerated and ruled out by Mistress Ford, and the expedient of the disguise has been hit upon, we reach the following exchange:

MISTRESS FORD I would my husband would meet him in this shape. He cannot abide the old woman of Brentford. He swears she's a witch, forbade her my house, and hath threatened to beat her.

MISTRESS PAGE Heaven guide him to thy husband's cudgel, and the devil guide his cudgel afterwards!

MISTRESS FORD But is my husband coming?

MISTRESS PAGE Ay, in good sadness is he, and talks of the basket too, howsoever he hath had intelligence.

MISTRESS FORD We'll try that; for I'll appoint my men to carry the basket again, to meet him at the door with it as they did last time.

MISTRESS PAGE Nay, but he'll be here presently. Let's go dress him like the witch of Brentford.

MISTRESS FORD I'll first direct my men what they shall do with the basket.

The point of this is not to surprise us with Mistress Page's knowledge, but to prepare us for Ford's cudgelling of Falstaff, which will seem funnier when it happens because the wives' enthusiasm has coloured our expectation. It is Mistress Ford who is surprised by Mistress Page's knowledge: her first quoted speech is just a piece of wishful thinking, but Mistress Page's reply promises that it will come true, so that Mistress Ford's question calls for a tone of joyous anticipation. The imminence of Ford's arrival now—and we forget that it was announced as imminent fifty lines earlier—allows us to feel excitement as we watch the wives devise and execute their plans just in time for his reception. This excitement is not tainted by any real anxiety lest Ford should arrive too soon and spoil the joke.

A joke it is, of course, as Mistress Page's couplets before going to disguise Falstaff emphasize; but it is also—in its effect, though it would have been quite wrong to have made the wives consciously aim at that effect—part of the cure of Ford's jealousy. His fever now is higher than it was the day before, because all he knew then was that Falstaff intended to be in the house, but now he knows that he was indeed there and how he escaped. Therefore he calls forth his wife and, when she appears, pours angry sarcasm on her:

> Come hither, Mistress Ford, Mistress Ford the honest woman, the modest wife, the virtuous creature, that hath the jealous fool to her husband! I suspect without cause, mistress, do I?
> MISTRESS FORD Heaven be my witness you do, if you suspect me in any dishonesty.

The beauty of her reply is that its earnest sincerity actually allows her to equivocate, because she does have Falstaff in the house even though she has never intended to commit adultery; our expectation of seeing Falstaff appear in his disguise ensures that we do not miss the piquancy of it, though the actress cannot, and should not try to, bring it to our notice. Ford, still holding the centre of the stage, now throws out all the basket's contents; and when, his search fruitless, he proposes to search upstairs again, his wife's summons to Mistress Page to bring down the old woman keeps him there, working himself up to a fine rage against the 'old cozening quean'. At this point he produces his cudgel, while Mistress Ford, by begging the others not to let him 'strike the old woman', virtually eggs him on. Falstaff's appearance releases the spring that sets Ford in motion. The cudgelling is brisk, like Ford's verbal abuse, which keeps time to the blows, and in a moment Falstaff is gone. To drag it out is fatal to the true comic effect, just as fatal as it is to the first buck-basket scene if the point of rest mentioned earlier (p. 19), when the wives review that situation, is accompanied by continual entrances and exits by the searchers, or by loud off-stage noises of objects being moved and overturned. It is this labouring of the physical comedy that has helped to get the play the undeserved reputation of a knockabout farce.[1]

When the two scenes in Ford's house are compared, more and more signs of Shakespeare's judgement are seen. Besides the reappearance of the buck-basket, this time as the wives' bait for Ford, the cudgelling of Falstaff is an appropriate new development. It allows Ford to let off steam at Falstaff's expense, even though he does not recognize Falstaff and is therefore on the receiving end of irony even while he is on the handing-out end of punishment. Not the least important of the differences affects the end of the scene. Ford and his neighbours are not shown returning empty-handed from this second search of the house, which would be an anti-climax lacking the comedy of the corresponding anti-climax in 3.3; instead the wives resolve to enlighten their husbands about Falstaff's misadventures, and leave the stage to do so, and to devise a final jest against him. There would be no theatrical satisfaction for us in witnessing the mutual explanations (for Ford must on the same occasion divulge his disguise as Brook).

The comic physical activity and the situational irony, though

[1] The reappearing searchers figured in the Royal Shakespeare Company's production of 1968, the off-stage noises in that of 1985. Falstaff's flight as Mother Pratt has often been followed, at the end of the scene, by an additional episode showing him pursued through the streets by children and other townspeople: it was introduced by Tree and continued by Bridges-Adams, was incorporated into the stage directions of French's Acting Edition (London, 1928), and was still being performed at the Festival Theatre, Stratford, Ontario, in 1967, when it was transferred from the stage to the auditorium. The tradition of making Caius and Evans superfluously come to blows in 3.1, notoriously overplayed in Frank Benson's productions from 1887 onwards, dates back at least to W. Oxberry's edition (London, 1820), 'faithfully marked with the stage business, and stage directions, as it is performed at the Theatres Royal'. In Tree's production of 1912, during the buck-basket scene, Ford gave Caius a push which successively brought down him, Evans, and Page. Obviously there must be stage business, but it needs to grow more naturally from the dramatic action than this.

3. Peggy Ashcroft and Ursula Jeans as Mistress Page and
Mistress Ford, Old Vic, 1951. Director: Hugh Hunt (4.2.186–8)

entertaining in themselves, cannot be separated from the characterization of the persons concerned in them. Falstaff, as created in
1 Henry IV, is this play's keystone. His huge bulk and his comic
cowardice, both exploited in the robbery at Gadshill and at the
battle of Shrewsbury, are exploited again in the two buck-basket
scenes, and to a lesser degree in the final scene because there he is
not the whole object of attention. As has been well pointed out,
his bulk 'provides a comic equivalent for the moral indignation
felt at the idea of adultery', and helps to ensure that 'the assertion
of chastity is achieved without preaching, and in a spirit of fun'.[1]
The wives, comparing their letters from Falstaff, are vivaciously
witty at his expense: 'I had rather be a giantess and lie under
Mount Pelion.' The allusion is inconsistent with what we assume,

[1] Leggatt, p. 146.

indeed with what we can deduce, of Mistress Page's education;[1] but the inconsistency—though of course our attention is not deliberately directed to it—is positively valuable in keeping Falstaff's intended adultery on the level of the fantastic. The idea of lying with, or on, a woman, which in Iago's mouth is able to madden Othello by its actuality, becomes ludicrous and unreal when applied to Falstaff. That his courtship of the wives is really aimed at their husbands' money makes it not more sordid but, curiously, more innocent. Falstaff can be acted as lustful in his hopes and angry in his disappointments, but this theatrical interpretation has been rare, which suggests that most actors find it contrary to the prevailing spirit of the play.[2] It is probably going too far to say that Falstaff's true motive gives him an advantage over the wives, who never discover it;[3] but it does give him a measure of immunity to the insults that are finally heaped on him (somewhat in Prince Henry's manner) as a would-be seducer who is ridiculously fat. Moreover, he rises above his disasters by the eloquence and imagination with which he reacts to them. When next seen after leaving Ford's house in the buck-basket he soliloquizes about his experience. One image leads to another— the barrow of butcher's offal leads to the buttered brains, the dog he will give them to leads to the blind puppies going to drowning, the drowning leads to the mountain of mummy. Then, after his dialogue with Mistress Quickly, a dialogue with its own imaginative fertility ('swallowed snowballs for pills', 'no pullet-sperm in my brewage', 'my belly full of ford'), he describes to the disguised Ford his experience with fresh detail, this time dwelling on his stewing in the heat of the buck-basket and so preparing the climax of his sudden cooling in the Thames 'like a horseshoe'. Though this is repugnance, there is relish in it, and his resolution is comically heroic: 'Master Brook, I will be thrown into Etna, as I

[1] Thomas Warton in 1781 drew attention to its incongruity (*The History of English Poetry*, iii. 494; cf. *Shakespeare: The Critical Heritage*, ed. Brian Vickers, vi: *1774–1801* (1981), p. 307). We can deduce that Mistress Page knows no Latin from her statement 'Sir Hugh, my husband says my son profits nothing in the world at his book', 4.1.13–14.

[2] James Henry Hackett, who played Falstaff in the USA from the 1830s to the 1860s, interpreted the part in this way (Shattuck, p. 27).

[3] Bertrand Evans, p. 102, speaks of 'their middle-aged vanity' and 'Falstaff's own well-guarded secret'. But Falstaff made no secret of it to Pistol and Nim in 1.3, and Mistress Page's first sentence in 2.1 shows that she has no illusions about her beauty.

have been into Thames, ere I will leave her thus.' His physical experiences, though he relives them in his narrations, leave no injuries: a production which showed him getting out of bed in his shirt and sitting with his feet in a mustard-bath seemed to overstress the consequences of his being thrown in the Thames, and when Mistress Quickly came and dried his feet one had an uncomfortable premonition of her attendance at his death-bed in *Henry V*. This may or may not have been what the directors intended.[1] In general, however, he is represented on stage as being impervious to cold water and invulnerable to stout cudgels. He may have broken Slender's head, but Ford does not break his. This tradition seems to be right. Surely he should not come limping to Herne's Oak?

If Falstaff is the play's keystone, Ford is only slightly less important, and much depends on the actor's ability to make him both ridiculous and credible. It is all very well to say that his speech of contrition is only four and a half lines long: if those four and a half lines do not carry conviction the end of the play will suffer, for the restoring of peace begins here and must colour everything that remains to be shown. The ideal actor of Ford will always have suggested—not, of course, by playing against the firmly drawn outline of his role, but by his speech and bearing— that he is better than his thoughts, and that if only he could throw off his jealousy he would be an ideal husband. Sometimes he is played as a grotesque, with mechanical physical manner- isms to suggest that he is a puppet controlled by his ruling passion. This presentation destroys his human relationship with his wife and his neighbours, upon which much of the humour of his fruitless searches depends. The balance of these scenes is harder to strike than it might seem:

Master Ford (a hang-dog, sallow wife-beater, as played by Mr Edmund Willard) is depicted as torn between love and jealousy at the end of the buck-basket scene, when he makes a sheepish tender for his merry spouse's forgiveness, only to be repulsed with laughing contempt.[2]

If this is an accurate impression—always a question to be

---

[1] Royal Shakespeare Company, 1979, directed by Trevor Nunn and John Caird.

[2] Review of W. Bridges-Adams's production, Stratford-upon-Avon, 1921, *Birmingham Mail*, 26 Apr. 1921.

considered in assessing productions by their reviews—it suggests that Ford's characterization was misconceived and that his relations with his wife were incredibly presented. Such a man would not feel such a conflict of emotion, and his wife would not dare to treat him in that way. As for 'laughing contempt', there is nothing in the text to imply anything but silent reproach on her part. Yet a conflict between love and jealousy in Ford can be found in his speeches; his mood is established by his aside as he returns from the search:

I cannot find him. Maybe the knave bragged of that he could not compass.

He is beginning to doubt Falstaff's whole story of the assignation. The whole quartet of Fords and Pages need to be made fully human if the play is to be, on its own terms, believable. Touches like Mistress Ford's reply when Mistress Page declares that Page would no more be jealous than she unfaithful—'You are the happier woman'—make us desire to see the Fords happy together. The title calls both wives merry, and so, considered as a pair of plotters against Falstaff, they are; but there is room to distinguish between them, within the confines of the dramatic structure, though 'one of them should not be going to a holiday feast and the other to a funeral'.[1]

All the other persons in the play, except Anne Page and Fenton, are extravagantly drawn. This is a reason for distinguishing the Fords and Pages from them, rather than for throwing a hue of extravagance over all the character-playing. It is important that Caius's exhibition of fury over the discovery that he has a rival whom Sir Hugh Evans is helping should precede Ford's muted misgivings over Pistol's revelation. Caius and Evans, dissimilar though they are in circumstances and temperaments, are alike in being foreigners. Their unfailing misuse of language links them with Pistol, Nim, and Mistress Quickly:

[1] Review of Frank Benson's production, Stratford-upon-Avon, 1916, *Stratford-upon-Avon Herald*, 5 May 1916. It was Mistress Ford who was the lively one. In the Royal Shakespeare Company's 1968 production, Elizabeth Spriggs played Mistress Ford as 'a pale, rather simple middle-class housewife who warms only slowly and shyly to her friend Mistress Page's practical joke. In the awakening of her enjoyment and whole nature, the familiar situations become funnier and less cruel than they really are' (Ronald Bryden, *Observer*, 5 May 1968).

EVANS If there be anypody in the house, and in the chambers, and in the coffers, and in the presses, heaven forgive my sins at the day of judgement!

CAIUS By gar, nor I too. There is nobodies.

(Anyone who thinks it is unworthy of Shakespeare to indulge in this kind of humour should ponder the skill that has gone into Caius's comprehensively incorrect remark.) Their abortive duel unites them against the Host, and it is a nice touch if Evans, who is the more sympathetically drawn of the two, displays 'a caressing simplicity towards his new friend' at this point.[1] Whether their complicity in the affair of the Germans is conveyed to the audience in advance is a matter for the director. At Stratford-upon-Avon in 1979 Caius, wearing a dark cloak for his German disguise and carrying a similar cloak for Evans, entered at the end of the Latin lesson, helped Evans into his disguise, and moved with him to the inn, where Bardolph was heard to say (in a line adapted from the Quarto text), 'Sir, here be the Germans.' This made the situation clear with the minimum of alteration. But it is equally effective if the audience is left to puzzle (with the small part of its mind not elsewhere engaged) over the mysterious Germans until the triumphant speeches of Evans and Caius make it plain that this was their revenge.

When the Host is told by Bardolph that the Germans desire to have three of his horses, he says 'Let me speak with the gentlemen. They speak English?', and Bardolph replies 'Ay, sir.' But since this is just what Caius and Evans never do, except their own peculiar varieties of English, a scene in which they gull the Host is unimaginable. Trying to imagine it makes the final scene, in which Falstaff recognizes Evans as a Welsh fairy but not as the parson of Windsor, credible in comparison. The kind of belief that we accord to that scene has already been discussed (pp. 20–4), but a particular point requires consideration here. The Quarto's stage-direction is '*Enter . . . mistress Quickly, like the Queene of Fayries*', and the speech-prefixes in both the Quarto and the Folio confirm that she speaks the Fairy Queen's lines. Bertrand Evans interprets this as 'a deliberate surprise' and 'shock' for the audience; he points out that even Fenton, telling the Host of his

---

[1] The phrase is Leigh Hunt's, describing Benjamin Webster's performance in the role (review dated 4 Oct. 1830, rep. in *Dramatic Essays by Leigh Hunt*, ed. William Archer and Robert W. Lowe, 1894).

plan to elope with Anne Page, said that she was to 'present the Fairy Queen', and that the audience would therefore expect to see her do so. His outrageous conclusion is that

Coming as such a surprise, in such a setting, Mistress Quickly, more hag than queen, may be taken as a left-handed compliment, well deserved by her who had condemned Falstaff, of the race of Rosalind and Prospero, to play the role of Bottom.[1]

'I am Mistress Quickly; know you not that?' One can picture Elizabeth's reaction.[2] This interpretation—if, indeed, seriously intended—cannot be seriously entertained. But the point that we were expecting Anne is a good one:

The shock of seeing Mistress Quickly instead of Sweet Anne Page might have been avoided by but one sentence spoken by Fenton before the action.[3]

—one sentence that would have exploded our belief, if Mistress Quickly had been named.

> The children must
> Be practised well to this, or they'll ne'er do't,

says Ford. What amount of practice would Mistress Quickly require?

It is worth asking how recognizable Mistress Quickly would be in her disguise as the Fairy Queen, speaking lines utterly unlike her usual prose: a question worth asking, but an unanswerable one, since we can never know how the actor who first played her looked, in this scene or earlier ones. She has nothing to say in her own person on this occasion, nor has Pistol, who is given Hobgoblin's speeches in the Folio (Hobgoblin does not appear in the Quarto). Perhaps the point of the surprise is not that we see Mistress Quickly playing the Fairy Queen but that we do not see Anne doing so. During the fairy speeches our eyes will be busy

[1] Bertrand Evans, p. 117. He calls the line about Windsor Castle ('Worthy the owner, and the owner it') 'an equivocal utterance'.

[2] 'I am Richard II; know ye not that?' was her remark to the antiquary William Lambarde on 4 Aug. 1601, possibly alluding to a performance of Shakespeare's *Richard II* commissioned at the Globe by some of Essex's supporters on 7 Feb. 1601, the day before his rebellion was launched. But her following remark, 'This tragedy was played forty times in open streets and houses', makes the allusion obscure.

[3] Bertrand Evans, p. 117.

searching for 'the right Anne', and whether or not we pick her out before Fenton does we shall enjoy their elopement (and Slender's and Caius's mistakes).[1]

Editors who go against the Quarto and Folio in giving the Fairy Queen's lines to Anne Page are undoubtedly taking a liberty; but editors who follow those texts in giving the lines to Mistress Quickly may not have taken sufficient account of the fact that the texts are theatrical scripts, and that, if what Shakespeare intended was that the actor of Mistress Quickly should now come on again, without characterization, to speak the Fairy Queen's lines, there was no way of indicating this other than by naming him—which would look very odd in a published text for readers.[2] For directors too there is a problem: if not by Anne Page, should the Fairy Queen be played as if by some unspecified native of Windsor taking the role, or as if by Mistress Quickly herself, and, if the latter, is she to sink her personality in the role or to interpret the role as a vehicle for her personality? How that problem is solved greatly affects the impression made by the scene. To a much lesser extent the children impersonating the fairies present the same problem. They ought not to be so like real fairies that Oberon and Titania could not tell the difference, yet they ought not to be recognizable as a bunch of hobbledehoys, or they will be out of tune with the refinement of the language and the verse.

A feature of several recent productions has been the presence of a number of schoolboys, William Page's friends, at his Latin test, distracting him by playing ball with him, or supporting him by repeating all the Latin words; in 1979 at Stratford-upon-Avon

[1] Greg, p. 89, makes an important point: 'Slender abducts the Fairy Queen, supposing her to be Anne, and she turns out to be, not Mistress Quickly, but the Postmaster's boy.' He concludes that all that we are entitled to assume about the Fairy Queen is that she was played by 'the same boy' who acted Mistress Quickly. His argument is persuasive. The Quarto's stage direction (see collation at 5.5.101.1) is against it, it is true; but the Quarto is thoroughly muddled as to the colours to be worn by Anne Page and the others, and its stage direction here is undoubtedly influenced by the fact that Caius and Slender will soon be revealed to have abducted boys by mistake for Anne. The Quarto's stage direction does not, therefore, invalidate Greg's statement that Slender abducts the Fairy Queen, who was to be dressed in white (4.4.68–9, 4.6.34–7, though the Folio also muddles the statements about the colours after Slender and Caius have returned).

[2] The Quarto, being a reported text (or 'bad' quarto), is obviously not printed from Shakespeare's foul papers or from a theatrical manuscript, in either of which actors' names might appear. The Folio text has been thoroughly edited, in his distinctive manner, by the scribe Ralph Crane (see pp. 48–9).

the play opened with their rushing on stage as the bell rang for the end of school, Evans following and shooing them off. This device, as well as preparing for the child-fairies in advance, helps to create the sense of Windsor as a real town, an appropriate setting for Shakespeare's citizen comedy. Stage settings have often been rich in realistic detail with the same purpose. Costumes have usually been Elizabethan rather than late-medieval, even in the Victorian period when the *Henry IV* plays were costumed in the latter style.[1] This concentration on Elizabethan Windsor harmonizes with the profusion of homely objects and occupations in the imagery—feasting at a farm house, going a-birding, coursing hares with greyhounds, forging horseshoes, and so on— and the last scene ends with a general departure to Page's house to 'laugh this sport o'er by a country fire'.

Though it is a citizen comedy, *The Merry Wives of Windsor* does not obtrude the social and economic hostility frequent in this type of drama. Page objects to Fenton as a son-in-law because he 'is of no having' and has 'kept company with the wild Prince and Poins'. Fenton repeats to Anne her father's objections: Page, he says,

> tells me 'tis a thing impossible
> I should love thee but as a property

—that is, as a means to an end, the getting of money. Her teasing reply, 'Maybe he tells you true' (recalling Hermia on 'all the vows that ever men have broke', and Jessica on Lorenzo's 'many vows of faith, | And ne'er a true one'), prompts his ardent denial— coupled with the frank admission that he did begin his wooing because her father was rich. That Page favours Slender because he has three hundred pounds a year, even though he is a fool, and that Mistress Page, who can see Slender's folly, herself favours Caius, who is equally unsuitable, are rather the necessary conditions of the plot than serious reflections on the Pages' moral values or those of bourgeois society as a whole. Money is also featured in Falstaff's designs on the wives, and in Ford's first

[1] Peter Evans (see p. 25, n. 2) quotes a reviewer's praise, in Tree's 1902 production, of 'the beautiful fifteenth-century costumes, which have been purposely preferred to the customary Elizabethan habits' (*Illustrated London News*, 14 June 1902). Tree's 1888 production had been Tudor in costume and setting (Evans, pp. 61–2).

interview with Falstaff, but here again it is not a dominant theme but rather a means of setting events in motion. No director has tried to centre the play upon social conflict, though some have gestured towards it in their programme notes and interviews.[1] Feminist criticism has had little to say, and that little not illuminating, about the women's roles in the play and in the society that the play depicts.[2]

Occasionally *The Merry Wives of Windsor* has been staged, in the present century, in an un-Elizabethan manner. Komisarjevsky stressed its character as a theatrical comedy by dressing it in colourful costumes (Falstaff had a red jacket and white sidewhiskers) and giving it a setting of a range of brightly coloured doors, each representing a different house, between which there was frequent coming and going.[3] Oscar Asche staged it in modern dress in 1929, and Bill Alexander in the dress of the 1950s (a curious combination of the modern and the nostalgic) in 1985.[4] Both these productions made a feature of incongruity: in the

[1] Terry Hands (programme note, Royal Shakespeare Company, 1968) states that Falstaff, 'whose life has been spent on the fringes of the court', misinterprets the wives' behaviour and underrates their intelligence and their virtue: 'The play, therefore, has a central conflict between two different levels of society.' Bill Alexander (*New Society*, 11 Apr. 1985) is reported as attempting to bring out the analogy between Elizabeth's England, when the wealth of the aristocracy was at its height, and the new rich of the 1950s.

[2] Coppélia Kahn, *Man's Estate: Masculine Identity in Shakespeare* (Berkeley, Calif., 1981) concentrates on cuckoldry as a patriarchal neurosis. Marilyn French, *Shakespeare's Division of Experience* (1982), p. 108, finds that in scrupulously preserving their chastity the wives are conforming to the values of a patriarchal society, as does Anne Parten, 'Falstaff's Horns: Masculine Inadequacy and Feminine Mirth in *The Merry Wives of Windsor*', *Studies in Philology* 82 (1985), 184–99 (p. 190). A different but equally limited interpretation of the play has been put forward by Peter Erickson, 'The Order of the Garter, the Cult of Elizabeth, and Class–Gender Tension in *The Merry Wives of Windsor*', in *Shakespeare Reproduced. The Text in History and Ideology*, ed. Jean E. Howard and Marion F. O'Connor (1987), pp. 116–40: 'Ultimately my thesis involves making a connection between the wives and Queen Elizabeth: the female-controlled plotting within the play parallels the Queen-dominated court politics and arouses a similar male uneasiness' (pp. 118–19).

[3] *Scotsman*, 15 July 1935; *Birmingham Mail*, 20 Apr. 1935. The prompt-book is at the Shakespeare Centre, Stratford-upon-Avon.

[4] Oscar Asche's production (Apollo, London) is described by Gordon Crosse, *Shakespearean Playgoing, 1890–1952* (1953). pp. 91–2, and by J. L. Styan, *The Shakespeare Revolution* (Cambridge, 1977), p. 151. Bill Alexander's (Royal Shakespeare Company) is described in contemporary reviews (e.g. Stanley Wells, *Times Literary Supplement*, 19 Apr. 1985); the prompt-book is at the Shakespeare Centre, Stratford-upon-Avon.

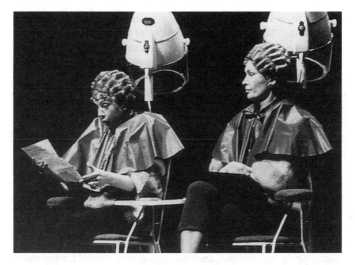

4. Janet Dale and Lindsay Duncan as Mistress Page and Mistress Ford, Royal Shakespeare Theatre, 1985. Director: Bill Alexander (2.1.68.1–2)

former Mistress Page gave her instructions to Mistress Quickly by telephone, and in the latter the wives exchanged Falstaff's letters while sitting under two hair-driers; a motor-cycle (Fenton's) appeared in the former, a Morris Minor (Shallow's or Slender's) in the latter. In both the language was from time to time adjusted, either to remove accidental incongruities (such as a reference to the 'great beard' of a beardless Falstaff) or to introduce deliberate ones (as when Falstaff, leaving the stage, called for a taxi). Needless to say, the sixteenth-century language and manners are continually in conflict with twentieth-century ones. The abortive duel, for which a private fist-fight was a plausible equivalent in the 1929 production, was disastrous in the 1985 one; with Caius in full fencing kit and Evans in a medley of sporting gear, no one could suppose that either took it seriously, and though it got the laughter that it was begging for there was not a trace of Shakespearian humour in it. The director would have done better to substitute pistols for rapiers and adjust the dialogue to this substitution. Modern-dress productions cannot cope with the final scene at all, which is unfortunate, since the final scene is what one is finally left with. In 1985 Herne's Oak was a stump about two feet high with an 'ancient monument' sign attached to it; park railings closed in the setting; most of the fairy speeches were omitted, the Fairy Queen did not arrive until too late because she had been drinking, Evans (costumed as the gnome Big-Ears from Enid Blyton's 'Noddy' books for children) presided, and the fairies seemed to be children dressed for a Hallowe'en party as various monsters and a conventional steeple-hatted witch or two. As a reviewer commented, this modernized production never had 'the chance to give the closing scene in Windsor Forest a brush with stranger non-human forces to precede the reconciliation'.[1]

In strong contrast, the scene was played with violence in Terry Hands's 1968 production. On the line 'With trial-fire touch me his finger-end' Evans, Nim, and Pistol dragged Falstaff by a halter towards Rugby, who held the fire; the halter broke, and Falstaff turned, only to be encircled by devils emerging from a trap, into which, after dancing round Falstaff, they prepared to throw him; Falstaff again broke loose, and was again surrounded for the song and dance; breaking through the ring, he gained the oak up-stage; the song and dance were repeated around the oak, while Slender, Caius, and Fenton led away their partners; then, with flashes and bangs, the oak caught fire, forcing Falstaff to climb up its inside and down its front, finally dropping to his knees centre stage.[2] Like much of the stage business in this production, this was hard-driven, but it did create its own kind of dramatic conviction in the audience.

The performance of the final scene just described had an undertone of real terror, though this was held in check by the extravagance of the present action and of much previous action. Falstaff was plainly being persecuted and put in fear for his life. The effect upon many spectators was somewhat disturbing, partly because they felt that they were accessories in the hunting down of an isolated human being. Some such feeling lies behind a modern critical approach which is concerned with the ritualistic aspect of the play. The originator of this approach is Northrop Frye, though his lightly ironic tone is to be contrasted with the earnestness with which others have pursued it. In *Anatomy of Criticism* Frye has a subsection called 'The Mythos of Spring: Comedy' as part of the section of the book which deals with

[1] Jeremy Kingston, *Times*, 30 Jan. 1986.
[2] Prompt-book at the Shakespeare Centre, Stratford-upon-Avon.

5. Falstaff and the wives at Herne's Oak (oil-painting (1789) by Robert Smirke (1752–1845), commissioned for John Boydell's Shakespeare Gallery, London, and exhibited there in 1789; now in the Art Gallery of the Royal Shakespeare Theatre)

'Archetypal Criticism'. Here he advances the theory that comedy continues to display its origin in festive ritual by the kinds of action and the character-types that it employs. One of these character-types is the *pharmakos* (defined by him as 'The character in an ironic fiction who has the role of a scapegoat or arbitrarily chosen victim'), and one of the kinds of action enacts 'the ritual theme of the triumph of life and love over the waste land'. Though it is the rejected Falstaff of the end of *2 Henry IV* to whom Frye applies the term *pharmakos*, he has a comment on *The Merry Wives of Windsor* which has been the basis of later criticism that sees Falstaff as a scapegoat:

In *The Merry Wives* there is an elaborate ritual of the defeat of winter known to folklorists as 'carrying out Death', of which Falstaff is the victim; and Falstaff must have felt that, after being thrown into the water, dressed up as a witch and beaten out of a house with curses, and finally supplied with a beast's head and singed with candles, he had done about all that could reasonably be asked of any fertility spirit.[1]

The theme of Falstaff as scapegoat seems to have attracted Frye's followers for two reasons. In the first place, it satisfies the craving for a deeper seriousness than is apparent. In the second place, it offers an alternative to the now exhausted critical tradition which finds Falstaff degraded from his former glories and which therefore belittles the play.

The fullest expression of the whole 'folk-ritual' aspect of *The Merry Wives of Windsor* is by Jeanne Addison Roberts.[2] Starting from the position that 'the major emphases of the play specifically reinforce the middle-class social values of its participants' and that Falstaff's courtship of the wives is 'sexually threatening to this social order', she maintains that Falstaff's horns are a symbol of sexual potency, and that their removal is a symbolic castration which at the same time transfers the sexual potency to Ford and eliminates the threat of cuckoldry. This resolution she sums up as follows:

On one level the old fertility god is sacrificed; order is restored to marriage, and posterity is assured. On another, rather uglier, level, social forces have focused their hostilities on a convenient butt and, having vented their explosive power, subside into calm normality.

She compares this treatment of the hearty Falstaff to that of the gloomy Shylock in *The Merchant of Venice*, finding that both plays—and even *Twelfth Night*, where the similar treatment of Malvolio is a subordinate element in the action—'in spite of the surface serenity of their endings, leave their audiences with a lingering uneasiness'.[3] Nothing makes some critics more uneasy

[1] *Anatomy of Criticism*, p. 183. The definition of *pharmakos* is on p. 367, and the allusion to the rejection of Falstaff on p. 45.

[2] Roberts, pp. 75–83, 110–18, 119–34.

[3] Roberts, pp. 81–2. She sees 'rebirth and baptisms' in 'the expulsion from the buck basket and the dip in the Thames', p. 77. Though in the play the only references to Actaeon treat him as an emblem of cuckoldry, she and some other critics treat him as an emblem of sexual potency. This is a modification of John M. Steadman's view that Falstaff's disguise is 'an obvious burlesque of the Actaeon myth' and that it parodies a 'familiar *exemplum* of lust' ('Falstaff as Actaeon: A

than a thoroughly happy ending, especially in our irony-obsessed modern age, so this conclusion is not surprising.

Roberts is also concerned with the seasonal aspect of the play. The 'defeat-of-winter' school would associate it with spring, but she associates it with autumn, and specifically with Hallowe'en (31 October, the night before Allhallowmas or All Saints' Day), mainly because spirits are said to be abroad then.[1] Her case is not at all compelling, and she allows that the indications in the text are indecisive. In fact they are inconsistent. Indoor fires are mentioned (1.4.7–8 and 5.5.235). Caius comments that it is very warm (1.4.46). Pistol, warning Ford of Falstaff's scheme, bids him 'Take heed, ere summer comes, or cuckoo-birds do sing' (2.1.115). Evans waits in the fields for Caius on a 'raw rheumatic day' (3.1.44). Clothes are sent to be washed and bleached beside the Thames (3.3.13). Page and his neighbours go birding, a sport that requires the bushes not to be in full leaf (3.3.219). Herne the Hunter, whom Falstaff is to impersonate, is said to walk 'all the winter-time, at still midnight' (4.4.27). If the German Duke is coming for a Garter Feast, it is in April; if for a Garter Installation, it is in June (4.5.80–2). It is very dark by ten o'clock (5.2.10–11). Falstaff, at midnight, prays Jove for a cool rut-time (5.5.13). The fairy Cricket is sent to inspect Windsor fireplaces (5.5.42); other fairies are told to create a fairy-ring and decorate it with appropriately coloured flowers (5.5.69). One must conclude that each of these passages is directed towards its particular context, not towards establishing the season. The question of the time of year in which to set the play never arose till changeable scenery was introduced, long after Shakespeare's day. The first winter setting of a production was Oscar Asche's in 1911 (Garrick, London), in which 'street and field were covered four inches deep in salt' and snowballs were thrown.[2] Before that

Dramatic Emblem', *Shakespeare Quarterly*, 14 (1963), 230–44: quotations from pp. 231, 237). Bullough, ii. 17–18, allows that 'Shakespeare had Ovid in mind', as Falstaff's allusions to Jove's metamorphoses indicate, but he is surely right in treating Falstaff's disguise and punishment lightly: 'When he dons the horns which he would have placed on Ford's brows he suffers the poetic justice of a failed Don Juan.'

[1] Roberts, pp. 78–80. She points out that the theatre programme for the Royal Shakespeare Company's 1968 production also dwelt on the folk-festival of Hallowe'en.

[2] Robert Speaight, *Shakespeare on the Stage* (1973), p. 130; Crosse, *Shakespearean Playgoing*, p. 27.

time, summer settings were traditional; since then, designers and directors have felt free to follow their inclination. It does not seem a matter of great importance compared with the all-important matter of how speech and action are handled. *The Merry Wives of Windsor* is a merry play, all the merrier for the gravity with which so many of the characters regard themselves, and the director's best course is not to be afraid of the obvious but to concentrate his efforts and those of his actors on bringing out, without labouring, the humour which is so abundant in it.[1]

The Quarto and Folio Texts

The First Quarto (Q, 1602) and the First Folio (F, 1623), which have already been mentioned, are the only texts of *The Merry Wives of Windsor* that have independent authority. A second quarto (Q2, 1619) is a reprint, with minor alterations, of Q; a third (Q3, 1630) is a similar reprint of F, and so are the three later folios (F2, 1632; F3, 1664; F4, 1685), each of which derives directly from its forerunner.

It was formerly believed that the very brief text printed in Q was Shakespeare's first version of the play, but it is now accepted that it is a corrupt text reconstructed from memory and, where memory failed, from invention. Highly unreliable though it is, therefore, it does reflect its compiler's knowledge of the play as it was performed, and so provides evidence which must be weighed by an editor alongside the evidence of F.

The text printed in F is nearly twice as long, and, having been supplied to the printer by Shakespeare's fellow sharers in the King's Men, carries good authority. Yet it has its own imperfections. Like the texts of the two plays which precede it in F, *The Tempest* and *The Two Gentlemen of Verona*, and that of *Measure for Measure* which follows it, it was evidently transcribed for printing by Ralph Crane, a professional scribe who had some conspicuous mannerisms, particularly his widespread use of parentheses and

---

[1] Hugh Hunt, *Old Vic Prefaces* (1954), p. 93, told his cast: 'I have, I think, good reason for insisting on a realistic interpretation, since this is our Festival play and there are some who would criticize the choice of so minor a play as *The Merry Wives of Windsor* for such an occasion [the Festival of Britain, 1951]. I would like to justify it by showing the English humour of the play—the merry England which has played so large a part in the building of our institutions and national character.'

of hyphens and his listing at the beginning of every scene the names of all the characters who were to appear in it.[1] Because of this mannerism of 'massed entries' no entries that occur during a scene (except '*Enter Fairies*' in the final scene) are marked, nor are exits other than those that end a scene. Other imperfections of the F text are its consistent substitution of Broom (*Broome*) for Brook (*Brooke* in Q) as Ford's assumed name, and its expurgations of language that was profane or might be thought profane.

There is no need to set down all the evidence that has been accumulated to prove that Q is a 'bad Quarto' and prints an imperfectly reconstructed text (a 'reported text') of the play. It is sufficient to illustrate from it three kinds of corruption characteristic of such reported texts.

Firstly, consistent action and dialogue in the original become inconsistent because of the reported text's omissions. In 1.4, when Caius has just discovered Simple hiding in the closet, Mistress Quickly explains to him, in F, that 'The young man is an honest man' who 'came of an errand to me from Parson Hugh', and Simple takes up the tale:

> To desire this honest gentlewoman, your maid, to speak a good word to Mistress Anne Page for my master in the way of marriage.

Caius absorbs this information ('Sir Hugh send-a you?') and orders Rugby to give him some paper, on which he writes his challenge to the parson. In Q Caius directly accuses Simple of being a thief; Simple replies

> O Lord sir no: I am no theefe,
> I am a Seruingman:
> My name is *Iohn Simple*, I brought a Letter sir
> From my M. *Slender*, about misteris *Anne Page*
> Sir: Indeed that is my comming.

Caius retorts 'I begar is dat all?', calls for pen and ink, and writes his challenge. Q has left out the fact that the letter was from Sir Hugh Evans, thus rendering Caius's challenge inconsequential, and in making Simple say that the letter was from Slender is inconsistent with its own version of 1.2, where it is clear that

---

[1] A full account of Ralph Crane and his transcripts of writings by Shakespeare and others is to be found in T. H. Howard-Hill, *Ralph Crane and Some Shakespeare First Folio Comedies* (Charlottesville, Va., 1972).

Evans wrote the letter ('tis about Maister *Slender*'). It is evident, then, that Q's version of 1.4 is a faulty reconstruction of the scene.

Secondly, fragments of the dialogue of the original text turn up in the wrong place in the reported text. Thus Falstaff's remarks, after being first thrown in the Thames and later cudgelled, about how he would be mocked at court if his discomfiture came to be known (4.5.88–94), are transferred in Q to the final scene and applied to his being imposed on by the pretended fairies; the dialogue between Shallow and Page about the wisdom of not fighting duels and the natural urge to fight them (2.3.35–47), which belongs properly to the situation when Evans has failed to meet Caius at what the latter has been told is the appointed place, is moved in Q, with some further transposition of the order of the speeches, to the scene in which the duel is first being discussed (F's 2.1); two speeches from Slender's wooing scene (3.4.59–63) are used in Q to open his conversation with Anne Page near the end of the opening scene; the phrase 'a legion of angels' (1.3.50) lodged so firmly in the reporter's memory that he brought it in a second time when Falstaff is speaking to 'Master Brook' of Ford's 'masses of money' (2.2.257).

Thirdly, there are echoes of other plays in which the reporter may have acted. Nim repeatedly uses the phrase 'there's the humour of it', a corruption of his phrase 'that's the humour of it' in *Henry V* (a corruption shared by the 'bad quarto', printed in 1600, of that play, where it is always given in the wrong form); Pistol twice uses his *Henry V* word 'retort' and once his phrase from *2 Henry IV* 'When Pistol lies, do this'.

Besides the loose paraphrase which is a characteristic of reported texts, Q on three occasions substitutes entirely new dialogue for that of F: Fenton's dialogue with Anne Page (3.4), the dialogue in which Ford expresses his contrition and the Herne's Oak jest is plotted (4.4), and the speeches of the fairies in the final scene. On all these occasions verse is replaced by other verse, of a quality no better than might be expected of an actor who was used to appearing in verse plays: it is mostly end-stopped blank verse, sometimes falling into rhymed couplets, and in the fairies' dialogue there are over thirty lines of octosyllabic verse (one quatrain followed by fourteen couplets).

All these features of Q's text suggest that it was compiled from a report made by someone who knew the play tolerably well and knew some parts of it better than others. The relatively accurate reporting of the Host's speeches in particular gives good reason for believing that the actor who played this role was either the sole reporter or the principal one.[1] It is significant that the only other verse scene in the play besides the three mentioned as having been rewritten is that between Fenton and the Host (4.6), which has not been rewritten and is reported with some accuracy.

Though Q's text is very unlike F's there is little likelihood that it is based on a much revised version used in a public theatre as distinct from the original court version. Most of its shortening can be explained by the reporter's failure to remember the full text. This may also explain the omission of the whole of William's Latin lesson (F's 4.1), a useful scene which prevents two Falstaff scenes from occurring consecutively and with nothing but Ford's soliloquy to separate Falstaff's exit from his re-entry.[2] The first four scenes of Act 5, also omitted, are all very short, so nothing would have been gained by cutting them out, and one of them (Ford's final visit to Falstaff as Brook) is actually promised in Q's 'Let me alone, Ile to him once againe like *Brooke*, and know his mind whether heele come or not' (which corresponds to F's 4.4.73–4). Q's consistent alterations of Caius's 'closet' (in F's 1.4) to his 'counting-house' need not derive from a revised version, for the reporter may have performed in some play, such as *Arden of Faversham*, in which the off-stage room was so called; and Caius's command, in the scene corresponding to F's 2.3,

> *Iohn Rugbie* goe looke met your eies ore de stall,
> And spie and you can see de parson,

[1] Falstaff's speeches are often well reported too, but the fact that one is conspicuously misplaced makes it unlikely that the actor of Falstaff collaborated in compiling Q, as Oliver (p. xxvii) maintains. Falstaff is the chief character and his lines are particularly memorable, and the actor who played the Host may have had a comedian's special interest in the role.

[2] Q gets over the difficulty by transposing 3.5 and 3.4. Gerald D. Johnson thinks it 'very doubtful that a reporter would have rearranged the scenes' and that 'the reporter was attempting to follow an alternative version of the play that already included these changes' ('*The Merry Wives of Windsor*, Q1: Provincial Touring and Adapted Texts', *Shakespeare Quarterly*, 38/2 (1987), 154–65; p. 163). It is true that the two F scenes could be satisfactorily transposed, provided that Mistress Quickly's last two sentences in the final speech of 3.4, about her errand to Falstaff, which she performs in 3.5, were omitted. But why should William's Latin lesson have been cut? It has plenty of obvious verbal humour—more, in fact, than Catherine's English lesson in *Henry V* (3.4), which is conducted entirely in French and is not omitted from the 'bad quarto' (1600) of the play.

rather than implying that Caius owns a stall or shop, seems to involve a mishearing of 'stile', for the scene is in the fields, and in F's corresponding scene for Evans (3.1) Simple sees people coming from Frogmore 'over the stile'.[1] In the final scene the substituted 'fairy' speeches virtually rule out the possibility that a revised version of them lies behind Q, for in that case one would expect Q to reproduce some of the new Shakespearian lines, whereas Q's lines have a pedestrian self-consistency:

> Where is *Pead*? go you & see where Brokers sleep,
> And Foxe-eyed Seriants with their mase,
> Goe laie the Proctors in the street,
> And pinch the lowsie Seriants face:
> Spare none of these when they are a bed,
> But such whose nose looks plew and red.

The last quoted line echoes Fluellen's description of Bardolph (*Henry V*, 3.6.105–6), and therefore supports the inference that this long verse passage was entirely the invention of the reporter, being typical of a reported text. To argue that Shakespeare did not provide completely new speeches for the fairies, either about brokers and serjeants or about anything else, need not imply that the Fairy Queen's topical allusions to the Garter Knights' stalls in St George's Chapel at Windsor Castle were still being made on the public stage: she has enough to say without them, and, as has been stated already (p. 3), they have usually been omitted in performance.

The purpose for which Q was compiled is a matter of opinion. It may have been intended to provide a script for acting troupes to perform: the omission of William's Latin lesson and of Robin's speeches can be interpreted as saving two speaking parts for boy actors.[2] On the other hand, a number of boys are required to play

---

[1] Similar errors in Q are 'sir *Yon* [= You]' for 'Sir Hugh' (B3) and 'bullies taile' for 'bully stale' (D1ᵛ), which show that dictation was part of the process in compiling the text. The line 'And by my sword [for 'side'] were [for 'wear'] steel' (B2ᵛ) suggests, in its first error, just the same peculiarity of the reporter's accent that caused the stall/stile error.

[2] No significant reduction of the number of actors required is possible. The F text has 22 speaking parts, the Q text 19 (William absent, Robin silent, only one of the two Servants speaking). F's 22 parts could be played by 18 actors (e.g. Simple doubling John, Bardolph doubling Robert, Nim doubling Fenton, Robin doubling William); Q's 19 parts require 16 actors, and the time available for costume-changes is considerably reduced by the shortening of the dialogue.

fairies in the final scene, Robin has to appear in the scene where Falstaff gives him the letters to deliver, Robin and William could have been doubled by one boy actor (and both, at a pinch, by the actor of Anne Page, if William were dropped from the fairy troupe in the last two scenes), and William's Latin lesson may have been omitted either because the reporter could not remember enough of it or because he did not think it particularly amusing, either of which reasons may also explain the omission of most of the opening dialogue with the 'luces' joke. It is just as likely that Q was compiled for sale to readers. The title-page does its best to promise entertainment:

A | Most pleasaunt and | excellent conceited Co-|medie, of Syr *Iohn Falstaffe*, and the | merrie Wiues of *Windsor*. | Entermixed with sundrie | variable and pleasing humors, of Syr *Hugh* | the Welch Knight, Iustice *Shallow*, and his | wise Cousin M. *Slender*. | With the swaggering vaine of Auncient | *Pistoll*, and Corporall *Nym*. | By *William Shakespeare*. | As it hath bene diuers times Acted by the right Honorable | my Lord Chamberlaines seruants. Both before her | Maiestie, and else-where. | [ornament] | LONDON | Printed by T. C. for Arthur Iohnson, and are to be sold at | his shop in Powles Church-yard, at the signe of the | Flower de Leuse and the Crowne. | 1602.

The error in calling Sir Hugh Evans a knight instead of a parson was presumably the publisher's.[1] The statement about performances 'both before Her Majesty and elsewhere' implies that the reader is being given the whole text of the play, and nothing suggests that there has been any authorized revision for public performance (nor, of course, any unauthorized revision for the present publication).

The authorized text printed in F took the form, as has been said, of a transcript by Ralph Crane, who had also transcribed the other three comedies placed with this play at the beginning of the Folio. All are divided into acts and scenes, and the other three have a final list of characters, for which there was no room on the last page of *The Merry Wives of Windsor*. The publishers' evident desire for consistency in presentation (probably emulating Ben

---

[1] The play had been entered to John Busby in the Stationers' Register on 18 Jan. 1602 and on the same date transferred to Arthur Johnson, a transfer sometimes interpreted as a manoeuvre to disguise Busby's involvement with a pirated text, but more probably indicating a joint venture (Jowett, p. 340).

Jonson's folio *Works* of 1616) combined with Crane's own mannerisms makes it difficult to establish what kind of copy Crane had before him. There are, however, signs suggesting that it was Shakespeare's manuscript rather than the company's prompt-book. Firstly, Page's Christian name is given as Thomas in 1.1, but by 2.1 it has become George.[1] Secondly, the 'massed entry' at the beginning of 1.3 is *'Enter Falstaffe, Host, Bardolfe, Nym, Pistoll, Page'*, where *'Page'* is not the Windsor citizen but Falstaff's page, who has no name as yet (nor has he in *2 Henry IV*, assuming the page there to be the same character), but acquires the name Robin by 2.2 and retains it in his two later scenes. Thirdly, in 1.3 Nim says that he is going to betray Falstaff's plan to Ford and Pistol says that he will betray it to Page, whereas in 2.1 it is Pistol who informs Ford and Nim who informs Page; this inconsistency is not found in Q, which transposes the names of Ford and Page in the earlier scene and in so doing probably reflects what was done in performance. These are indications that Crane's copy was less likely to have been a professionally prepared prompt-book, in which the two latter irregularities might be expected to have been put right even if the first had been allowed to stand, than Shakespeare's manuscript, from which the company's prompt-book would in due course be prepared. It is believed that *The Two Gentlemen of Verona* and *Measure for Measure*, which contain similar inconsistencies, were also transcribed from Shakespeare's manuscripts of them.

One other inconsistency seems likely to have been left standing in the prompt-book and in performance because there would have been considerable difficulty and little dramatic advantage in altering it. As P. A. Daniel first pointed out, the treatment of time is consistent up to Falstaff's buck-basket escape and the dinner at Ford's that follows, but thereafter becomes inconsistent.[2] The wives arrange for Mistress Quickly to give Falstaff an appointment for 'tomorrow eight o'clock', but when she arrives to find Falstaff swallowing sack to counteract the cold Thames water she wishes him good morrow, tells him that Ford 'goes this morning a-

---

[1] Jowett, who argues for prompt-book copy, suggests that F's *Thomas* may result from a misreading of Geo in Shakespeare's handwriting as Tho.

[2] P. A. Daniel, introduction to *The Merry Wives of Windsor* (photolithographic facsimile of Q [1881]), p. viii.

birding', and fixes the appointment 'between eight and nine'. Ford next enters, disguised as Brook, to learn how Falstaff has fared; at their first meeting Falstaff had insistently bidden him 'Come to me soon at night', but now he repeats to him Mistress Quickly's message, and, being told by Ford that it is 'past eight already', goes to keep his appointment, Ford following. Then, after emptying the buck-basket, Ford declares to Page 'there was one conveyed out of my house yesterday in this basket'. Q's version of the Falstaff/Mistress Quickly/Ford scene (F's 3.5) is similar except that Mistress Quickly gives Falstaff an appointment for 'to morrow', which is inconsistent with what follows, whereas in F the inconsistency is with what has gone before. Daniel observed that consistency could be maintained in F by splitting the scene into two and setting the two dialogues on consecutive days, changing Mistress Quickly's speeches to bring them into line with this, but that to have two consecutive scenes for Falstaff would be contrary to stage practice. He might have added that the rearrangement would draw attention to Ford's failure to visit Falstaff as Brook on the evening of the first day. As it is, Shakespeare plays fast and loose with time but maintains dramatic pace.

F's inconsistency over the costumes required for Fenton's elopement with Anne, and for Caius's and Slender's unsuccessful abductions, in the final scene is a different matter. Here everything is consistent until the return of Slender and Caius. Then Slender complains that he has not got Anne although he took the fairy 'in greene', Mistress Page explains his error by telling Page that she put Anne 'into white', and Caius complains that he has not got Anne although (as his reply to Mistress Page confirms) he took the fairy 'in white'. This is inexplicable unless (as Oliver suggests, calling the suggestion 'a desperate hypothesis') Crane deliberately transposed 'green' and 'white' in his transcript, 'thinking that Slender was bound to get his instructions wrong', and then made the opposite transposition for consistency's sake. Whatever the reason for the error, it can hardly derive from Shakespeare's manuscript, since it has been made clear over and over again that the original plan is for Anne to be dressed in white as the Fairy Queen, that Page thereupon arranges for Slender to abduct Anne in white, and that by Mistress Page's substituted scheme Caius is to abduct Anne in green. What colour she eventually wears in order to elude her two unwelcome suitors and be recognized by Fenton is not, and does not need to be, stated in Fenton's dialogue with the Host (4.6). Q utterly garbles this: when the original plan is formulated Page (evidently in an aside) determines to dress Anne in white so that Slender may abduct her; Mistress Page has already (evidently in another aside) determined that Caius shall abduct Anne on this occasion, though without reference to her costume; later Fenton tells the Host that Anne's father means to dress her in white to be abducted by Slender, that her mother means to dress her in red to be abducted by Caius, and that he, Fenton, will be sure to know her 'by a robe of white, the which she weares'; finally Caius makes his complaint without reference to Anne's costume, and Slender makes his because 'I came to her in red as you bad me, and I cried mum, and hee cried budget, so well as euer you heard'—incidentally giving one more proof that Q's text is a corrupt version of F's, since this is the first that we hear of Slender's mum-budget password in Q.

In addition to the confusion over the colours in the last scene, two characteristics of F's text cannot reflect Shakespeare's original intentions, though it is best to reserve judgement on whether the first of them can have appeared in Shakespeare's manuscript, assuming that to have been what lay before Crane. These are the substitution of Broom for Brook as Ford's assumed name and the expurgation of profane language.

That Shakespeare intended Ford to call himself Brook is both obvious and provable. A ford goes through a brook, and Ford's choice of an appropriate false name is consistent with Falstaff's quibble (3.5.34–5), when brought a message from Mistress Ford,

Mistress Ford? I have had ford enough. I was thrown into the ford. I have my belly full of ford.

So much for obviousness. The proof lies in Falstaff's other quibble, when sent an introductory draught of sack by Master Brook (2.2.143–4):

Such Brooks are welcome to me, that o'erflows such liquor.

This reading, accepted by all editors as correct, is a conflation of Q's 'Such *Brookes* are alwaies welcome to me' and F's 'such *Broomes* are welcome to mee, that ore'flowes such liquor'.

Q preserves the name but leaves out the emphatic part of the joke; F preserves the joke intact but corrupts the name.[1]

Why and when the substitution was made is unknown. The natural, and probably correct, inference is that it was made either to avoid offending the Brooke family or in consequence of having offended them.[2] Green believes that Shakespeare chose Ford's false name without remembering that it was the surname of the Lords Cobham, one of whom had had Oldcastle renamed Falstaff, and that the substitution was voluntarily made in time for the first performance. Taylor believes that Shakespeare chose the name provocatively and that the substitution was indirectly compelled by Henry Brooke after his marriage in 1601. Oliver is inclined to accept Alfred Hart's explanation that the substitution was made for a performance before James I on 4 November 1604 because the name Brooke 'might revive unpleasant memories' of two political plots for which, in the previous December, Henry Brooke and his brother George had been sentenced to death.[3] As for the date of the substitution, one's first thought is that it must have happened between the publication of Q and that of F, but one's second thought is that it may have been only a temporary measure for the original court performance (assuming the 'Garter play' theory to be correct), after which the name Brooke could go on being used in the public theatre. The suppression of the name Oldcastle is not comparable: Oldcastle is a distinctive name and belonged to a historical individual, but Brook is a common name and is assumed by a character who is himself fictitious. If the substitution was only a temporary measure, and if the play had been composed to such an imminent deadline that, for once, Shakespeare's manuscript had to serve as the prompt-book for the court performance, the substitution could have been made there, and there Crane would find it. Meanwhile, soon after the court performance, the company's prompt-book would be made, with Brook restored and the joke about liquor once more making sense. Since it makes no sense with Broom it would have had to

---

[1] Q's incorrect reporting of this significant speech throws further doubt on Oliver's theory that the actor of Falstaff was a reporter.

[2] See pp. 9–11, and Green, pp. 107–20; Oliver, pp. lvi–lviii; Taylor, 'William Shakespeare, Richard James, and the House of Cobham', pp. 349–54.

[3] Alfred Hart, *Stolne and Surreptitious Copies* (Melbourne, 1942), pp. 89–90. George Brooke was executed, but Henry was reprieved, imprisoned, and expelled from the Order of the Garter.

be dropped for the court performance; it therefore ought to have been struck out of Shakespeare's manuscript if that were serving as the temporary prompt-book, but human behaviour is not always strictly methodical, and it could have been safely left to the actor of Falstaff to remember to cut the sentence. Why, then, did not Heminges and Condell correct Crane's Broom back to Brook, either at the transcript stage or at the proof stage? How serious an objection this is depends upon what part they may have taken in checking copy for the printer or in checking the printer's proofs. Even if they did undertake one or both of these operations for *The Merry Wives of Windsor*, they may have felt that Ford's assumed name was not important enough to alter, especially as Broom had been used once before in a performance.[1] The explanation of the Brook/Broom discrepancy here offered is not free from difficulties,[2] but it seems more credible than that after acting the play with the name Brook for three or four years the company allowed Henry Brooke to intimidate them (on grounds that could only make him appear ridiculous) into changing it to Broom, and then went on acting the play in that form for another twenty years even though Henry Brooke and his brother had been thoroughly discredited in 1603.[3]

The inference that Crane's copy was Shakespeare's manuscript also affects the matter of F's expurgations, since they consequently have to be inferred to have been made either by Crane or by someone working over the manuscript for this purpose before Crane began to transcribe it. The expurgation of profanity was a consequence of the Act to Restrain Abuses of Players (May 1606), which provided a penalty of £10 for 'jestingly or profanely'

[1] They tolerated or overlooked a much more important change of name in *Cymbeline* if, as the Oxford Shakespeare indicates, the heroine's name should have been Innogen and not Imogen.

[2] For example, as Stanley Wells points out to me, if somebody (possibly Shakespeare) was careful enough to alter every occurrence of the frequently recurring name Brook he might be expected to correct the inconsistencies mentioned above, in particular the transposition of Ford and Page in 1.3 and the confusion over the colours in 5.5. In defence of my hypothesis I might argue that the expurgation of the name Brook may have been a special operation, and that, as the name occurs only in six of the twenty-three scenes, usually in heavy concentrations, Crane, when he came to copy the manuscript, would remember that Broom was to be substituted even if Brook had been left standing in the manuscript now and then.

[3] Hart's explanation, that Broom was substituted to spare James I's sensibility in 1604, is open to the same objection as Taylor's.

speaking or using 'the holy name of God, or of Christ Jesus, or of the Holy Ghost, or of the Trinity' in performances. Though the act was aimed at the stage, not at printed playbooks, it was natural that plays being printed for the first time since it became law should be overhauled by their publishers. As regards F, its publication implied that its texts were currently being performed by the King's Men in their printed form, and Heminges and Condell may have encouraged the expurgation of profanity. *Measure for Measure* (1604), which Crane transcribed from what was probably Shakespeare's manuscript, has (2.4.4–5)

> Heaven in my mouth
> As if I did but only chew his name,

where the original must have read 'God in my mouth'. Similarly, in *The Merry Wives of Windsor* (2.2.50–1), when Falstaff has reassured Mistress Quickly that nobody hears them but Pistol and Robin who are his own people, she replies, in F,

Are they so? heauen-blesse them, and make them his Seruants.

In Q her reply is

Are they so? Now God blesse them, and make them his seruants.

Q's reading 'God' is evidently that of the original, and is supported by the fact that in two scenes of *The Famous Victories of Henry the Fifth*, one of Shakespeare's sources for the English history plays that he was then writing, Henry IV addresses Prince Henry in the same formula:

> Stand up my son, and do not think thy father,
> But at the request of thee my sonne, wil pardon thee,
> And God blesse thee, and make thee his servant.[1]

When Falstaff tells 'Master Brook' how he was conveyed into a buck-basket (3.5.80), and Ford repeats the word, F makes him reply

Yes: a Buck-basket: ram'd mee in with foule Shirts and Smockes, Socks, foule Stockings, greasie Napkins, that (Master *Broome*) there was the rankest compound of villanous smell, that euer offended nostrill.

[1] Scene vi (ll. 577–9); also Scene viii (ll. 671–3). Printed in Bullough, iv. 316, 318.

Q's version is

> By the Lord a buck-basket, rammed me in
> With foule shirts, stokins, greasie napkins,
> That M. *Brooke*, there was a compound of the most
> Villanous smel, that euer offended nostrill.

Though Q does not get the whole passage word-perfect, it is reported well enough at this point to make its 'By the Lord' convincing. F's 'Yes' is a palpable substitution; were Falstaff to reply without an oath, 'A buck-basket' would be stronger, like his immediately preceding reply to Ford's 'What? While you were there?'

While I was there.

(substantially the same in Q: 'While ye were there?' 'Whilst I was there.'). 'Yes' is so feeble that it must be put down to editorial expurgation; one cannot imagine Shakespeare, or any member of the King's Men, writing it in a revised prompt-book.

Though F has been expurgated, Q cannot be relied on to supply its deficiencies because, as Oliver points out, reporters 'improvise asseverations more readily than most other phrasing'. A typical instance of such improvisation is Anne Page's

> O God how many grosse faults are hid
> And couered in three hundred pound a yeare?

where the right reading is (as in F, 3.4.32–3)

> O, what a world of vile ill-favoured faults
> Looks handsome in three hundred pounds a year!

Even Falstaff, though given to profanity as Anne Page is not, is not likely to reply to Ford's invitation to ease him of the burden of his bag of money (2.2.165–6 in F) with

> O Lord, would I could tell how to deserve
> To be your porter.

where F gives him the ceremonious phrase

Sir, I know not how I may deserve to be your porter.

Sometimes, however, it is very difficult to decide whether to follow F or admit a profanity from Q. When Falstaff asks Mistress

Quickly whether Mistress Ford and Mistress Page have told each other that they love him, she replies (in F, 2.2.105–6)

That were a iest indeed: they haue not so little grace I hope, that were a tricke indeed:

and goes on, in a long speech, to urge him to send Robin to Mistress Page (all of which, like Robin's presence in the scene, is omitted in Q). Q's words corresponding to those quoted from F are

O God no sir: there were a iest indeed.

The oath is spontaneous enough, and 'in character' enough, to be authentic; and yet F's repeating of its first phrase with a slight variation sounds authentic too, and the implied denial in the middle phrase may make an opening flat denial superfluous. To complicate matters, bearing in mind that compilers of reported texts often introduce expressions from other plays, we may notice that in the opening scene of Jonson's *Every Man in his Humour* (Q, 1601), a play in the repertory of the Lord Chamberlain's Men, Lorenzo Senior gives his servant Musco a letter that has just been brought for his son Lorenzo Junior, adding that he is not to tell the son that the father has opened it. Musco replies

O Lord sir, that were a iest indeed.

In the circumstances it seems safer to follow F here. Each case of possible expurgation has to be separately considered in this way by an editor, unless he decides to stick to F for fear of introducing unauthorized profanities from Q.

The final characteristic of Crane's transcript to be considered is his omission of stage directions, other than 'massed entries' and end-of-scene exits. In the absence of stage directions in F, Q's stage directions become particularly interesting, though they are not necessarily reliable. For an editor the problem is similar to the problem presented by the expurgations. On the one hand, the reporter undoubtedly knew the play on the stage; on the other, he was putting together what he could remember of the text, and his stage directions had to accommodate themselves to what was left of it when his memory and invention had done their best. They had also to accommodate themselves to the space on the page. Thus in the equivalent of 1.3 the direction '*Exit Falstaffe, and the Boy*', placed at the end of the speech in which Falstaff

the merry Wiues of Windsor.

My name is Iohn Simple, I brought a Letter sir
From my M. Slender, about mistris Anne Page.
Sir: Indeed that is my comming,
Doc. I begar is dat all: Iohn Rugby giue a ma pen
An Inck: tarche vn pertit tarche a little.
            The Doctor writes.
Sim. O God what a furious man is this?
Qui. Nay it is well he is no worse:
I am glad he is so quiet.
Doc. Here giue dat same to sir Hu, it ber ve chalenge
Begar tell him I will cut his nase, will you? (may.
Sim. I sir, Ile tell him so.
Doc. Darbevell, my Rapier Iohn Rugby, follow
Qui. Maister, Ile doo what I can for him,   Exit Doctor.
And so farewell.
Sim. Mary, will I, I am glad I am got hence.
                Exit omnes.

Enter Mistresse Page, reading of
            a Letter.

Mist. Pa. Mistresse Page I loue you: Aske me no
Because they impossible to alledge. Your faire, (treason,
And I am fat. You loue sacke, so do I.
As I am sure I haue so mind but to loue,
So I know you haue no hart but to grant (knowes
A souldier doth not vse many words, where a
A letter may serue: so ba sentence: I loue you,
And so I leaue you,   Yours Sir Iohn Falstaffe.   Now.

6. A page (B4ᵛ) from the Quarto of 1602

Fen. Well, fare-well, I am in great haste now.
Qui. Fare-well to your Worship: truely an honest
Gentleman: but Anne loues hiim not: for I know Ans
minde as well as another do's: our vpon't: what haue I
forgot.   Exit.

Actus Secundus. Scoena Prima.

Enter Mistris Page, Mistris Ford, Master Page, Master
Ford, Pistoll, Nim, Quickly, Host, Shallow.

Mist. Page. What, haue scap'd Loue-letters in the
holly-day-time of my beauty, and am I now a subiect
for them? let me see?

Aske me no reason why, I loue you, for though Loue vse Reason for his precisian, hee admits him not for his Counsailour:
you are not yong, no more am I: goe to then, there's simpathie:
you are merry, so am I: ha, ha, then there's more simpathie:
you loue facke, and so do I: would you desire better simpathie?
Let it suffice thee (Mistris Page) at the least if the Loue of
Souldier can suffice, that I loue thee: I will not say pitty mee,
'tis not a Souldier-like phrase; but I say, loue me:
By me, thine owne true Knight, by day or night:
Or any kinde of light, with all his might,
For thee to fight.   Iohn Falstaffe.

What a Herod of Iurie is this? O wicked, wicked world:

7. Part of a page (D4ᵛ) from the Folio of 1623

62

gives the letters to Robin, need mean no more than that after the end of the speech Pistol and Nim are left alone to plot their revenge; it does not oblige Robin to leave the stage when Falstaff does (and his exit, and Falstaff's abuse of Pistol and Nim, are more effective if he leaves the stage directly after he has been given the letters). In the equivalent of 2.1 the opening direction is unexceptionable ('*Enter Mistresse* Page, *reading of a Letter*'), and so is the placing of Mistress Ford's entry at the end of Mistress Page's soliloquy, but if there had been any further directions about the two letters they would have been at variance with the scene in F: there Mistress Ford makes no reference to Mistress Page's letter, for the good reason that Mistress Page does not show it her until after she has shown her own letter; but in Q Mistress Ford enters with the greeting

> How now Mistris *Page*, are you reading
> Loue Letters? How do you woman?

and it is she who matches Mistress Page's letter, not Mistress Page who matches hers. This freedom taken by Q with the text in 2.1 must cast doubt on the stage directions in the final scene, which has been even more thoroughly rewritten. The direction '*Falstaffe pulles of his bucks head, and rises vp. And enters* M. *Page*, M. *Ford, and their wiues*, M. *Shallow, Sir Hugh.*', besides bringing in Shallow where F does not, calls for an action on Falstaff's part which fits Page's greeting,

Why how now sir *Iohn*, what a pair of horns in your hand?

But there is nothing in F's text to suggest that Falstaff has pulled off his horns before he is confronted by the Fords and the Pages, and an editor must decide for himself what the appropriate directions are.[1]

---

[1] He must also decide whether Falstaff wears a simple pair of horns or an imitation buck's head. See Appendix C.

EDITORIAL PROCEDURES

THE text of this edition is necessarily based on that of the Folio (F), which is taken to be an essentially faithful transcript of Shakespeare's manuscript although it is heavily marked by the editorial mannerisms of Ralph Crane the scribe. The Quarto (Q), though a very corrupt text, has considerable importance and has had to be compared with F throughout. This situation has created a problem in compiling the collation. To collate all Q's variant readings would take up a great amount of space and would often be unprofitable, since most of them can be attributed to the reporter's failure to remember the text accurately. Accordingly only such Q readings as seem to be relevant to readings in F have been collated. When the collation lists a F reading without a Q one the reader is to understand that the passage in question is either very differently expressed in Q or entirely absent from it.

The practice of the Oxford Shakespeare with regard to stage directions in the text is to place them in broken brackets (⌈ ⌉) if they are matters of editorial opinion (for instance, if there is room for doubt as to what the action should be or where it should occur) and not to single them out in this way if they are indisputably implied by the dialogue. This practice is followed in this edition. All indications of speech direction (e.g. '(*to Shallow*)') and all asides are editorial unless otherwise stated; they are collated only when original to this or other recent editions, or if they seem disputable. The first editor to list the persons of the play was Rowe in 1709. The list in the present edition is adapted from that of Hibbard.

Punctuation and spelling have been modernized. When the punctuation of F has been changed in such a way as to affect the sense or the syntax it is collated; otherwise it is silently brought into consistency with modern usage. The modernizing of spelling is a more difficult matter for an editor. The Oxford Shakespeare's practice is to adjust obsolete, variant, or ambiguous spellings to appropriate modern ones.[1] In editing *The Merry Wives of Windsor*

---

[1] The subject of modernization is discussed by Stanley Wells, 'Modernizing Shakespeare's Spelling', in Stanley Wells and Gary Taylor, *Modernizing Shakespeare's Spelling, with Three Studies in the Text of 'Henry V'* (Oxford, 1979) and in ch. 1 of his *Re-Editing Shakespeare for the Modern Reader* (Oxford, 1984).

it has often been hard to decide when to retain a F spelling and when to change it, and I cannot claim to be wholly satisfied with all the decisions that I have reached. Where modernizing simply involves abandoning an archaic spelling (accoutrement, 4.2.4; accustrement F, accoustrement F2), or where only a minor point of pronunciation may be in question (yellowness, 1.3.94; yellownesse F), one is following the example of most previous editors in using the modern form of the word. Similarly, as by most previous editors, at 3.3.75 and 4.2.51 F's 'lime-kill' and 'kill-hole' have been modernized, even though the 'kill' form, to judge from its frequency, was Shakespeare's own spelling. Such proper names as Cotswold (1.1.82: *Cotsall* F), Brentford (4.2.66 etc.: *Brainford* F), and Colnbrook (4.5.73: *Cole-brooke* F) have been spelt in the modern way (though I understand that their local pronunciation still approximates to the old spelling), but Readings (4.5.72: *Readins* F, Readings Q) has been retained because the final *s* is consistent with Evans's mannerism elsewhere. At 3.3.38 I modernize F's 'pumpion' to 'pumpkin' with some reluctance, partly because I am not quite sure that the modern form had been introduced in Shakespeare's time (though *OED* shows that it was in use by 1647) and partly because in *Love's Labour's Lost* a Shakespearian joke depends on the older form of the word. At 3.1.59 I read 'mess of porridge' (messe of porredge F) rather than 'mess of pottage' precisely because both forms were current in Shakespeare's time and because it is the latter form that is used in a contemporary translation of Genesis 25; I think that there may be some significance in Evans's using the other form (see commentary). Evans's Welsh pronunciation, fitfully indicated in F, has been equally fitfully indicated in this edition: consistent substitution of *p* for *b*, *c* for *g*, and *t* for *d* would be to labour the point. Caius's French, when he is evidently speaking French and not Franglais, has been modernized; but when he says to the Host 'it is tell-a me dat you make grand preparation ...' (4.5.80–1) the last two words quoted have been left in English spelling even though the sense of the first of them is clearly French; this indicates that he pronounces the words in the English way but with a French accent rather than that he says '*grand(e) préparation*'. Wherever modernization of spelling seems significant enough to mention, the F spelling is collated.

The collation, while recording substantive departures from F's

66

readings, does not take account of most of the merely mechanical errors in F, which have no significance and cannot be seriously entertained as readings. Some examples are the following: Gater (Garter, 1.1.128), hononor (honor, i.e. honour, 2.2.20), foolish-ion Carion (foolish carrion, 3.3.181), *Fenter* (Fenton, 3.4.66), Oh, heere be comes (O here he comes, 3.5.56), direct direct my men (direct my men, 4.2.89), thi is (this is, 4.2.140), Mote fertile-fresh (More fertile-fresh, 5.5.67). However, occasionally an error of this sort is collated: for instance, 'We cannot misuse enough' (for 'We cannot misuse him enough', 4.2.91–2) reinforces the argument that words may have been omitted elsewhere. The frequent appearances of hyphens in F are recorded only when they may be material to the interpretation of the sense. The abbreviation M., used regularly in F for Master and occasionally for Mistress, has not been collated except where its sense is debatable.

The greater part of the play is in prose, and so the question of indicating the syllabic value, for metrical purposes, of the past forms of verbs rarely arises; when it does, an accent is placed on the sounded syllable (sealèd bags, 3.4.16). Elisions within words are retained when a line of verse might be wrongly pronounced without them (dean'ry, 4.6.30; *Deanry* F); in prose they are disregarded (deanery, 5.5.198; Deanrie F). The lineation in the few passages of sustained verse presents no problems; when there has been variance of editorial opinion (e.g. 4.6.25) it is shown in the collation. Other irregularities of lineation, such as the printing of verse as prose and of prose as verse (including one-line prose speeches which are turned up or turned down at the end as though they were verse), are listed in Appendix D.

Abbreviations and References

Line-numbers and quotations from other Shakespeare plays are taken from *William Shakespeare: The Complete Works* (The Oxford Shakespeare), general editors Stanley Wells and Gary Taylor (Oxford, 1986); all references to *King Lear* are to *The Tragedy of King Lear* in that edition (based on the First Folio text of 1623). Quotations from the Bible, unless otherwise stated, are taken from the Bishops' Bible (1568). Titles and illustrative quotations are normally given in modern spelling and with modern punctuation, except the quotations from the First Quarto of *The Merry*

Wives of Windsor. The place of publication is London unless otherwise stated. In the collation, dates are added when editions later than the first are referred to. F1 is specified when the First Folio needs to be distinguished from the others, and Q1 when the First Quarto needs to be distinguished from the others.

EDITIONS OF SHAKESPEARE

Q, Q1	The First Quarto (1602)
Q2	The Second Quarto (1619)
F, F1	The First Folio (1623)
Q3	The Third Quarto (1630)
F2	The Second Folio (1632)
F3	The Third Folio (1663)
F4	The Fourth Folio (1685)
Alexander	Peter Alexander, *Complete Works* (1951)
Bowers	Fredson Bowers, *The Merry Wives of Windsor*, in *Complete Works*, gen. ed. Alfred Harbage, revised Pelican Shakespeare (Baltimore and London, 1969)
Cambridge	W. G. Clark and W. A. Wright (and, vol. i, John Glover), *Works*, The Cambridge Shakespeare, 9 vols. (Cambridge, 1863–6)
Capell	Edward Capell, *Comedies, Histories, and Tragedies*, 10 vols. (1767–8)
Clarke	Charles and Mary Cowden Clarke, *Dramatic Works*, 4 vols. (1864)
Collier	John Payne Collier, *Works*, 8 vols. (1842–4)
Collier 1853	John Payne Collier, *Plays* (1853)
Craig	William J. Craig, *Works* (1891)
Daly	*Shakespeare's Comedy of The Merry Wives of Windsor*. A facsimile of the First Quarto (1602), together with a reprint of the prompt-copy prepared for use at Daly's Theatre. The alterations and emendations by Augustin Daly. Introduction by William Winter (New York, 1886)
Dyce	Alexander Dyce, *Works*, 6 vols. (1857)
Dyce 1866	Alexander Dyce, *Works*, 9 vols. (1864–7)
Furnivall	F. J. Furnivall, *The Merry Wives of Windsor*, The Old-Spelling Shakespeare (London and New York, 1908)
Greg	W. W. Greg, *The Merry Wives of Windsor, 1602* (Oxford, 1910)

Halliwell	J. O. Halliwell, *Complete Works* (London and New York, 1850)
Hanmer	Thomas Hanmer, *Works*, 6 vols. (Oxford, 1743–4)
Harness	William Harness, *Dramatic Works*, 8 vols. (1825)
Hart	H. C. Hart, *The Merry Wives of Windsor*, Arden Shakespeare (1904)
Hibbard	G. R. Hibbard, *The Merry Wives of Windsor*, New Penguin Shakespeare (Harmondsworth, Baltimore, and Ringwood, 1973)
Irving/Marshall	Sir Henry Irving and Frank A. Marshall, *Works*, The Henry Irving Shakespeare (second edition), 14 vols. (1906)
Johnson	Samuel Johnson, *Plays*, 8 vols. (1765)
Keightley	Thomas Keightley, *Plays*, 6 vols. (1864)
Kittredge	G. L. Kittredge, *Complete Works* (Boston, 1936)
Malone	Edmond Malone, *Plays and Poems*, 10 vols. (1790)
NCS	Sir Arthur Quiller-Couch and John Dover Wilson, *The Merry Wives of Windsor*, The New Shakespeare (Cambridge, 1921)
Neilson	William A. Neilson, *Works* (Boston, 1906)
Oliver	H. J. Oliver, *The Merry Wives of Windsor*, Arden Shakespeare (1971)
Oxberry	W. Oxberry, *The Merry Wives of Windsor*, Oxberry's New English Drama, vol. 8 (1820)
Oxford	Stanley Wells and Gary Taylor, gen. eds., with John Jowett and William Montgomery, *Complete Works*, The Oxford Shakespeare (Oxford, 1986)
Pope	Alexander Pope, *Works*, 6 vols. (1723–5)
Rann	Joseph Rann, *Dramatic Works*, 6 vols. (Oxford, 1786–94)
Reed	Isaac Reed, *Plays*, 10 vols. (1785)
Riverside	G. Blakemore Evans (textual editor), *The Riverside Shakespeare* (Boston, 1974)
Rowe	Nicholas Rowe, *Works*, 6 vols. (1709)
Rowe 1714	Nicholas Rowe, *Works*, 8 vols. (1714)
Singer	S. W. Singer, *Works*, 10 vols. (1826)
Sisson	Charles J. Sisson, *Complete Works* (1954)
Staunton	Howard Staunton, *Plays*, 3 vols. (1858–60)
Steevens	Samuel Johnson and George Steevens, *Plays*, 10 vols. (1773)

Steevens 1778 Samuel Johnson and George Steevens, *Plays*, 10 vols. (1778)

Steevens 1793 George Steevens, *Plays*, 15 vols. (1793)

Theobald   Lewis Theobald, *Works*, 7 vols. (1733)

Warburton   William Warburton, *Works*, 8 vols. (1747)

Wheatley   Henry B. Wheatley, *The Merry Wives of Windsor* (1886)

White   Richard Grant White, *Works*, 12 vols. (Boston, 1857–66)

OTHER WORKS

Abbott   E. A. Abbott, *A Shakespearian Grammar*, second edition (1870)

Arden of Faversham   *The Tragedy of Master Arden of Faversham*, ed. M. L. Wine, The Revels Plays (1973)

Baldwin   T. W. Baldwin, *William Shakespeare's 'Small Latine & Lesse Greeke'* (Urbana, Ill., 1944)

Bullough   Geoffrey Bullough, *Narrative and Dramatic Sources of Shakespeare*, 8 vols. (1957–75)

Capell, *Notes*   Edward Capell, *Notes and Various Readings to Shakespeare*, 3 vols. (1783)

Cercignani   Fausto Cercignani, *Shakespeare's Works and Elizabethan Pronunciation* (Oxford, 1981)

Chambers   E. K. Chambers, *The Elizabethan Stage*, 4 vols. (Oxford, 1923)

Chapman   *The Plays of George Chapman. The Comedies*, gen. ed. Allan Holaday (Urbana, Ill., 1970)

Chaucer   *Works*, ed. F. N. Robinson (Boston, 1933)

Daniel   P. A. Daniel, *Notes and Conjectural Emendations of Certain Doubtful Passages in Shakespeare's Plays* (1870)

Dekker, *Shoemaker's Holiday*   Thomas Dekker, *The Shoemaker's Holiday*, ed. R. L. Smallwood and Stanley Wells, The Revels Plays (Manchester and Baltimore, 1979)

Dent   R. W. Dent, *Shakespeare's Proverbial Language: An Index* (Berkeley, Los Angeles, and London, 1981)

Douce   Francis Douce, *Illustrations of Shakespeare* (1807)

Dyce, *Remarks*   Alexander Dyce, *Remarks on Mr J. P. Collier's and Mr C. Knight's editions of Shakespeare* (1844)

Evans   Bertrand Evans, *Shakespeare's Comedies* (London, Oxford, and New York, 1960)

Edward III	*The Reign of King Edward the Third* (1596), in *The Shakespeare Apocrypha*, ed. C. F. Tucker Brooke (Oxford, 1908)
Farmer	Richard Farmer, *An Essay on the Learning of Shakespeare* (Cambridge, 1767)
Fripp	E. I. Fripp, *Shakespeare: Man and Artist*, 2 vols. (1938)
Golding	*Shakespeare's Ovid: being Arthur Golding's Translation of the Metamorphoses*, ed. W. H. D. Rouse (1961)
Green	William Green, *Shakespeare's 'Merry Wives of Windsor'* (Princeton, 1962)
Hotson	Leslie Hotson, *Shakespeare versus Shallow* (1931)
Jackson	Zachariah Jackson, *Shakespeare's Genius Justified* (1819)
Jonson	*Ben Jonson*, ed. C. H. Herford and Percy and Evelyn Simpson, 11 vols. (Oxford, 1925–52)
Jowett	John Jowett, textual notes on *The Merry Wives of Windsor*, in *William Shakespeare: A Textual Companion*, S. Wells and G. Taylor (Oxford, 1987), pp. 340–50.
Lambrechts	Guy Lambrechts, 'Proposed New Readings in Shakespeare', *Bulletin de la Faculté des Lettres de Strasbourg*, 63 (1965), 946–7
Lyly	*The Works of John Lyly*, ed. R. W. Bond, 3 vols. (Oxford, 1902)
Marlowe, *Doctor Faustus*	Christopher Marlowe, *The Tragical History of the Life and Death of Doctor Faustus*, ed. J. D. Jump, The Revels Plays (Manchester and Baltimore, 1976)
Marlowe, *The Jew of Malta*	Christopher Marlowe, *The Jew of Malta*, ed. N. W. Bawcutt, The Revels Plays (Manchester and Baltimore, 1978)
Medwall, *Fulgens and Lucrece*	Henry Medwall, *Fulgens and Lucrece*, in *Five Pre-Shakespearean Comedies*, ed. F. S. Boas (1934)
N & Q	*Notes and Queries*
Nashe	*The Works of Thomas Nashe*, ed. R. B. McKerrow (1904–10) . . . With supplementary notes . . . by F. P. Wilson, 5 vols. (Oxford, 1958)
Naylor	Edward W. Naylor, *Shakespeare and Music* (London and Toronto, 1931)
Noble	Richmond Noble, *Shakespeare's Biblical Knowledge and Use of the Book of Common Prayer* (1935)
OED	*The Oxford English Dictionary*, 13 vols. (Oxford 1933), and supplements 1–4 (1972–86)

Onions	C. T. Onions, *A Shakespeare Glossary*, enlarged and revised by Robert D. Eagleson (Oxford, 1986)
RES	*Review of English Studies*
Roberts	Jeanne Addison Roberts, *Shakespeare's English Comedy: 'The Merry Wives of Windsor' in Context* (Lincoln, Nebr., and London, 1979)
Schmidt	Alexander Schmidt, *A Shakespeare Lexicon*, revised by G. Sarrazin, 2 vols. (Berlin, 1962)
Shakespeare's England	*Shakespeare's England: An Account of the Life and Manners of his Age*, ed. Sidney Lee and C. T. Onions, 2 vols. (Oxford, 1916)
Shattuck	C. H. Shattuck, 'Six Episodes in the Life of a Play', in *The Merry Wives of Windsor*, gen. ed. Francis Fergusson, The Laurel Shakespeare (New York, 1966)
Sisson (*New Readings*)	C. J. Sisson, *New Readings in Shakespeare*, 2 vols. (Cambridge, 1956)
Tilley	M. P. Tilley, *A Dictionary of the Proverbs in England in the Sixteenth and Seventeenth Centuries* (Ann Arbor, 1950)
Tyrwhitt	Thomas Tyrwhitt, *Observations and Conjectures upon Some Passages of Shakespeare* (1766)
Vickers	Brian Vickers, *The Artistry of Shakespeare's Prose* (1968)
Walker	W. S. Walker, *A Critical Examination of the Text of Shakespeare*, 3 vols. (1860)
Walter	Shakespeare, *Henry V*, ed. J. H. Walter, Arden Shakespeare (1955)

The Merry Wives of Windsor

THE PERSONS OF THE PLAY

Master George PAGE, a citizen of Windsor
MISTRESS Margaret (Meg) PAGE, his wife
ANNE (Nan) Page, their daughter
WILLIAM Page, their son, a schoolboy
Master Francis (Frank) FORD, another citizen of Windsor
MISTRESS Alice FORD, his wife

JOHN
ROBERT } Ford's servants

Sir Hugh EVANS, a Welsh parson
Doctor CAIUS, a French physician and suitor for the hand of Anne Page
MISTRESS QUICKLY, Doctor Caius's housekeeper
John RUGBY, Doctor Caius's servant
The HOST of the Garter Inn
Several children of Windsor

Master FENTON, a young gentleman and suitor for the hand of Anne Page

Sir John FALSTAFF
ROBIN, Falstaff's page
BARDOLPH
PISTOL } Falstaff's followers
NIM

Master Robert SHALLOW, a country justice of the peace
Master Abraham SLENDER, Shallow's nephew and suitor for the hand of
Anne Page
Peter SIMPLE, Slender's servant

The Merry Wives of Windsor

1.1 *Enter Justice Shallow, Slender, and Sir Hugh Evans*

SHALLOW Sir Hugh, persuade me not. I will make a Star
  Chamber matter of it. If he were twenty Sir John
  Falstaffs, he shall not abuse Robert Shallow, Esquire.

SLENDER In the county of Gloucester, Justice of Peace and
  coram.   5

SHALLOW Ay, cousin Slender, and Custalorum.

SLENDER Ay, and Ratolorum too; and a gentleman born,

1.1] F (*Actus primus, Scena prima.*)   0.1 *Enter Justice Shallow, Slender, and Sir Hugh Evans*]
ROWE; *Enter Iustice* Shallow, Slender, *Sir* Hugh Euans, *Master* Page, Falstoffe, Bardolph, Nym,
Pistoll, Anne Page, *Mistresse* Ford, *Mistresse* Page, Simple. F; *Enter Iustice* Shallow, *Syr* Hugh,
Maister Page, *and* Slender. Q

1.1 In Q Page enters with the other three,
joins with Evans in trying to placate
Shallow, and agrees to Slender's court-
ship of Anne ('and if my daughter | Like
him so well as I, wee'l quickly haue it a
match'). Falstaff enters with his followers, and a dialogue corresponding to
ll. 100–70 takes place. Mistress Ford,
Mistress Page, and Anne enter, and soon
everyone leaves the stage but Anne and
Slender, who begins his courtship in a
passage corresponding to 3.4.59–63;
the equivalent of ll. 257–89 follows.

1 **Sir Hugh** 'Sir', applied as here to a
clergyman, translates the academic title
dominus and indicates that Evans holds a
university degree.

persuade i.e. to overlook my grievance

1–2 **a Star Chamber matter** a matter for the
Court of Star Chamber. The history of this
special court of law is complicated (see
Encyclopaedia Britannica, 11th edn.,
1910–11, xxv, 795–6, 'Star Chamber'),
but the following points are relevant to
this scene: the royal council, or a com-
mittee of it, tried cases there; it was in
existence before the time of Henry IV and
continued after that of James I (being
abolished in 1641); among the cases
brought before it were abuses of power by
the nobility and gentry, and cases of riot
and unlawful assembly. The name Star
Chamber is derived from the gilded stars

decorating the interior roof of the room, in
Westminster Palace, where the court met.

3 **abuse** wrong (as in ll. 93, 96, 98)
Esquire a gentleman of the highest rank
below a knight

5 **coram** 'a well-established corruption for
quorum, the first word of the clause in the
Commission which named the justices—
"*quorum vos . . . unum esse volumus* [of
whom we wish you to be one]"' (Hart,
who quotes the phrase 'a Justice . . . of
Peace and of Coram' from Nashe, *Pierce
Penniless*, 1592). The quorum were a
number of select justices, chosen for their
ability and knowledge, whose presence
was necessary to constitute a bench.

6 **cousin** kinsman. Shallow seems to be
Slender's uncle, in the precise modern
sense of the word (see 3.4.38–41), or
perhaps his great-uncle, if he really is
over eighty years old (3.1.52).
Custalorum *custos rotulorum* (keeper of
the rolls), the chief justice of peace in his
county, 'having in his care the records of
the sessions' (Hibbard). The corruption of
the Latin phrase seems to be Shallow's
rather than one in common use; not in
OED.

7 **Ratolorum** 'Slender, not understanding
that "custalorum" means "*custos rotulorum*", tries to bring that office in, and,
typically, gets it wrong' (Oliver).
a gentleman born Slender continues to

77

Master Parson, who writes himself Armigero—in any
bill, warrant, quittance, or obligation, Armigero.

SHALLOW Ay, that I do, and have done any time these   10
three hundred years.

SLENDER All his successors gone before him hath done't,
and all his ancestors that come after him may. They
may give the dozen white luces in their coat.

SHALLOW It is an old coat.

EVANS The dozen white louses do become an old coat well.
It agrees well passant. It is a familiar beast to man, and
signifies love.

---

relish this expression at l. 254.
Shakespeare made comic capital out of it
again in *Winter's Tale* 5.2.126–37.

8 **writes** designates
   Armigero Hart shows that in 1589 *armiger* is given as the Latin translation of
   esquire, but seems reluctant to accept
   Steevens's (1793) explanation that Slender 'had seen the Justice's attestations,
   signed—"*jurat coram me*, Roberto Shallow, *Armigero* [he swears before me,
   Robert Shallow, Esquire]"; and therefore
   takes the ablative for the nominative case
   of Armiger', which is surely correct,
   being much more probable than that
   Shallow would use the Italian adjective
   armigero (valiant in arms, warlike, mar-
   tial), as Hart suggests.
9 **bill** either a 'deed' in the legal sense (*OED
   sb.* 1d) or a 'bill of exchange' or money
   order (*OED sb.* 9)
   quittance receipt
   obligation bond
10–11 **Ay ... years** 'Shallow means that his
   family has borne arms for three centuries' (Hibbard); but what he *says* is that
   he personally has been subscribing documents in this manner for that length of
   time.
12–13 **All . . . may** Slender, like Dogberry
   and Elbow, 'misplaces' (*Measure* 2.1.86)
   or transposes words and thus produces
   violent incongruities of sense.
12 **hath** have (Abbott 334)
14 **give** (heraldic) display in a coat of arms
   luces pike (the voracious freshwater fish
   Esox lucius). Hart quotes Harrison's *Description of England* (1577): 'The pike, as
   he ageth, receiveth diverse names', *viz.*
   fry, gilthead, pod, jack, pickerel, pike, 'and
   last of all to a luce'. Three silver luces are

conspicuous in the arms of the Lucy family
(see Introduction, pp. 6–7, and Ill. 2);
irrespective of any such allusion, a round
dozen are needed in the Shallows' arms in
order to justify Evans's misunderstanding.
16 **louses** Hibbard wonders whether Evans is
   punning, but surely the humour depends
   on his innocent seriousness. It is true that
   Evans would hardly expect Shallow to
   say 'louses' instead of 'lice', but the fact
   that we accept Evans's 'louses' as his own
   version of 'lice' gets us over that small
   difficulty.
   old coat Evans mistakes Shallow's *old
   coat* (ancient coat of arms) as meaning an
   old article of clothing.
17 **It** the louse
   passant (heraldic) walking. For the sake
   of the comic incongruity of the louse as a
   heraldic beast Evans is made to use the
   heraldic participle, though without
   comic intent on his part. There is no need
   to conjecture, with Oliver, that he may
   mean *passant* in the old sense 'exceed-
   ingly, surpassingly' (*OED a.* 1 : last example quoted 1485).
   a familiar beast to man Evans's unconsciously comic idea is illustrated in Marlowe's *Doctor Faustus* (before 1593),
   where Wagner threatens the clown
   Robin: '. . . I'll turn all the lice about me
   into familiars [i.e. attendant devils in
   animal form] and make them tear thee in
   pieces.' *Robin.* 'Nay sir, you may save
   yourself a labour, for they are as familiar
   with me as if they paid for their meat and
   drink, I can tell you' (Sc. 4. 21–5). There
   may also be a connection with the
   proverb 'A louse is a gentleman's companion' (Tilley L471 : Dent records its
   occurrence in 1594).
18 **signifies love** Evans uses the language of

SHALLOW The luce is the fresh fish. The salt fish is not an
old coat.   20

SLENDER I may quarter, coz.

SHALLOW You may, by marrying.

EVANS It is marring indeed, if he quarter it.

SHALLOW Not a whit.

EVANS Yes, py'r Lady. If he has a quarter of your coat,
there is but three skirts for yourself, in my simple
conjectures. But that is all one. If Sir John Falstaff have
committed disparagements unto you, I am of the
Church, and will be glad to do my benevolence to make
atonements and compromises between you.   30

SHALLOW The Council shall hear it; it is a riot.

EVANS It is not meet the Council hear a riot. There is no
fear of Got in a riot. The Council, look you, shall desire
to hear the fear of Got, and not to hear a riot. Take your
'visaments in that.

SHALLOW Ha! O' my life, if I were young again, the sword
should end it.

19–20 The luce . . . coat] This edition (*conj.* Johnson); The Luse is the fresh-fish, the salt-fish, is
an old Coate F; The luce is the fresh fish—the salt fish is an old cod NCS; The luce is the fresh
fish, the salt fish—is an old coat SISSON   25 py'r Lady] CAPELL; per-lady F

the emblem books; he is probably thinking of St John's exhortation to brotherly
love among the faithful, 1 John 4: 7–21.

19–20 **The salt fish is not an old coat** No
satisfactory explanation of the F reading
has ever been proposed. (See Appendix
A.) Johnson's emendation, though it does
not display Shakespearian wit, is consistent with the fatuity uttered by
Shakespeare's scatterbrains: Shallow,
having informed Evans that he was talking of the luce (a freshwater fish) and not
of the louse, gratuitously adds that the
salt (i.e. salted) fish is not an old coat (i.e.
an ancient coat of arms), when nobody
would suppose that it was in this sense a
coat at all, either new or old. F accidentally omits 'not' at 4.2.166, so it is
reasonable to suppose that it may also
have done so here.

21 **quarter** add another family's coat of arms
to our family's (by marrying). The two
coats each appeared twice on the result-
ing shield. Slender's remark does not
follow from Shallow's; it is introduced
merely to give rise to another misunder-

standing by Evans.

21 **coz** cousin (as in l. 7), abbreviated famili-
arly

22 **marrying** Oliver cites the proverb 'Marrying is marring' (Tilley M701). Compare
All's Well 2.3.295: 'A young man married is a man that's marred.'

24 **Not a whit** not at all

26 **skirts** parts of a coat below the waist

27 **conjectures** The first instance of Evans's
characteristic use of the plural form with
the singular sense: compare *disparagements*, *atonements*, *compromises*, all
always singular elsewhere in the plays.

30 **atonements** reconciliation (with Evans's
plural)

31 **Council** the royal council (in session in
Star Chamber). The NCS editors state that
Evans's reply refers to 'an ecclesiastical
"council" or synod'; they thus destroy
the humour of making the fear of God a
Star Chamber matter.

35 **'visaments** i.e. advisement (with Evans's
plural). The sense is 'be advised of that',
'consider that'.

36 **O' my life** on my life (i.e. as sure as I live)

EVANS It is petter that friends is the sword and end it. And
there is also another device in my prain, which perad-
venture prings goot discretions with it. There is Anne   40
Page, which is daughter to Master George Page, which
is pretty virginity—

SLENDER Mistress Anne Page? She has brown hair, and
speaks small like a woman?

EVANS It is that fery person for all the 'orld, as just as you
will desire. And seven hundred pounds of moneys, and
gold, and silver, is her grandsire upon his death's-bed—
Got deliver to a joyful resurrections!—give, when she is
able to overtake seventeen years old. It were a goot
motion if we leave our pribbles and prabbles, and desire   50
a marriage between Master Abraham and Mistress
Anne Page.

SLENDER Did her grandsire leave her seven hundred
pound?

EVANS Ay, and·her father is make her a petter penny.

⌈SHALLOW⌉ I know the young gentlewoman. She has
good gifts.

41 George] THEOBALD; *Thomas* F   42 virginity—] This edition; virginity. F   44 woman?]
HIBBARD (*conj.* Lambrechts); woman. F   53 SLENDER] F; *Shal⟨low⟩.* CAPELL   56 ⌈SHALLOW⌉]
CAPELL; *Slen⟨der⟩.* F

38 **sword** NCS emends to 'swort' to give a
'quibble upon "sort" (= issue, upshot)',
but this sense of 'sort' as a substantive is
not supported by *OED* (*sort sb.*¹ is always
used in a sense closely related to lot,
share, fortune, condition, etc.), and, in
any case, Evans is not a quibbler but a
literal-minded man (hence the humour of
his inept metaphor here).

41 **George** F's *Thomas* probably reproduces
what Shakespeare wrote (compare the
inconsistency between George Seacole
and Francis Seacole in *Much Ado* 3.3.10
and 3.5.54), but there is no benefit in
retaining it on this one occasion (e.g. to
imply that Evans does not know the
name of one of his neighbours).

41–2 **which is pretty virginity** Evans's
meaning is clear, but his awkward repetition of *which is* makes it appear that he is
misapplying this phrase to Anne's father.

44 **small** in a treble voice
woman? Evans's reply suggests that
Slender is seeking confirmation rather
than making a statement.

45–6 **It . . . desire** Evans emphasizes the
point by making it three times, and reacts
as though Slender had described Anne
vividly.

50 **pribbles and prabbles** 'A redundancy for
"brabbles" i.e. brawls' (Hart). Compare
4.1.45 and 5.5.159.

51 **Abraham** The patriarch's name is a
humorously incongruous one for Slender
to bear. Note that Shallow solemnly
addresses him by it at l. 213, where the
context suggests male sexual potency,
though Shallow is making no such suggestion.

53–4 **Did . . . pound?** Some editors give this
to Shallow (expressing cupidity), but it is
appropriate enough to Slender (expressing vacuity).

55 **a petter penny** more besides. Proverbial
(Tilley P189).

56–7 ⌈SHALLOW⌉ **I know . . . gifts** Slender
has already indicated that he knows
Anne—and has done so in terms that
show him to be incapable of offering a
judgement of her qualities (*good gifts*). It is

EVANS Seven hundred pounds, and possibilities, is goot
gifts.

SHALLOW Well, let us see honest Master Page. Is Falstaff 60
there?

EVANS Shall I tell you a lie? I do despise a liar as I do
despise one that is false, or as I despise one that is not
true. The knight Sir John is there; and I beseech you be
ruled by your well-willers. I will peat the door for Master
Page. (*He knocks*) What ho! Got pless your house here!
Enter Page

PAGE Who's there?

EVANS Here is Got's plessing and your friend, and Justice
Shallow, and here young Master Slender, that peradventures shall tell you another tale, if matters grow to 70
your likings.

PAGE I am glad to see your worships well. I thank you for
my venison, Master Shallow.

SHALLOW Master Page, I am glad to see you. Much good
do it your good heart! I wished your venison better; it
was ill killed. How doth good Mistress Page?—And I

---

66 *He knocks*] ROWE; *not in* F   66.1 *Enter Page*] ROWE; *after* 71 COLLIER 1853; *not in* F   67
PAGE Who's] *as* F; *Page (above, at the window)*. Who's COLLIER 1853; *Page (within)*. Who's
DYCE   69–70 That peradventures ... likings] F; *as aside* OXFORD

probable that the scribe or compositor
accidentally repeated the speech-prefix of
ll. 53–4.

58 **possibilities** pecuniary prospects (*OED,
possibility sb.* 3c: both the singular and
plural forms are recorded, so this need
not be one of Evans's peculiar plurals)

65 **your well-willers** those who wish you
well. The expression is not peculiar to
Evans, and the sense seems to be genu-
inely plural here.

66.1 *Enter Page* Page speaks as he opens the
door in response to the knock. If he speaks
within, and opens the door only after
Evans has identified himself and the other
two visitors, he seems unnecessarily sus-
picious.

69–71 **that . . . likings** Evans can say this
either aside to Shallow or directly to Page.
In the former case, he makes a roguish
reference to their preconceived plan; in
the latter case, he is so eager for the plan
that he begins blurting it out to Page.

70 **tell you another tale** have something

more to say to you. A common expression
(Tilley T49).

71 **likings** Elsewhere singular in
Shakespeare except in *Othello* 3.1.47,
where the Quarto (1622) and Folio
agree, but where the latter text may be
influenced by the former, and the former's reading may be an error. On the
present occasion Evans possibly means
the *likings* of both Page and Slender; if he
means only Page's, the plural form is
probably his verbal mannerism.

76 **ill killed** not killed in the proper manner.
Oliver interprets this as meaning that the
particular deer may have had too much
blood drained away too soon, which
would impair its eating quality. But perhaps Shallow means that this was not the
most suitable deer (i.e. not the fattest) of
his herd for killing. Why he has sent the
venison to Page (who has only just been
proposed, by Evans, as Slender's father-
in-law) is not clear, nor is it more than
conjecture that the deer was killed by
Falstaff.

thank you always with my heart, la, with my heart.

PAGE Sir, I thank you.

SHALLOW Sir, I thank you; by yea and no, I do.

PAGE I am glad to see you, good Master Slender.   80

SLENDER How does your fallow greyhound, sir? I heard
say he was outrun on Cotswold.

PAGE It could not be judged, sir.

SLENDER You'll not confess, you'll not confess.

SHALLOW That he will not. ⌈*Aside to Slender*⌉ 'Tis your
fault, 'tis your fault. ⌈*To Page*⌉ 'Tis a good dog.

PAGE A cur, sir.

SHALLOW Sir, he's a good dog and a fair dog. Can there be
more said? He is good and fair. Is Sir John Falstaff here?

PAGE Sir, he is within; and I would I could do a good office   90
between you.

EVANS It is spoke as a Christians ought to speak.

SHALLOW He hath wronged me, Master Page.

PAGE Sir, he doth in some sort confess it.

SHALLOW If it be confessed, it is not redressed. Is not that
so, Master Page? He hath wronged me, indeed he hath,
at a word he hath. Believe me—Robert Shallow,

---

82 Cotswold] F (*Cotsall*)   85 *Aside to Slender*] This edition; *not in* F   86 *To Page*]
OXFORD; *not in* F   97 hath. Believe me—Robert] F (hath : beleeue me, *Robert*); hath, believe
me; Robert DYCE 1866

77 **la** An intensive interjection, used in this
play by Shallow, Slender, and Mistress
Quickly.

79 **by yea and no** This mild asseveration,
used also by Mistress Quickly in this play,
seems to have originated with the commandment 'Swear not at all ... But let
your communication be Yea, yea; nay,
nay; for whatsoever is more than these
cometh of evil' (Matthew 5 : 34, 37).

81 **fallow** fawn-coloured

82 **Cotswold** a range of hills in Gloucestershire

83 **judged** positively decided. Page probably
means that the hare being coursed doubled back into the mouth of the rival
dog.

85–6 **'Tis your fault** you are to blame (i.e. for
teasing him; not he for not confessing his
dog's inferiority). Hart, comparing
3.3.206 and *Pericles* Sc.16.71, glosses
fault as 'misfortune, loss', but *OED* does
not support this gloss, and the usual

senses of *fault* are appropriate to the
instances that Hart cites. NCS interprets
fault as 'a check caused by failure of
scent', but Hibbard rightly rejects this
'because greyhounds hunt [hares] by
sight not scent', as Shallow would know.
Hibbard takes the phrase to mean 'You
are mistaken, you are in the wrong' (i.e.
in believing that Page's dog was outrun),
but Shakespeare does not apply *fault* to a
mistake of understanding.

89 **good and fair** NCS quotes the phrase 'the
tokens whereby a man may knowe a
good and fayre hound' from George Turberville's *The Noble Art of Venery or Hunting* (1575).

94 **in some sort** to some extent. Page is being
diplomatically evasive.

95 **If ... redressed** A sharply expressed variation on the proverb 'Confession of a fault
is half amends' (Tilley C 589: from
1592).

97 **at a word** in short, in a word (*OED word*

Esquire, saith he is wronged.

    Enter Sir John Falstaff, Pistol, Bardolph, and Nim

PAGE Here comes Sir John.

FALSTAFF Now, Master Shallow, you'll complain of me to   100
the King?

SHALLOW Knight, you have beaten my men, killed my
deer, and broke open my lodge.

FALSTAFF But not kissed your keeper's daughter?

SHALLOW Tut, a pin! This shall be answered.

FALSTAFF I will answer it straight. I have done all this.
That is now answered.

SHALLOW The Council shall know this.

FALSTAFF 'Twere better for you if it were known in
counsel. You'll be laughed at.   110

EVANS *Pauca verba*, Sir John, good worts.

FALSTAFF Good worts? Good cabbage!—Slender, I broke
your head. What matter have you against me?

SLENDER Marry, sir, I have matter in my head against you,

98.1] Q; *not in* F   101 King?] F; Councell, I heare? Q   109 if it were] F; twere Q
110 counsel] Q (counsell); coun-|cell F

sb. 13a). '[Shallow's] repetitions are con-
stant, sharper than ever as he stands on
his dignity' (Vickers, p. 143).

98.1 *Nim* The verb *nim* ('take'), archaic by
late 16th c., then acquired the sense
'steal, filch, pilfer' (*OED v.* 3: first example 1606). The noun *nim* ('a thief', *OED*:
one example only, 1630) is derived from
the verb. Shakespeare no doubt also
named his character from the verb. The
name is spelt both *Nim* and *Nym* in both Q
and F.

101 *King* See Introduction, p. 11.

103 **lodge** house in a forest (here, in a park)
used in connection with hunting (*OED sb.*
2), and here 'occupied by the keeper'
(Hibbard)

104 **kissed your keeper's daughter** Probably
alluding not to 'some lost ballad' (NCS)
but to Robert Greene's *Friar Bacon and
Friar Bungay* (c.1590), 1.1.1–25, where
Prince Edward, after a successful day's
hunting at Fressingfield, has become melancholy after he 'got to the keeper's
lodge', and his fool Rafe asks him 'I
prithee tell me, Ned, art thou in love with
the keeper's daughter?' (as indeed he is).

105 **Tut, a pin!** Shallow makes an angry
dismissive noise and calls Falstaff's levity
worthless (*OED pin sb.* 3b).
answered compensated for

106 **straight** immediately

107 **answered** rejoined to

109–10 **in counsel** in secret (*OED counsel sb.*
5c)

111 *Pauca verba* (Latin) few words [i.e. are
best (Tilley W798)]. Evidently a frequent
expression: Hart cites Jonson, who calls it
'the bencher's [i.e. of one sitting on a
tavern bench] phrase' in *Every Man in his
Humour* 3.4.58–9 (1601), 4.2.40–1
(1616). Holofernes the schoolmaster
uses it in *LLL* 4.2.162. In translating it,
Evans substitutes *good* for 'few', thus
allowing Falstaff to play upon his mispronunciation of *words*.

112 **cabbage** (plural) synonymous with
worts

112–13 **broke your head** gave you a blow
on the head which made it bleed
matter 'subject of complaint' (Hibbard)

113 **matter** '(1) matter of consequence; (2)
pus' (Hibbard). Compare *LLL*
3.1.115–16, for the same pun.

and against your cony-catching rascals, Bardolph, Nim,
and Pistol.

BARDOLPH You Banbury cheese!

SLENDER Ay, it is no matter.

PISTOL How now, Mephostophilus?

SLENDER Ay, it is no matter.   120

NIM Slice, I say. *Pauca, pauca.* Slice, that's my humour.

SLENDER (*to Shallow*) Where's Simple, my man, can you
tell, cousin?

EVANS Peace, I pray you. Now let us understand. There is
three umpires in this matter, as I understand—that is,
Master Page, *fidelicet* Master Page; and there is myself,
fidelicet myself; and the three party is, lastly and finally,
mine host of the Garter.

PAGE We three to hear it, and end it between them.

115–16 and against ... Pistol.] *as* F; and your cogging companions, *Pistoll* and *Nym*. They
carried mee to the Tauerne and made mee drunke, and afterward picked my pocket. Q

115 **cony-catching** cheating (literally 'rab-
bit-catching'; pronounced 'cunny-
catching'). Robert Greene's pamphlets *A
Notable Discovery of Cozenage* and *The
Second Part of Cony-Catching* (both 1591)
had given the term wide currency.

116 **Pistol** The résumé of Slender's misfortune, as given in Q at this point, is
probably an addition. It would be difficult
to explain its omission from the F text if it
had been in the scribe's or compositor's
copy. As Hart says, 'it is not necessary,
since we can gather all this from the
subsequent dialogue, and Sir John knows
his followers' doings no doubt.' There is
more dramatic power in making Bardolph, Pistol, and Nim respond immediately to Slender's mention of them.

117 **Banbury cheese** Cheeses made at Banbury were proverbially thin ('as thin as
Banbury cheese', Tilley C268: from
1562), being 'made about an inch in
thickness' (Wheatley). See also *OED Banbury cheese*. The allusion is to Slender's
physical slenderness; also, perhaps, implying that his face is pale, a taunt which
would come appropriately from Bardolph.

119 **How now, Mephostophilus** Not a quotation from Marlowe's *Doctor Faustus*,
though delivered as if it were. The corruption of the name Mephostophilis (which
would be generally familiar) is presumably Pistol's error.

121 **Slice** In conjunction with *pauca, pauca*
(few [words]), this clearly means that
Nim's fancy (*humour*) is for sword-strokes
and not for words. There is no need to
connect his verb with slicing a Banbury
cheese.

humour Nim's devotion to this word, in
Merry Wives and *Henry V*, reflects contemporary fashion: see the long discussion between the speakers in the Induction of Jonson's *Every Man out of his
Humour*. Originally meaning moisture,
and then one of the bodily fluids (blood,
phlegm, choler, melancholy) the respective proportions of which determined a
person's disposition, it consequently became applied to the habitual disposition
itself, to a temporary mood, and to a
fancy or whim.

122–3 **Where's Simple ... cousin?** Slender
seems to be anticipating a fray and
looking for support.

124 **understand** i.e. understand the situation

126 **fidelicet** (Latin) *videlicet* (namely)

127 **lastly and finally** Evans's tautology. His
laboriously inept setting-forth of the situation may be compared with Dogberry's
enumeration of the offences committed
by Borachio and Conrad, *Much Ado*
5.1.208–12.

129 **them** Shallow and Falstaff, the chief
parties in the dispute

EVANS Fery goot. I will make a prief of it in my notebook,   130
and we will afterwards 'ork upon the cause with as
great discreetly as we can.   *He writes*

FALSTAFF Pistol!

PISTOL He hears with ears.

EVANS (*aside*) The tevil and his tam! What phrase is this?
'He hears with ears'? Why, it is affectations.

FALSTAFF Pistol, did you pick Master Slender's purse?

SLENDER Ay, by these gloves did he, or I would I might
never come in mine own great chamber again else; of
seven groats in mill-sixpences, and two Edward shovel-   140
boards that cost me two shilling and twopence apiece of
Yed Miller, by these gloves.

FALSTAFF Is this true, Pistol?

EVANS (*aside*) No, it is false, if it is a pickpurse.

---

132 *He writes*] NCS; *not in* F   135 *aside*] This edition; *not in* F   136 ears?] DALY; eare?
F   141 shilling] F; shillings HIBBARD   142 Yed] F (*Yead*); Ed OXFORD   144 *aside*] This
edition; *not in* F

130 **prief** brief, summary. In *LLL* 5.1.15.1
another parson, Sir Nathaniel, '*draws out
his table-book*' to note down Holofernes'
word 'peregrinate'.

134 **He hears with ears** Compare 'Hear
diligently my words, and ponder my
sayings with your ears' (Job 13: 17) and
'We have heard with our ears' (Psalms
44: 1; this is one of the 'sentences after
the first collect' after the Litany in the
Book of Common Prayer, 1559). Noble
(p. 181) suggests that Evans is exposing
his ignorance. But Pistol's expression,
with its theatrical use of the third person
pronoun and its omission of the
possessive adjective, is undeniably
affected.

135 **the tevil and his tam** the devil and his
dam (i.e. mother). A frequent expression
(Tilley D225).

136 **ears** There is no reason why Evans
should immediately repeat Pistol's expression inaccurately (as in F), especially
as his own mannerism is to turn singular
nouns into plural ones, not *vice versa*. It
is amusing (perhaps intentionally so)
that in commenting on Pistol, the great
blank-verse speaker, Evans unwittingly
creates two lines of blank verse in his own
prose.

139 **great chamber** the principal room of a
house

140 **seven groats in mill-sixpences** A groat
was a coin worth 4*d*. Mill-sixpences
were manufactured (in a stamping mill)
in the attempt 'to replace the irregular
products of hammering by machine-
made coins with hard clear edges, and
so to make the offence of clipping easier
of detection' (*Shakespeare's England*,
i.343). Since 2*s*. 4*d*. is a sum not di-
visible by six, Slender is miscalculat-
ing.

140-1 **Edward shovel-boards** large shillings
of Edward VI's reign (1547-53), which
when worn smooth with age were used
for sliding along a *shovel-board* (a long
polished board marked with numbered
lines at its far end) in the game so called.
The game was also called 'shove-groat'
(as in modern shove-halfpenny): 'a
shove-groat shilling' is mentioned in *2
Henry IV* 2.4.189-90.

142 **Yed Miller** Edward Miller; or, perhaps,
Edward the miller (compare 'William
Cook', *2 Henry IV*, 5.1.9-24).

144 **No ... pickpurse** Evans's comment
interprets 'true, Pistol?' as 'true Pistol?'
(i.e. honest Pistol).

PISTOL

Ha, thou mountain-foreigner?—Sir John and master
  mine,

I combat challenge of this latten bilbo.

(*To Slender*) Word of denial in thy *labras* here!

Word of denial! Froth and scum, thou liest!

SLENDER (*pointing to Nim*) By these gloves, then 'twas he.

NIM Be advised, sir, and pass good humours. I will say   150
'marry trap' with you, if you run the nuthook's humour
on me; that is the very note of it.

SLENDER By this hat, then he in the red face had it. For
though I cannot remember what I did when you made
me drunk, yet I am not altogether an ass.

FALSTAFF What say you, Scarlet and John?

BARDOLPH Why, sir, for my part, I say the gentleman had
drunk himself out of his five sentences—

EVANS (*aside*) It is 'his five senses'. Fie, what the ignorance
is!   160

BARDOLPH And being fap, sir, was, as they say, cashiered;

---

145 mountain-foreigner?] This edition; mountaine Forreyner: F; mountain-foreigner!
HANMER   146 latten] Q (laten); Latine F   149 *pointing to Nim*] HIBBARD; *not in* F   150
advised] F (auis'd)   150–1 I say ... you] JOHNSON; say marry trap with you F; say 'marry trap
with you' Q; say mary trap Q   158 sentences—] This edition; sentences. F   159
aside] This edition; *not in* F

145 **mountain-foreigner** Welshman (derogatory). In *Henry V* Pistol is reported as
  calling Fluellen 'mountain-squire'
  (5.1.34). Pistol seems to have only half
  heard Evans, for his aggression is not
  diverted from Slender.
146 **I combat challenge** I demand a trial by
  combat
  latten bilbo sword (the name deriving
  from the Spanish town Bilbao, famous for
  swords) of base metal. 'Pistol calls Slender a worthless sword, with a reference to
  his leanness' (Hart).
147 **labras** intended for Spanish *labios*, earlier *labros* (lips) and no doubt confused
  with *palabras*, words.
150 **Be ... humours** think carefully and be
  agreeable
150–1 **I will ... you** The sense of this, and
  whether *marry trap with you* or only the
  first two words of it (as in Q) is what
  Nim proposes to say to Slender, are not
  clear. The mood of his speech would
  suggest that his meaning is 'I will pay you
  out'.

151–2 **run ... me** 'threaten me with the
  constable' (Hibbard). The original sense
  of *nuthook*, a hooked stick for pulling
  down branches of nuts, led to the derogatory sense, which also occurs in *2 Henry
  IV* 5.4.7.
152 **very note** right tune, i.e. truth
155 **not altogether an ass** Dent (A231.1)
  compares *The Pedlar's Prophecy* (anon.,
  pr. 1595), l. 479: 'What, man, think not
  that I am altogether a fool'.
156 **Scarlet and John** Will Scarlet and Little
  John, two of Robin Hood's 'merry men';
  compare the snatch 'And Robin Hood,
  Scarlet, and John' (from the ballad of
  Robin Hood and the Pinder of Wakefield)
  which Silence sings in *2 Henry IV*
  5.3.104. Here addressed as a nickname,
  synonymous with 'red face', to Bardolph.
161 **fap** drunk. Sisson (*New Readings*, p. 64)
  notes that Hilda Hulme found the word in
  17th-c. West Midlands churchwardens'
  accounts. *OED* gives only this example
  and another of 1818 which is probably
  derived from it.

and so conclusions passed the careers.

SLENDER Ay, you spake in Latin then too. But 'tis no
matter. I'll ne'er be drunk whilst I live again but in
honest, civil, godly company, for this trick. If I be drunk,
I'll be drunk with those that have the fear of God, and
not with drunken knaves.

EVANS So Got 'udge me, that is a virtuous mind.

FALSTAFF You hear all these matters denied, gentlemen.
You hear it.   ⌜*Exeunt Bardolph, Pistol, and Nim*⌝   170
          Enter Anne Page, with wine

PAGE Nay, daughter, carry the wine in; we'll drink
within.   *Exit Anne Page*

SLENDER O heaven, this is Mistress Anne Page!
          ⌜*Enter Mistress Ford and Mistress Page*⌝

PAGE How now, Mistress Ford?

FALSTAFF Mistress Ford, by my troth, you are very well
met. By your leave, good mistress.
          He kisses her

162 careers] F (Car-eires)   170 *Exeunt ... Nim*] DALY; *not in* F   170.1] ROWE; *Enter Mistresse* Foord, *Mistresse* Page, *and her daughter* Anne. Q; *not in* F   172 *Exit Anne Page*] THEOBALD; *not in* F   173.1] ROWE; *not in* F   176.1] Q (*Syr* Iohn kisses her.); *not in* F

161 **cashiered** The main meaning of the word (*OED v.* 1) is 'dismissed from service', with its figurative extension 'got rid of'. This seems a better explanation than Schmidt's generally accepted one (recorded in *OED, v.* 5) that it is Bardolph's slang term for 'deprived of cash'. If Bardolph is saying that Slender, being drunk, was turned out of an alehouse, he is probably implying that Slender lost his purse rather than was robbed of it. Emrys Jones, *Scenic Form in Shakespeare* (Oxford, 1971), p. 127, notes 'the "cashiering" of a man who has been made drunk' as a reminiscence of *Merry Wives* in *Othello*.

162 **conclusions passed the careers** conclusions ran their courses (figurative expression from horsemanship). Bardolph is not trying to give a definite account but a vague one, as one might say 'one thing led to another'.

168 **mind** intention

170 *Exeunt ... Nim* Daly, whose realistic setting has Page's house at stage left and the Garter Inn at stage right, directs Bardolph, Nim, and Pistol to leave one after another for the inn, from which

they had entered earlier, Falstaff (accompanied by Robin) having entered from Page's house. On an unlocalized stage it will not seem incongruous if they enter with Falstaff as from Page's house, for such an entrance establishes that they are his followers, but it will seem incongruous if they go out at l. 179.1 with the dinner-party like invited (or uninvited) guests. Falstaff's speech closing the conversation (ll. 169–70) allows him to give them a hint, by a gesture, to take themselves off. Their exit by one door coincides with Anne's entrance by the other.

170.1 *Enter . . . wine* This entry, and the subsequent entry of Mistress Ford and Mistress Page, are supplied by Rowe. They allow Anne to enter as from Page's house, and Mistress Ford and Mistress Page to enter as from elsewhere in the town (Mistress Page having perhaps gone to Mistress Ford's house to fetch her).

176.1 *He kisses her* i.e. in formal salutation, as was the custom in England in the 16th c.

PAGE Wife, bid these gentlemen welcome.—Come, we
   have a hot venison pasty to dinner. Come, gentlemen, I
   hope we shall drink down all unkindness.

                              Exeunt all except Slender
SLENDER I had rather than forty shillings I had my book of   180
   Songs and Sonnets here.

         Enter Simple
   How now, Simple, where have you been? I must wait
   on myself, must I? You have not the *Book of Riddles*
   about you, have you?

SIMPLE *Book of Riddles?* Why, did you not lend it to Alice
   Shortcake upon Allhallowmas last, a fortnight afore
   Michaelmas?

         Enter Shallow and Evans
SHALLOW Come, coz; come, coz; we stay for you. (*Drawing
   him aside*) A word with you, coz; marry, this, coz; there
   is as 'twere a tender, a kind of tender, made afar off by   190
   Sir Hugh here—do you understand me?

SLENDER Ay, sir, you shall find me reasonable. If it be so, I
   shall do that that is reason.

SHALLOW Nay, but understand me.

SLENDER So I do, sir.

179.1 *Exeunt ... Slender*] *as* NCS; *Exit all, but* Slender *and mistresse* Anne. Q; *Ex.* Fal. Page, &c.
Manent Shallow, Evans, *and* Slender. ROWE; *not in* F   181.1] ROWE; *not in* F   187
Michaelmas] F; Martlemas THEOBALD   187.1] *as* NCS; *not in* F   188–9 *Drawing him aside*]
as OXFORD; *not in* F   191 here—] This edition; here: F

178 **to** for
179 **drink down all unkindness** Compare
    Caesar 4.3.212–3: 'Give me a bowl of
    wine. | In this I bury all unkindness,
    Cassius.'
180 **I had rather than forty shillings** Sir
    Andrew uses the same expression in
    Twelfth Night 2.3.19–20.
180–1 **book of** *Songs and Sonnets Songs and
    Sonnets*, a collection mainly of love-poems
    by Surrey, Wyatt, Vaux, and others, was
    published by Richard Tottel in 1557 and
    reprinted at regular intervals to 1587. The
    term *songs and sonnets* was in common
    use from the 1580s (Hart gives exam-
    ples). Slender, reminded of his projected
    courtship of Anne Page by the sight of
    her, wishes for such aids to conversation
    as his books of love-poems and riddles.
183 *Book of Riddles* Not identified. The
    earliest modern English riddle-book

known was printed in 1511; another,
not extant, was in existence by 1575,
and a third survives in an edition of 1629
(Hart gives details).
186–7 **Allhallowmas . . . Michaelmas**
    Allhallowmas (All Saints' Day) is 1 Nov.;
    Michaelmas (St Michael and All Angels'
    Day) is 29 Sept. Simple perhaps means to
    say Martlemas (St Martin's Day, 11
    Nov.), which *is* about a fortnight after
    Allhallowmas. But Theobald was not
    justified in emending, since it is unlikely
    that the scribe or the compositor would
    make the mistake.
188 **stay** are waiting
189 **marry** indeed (an asseveration deriving
    from 'Mary', i.e. the Blessed Virgin)
190 **tender** offer (i.e. of marriage, on Slen-
    der's behalf)
    afar off indirectly, 'in a roundabout man-
    ner' (Hibbard)

EVANS Give ear to his motions. Master Slender, I will
  description the matter to you, if you be capacity of it.
SLENDER Nay, I will do as my cousin Shallow says. I pray
  you pardon me. He's a justice of peace in his country,
  simple though I stand here.   200
EVANS But that is not the question. The question is
  concerning your marriage—
SHALLOW Ay, there's the point, sir.
EVANS Marry is it, the very point of it—to Mistress Anne
  Page.
SLENDER Why, if it be so, I will marry her upon any
  reasonable demands.
EVANS But can you affection the 'oman? Let us command
  to know that of your mouth, or of your lips—for divers
  philosophers hold that the lips is parcel of the mouth.   210
  Therefore, precisely, can you carry your good will to the
  maid?
SHALLOW Cousin Abraham Slender, can you love her?
SLENDER I hope, sir, I will do as it shall become one that
  would do reason.
EVANS Nay, Got's lords and his ladies, you must speak

---

196 motions. Master Slender, I] F (motions; (Mʳ. *Slender*) I); motions, Mr. *Slender:* I
ROWE   202 marriage—] This edition; marriage. F

196 **motions** proposal (with Evans's plural)
198–9 **I pray you pardon me** This phrase
  often, as here, carries an assertive tone;
  compare Oswald's reply to Lear's abuse:
  'I am none of these, my lord, I beseech
  your pardon' (*Lear* 1.4.80–1).
199 **country** county, district
200 **simple though I stand here** A modest (or
  mock-modest) expression common at the
  time: 'undistinguished though I am (or
  seem to be)' (*OED simple a.* 4c.).
201 **that** either (a) Shallow's being a justice
  of peace or (b) the settling of Slender's
  grievance
207 **demands** authoritative requests (*OED
  demand sb.* 1)
208 **command** Does Evans mean 'desire',
  'beg'?
209 **divers** some. There is no point in seeking
  Evans's source for this distinction without a difference between the lips and the
  mouth. Touchstone's learned allusion to
  the heathen philosopher and the grape
  (*As You Like It* 5.1.31–5) is a comparable
  piece of nonsense.

210 **parcel** part
211 **carry your good will to** Evans means
  'feel affection towards', but in everything
  he says hereabouts there is a sexual
  innuendo of which he is unaware. Here
  will also means the male sexual organ.
  Compare *Much Ado* 5.4.28–30: 'But for
  my will, my will is your good will | May
  stand with ours this day to be conjoined
  | In the state of honourable marriage.'
  The unintended ambiguity is reinforced
  by 'precisely', which means both 'in
  definite terms' (*OED* 1b) and 'with strict
  propriety' (*OED* 3).
216 **Got's lords and his ladies** Not found
  elsewhere, nor previously explained, this
  is a nonce-oath dictated by the context of
  unintentional innuendo. 'Lords and ladies' is a popular name for *Arum macula-
  tum*, which is also called 'wake robin' and
  'cuckoo-pint'. The 'i' of 'pint' in the last-
  mentioned word is pronounced short,
  'pint' being an abbreviation of 'pintle',
  i.e. penis. The name 'cuckoo-pint' derives
  from the shape of the flower, in which the

possitable if you can carry her your desires towards her.

SHALLOW That you must. Will you, upon good dowry, marry her?   220

SLENDER I will do a greater thing than that upon your request, cousin, in any reason.

SHALLOW Nay, conceive me, conceive me, sweet coz; what I do is to pleasure you, coz. Can you love the maid?

SLENDER I will marry her, sir, at your request; but if there be no great love in the beginning, yet heaven may decrease it upon better acquaintance, when we are married and have more occasion to know one another. I hope upon familiarity will grow more contempt. But if you say 'marry her', I will marry her; that I am freely   230 dissolved, and dissolutely.

EVANS It is a fery discretion answer, save the fall is in the

229 contempt] THEOBALD; content F   232 fall] F; faul' HANMER; fault COLLIER

large erect spadix is conspicuous. See the illustration, under the heading 'Aroideae' in *Encyclopaedia Britannica*, 11th ed., 1910–11, ii. 640; and see *OED cuckoo-pint, cuckoo-pintle,* and *pintle.*

217 **possitable** i.e. positively

217–18 **carry her . . . towards her** direct your desire (with Evans's plural) towards her. The redundant *her* immediately after *carry* is idiomatic and represents the old dative case (Abbott 220).

219 **upon good dowry** provided that her father gives a good marriage-portion with her

221–2 **I will . . . reason** Slender treats marriage as a self-sacrifice that he is prepared to make.

223 **conceive me** understand my meaning (*OED conceive v.* 9)

227 **decrease** Slender's error for 'increase'

229 **contempt** Theobald's emendation, though modern editors (Oliver, Hibbard) reject it, must be right. Why should Slender make a sensible statement immediately after making a silly one? Oliver's suggestion that he means *contempt* but mistakenly says *content* is unprofitably tortuous and would be impossible to convey in performance, when—such is the familiarity of the proverb 'familiarity breeds contempt' (Tilley F47: from 1576)—the audience will think they

hear *contempt* whichever word the actor uses.

231 **dissolved, and dissolutely** meaning 'resolved' and 'resolutely'. Hart (perhaps overlooking the transpositions at ll. 12–13) observes that Slender has elsewhere no malapropisms. This burst of them is, as Oliver says, 'for the sake of the laugh'. That Evans, whose own usage is thoroughly eccentric, should at this moment notice one mistake in Slender's completes the humour. Two fundamental senses of 'resolve' (*OED v.* 1, dissolve; 2, disintegrate) show that the words were much more closely related in Shakespeare's time than now. The following juxtaposition in *Edward III* (printed 1596) is notable: '*King.* What saies my faire loue? is she resolute? | *Countess.* Resolute to be dissolude' (i.e. dissolv'd: 2.2.168–9). In 1 *Henry IV* 1.2.33–5 there is an antithesis between 'most resolutely snatched' and 'most dissolutely spent'. Lyly had brought the words antithetically together in *Euphues*: 'How dissolute have I been in striving against good counsel, how resolute in standing in mine own conceit!' (Lyly, i. 250).

232 **save the fall is** excepting the fault that is. *OED* does not list any such sense as 'mistake' under *fall*, and Oliver's suggestion that it is analogous to the modern

'ord 'dissolutely'. The 'ort is, according to our meaning,
'resolutely'. His meaning is good.

SHALLOW Ay, I think my cousin meant well.

SLENDER Ay, or else I would I might be hanged, la!

>   *Enter Anne Page*

SHALLOW Here comes fair Mistress Anne.—Would I were
young for your sake, Mistress Anne!

ANNE The dinner is on the table. My father desires your
worships' company.   240

SHALLOW I will wait on him, fair Mistress Anne.

EVANS 'Od's plessèd will! I will not be absence at the
grace.   *Exeunt Shallow and Evans*

ANNE Will't please your worship to come in, sir?

SLENDER No, I thank you, forsooth, heartily; I am very
well.

ANNE The dinner attends you, sir.

SLENDER I am not a-hungry, I thank you, forsooth. (*To
Simple*) Go, sirrah, for all you are my man, go wait upon
my cousin Shallow.   *Exit Simple*   250
A justice of peace sometime may be beholden to his
friend for a man. I keep but three men and a boy yet, till

---

233 our meaning] F; your meaning This edition *conj.*   236.1] ROWE; *not in* F   243 *Exeunt
... Evans*] ROWE; *not in* F   250 *Exit Simple*] THEOBALD; *not in* F   251 beholden] F
(beholding)

'slip' is improbable. But nor does *OED*
give *fall* as a variant of *fault*. In *fault* the
letter l, though introduced for etymologi-
cal reasons during the 15th c., seems
usually not to have been pronounced till
the end of the 18th c. This makes it
improbable that *fall* is Evans's distinctive
pronunciation of *fault*. NCS, suggesting
that it is, also suggests that *fall* may be a
'misprint for "falt", a 16th cent. spelling'; but the fact that the word is always
spelt 'fault' in F's text of the play, and in
F's text of *Two Gentlemen* (another Crane
transcript), in both of which it frequently
occurs, makes this suggestion improbable. Though the general sense is clear, the
exact sense therefore remains doubtful.

233 **our meaning** If F is right, this must
mean 'our interpretation'. This sense is
not given in *OED*, but as the speaker is
Evans one hesitates to emend. Even so, it
is strange that in *His meaning is good*

Evans uses the word correctly. His speech
will perhaps be more effective on stage if
he addresses his second sentence to Slender (changing *our* to *your*) and his third
sentence to Shallow.

237–8 **Would ... sake** as Oliver notes, a
cliché (Tilley S68)

245–6 **I am very well** I am very comfortable
(i.e. out here where I am)

249 **for all** although
wait upon attend upon (i.e. at dinner).
Such attendance would be superfluous
and irregular, but Slender makes the
order serve to introduce his boast about
his social status.

251 **beholden** under an obligation

252 **friend** kinsman (*OED sb.* 3)

252–3 **till my mother be dead** 'Slender's
mother evidently curbs his desire to cut a
figure' (Hibbard), and his remark shows a
comic lack of feeling. That his father is
already dead appears from 3.4.36–7.

my mother be dead. But what though? Yet I live like a
poor gentleman born.

ANNE I may not go in without your worship; they will not
sit till you come.

SLENDER I'faith, I'll eat nothing; I thank you as much as
though I did.

ANNE I pray you, sir, walk in.

SLENDER I had rather walk here, I thank you. I bruised my   260
shin th'other day with playing at sword and dagger
with a master of fence—three veneys for a dish of
stewed prunes—and, by my troth, I cannot abide the
smell of hot meat since. Why do your dogs bark so? Be
there bears i'th' town?

ANNE I think there are, sir; I heard them talked of.

SLENDER I love the sport well, but I shall as soon quarrel at
it as any man in England. You are afraid if you see the
bear loose, are you not?

· 260–4 I had ... since.] F; No faith not I. I thanke you, | I cannot abide the smell of hot meate |
Nere since I broke my shin. Ile tel you how it came | By my troth. A Fencer and I plaid three venies
| For a dish of stewd prunes, and I with my ward | Defending my head, he hot my shin. Yes faith.
Q   264 hot meat since.] F; COLLIER 1853 adds 'Dogs bark.'

253 **what though?** what does it matter?

257 **I'll eat nothing** I'll not go in and eat.
Slender is too obtuse to respond to Anne's
gentle pressure.

260–1 **I bruised my shin** Since a master of
fence would not strike at his opponent's
shin, Slender must mean that he hit his
own shin accidentally. This would be like
his incompetence, and is much better
than Q's pun 'he hot my shin' ('hot'
being a past tense, now obsolete, of 'hit').

261 **playing at sword and dagger** engaging
in a fencing-match in which both contes-
tants had swords in their right hands and
daggers in their left. George Silver, Para-
doxes of Defence (1599), distinguishes between 'sword and dagger' and 'rapier and
dagger': the rapier was narrower, and
the fencing-schools insisted on the thrust,
whereas for the broader sword they insisted on the cut—wrongly, in Silver's
opinion (see *Shakespeare's England*, ii.
399). Both sports were practised by
gentlemen, and Hart (followed by Oliver)
is mistaken in inferring that rapier-and-
dagger fighting (he contrasts it with
sword-and-buckler fighting, and takes no
account of sword-and-dagger fighting)
was 'the fashion amongst serving-men'.

262 **master of fence** Fully accredited fencing-
masters were incorporated under Letters
Patent of July 1540 by Henry VIII
(*Shakespeare's England*, ii. 389).
veneys bouts (Fr. *venues*)

263 **stewed prunes** Shakespeare's other references to stewed prunes (1 Henry IV
3.3.112–13, 2 Henry IV 2.4.142,
Measure 2.1.88), all in derogatory contexts, associate them with brothels. Slender is unaware of the association (which
is also found in Lodge's Wit's Misery,
1596, as Steevens pointed out in connection with the 1 Henry IV passage).

263–4 **I cannot ... since** The point, such as
it is, of Slender's anecdote, when it is
reached, turns out to be an absolute *non
sequitur*, whether *meat* means specifically
butcher's meat or food in the general
sense.

264 **Why do your dogs bark so?** There is no
need for an off-stage dog to give Slender
his cue, for the laughter at his last remark
will cover the pause in which he hears
the barking, which he implies has been
going on for some time.

267 **the sport** bear-baiting

267–8 **quarrel at it** quarrel with other spectators while watching it. The NCS editors

ANNE　Ay, indeed, sir.　　　　　　　　　　　　　　270

SLENDER　That's meat and drink to me, now. I have seen Sackerson loose twenty times, and have taken him by the chain. But I warrant you, the women have so cried and shrieked at it that it passed. But women, indeed, cannot abide 'em—they are very ill-favoured rough things.

　　　Enter Page

PAGE　Come, gentle Master Slender, come; we stay for you.

SLENDER　I'll eat nothing, I thank you, sir.

PAGE　By cock and pie, you shall not choose, sir! Come, come.　　　　　　　　　　　　　　280

SLENDER　Nay, pray you lead the way.

PAGE　Come on, sir.

SLENDER　Mistress Anne, yourself shall go first.

ANNE　Not I, sir. Pray you, keep on.

SLENDER　Truly, I will not go first, truly, la! I will not do you that wrong.

ANNE　I pray you, sir.

SLENDER　I'll rather be unmannerly than troublesome. You do yourself wrong, indeed, la!

　　　Exeunt ⌈Slender first, the others following⌉

276.1] Q; *not in* F　　283 Mistress Anne] F; Nay be God misteris *Anne* Q　　289.1 *Exeunt ...*
following] OXFORD; *Exeunt.* F; *Exit omnes.* Q

and Hibbard interpret 'decry it, object to it' (*OED quarrel v.* 1c) and represent Slender as a puritan. They either overlook 'I love the sport well' or make Slender incredibly self-contradictory. Slender is like Sir Andrew Aguecheek in his readiness to quarrel (*Twelfth Night* 1.3.28), and would probably share his attitude towards puritans (*Twelfth Night* 2.3.136).

271　**That's meat and drink to me** Proverbial (Tilley M842); compare *As You Like It* 5.1.10.

272　**Sackerson** one of the bears kept at the Bear Garden in Southwark. He is mentioned in Sir John Davies's *Epigrams* (*c.*1598) and elsewhere.

274　**passed** was beyond belief. Compare 4.2.111, 124.

275　**ill-favoured** ugly-looking

279　**By cock and pie** *OED* (*cock-and-pie sb.*) says that this asseveration is 'supposed to

be orig. COCK sb.⁸ and PIE, the ordinal of the Roman Catholic Church'. About *cock* (euphemism for 'God') there can be no doubt, but there is no evidence that *pie* in this oath means anything but a *pie* of pastry, which might naturally follow from *cock* (the fowl). Shallow uses this mild oath in *2 Henry IV* 5.1.1.

279　**you shall not choose** I insist (an established phrase of courtesy)

288　**I'll rather ... troublesome** Proverbial (Tilley U15).

288–9　**You do yourself wrong** The common phrase recurs at 3.3.156–7, 3.3.195–6, and (as 'do not yourself wrong') in *2 Henry IV* 3.2.251.

289.1　'When she finally persuades Slender to walk before her into the house, we editors had written (but afterwards in cowardice erased) a stage direction *He goes in; she follows with her apron spread, as if driving a goose*' (NCS, p. xxxv).

1.2   *Enter Evans and Simple*

EVANS Go your ways, and ask of Doctor Caius's house
which is the way. And there dwells one Mistress
Quickly, which is in the manner of his nurse, or his dry
nurse, or his cook, or his laundry, his washer, and his
wringer.

SIMPLE ⌜*going*⌝ Well, sir.

EVANS Nay, it is petter yet. Give her this letter, for it is a
'oman that is altogethers acquaintance with Mistress
Anne Page, and the letter is to desire and require her to
solicit your master's desires to Mistress Anne Page. I   10
pray you be gone.   ⌜*Exit Simple*⌝

1.2] F (*Scena Secunda.*)   0.1] F; *Enter sir* Hugh *and* Simple, *from dinner.* Q   3–5 which is . . .
wringer] F; his woman, or his try nurse Q   6 ⌜*going*⌝] This edition; *not in* F   8 that is
altogethers] This edition; that altogeathers F; that altogether's STEEVENS 1778 (*conj.* Tyrwhitt)   11 *Exit Simple*] OXFORD; *not in* F

1.2.1–2 **ask . . . way** Evans's eccentric style:
he means 'ask the way to Doctor Caius'
house', but he tells Simple to ask the
house for directions.

1 **Caius** The modern pronunciation is 'to
rhyme with "try us"' (Hibbard). The
Elizabethan pronunciation was to rhyme
with 'play us'. (The modern pronunciation of Gonville and Caius College,
Cambridge, is 'keys', 'Caius' and 'keys'
having both been pronounced 'kays'
in the 16th c.) Why Shakespeare chose
the name is unknown. John Caius
(1510–73), who refounded the
Cambridge college, was not French but
English, but he was a physician, and
Shakespeare may have remembered his
name though intending no personal allusion. Caius is also the name that Kent
adopts when disguised (*Lear* 5.3.259).

3 **nurse** Caius himself calls her his nurse at
3.2.57. She is evidently his housekeeper.
Q substitutes for Evans's whole list 'his
woman, or his try nurse', but this gives
no grounds for supposing that F's *nurse* is
an error for *woman* (or for *'oman*). Perhaps the point of Evans's specification of
nurse as well as *dry nurse* is to make the
audience smile at his unintended suggestion that Caius needs a wet-nurse, i.e. is a
baby.

4 **laundry** Evans's error for 'laundress'
(OED *laundry sb.* 3: the only example in
this sense).

6 **Well, sir.** This reply, with Evans's rejoinder, may imply that Simple is
going before he has received the instruction which is the point of his journey; when Evans says 'I pray you be
gone' Simple may be standing waiting
for further instructions after Evans
has visibly finished. But if so, the business does not survive in Q, which puts
all Evans's instructions into his first
speech.

8 **is altogethers acquaintance** is thoroughly acquainted. OED records *altogethers* (last example 1586) as being
formed 'from ALL + TOGETHERS a variant
of TOGETHER, with genitival ending: cf.
afterward, -s.' Evans, being fond of words
ending in *s*, would naturally use this
word, so it is more likely that F has
omitted *is* than that *altogethers* should be
read as *altogether's*.

11 *Exit Simple* F ends this scene with *Exeunt*, but it seems less natural that Evans
should inform Simple of his intention to
return to dinner than that he should say
it to himself or to the audience. That F
punctuates 'be gon: I' is no objection: at
the end of 3.4 Mistress Quickly's speech
begins in F 'Now heauen send thee good
fortune, a kinde heart he hath', and
continues for another eight lines to *Exeunt*, Fenton having left the stage at
'fortune'.

I will make an end of my dinner; there's pippins and
cheese to come.   *Exit*

1.3   *Enter Falstaff, Host, Bardolph, Nim, Pistol, and*
       Robin

FALSTAFF Mine host of the Garter—

HOST What says my bully rook? Speak scholarly and
wisely.

FALSTAFF Truly, mine host, I must turn away some of my
followers.

HOST Discard, bully Hercules, cashier. Let them wag; trot,
trot.

FALSTAFF I sit at ten pounds a week.

HOST Thou'rt an emperor—Caesar, Kaiser, and Feezer. I

13 *Exit*] OXFORD; *Exeunt.* F

1.3] F (*Scena Tertia.*)   0.1–2] F (*Enter Falstaffe, Host, Bardolfe, Nym, Pistoll, Page.*); *Enter sir*
Iohn Falstaffes Host of the Garter, Nym, Bardolfe, Pistoll, *and the boy.* Q; *Enter Sir John Falstaff,*
Bardolph, Nim, Pistol, and Robin OXFORD   Robin] ROWE; *Page* F; *the boy* Q   1 Garter—] This
edition; Garter? F; Garter. Q; Garter! *Enter the Host of the Garter* OXFORD   9 Kaiser] F
(*Keiser*) Q (*Kesar*)   Feezer] This edition (*after* F, *Pheazar*); *Phesser* Q; pheezer OXFORD

12–13 **pippins and cheese** apples and
cheese. Hart illustrates that these were
the usual finish to a meal, and adds
'Evans, the Welshman, would be sure to
recollect the cheese.'

1.3.2 **bully rook** *bully* (*OED sb.*[1] 1) is 'a
term of endearment and familiarity,
originally applied to either sex'.
Shakespeare has 'bully Bottom' (*Dream*
3.1.7, 4.2.18), 'the lovely bully' (Pistol's
phrase for the King, *Henry V* 4.1.49), and
'bully-monster' (of Caliban, *Tempest*
5.1.261); the Host uses *bully* frequently,
both alone and in conjunction with *rook*,
Hercules, Hector, doctor, stale, knight, and
Sir John. The sense of *rook* here is obscure. The sense most common in
Shakespeare's time was 'gull, simpleton'
(*OED sb.*[1] 2c, first example 1598); only
later did it come to mean 'cheat, swind-
ler, or sharper, spec. in gaming' (*OED sb.*[1]
2b, first unequivocal example 1662: the
example of 1577 may be a miswriting of
'rooge', i.e. rogue). If it means 'gull', why
does Falstaff not resent it, and if it is used
'with jocular irony' (Oliver) what is the
point of the irony? The sense 'castle' (in
chess) has no evident personal application, e.g. to Falstaff's original name in the
Henry IV plays, Oldcastle, since the Host
in three consecutive speeches in 2.1
addresses Page, Shallow, and Ford as
bully rook. OED glosses 'bully-rock, bully-
rook' as '1. = BULLY sb.[1]; jolly comrade,
boon companion' (this example and one
other, 'Bully Rocks', 1697) and
'2. = BULLY sb.[1] 3; a bravo, hired ruffian'
(first example 1653). Though *OED* hy-
phenates, F does not, which, given
Crane's fondness for introducing hyphens, indicates that *bully rook* was a
two-word phrase in the copy that he was
transcribing.

4 **turn away** synonymous with *discard* and
cashier in the Host's reply

6 **wag** go, depart, be off (*OED v.* 7)

8 **sit at** dwell here at the rate of (*OED sit v.*
8)

9 **Kaiser** emperor (of any nation). Often
found alliteratively associated with
'king', e.g. Spenser, *Faerie Queene* II.vii. 5.
Feezer Malone explains as the Host's
coinage from the verb *feeze*, as in the
phrase 'I'll feeze you', i.e. 'I'll do for you,
settle your business, sort you out' (*OED v.*
3), used by Sly in *Shrew*, Induction 1.1,
where F spells 'pheeze'. The modern
equivalent title might be 'Thumper'. Hart
interprets it as a corruption of 'Vizier',
but a viceroy would be too anticlimactic a
conclusion for the Host's triad of epithets.

will entertain Bardolph; he shall draw, he shall tap.   10
Said I well, bully Hector?

FALSTAFF Do so, good mine host.

HOST I have spoke. Let him follow. (*To Bardolph*) Let me see
thee froth and lime. ⌈*To Falstaff*⌉ I am at a word. (*To
Bardolph*) Follow.   *Exit*

FALSTAFF Bardolph, follow him. A tapster is a good trade.
An old cloak makes a new jerkin; a withered serving-
man a fresh tapster. Go, adieu.

BARDOLPH It is a life that I have desired. I will thrive.

                                                              Exit

PISTOL

O base Hungarian wight, wilt thou the spigot wield?   20

NIM He was gotten in drink. Is not the humour conceited?

FALSTAFF I am glad I am so acquit of this tinderbox. His
thefts were too open. His filching was like an unskilful
singer—he kept not time.

---

14 lime] Q (lyme); liue F   *To Falstaff*] This edition; *not in* F   15] Q (*Exit Host.*); *not in* F
19.1 *Exit*] Q (*Exit Bardolfe.*); *after* 20 DYCE; *not in* F   20 Hungarian] F; gongarian Q
21 He was ... conceited?] F; His minde is not heroick. And theres the humor of it. Q

10 **draw** draw liquor from a barrel by means
   of a tap; synonymous with *tap* (*OED tap*
   *v.*¹ 4c)
14 **froth** pour out beer in such a way as to
   make it frothy on top (thus avoiding
   giving full measure)
   lime adulterate wine by adding lime
   (calcium carbonate) 'to mitigate and al-
   lay the tartness' (*Pliny's Natural History*,
   trans. Philemon Holland, 1601, quoted
   by Hart), not to make it sparkle as has
   sometimes been suggested. The Q reading
   must be preferred to the F one, since *froth*
   and lime is in the Host's style (like *he shall*
   draw, he shall tap), and also since it refers
   to tricks of the trade in both its aspects,
   ale-selling and wine-selling.
   I am at a word Synonymous with *I have*
   spoke. Compare 'Go to, I have spoke at a
   word' (Shallow in *2 Henry IV* 3.2.294).
   The sense is 'Without wasting more
   words, I mean what I say'.
17 **An old ... jerkin** i.e. by being remade in
   the form of a jerkin (short close-fitting
   jacket)
17–18 **a withered ... tapster** i.e. by reaching
   the end of one occupation and the beginning of a new one; compare the proverb
   'An old serving man, a young beggar'

(Tilley S255).
20 An iambic hexameter line in Pistol's
   theatrical style. *Hungarian* probably involves a pun on 'hungry' (Hart gives
   contemporary examples); *wight* (man) is
   archaic, as in l. 34; the *spigot* (*OED sb.* 2)
   is the tap of a barrel, incongruously
   spoken of as if a weapon or a substitute
   for one.
21 **gotten in drink** begotten by a drunken
   father, or between two drunken parents.
   Compare the plural pronoun in *Winter's*
   Tale 3.3.73–4: 'They were warmer that
   got this than the poor thing is here'.
   Is not the humour conceited? 'Isn't that
   notion witty?' Nim's wit may lie in
   implying that in becoming a tapster
   Bardolph is unmanly (as in the proverb
   (first recorded in 1606) 'Who goes drunk
   to bed begets but a girl', Tilley B195), or
   in implying that there is a hereditary
   connection between Bardolph's new
   trade and his red nose. The latter is the
   more probable, for in *2 Henry IV*
   4.2.90–1 Falstaff says that it is abstainers
   who beget 'wenches'.
24 **he kept not time** i.e. he stole on unsuitable occasions

NIM The good humour is to steal at a minute's rest.

PISTOL 'Convey', the wise it call. 'Steal'? Foh, a *fico* for the
phrase!

FALSTAFF Well, sirs, I am almost out at heels.

PISTOL

Why then, let kibes ensue.

FALSTAFF There is no remedy: I must cony-catch, I must   30
shift.

PISTOL

Young ravens must have food.

FALSTAFF Which of you know Ford of this town?

PISTOL

I ken the wight. He is of substance good.

FALSTAFF My honest lads, I will tell you what I am about.

PISTOL Two yards and more.

FALSTAFF No quips now, Pistol. Indeed I am in the waist
two yards about; but I am now about no waste—I am
about thrift. Briefly, I do mean to make love to Ford's
wife. I spy entertainment in her. She discourses, she   40
carves, she gives the leer of invitation. I can construe

25 minute's] F, Q (minutes); minim's COLLIER 1853 (*conj*. Langton); minim- NCS   26–7] *as
prose* F; *as two lines, breaking after* 'Foh' HIBBARD; *as one verse line* This edition *conj*.

25 **good humour** 'right trick of the trade'
(Hibbard)
at a minute's rest in the small space of a
minute. Nim develops (in *rest*) Falstaff's
simile drawn from music. Q confirms F's
reading.

26–7 Pistol's speech could conceivably be a
fourteener, or else a line and a half of
blank verse (with '*Steal*'? *Foh* equivalent
to an iambic foot each, like 'Rage! Blow!'
in *Lear*, 3.2.1), but it is perhaps better to
take it as prose including two strongly
rhythmical phrases.

26 **Convey** The euphemism (*OED v.* 6b) had
been current for over a hundred years.
fico (Italian) fig. The contemptuous
phrase 'A fig [or "a fico"] for it!' (Tilley
F210) was in general use from 1576
(*OED fico* 2, *fig sb.*[1] 4). The fig [or 'the
fico'] was also a contemptuous gesture
(*OED fico* 3, *fig sb.*[2]) made either by
thrusting the thumb between two of the
closed fingers or by thrusting it into the
mouth. If Pistol makes a gesture here it is
probably the former.

28 **out at heels** penniless: proverbial (Tilley

H389). Pistol's reply takes the cliché in
the literal sense from which it originated.

29 **Why then, let kibes ensue** A typical idiom
and cadence for Pistol; compare *2 Henry
IV* 5.3.109: 'Why then, lament therefor',
and *Henry V* 3.6.50: 'Why then, rejoice
therefor.'
kibes sore patches on the heels, caused by
cold

31 **shift** improvise; here with the additional
force of 'cheat'.

32 **Young ravens must have food** 'Small
birds must have meat' was proverbial
(Tilley B397), and Shakespeare alludes to
Psalm 147: 9 ('He giveth to the beast his
food, and to the young ravens which
cry') here and in *As You Like It* 2.3.44.

34 Blank verse, as the archaic diction and
inverted word-order emphasize.

35 **about** doing (Falstaff's sense); round
about, in circumference (Pistol's sense).
Falstaff continues the quibbling with his
pun on *waist/waste*.

40 **entertainment** welcoming behaviour

41 **carves** Not positively explained. There
must be a connection with carving meat

the action of her familiar style; and the hardest voice of her behaviour, to be Englished rightly, is 'I am Sir John Falstaff's'.

PISTOL ⌈*aside to Nim*⌉ He hath studied her will, and translated her will—out of honesty into English.

NIM ⌈*aside to Pistol*⌉ The anchor is deep. Will that humour pass?

FALSTAFF Now, the report goes she has all the rule of her husband's purse: he hath a legion of angels.   50

PISTOL

As many devils entertain, and 'To her, boy!', say I.

NIM The humour rises; it is good. Humour me the angels.

FALSTAFF (*showing letters*) I have writ me here a letter to her; and here another to Page's wife, who even now gave me good eyes too, examined my parts with most

---

45 *aside to Nim*] This edition; *not in* F   45–6 studied ... will—] F (studied her will; and translated her will:); studied her well, Q; studied her well and translated her will, WHITE; studied her well and translated her ill, CAMBRIDGE *conj.*   47 *aside to Pistol*] This edition; *not in* F   50 he] F; She Q   a legion] ROWE 1714; a legend F; legians Q   53 *showing letters*] OXFORD; *not in* F

(and helping others to it) at table, but the placing of the word in the sequence *discourses ... carves ... invitation* suggests that there was a figurative sense: *OED carve v.* 13 records Schmidt's conjectural explanation 'to show great courtesy and affability'.

41 **leer** look
   construe (*a*) interpret (*OED v.* 7); (*b*) translate from a foreign language (*OED v.* 3), which leads on to *voice, Englished rightly*, and *translated*.

42 **action** working
   familiar style (*a*) affable behaviour (*OED familiar a.* 7); (*b*) plain, easily understood expression (*OED familiar a.* 6c)
   hardest (*a*) least encouraging in appearance (*b*) most difficult to construe
   voice (*a*) expression (*b*) grammatical voice (active, passive, or middle)

45–6 **He ... English** Though various emendations have been proposed, Pistol's quibble requires the repetition of *will*, a word which could carry many senses (wish, wilfulness, sexual desire, sexual parts, last will and testament). Perhaps the meaning is 'He has had his eye on her sexual parts (figuratively), and has translated (in the sense in which Bottom was "translated", *Dream* 3.1.113) her wish,

out of chastity into very plain speaking (i.e. "I am Sir John Falstaff's").'

47 **The anchor is deep** Not positively explained. 'The natural interpretation is that just as a deep anchor normally holds firmly, so Falstaff's ideas are firm' (Oliver).

47–8 **Will that humour pass?** 'What do you think of that for a neat phrase?' (Hibbard).

50 **legion** great number (*OED sb.* 3: from Mark 5: 8–9, where the 'unclean spirit', being asked his name, replies 'My name is Legion, for we are many', and where the side-note in the Geneva Bible states 'A legion contained above 6000 in number'). There is also an allusion to Matthew 26: 53 ('twelve legions of angels'), and a pun on *angels* meaning 'gold coins' (named from the figure of the archangel Michael stamped upon them).

51 Another of Pistol's theatrical iambic lines (compare l. 20), this time a fourteener. 'Employ as many devils, and I say, assail her.'

52 **The humour ... angels** Given Nim's freedom of usage, this seems to mean 'The plot takes shape—it is good. Get hold of the money.' The use of *me* here and in Falstaff's next speech is emphatic (Abbott 220).

judicious œillades. Sometimes the beam of her view
gilded my foot, sometimes my portly belly.

PISTOL ⌈*aside to Nim*⌉

Then did the sun on dunghill shine.

NIM ⌈*aside to Pistol*⌉ I thank thee for that humour.

FALSTAFF O, she did so course o'er my exteriors, with such   60
a greedy intention, that the appetite of her eye did seem
to scorch me up like a burning-glass. Here's another
letter to her. She bears the purse too. She is a region in
Guiana, all gold and bounty. I will be cheaters to them
both, and they shall be exchequers to me. They shall be
my East and West Indies, and I will trade to them both.
⌈*To Nim*⌉ Go, bear thou this letter to Mistress Page, ⌈*to
Pistol*⌉ and thou this to Mistress Ford. We will thrive,
lads, we will thrive.

PISTOL

Shall I Sir Pandarus of Troy become,   70
And by my side wear steel? Then Lucifer take all!
He gives back the letter

56 œillades] HANMER (*conj.* Pope); illiads F   58 *aside to Nim*] HIBBARD (*conj.* Walker); *not in*
F   59 *aside to Pistol*] HIBBARD (*conj.* Walker); *not in* F   67 *To Nim*] FURNIVALL; *to Pistol*
NCS; *not in* F   68 *to Pistol*] FURNIVALL; *to Nym* NCS; *not in* F   71.1] *as* OXFORD; *not in* F

56 **œillades** (French) amorous glances. First
recorded as used by Greene in 1592
(*OED*); Shakespeare uses it again in *Lear*
4.4.25. The Elizabethan pronunciation is
shown by the F spelling 'illiads' ('Eliads'
in *Lear*).
beam sunbeam

58 **Then … shine** Compare Lyly, *Euphues*
(Lyly, i. 193): 'The sun shineth upon the
dunghill and is not corrupted.' Proverbial
(Tilley S982).

60 **course o'er** run through, one after
another (*OED course v.* 5c: first example)

61 **intention** intent observation (*OED sb.* 1)

64 **Guiana** The country between Venezuela
and Brazil on the north-east coast of
South America. Spanish and English ex-
plorers sought there for the fabled 'golden
city' El Dorado. Ralegh made an expedi-
tion in 1595 and on his return published
The Discovery of Guiana, which, because of
its exaggerations, was received with incredulity.
cheaters escheators, officials who notified
their supervisor the escheator-general of
'escheats', i.e. estates in their district

which fell due to the Crown (e.g. for lack
of succession). The abbreviated form, in
use from the 14th c., was by now acquiring a punning sense, as here and in *Titus*
5.1.111. Both Q and F give the plural
form, though logically the singular form
would be required.

67 **To Nim** In this edition the first letter is
given to Nim because it is he who warns
Mistress Page's husband in 2.1. See l. 88
below.

70–1 'Shall I, a soldier, descend to playing
the pander? The devil take me, body and
soul, if I do!' Not a quotation but the
spontaneous eloquence of Pistol's indignation. The second line of the two is
another iambic hexameter.

70 **Pandarus** The go-between in Troilus's
courtship of Cressida, in Chaucer's poem
and (after *Merry Wives*) Shakespeare's
play on the subject. *Sir* is Pistol's title for
him (compare 'Sir Actaeon', 2.1.111),
whereas he is to be 'lord Pandarus' in
Troilus 3.1.11 and in *Twelfth Night*
3.1.50.

NIM I will run no base humour. Here, take the humour-
letter. (*He gives it back*) I will keep the haviour of
reputation.

FALSTAFF (*to Robin, giving him the letters*)
  Hold, sirrah, bear you these letters tightly;
  Sail like my pinnace to these golden shores.
                                              ⌜*Exit Robin*⌝
  Rogues, hence, avaunt! Vanish like hailstones, go!
  Trudge, plod away o'th' hoof, seek shelter, pack!
  Falstaff will learn the humour of the age,
  French thrift, you rogues—myself and skirted page.   80
                                              ⌜*Exit*⌝

---

73 *He ... back*]' *as* OXFORD; *not in* F   75 *to ... letters*] This edition; *To Robin* THEOBALD; *He gives Robin the letters (after* 76*)* OXFORD; *not in* F   76.1 *Exit Robin*] OXBERRY; *not in* F   78 o'th'] F2 (oth'); ith' F   79 humour] Q (humor); honor F   80.1 *Exit*] DYCE; *Exit Falstaffe, and the Boy.* Q; *not in* F

72–3 **humour-letter** At 2.1.121 Nim calls it *the humoured letter*, again with no clear sense. See l. 52 and n.

73–4 **keep the haviour of reputation** maintain my respectable conduct

75 **Hold, sirrah ... tightly** This is a satisfactory line of verse because the deliberate action of handing over the letters fills the gap in the metre. 'Falstaff's transition to verse ... is unexpected but not inexplicable. Again half-seriously speaking of his plan as if it were the equivalent of a romantic voyage to reach Eldorado, he adopts for the minute the manner of Pistol' (Oliver).
  tightly soundly, properly, well (*OED*), as in 'He will clapper-claw thee tightly, bully', 2.3.59.

76 **pinnace** a small and therefore fast-sailing ship. The simile has a parallel in *Troilus* 1.1.100–5, where 'this sailing Pandar' is Troilus's 'barque', trading for him to 'India', Cressida's bed.

76.1 **Exit Robin** No direction (as usual) is given in F. Q has *Exit Falstaffe, and the Boy* at the end of the speech, but this is merely the most convenient place at which to print Robin's exit. It is more natural that Robin should immediately obey his orders, and that Falstaff should then turn on Pistol and Nim, than that Robin should linger and then go out either with Falstaff or separately.

77 **avaunt** begone

78 **o'th' hoof** on the hoof, i.e. on your feet.

F's reading (= 'in the hoof') is without parallel and must be an error which F2 corrects.

78 **pack** be off

79 **humour** habit, fashion. Q's reading is consistent with both *learn* and *French thrift*, while F's is consistent with neither. F's 'honor' would be an easy misreading of 'humor' (F's more frequent spelling than 'humour' in this scene); the same misreading occurs in Q's version of 1.1.150–2, where Nim says 'Syr my honor is not for many words, | But if you run bace humors of me, | I will say mary trap. And there's the humor of it.'

80 **French thrift** The expression seems to be Falstaff's own, not one in general use, and it is not clear whether it alludes to a known custom of France (no satisfactory evidence has been produced) or to French economy in general (not referred to elsewhere by Shakespeare). In *LLL* Armado, a Spaniard, is attended by a single page, Mote. Compare Chapman, *Monsieur D'Olive* (printed 1606) 3.1.76–9: 'With our great lords, followers abroad and hospitality at home are out of date. The world's now grown thrifty. He that fills a whole page in folio with his style thinks it veriest noble to be manned with one bare page and a pander.'
  skirted wearing a long coat belted about the waist, in the manner of servants. Compare the traditional bluecoat uniform of Christ's Hospital.

PISTOL

Let vultures gripe thy guts! For gourd and fulham
    holds,
And high and low beguiles the rich and poor.
Tester I'll have in pouch when thou shalt lack,
Base Phrygian Turk!

NIM I have operations which be humours of revenge.

PISTOL

Wilt thou revenge?

NIM   By welkin and her stars!

PISTOL

With wit or steel?

NIM   With both the humours, I.
I will discuss the humour of this love to Page.

81 fulham] F (fullam)   85 operations] F (opperations,); operations in my head, Q   be]
F; are Q   86 stars] COLLIER 1853; Star F; Fairies Q   88 Page] Q; Ford F

81 **Let vultures gripe thy guts!** Compare
Pistol's imprecation in *2 Henry IV*
5.3.138: 'Let vultures vile seize on his
lungs also!' Not a parody of any particular passage in drama but typical of Pistol's theatrical clichés. The line is another
iambic hexameter.
    gourd 'a kind of false dice' (*OED*, which
compares Old Fr. *gourd*, a swindle, 'four-
berie')
    fulham 'a die loaded at the corner (a high
fulham was loaded so as to ensure a cast
of 4, 5, or 6; a low fulham, so as to ensure
a cast of 1, 2, or 3)' (*OED*)
    holds hold good, prevail (Abbott 333,
third person plural in -s).
82 **high and low** dice so cut or loaded as to
turn up high and low numbers respectively. Pistol's line continues with a reminiscence of Psalm 49: 2: 'Both high and
low, both rich and poor | That in the
world do dwell' (in the metrical version;
in the Book of Common Prayer (1559)
the two phrases are the same, though the
Geneva Bible has 'low and high'), as was
shown by Fripp, i. 86–7.
83 **Tester** sixpenny piece
84 **Phrygian Turk** From the references to
Phrygia in *Troilus* (e.g. 4.7.106–7: 'The
fall of every Phrygian stone will cost | A
drop of Grecian blood') it is evident that
Shakespeare   meant   Pistol's   abuse
(= base Trojan Turk) to be ridiculous.
85 **operations** workings; in his head, as Q
unnecessarily spells out. 'Nym means

that, of course, but he was the last person
to say so' (Hart).
86 **welkin** the sky. Here equivalent to
'heaven'.
    stars The plural form is more probable
than the singular, even allowing for the
fact that Nim is the speaker. When
Shakespeare mentions a star he defines it,
e.g. 'th' unfolding star' (*Measure*
4.2.202), 'the North Star' (*Much Ado*
2.1.234), 'sailing by the star' (i.e. the
pole star, *Much Ado* 3.4.53), 'the wat'ry
star' (i.e. the moon, *Winter's Tale* 1.2.1).
Q's 'Fairies' may be a misreading of
'starres'.
88 **discuss** make known (*OED v.* 5). The
word is used only by Shakespeare's comic
characters—Nim here, the Host at 4.5.2,
Fluellen (*Henry V* 3.3.7), and Pistol
(*Henry V* 4.1.38, 4.4. 5, 29)).
    Page F, in this and the two following
speeches, makes Nim say that he is going
to Ford, and Pistol that he is going to
Page. In Q, where Nim has no third
speech, the names are transposed. Since
the transposition is consistent with 2.1
it may be supposed to reflect what was
done in the theatre. The F readings
(unless they reflect threefold error by the
scribe, which is almost impossible, or his
deliberate alteration of the second and
third after mistranscribing the first,
which is hardly more likely) must arise
from Shakespeare's first thoughts as recorded in his foul papers. To make the

PISTOL

And I to Ford shall eke unfold

  How Falstaff, varlet vile,   90

His dove will prove, his gold will hold,

  And his soft couch defile.

NIM My humour shall not cool. I will incense Page to deal
with poison. I will possess him with yellowness, for this
revolt of mine is dangerous. That is my true humour.

PISTOL

Thou art the Mars of malcontents. I second thee. Troop

  on.   *Exeunt*

1.4   *Enter Mistress Quickly and Simple*

MISTRESS QUICKLY (*calling*) What, John Rugby!

  ⌜*Enter Rugby*⌝

I pray thee, go to the casement and see if you can see my
master, Master Doctor Caius, coming. If he do, i'faith,

---

89 Ford] Q; *Page* F   93 Page] RANN; *Ford* F   94 yellowness] F (yallow- | nesse); Iallowes
Q this] POPE; the F   95 mine] F; mien THEOBALD; men JOHNSON *conj.*; mind JACKSON
conj.; mine anger CAMBRIDGE *conj.*   96] F; *Exit omnes.* Q
    1.4.] F (*Scœna Quarta.*)   0.1] Q; *Enter Mistris Quickly, Simple, Iohn Rugby, Doctor, Caius,
Fenton.* F   1 *calling*] NCS; *not in* F   1.1] WHEATLEY; *not in* F

transposition causes two slight difficulties. Firstly, it is Ford, not Page, who will
be made jealous; but the audience has
not yet seen Ford, and knows nothing
about his disposition, and, besides, Nim's
words are no guarantee that Page will
actually become jealous. Secondly, the
fact that Pistol is the first to reject his
letter may imply that he was given the
first letter, and that therefore it was to
Mistress Page; but the scene acts equally
well if Nim is given the letter to Mistress
Page and takes it, but then follows
Pistol's example in rejecting it. On balance, it seems better to emend F by
following Q than to end 1.3 with a firm
resolution reached, and then in 2.1 to
present an incongruous sequel.

89–92 Fripp, i. 87, compares the metrical
version of Psalm 50: 18: 'When thou
dost them behold, | That wives and maids
defile, | Thou lik'st it well, and waxest
bold | To use that life most vile.' Pistol
loads his doggerel with internal rhymes
(l. 91) and alliteration (*varlet vile*; in this

respect *Ford . . . unfold* is an improvement
on *Page . . . unfold*).
91 **prove** test (sexually)
94 **yellowness** jealousy (*OED* 2: first reference). Compare *Winter's Tale* 2.3.107:
'No yellow in't' (i.e. no jealousy in the
mind).
94–5 **this revolt of mine** Compare 'this revolt of thine', *Henry V* 2.2.138. The noun
revolt with the possessive adjective is
frequent in Shakespeare. If the rest of the
phrase is correct, F's 'the' must be wrong
and Pope's emendation necessary; if F's
'the' is accepted as correct it becomes
necessary to emend 'mine' or to add
something after it (the Cambridge editors
suggest that 'anger' was omitted because
of the presence of *dangerous* immediately
afterwards).
96 **the Mars of malcontents** the most warlike
rebel of all. *OED* (*malcontent sb.* 1) records
that the 1587 edition of Holinshed's
Chronicle substitutes 'mal-contents' in a
context where the 1577 edition had
'Rebels'. Pistol ends the scene with an
iambic fourteener.

and find anybody in the house, here will be old abusing
of God's patience and the King's English.

RUGBY I'll go watch.

MISTRESS QUICKLY Go; and we'll have a posset for't soon at
night, in faith, at the latter end of a sea-coal fire.

⌈*Exit Rugby*⌉

An honest, willing, kind fellow as ever servant shall
come in house withal; and, I warrant you, no tell-tale,   10
nor no breed-bate. His worst fault is that he is given to
prayer; he is something peevish that way, but nobody
but has his fault. But let that pass.—Peter Simple you
say your name is?

SIMPLE Ay, for fault of a better.

MISTRESS QUICKLY And Master Slender's your master?

SIMPLE Ay, forsooth.

MISTRESS QUICKLY Does he not wear a great round beard
like a glover's paring-knife?

---

4 be old] POPE; be an old F   7 Go;] F (Goe,); Do, This edition *conj.*   8.1 *Exit Rugby*]
ROWE; *not in* F

1.4.4 **old** great, extreme (*OED a.*¹ 6).
Shakespeare's other instances (*Merchant*
4.2.15, *Much Ado* 5.2.87, *Shrew* 3.2.30,
2 Henry IV 2.4.17, *Macbeth* 2.3.2) and all
OED's instances are without the indefinite article, which may be a scribal
interpolation; compare the indefinite article at 2.1.21 in F.

5 **King's English** Hart gives instances of
the use of this proverbial expression
(Tilley K80) in Elizabeth I's reign,
though he also points out that Nashe
(*Strange News*, 1593) has 'abusing the
Queen's English'.

7 **Go** This form of assent to Rugby's offer
seems to me rather unnatural, and I
wonder whether it should be emended to
'Do'.

posset 'A drink composed of hot milk
curdled with ale, wine, or other liquor,
often with sugar, spices, or other ingredients' (*OED*)

for't Perhaps equivalent to 'to com-
pensate us for the pains we are taking
now'.

7–8 **soon at night** before the night is much
advanced (*OED soon* 3). Compare *Romeo*
2.4.76.

8 **sea-coal** mined coal (superior to char-
coal) brought by sea from Newcastle
upon Tyne and elsewhere

8.1 Rugby's exits and entrances partly de-
pend upon the stage setting assumed by
editors: in NCS the window at which he is
posted is on stage and he therefore does
not leave the stage until he follows Caius
out (l. 120.1).

11 **breed-bate** trouble maker. Compare *2
Henry IV* 2.4.250–1, 'breeds no bate'.

12 **peevish** Usually glossed as 'silly, foolish'
(*OED a.* 1), but the more frequent sense in
Shakespeare is 'perverse, refractory'
(*OED a.* 4), e.g. *Two Gentlemen* 3.1.68
('peevish, sullen, froward'), *Shrew*
5.2.162 ('froward, peevish, sullen,
sour'), and *1 Henry IV* 3.1.194 ('a peevish self-willed harlotry'), which is more
incongruous, and more amusing, in this
context.

12–13 **nobody but has his fault** proverbial
(Tilley M116)

15 **for fault of a better** proverbial (Tilley
F106)

19 **glover** leather-worker (like Shakespeare's father, as Oliver notes)

SIMPLE No, forsooth. He hath but a little wee face, with a   20
little yellow beard, a Cain-coloured beard.

MISTRESS QUICKLY A softly-sprited man, is he not?

SIMPLE Ay, forsooth. But he is as tall a man of his hands as
any is between this and his head. He hath fought with a
warrener.

MISTRESS QUICKLY How, say you?—O, I should remember

---

20 wee] F (wee-); whey- CAPELL   21 Cain-coloured] F (Caine colourd); kane colored
Q; cane-colour'd ROWE 1714   26 How, say you?] This edition; How say you: F

20 **wee** tiny. F's reading 'wee-face' (the
hyphen is explicable as the scribe Crane's
characteristic insertion) has been
doubted because *wee* is not used elsewhere by Shakespeare and 'seems to
have been hardly in use in the south at
the beginning of the seventeenth century, except in the phrase of distance, "a
wee bit"' (Hart); it was a northern form
(*OED*'s one instance dated 1450, cited by
Oliver against Hart, is in a Scottish
poem). The emendation *whey*, derived
from Q's phrase hereabouts for Mistress
Quickly, 'And he has as it were a whay
coloured beard', is open to at least two
objections: a misreading of the common
'whay' or 'whey' as the uncommon 'wee'
is improbable; and 'whey-face' (*Macbeth*
5.3.19) is too figurative for Simple (*OED*
gives no instance of 'whey-face' earlier
than *Macbeth*, from which later instances
may derive). Simple would be more likely
to join two synonyms together, as in
'little tiny', which occurs twice in 2
Henry IV and once each in *Twelfth Night*
and *King Lear*, but a misreading of 'tiny',
'tinie', 'tine', or 'tyne' as 'wee' is highly
improbable. The expression 'little wee' is
supported by Thomas Heywood's *The
Fair Maid of the West, Part 1* (1631:
Dramatic Works [ed. R. H. Shepherd],
1874, ii. 277), where Bess Bridges's
thirteen-year-old tapster Clem (not a nor-
therner) tells her that his father 'was
nothing so tall as I, but a little wee man
and somewhat huck-backed' (i.e. hunch-
backed). This may derive from the present passage (as the hyphenated 'wee-
man' of Q 1631 suggests), with which, if
so, Heywood found no difficulty.

21 **Cain-coloured** *OED* (*Cain* 2, this example
only) defines as '"red" or reddish-
yellow', probably following Theobald,
who says, of this passage, that 'Cain
and Judas, in the tapestries and pictures

of old, were represented with yellow
beards.' But Judas's hair was supposedly
red ('I ever thought by his red head he
would prove a Judas', Marston, *The Insa-
tiate Countess* 2.2.36), and 'Judas-
coloured' is so defined in *OED* (*Judas* 4).
Bottom's catalogue of beards (*Dream*
1.2.86–9) implies that the various
shades he mentions were distinct. Steevens took Bottom's 'strawcolour' to be
analogous to Simple's 'cane-coloured',
i.e. the yellow colour of a cane. Though
there is no firm evidence for the colour of
Cain's beard in art, F's 'Caine' (Q 'kane')
seems the right reading. Hart's suggestion that 'cane' is related to the Hiberno-
English *cane*, from Irish *caithne* (wild
arbutus) is strained, for the yellow dye in
which its rind was used along with poplar
bark and leaves was 'of a saffron colour'
(Camden's *Britannia*, trans. Philemon
Holland, 1610, p. 144), and 'saffron' is
used four times by Shakespeare, who
would be likely to use it here if that was
the colour he meant.

22 **softly-sprited** soft-spirited, of a mild disposition (*OED*'s only example)

23 **as tall a man of his hands** as brave a
fighter. A common phrase (Tilley M163).

24 **between this and his head** 'in these parts'
(Hibbard). Proverbial (Dent H237.1). Tilley (H429: 'From hence to [some distant
place]') cites 'between this and your own
skins' from the anonymous play *King
Darius* (1565).

25 **warrener** gamekeeper in charge of a
warren (an enclosure devoted to the
preservation of rabbits)

26 **How, say you?** 'Indeed, do you say so?';
an exclamation of admiration and surprise, equivalent to the modern 'You
don't say so!'

26–7 **I should remember him** 'Now I can call
him to mind'

him. Does he not hold up his head, as it were, and strut
in his gait?

SIMPLE Yes, indeed does he.

MISTRESS QUICKLY Well, heaven send Anne Page no worse   30
fortune! Tell Master Parson Evans I will do what I can
for your master. Anne is a good girl, and I wish—

RUGBY (*within*) Out, alas! Here comes my master.

MISTRESS QUICKLY We shall all be shent. Run in here, good
young man; go into this closet. He will not stay long.

        She shuts Simple in the closet

What, John Rugby! John, what, John, I say!

        ⌈*Enter Rugby*⌉

⌈*Speaking loudly*⌉ Go, John, go enquire for my master.

                                            ⌈*Exit Rugby*⌉

I doubt he be not well, that he comes not home.

(*Sings*) And down, down, adown-a (*etc.*)

        Enter Doctor Caius

CAIUS Vat is you sing? I do not like dese toys. Pray you go   40
and vetch me in my closet *une boîte en vert*—a box, a

---

33 *within*] This edition; *Enter Rugby.* ROWE; *not in* F   master.] F; master. *Exit.*
ROWE   35.1] ROWE (*after* 'closet', 35); *He steps into the Counting-house.* Q; *not in* F   36.1]
OXFORD; *not in* F   37 *Speaking loudly*] OXFORD; *not in* F   37.1 *Exit Rugby*] OXFORD (*after*
'home'); *not in* F   39 *Sings*] *as* THEOBALD; *not in* F   39.1 *Enter Doctor Caius*] ROWE; *And she
opens the doore.* Q; *Caius enters*; *she feigns not to see him* NCS (*after* 'I say!', 37)   40 dese toys]
THEOBALD; des-toyes F   41 *une boîte en*] HART; vnboyteene F; *un boîtier* ROWE; *une boîtine*
IRVING/MARSHALL   vert] CAMBRIDGE; verd F

---

33 **Out, alas!** an exclamation of alarm, like
'Out upon't!' (ll. 157–8)

34 **shent** blamed

35 **closet** Probably in its usual sense in
Shakespeare, a small private room (*OED
sb.* 1), though *OED* gives this passage
under *sb.* 3a (= a cupboard). Throughout
the scene Q subsititutes 'counting house'
for 'closet': see Introduction, p. 51.

37–8 **Go, John, go . . . home** Mistress Quickly
says this in a loud voice in order to
prevent Caius from suspecting that she
knows of his return. The NCS editors,
who first indicated this, did so by making
Caius enter after 'What, John, I say!'

38 **doubt** fear

39 **And down . . . etc.** The refrain of some
song. Compare *Hamlet* 4.5.171–2. 'The
implication of *etc.* would seem to be that
Mistress Quickly goes on repeating the
refrain until Caius interrupts her' (Hibbard). This is an argument against his
premature entry as in NCS.

41 ***une boîte en vert*** F's *verd* is the usual
spelling of *vert* at the time: compare
Cotgrave's *Dictionary*, 1611. F's *vnboyteene* is hard to interpret. The NCS editors
suggest that it is a misreading of *vnboy-
teere*, i.e. *un boîtier*, a surgeon's box of
instruments. But this would probably be
too big to go in Caius's *pochette*, and he
would not be likely to have several of
them, of different colours. His explanation of his unexpected return in Q, 'I
begar I be forget my oyntment', suggests
that the box is a small one. *Une boîtine*, i.e.
a little box, is possible, but no such
French word exists, and the fact that
Caius translates his expression as a green
box but not as a little green box tells
against this reading. *En vert* (in green) is
not idiomatic French, but it may have

green-a box. Do intend vat I speak? A green-a box.

MISTRESS QUICKLY Ay, forsooth, I'll fetch it you. (*Aside*) I
am glad he went not in himself. If he had found the
young man, he would have been horn-mad.

She goes to the closet

CAIUS Fe, fe, fe, fe! *Ma foi, il fait fort chaud. Je m'en vais à la
cour—la grande affaire.*

MISTRESS QUICKLY Is it this, sir?

She shows him the box

CAIUS *Oui, mettez-le à ma pochette. Dépêche*, quickly. Vere is
dat knave Rugby?   50

MISTRESS QUICKLY What, John Rugby! John!

Enter Rugby

RUGBY Here, sir.

CAIUS You are John Rugby, and you are Jack Rugby.
Come, take-a your rapier, and come after my heel to the
court.

---

43 *Aside*] POPE; *to Rugby* NCS; *not in* F   45.1 *She ... closet*] NCS; *not in* F   46–7 *Ma foi ...*
affaire] *as* ROWE 1714; *mai foy, il fait for ehando, le man voi a le Court la grand affaires* F; *ma foi, il*
fait fort chaud. Je m'en vais voir à la court la grande affaire OLIVER   48.1] This edition; *not*
in F   49 *mettez-le*] *as* THEOBALD; *mette le* F   *à ma pochette. Dépêche*, quickly] OXFORD; *au mon*
pocket, de-peech quickly F; *au mon pocket, dépêche Quickly* NCS   51.1 *Enter Rugby*]
WHEATLEY; *not in* F

been the expression that Shakespeare
wrote.

42 **Do intend vat I speak?** Caius, imagining
that he is now speaking English, means
'Do you hear (French *entendre*) what I
say?' She is, of course, paralysed by the
thought that Simple is in the closet.

45 **horn-mad** fighting-mad with rage, like a
horned beast in mating-season. A
proverbial expression (Tilley H628), usually in a context of sexual jealousy and
cuckoldry, as in 3.5.139, *Errors*
2.1.56–8, and *Much Ado* 1.1.251.

46 **il fait fort chaud** Caius probably feels hot
because he has hurried home, rather
than because of the fire that may be
burning there, since he does not directly
complain of it.

46–7 **Je ... affaire** 'I'm going to the court—
important business' (Hibbard). Oliver,
postulating that F omitted a word which
resembled *voi* (= *vais*), reads *vais voir* (i.e.
'I'm going to see the great affair at the
court'); this presumably refers to the
Garter ceremony—perhaps too directly

to be appropriate to the present context.

49 **mettez-le** The plural form of the imperative seems to have been more familiar to
Shakespeare than the singular (e.g.
Henry V 3.4.4: '*Je te prie, m'enseignez*'),
though he has *dépêche* at l. 52. The *tt*
sound in F's *mette* is clearly meant to be
pronounced.

à ma pochette 'in my (little) pocket'.
Whether Shakespeare intended a dimin-
utive of *poche* or thought that *pochette*
was French for pocket is uncertain. F's *au*
mon must be wrong: *au* is probably a
scribal misreading of an *a* with an upward final flourish (compare *mai* for *ma*,
l. 46). The spelling *pocket* probably arose
because the compositor misread italic
pochette as *pockette*, knew that this could
not be French, and so set the usual
English form of the word. As Jowett says,
'it is implausible for Caius to translate the
sentence's most difficult word alone'.

quickly Caius translates the sense of
dépêche for Mistress Quickly's benefit (and
the audience's).

53 **You ... Jack Rugby** NCS (glossary) inter-

RUGBY 'Tis ready, sir, here in the porch.

⌈*He fetches the rapier*⌉

CAIUS By my trot', I tarry too long. 'Od's me! *Qu'ai-je oublié?* Dere is some simples in my closet, dat I vill not for the varld I shall leave behind.

He goes to the closet

MISTRESS QUICKLY (*aside*) Ay me, he'll find the young man 60
there, and be mad.

CAIUS *O, diable, diable!* Vat is in my closet? Villainy!
Larron!

He pulls Simple out of the closet

Rugby, my rapier!

MISTRESS QUICKLY Good master, be content.

CAIUS Wherefore shall I be content-a?

MISTRESS QUICKLY The young man is an honest man.

CAIUS What shall de honest man do in my closet? Dere is
no honest man dat shall come in my closet.

MISTRESS QUICKLY I beseech you, be not so phlegmatic. 70
Hear the truth of it. He came of an errand to me from
Parson Hugh.

CAIUS Vell?

56.1 *He ... rapier*] OXFORD; *not in* F   57–8 *Qu'ai-je oublié*] F (*que ay ie oublie*)   59.1 *He ...
closet*] *as* HIBBARD (*Exit to the closet*); *after* oublié, 58 NCS; *not in* F   60 *aside*] OXFORD; *not in*
F   62 Villainy] F (Villanie); Villaine Q3   63 *Larron*] ROWE; La-roone F   63.1 *He pulls ...
closet*] *as* THEOBALD; *not in* F   73 Vell?] NEILSON; Vell. F

prets 'Jack' here as 'knave' (a frequent sense in the play), and it is true that Caius has just referred to 'dat knave Rugby'. On the other hand, Caius's English being what it is, he is not likely to make a linguistic quibble. In 2.3 and 3.1 he consistently addresses his man as 'Jack Rugby' without any derogatory intent. Since Mistress Quickly has consistently addressed Rugby as 'John' in this scene, twice immediately before Rugby now appears, Caius's statement seems best interpreted as that of a foreigner musing on the mysteries of the English tongue; compare his 'Jack dog; John ape', 3.1.77.

57 **trot'** troth

'Od's me The euphemistic *'od* for 'God' is common in oaths, and is used by Evans, Slender, and Mistress Quickly. 'God's me' (*1 Henry IV*, 2.4.91) is derived by *OED* (*God sb.* 8b) from 'God save me'.

58 **simples** medicines 'composed or con-

cocted of only one constituent, esp. of one herb or plant (*OED simple sb.* 6). Here, by dramatic irony, with unconscious reference to Simple.

62 **Villainy** The F spelling 'villanie' is repeated at 2.3.15, which suggests that it is not a compositor's error in either place (as in *Two Gentlemen* 3.1.325 where uncorrected F has 'villanie' and corrected F 'villaine') but represents some oddity of Caius's expression — either the abstract noun 'villainy' applied to a person or a Frenchified pronunciation of the English word 'villain'.

63 *Larron* (Fr.) thief

64 **Rugby, my rapier!** Whether Rugby hands the rapier to him or Mistress Quickly interposes before he can do so is at the actors' discretion.

70 **phlegmatic** Mistress Quickly's error for 'choleric', with a contrary sense: choler was hot and dry, phlegm cold and moist.

SIMPLE Ay, forsooth, to desire her to—

MISTRESS QUICKLY Peace, I pray you.

CAIUS Peace-a your tongue. (*To Simple*) Speak-a your tale.

SIMPLE To desire this honest gentlewoman, your maid, to
speak a good word to Mistress Anne Page for my master
in the way of marriage.

MISTRESS QUICKLY This is all, indeed, ~~la! But I'll ne'er put~~   80
~~my finger in the fire, an't need not.~~

CAIUS Sir Hugh send-a you?—Rugby, *baillez* me some
paper. (*To Simple*) Tarry you a little-a while.

    Rugby brings paper from the closet. Caius writes

MISTRESS QUICKLY (*aside to Simple*) I am glad he is so quiet. If
he had been thoroughly moved, you should have heard
him so loud and so melancholy. But notwithstanding,
man, I'll do your master what good I can. And the very
yea and the no is, the French doctor, my master—I may
call him my master, look you, for I keep his house, and I
wash, wring, brew, bake, scour, dress meat and drink,   90
make the beds, and do all myself—

76 *To Simple*] OLIVER, as Steevens (tongue.—Speak); *not in* F   81 an't] This edition; and
F   82 *baillez*] THEOBALD; ballow F; baille CAMBRIDGE   83 *To Simple*] HIBBARD; *not in*
F   83.1 *Rugby ... writes*] as OXFORD; *The Doctor writes.* Q; *not in* F   84 aside to Simple]
HIBBARD; *not in* F   85 thoroughly] F (throughly)   87 do your master] CAPELL; doe yoe
your Master F

76 **Peace-a ... tale** These two unidiomatic
commands, thus juxtaposed, suggest ob-
scenities of which Caius is unaware
(compare 'turd' for 'third', 3.3.223). The
first sounds as though he said 'Piss o'
your tongue'; the second can be heard as
an imperative, i.e. 'Let your tail speak'.

80–1 **I'll ... need not** A proverbial expression (Tilley F230) meaning 'I'll not meddle where I need not'. F's 'and' = and't,
i.e. if it.

82 *baillez* (French) bring; here in its usual
16th-c. sense of 'give'. As Oliver says, F's
'ballow' cannot be a misreading of *baillez*
or *baille*, but his conclusion that '"ballow" must be an anglicized form' of the
French verb, 'or Caius' attempt to find an
equivalent', does not follow. It is more
probably a more or less phonetic spelling
of the French verb. Theobald's emendation here is supported by Q's reading at
2.3.11, 'Bully moy, mon rapier *Iohn
Rugabie*', where '*Baillez-moi*' is clearly
intended.

83.1 Caius will have his pen and inkhorn in

his *pochette*. Q's stage direction *The Doctor
writes* implies the presence of a table and
a chair on stage for this scene. Similar
stage furniture is desirable in the scenes
which take place in the Garter Inn. See
2.2.162.1, 3.5.17.1.

86 **melancholy** Another unsuccessful effort
at 'choleric'; melancholy was cold and
dry.

notwithstanding Shakespeare, here and
at ll. 96 and 98, observes how un-
educated people, having caught hold of
an expression, use it repeatedly. Compare
Mistress Quickly's repetition of 'I warrant
you' five times in one speech, 2.2.57–74.

87 **do your master** In support of Capell's
emendation, Jowett convincingly argues
that the F compositor originally set 'doe
yoe' in error for 'doe your', that the proof-
reader demanded the correction of 'yoe'
to 'your', and that the compositor misun-
derstood his instruction and treated
'your' as an addition.

90 **dress** prepare

SIMPLE (*aside to Mistress Quickly*) 'Tis a great charge to come under one body's hand.

MISTRESS QUICKLY (*aside to Simple*) Are you advised o' that? You shall find it a great charge; and to be up early and down late. But notwithstanding—to tell you in your ear; I would have no words of it—my master himself is in love with Mistress Anne Page. But notwithstanding that, I know Anne's mind. That's neither here nor there.   100

CAIUS (*giving a letter to Simple*) You, jack'nape, give-a this letter to Sir Hugh. By gar, it is a shallenge. I will cut his troat in de Park, and I will teach a scurvy jackanape priest to meddle or make. You may be gone. It is not good you tarry here.   *Exit Simple*
~~By gar, I will cut all his two stones. By gar, he shall not have a stone to throw at his dog.~~

MISTRESS QUICKLY Alas, he speaks but for his friend.

CAIUS It is no matter-a ver dat. Do not you tell-a me dat I shall have Anne Page for myself? By gar, I vill kill de   110
jack priest; and I have appointed mine host of de Jarteer to measure our weapon. By gar, I will myself have Anne Page.

92 *aside to Mistress Quickly*] HIBBARD; *not in* F   94 *aside to Simple*] HIBBARD; *not in* F   101 *giving a letter to Simple*] OXFORD; *not in* F   105 *Exit Simple*] *as* NCS; *after* 'dog', 107 ROWE; *not in* F

94–5 **Are you . . . charge** 'You think so, do you? Yes, I can tell you, it is a real load.'

95 **charge** Oliver points out that though Mistress Quickly means a burden of trouble (*OED charge sb.* 8) the word also suggests a literal burden (*OED sb.* 1) and therefore a sexual sense. This is characteristic of her language, as in 'I have borne, and borne, and borne', 2 *Henry IV* 2.2.33–4.

99–100 **That's neither here nor there** 'But no matter for that.'

101 **jack'nape** jackanapes, monkey

102 **By gar** by God

104 **meddle or make** interfere (Tilley M852)

106 **stones** testicles

106–7 **he shall . . . dog** The usual form of this proverbial phrase (Tilley S880) is 'a dog', e.g. *As You Like It* 1.3.3. Perhaps *his* is an error induced by the preceding *his two stones* or the following *his friend*; but

since Caius is the speaker the eccentricity may be intended.

111 **jack priest** knave priest
Jarteer Garter (French *jarretière*). Caius omits *of* at 3.1.83 and 4.5.77.

112 **to measure our weapon** Not 'to act as my second' (Oliver) but 'to act as umpire in our duel' (Hibbard), i.e. to see fair play: see 2.1.187–8. Caius always uses the singular pronoun of himself; the singular form *weapon* for 'weapons' is either a textual error or one of his verbal eccentricities. Shakespeare uses *weapon* with a sexual innuendo (unconscious on the speaker's part) in *Romeo* 1.1.32 and 2.3.148, and again in 2 *Henry IV* 2.1.16 and 2.4.207; no doubt he means the audience to take this passage in the same way, prompted by Caius's repeated insistence that he alone shall have Anne Page.

MISTRESS QUICKLY Sir, the maid loves you, and all shall be
well. We must give folks leave to prate. What the good-
year!

CAIUS Rugby, come to the court with me. (*To Mistress
Quickly*) By gar, if I have not Anne Page, I shall turn
your head out of my door.—Follow my heels, Rugby.

MISTRESS QUICKLY You shall have Anne—   120

                 Exeunt Caius and Rugby

—ass-head of your own. No, I know Anne's mind for
that. Never a woman in Windsor knows more of Anne's
mind than I do, nor can do more than I do with her, I
thank heaven.

FENTON (*within*) Who's within there, ho?

MISTRESS QUICKLY Who's there, I trow?—Come near the
house, I pray you.

    Enter Fenton

115–16 good-year] CAPELL (good year); good-ier F   117–18 *To Mistress Quickly*] WHEATLEY,
as Steevens (me.—By); *not in* F   120–1 Anne—ass-head] OXFORD; *An*-fooles head F; An—
fool's head IRVING/MARSHALL (*conj.* Daniel)   120.1 *Exeunt Caius and Rugby*] IRVING/MARSHALL
(*conj.* Daniel); *after* 'Rugby', 119 ROWE; *Exit Doctor.* Q (*after line corresponding to* 119)   125
within] ROWE; *not in* F   126 there, I trow] F (there, I troa); there, trow HART *conj.*   127.1]
ROWE; *not in* F

114–15 **all shall be well** 'All shall be well
and Jack shall have Jill' (Tilley A164).
Compare *Dream* 3.3.45–8.

115 **give folks leave to prate** 'Give losers
leave to talk' is proverbial (Tilley L458).
Mistress Quickly is implying that Slender
is not a serious danger as a rival.

115–16 **What the good-year!** An expletive,
of uncertain origin, in use by the early
16th c.; *OED* conjecturally derives it from
early modern Dutch *wat goedtjaar*, which
may have originated as an exclamation
(= 'as I hope for a good year'). Mistress
Quickly uses it twice in 2 *Henry IV*
2.4.55–6, 174, and Borachio once in
Much Ado 1.3.1.

118–19 **turn your head out** An expression
peculiar to Caius ('turn you out' would be
normal), ridiculous because it makes one
visualize a separate head being ejected.
Compare the figurative 'thrust . . . out . . .
by the head and shoulders' at 5.5.147–8.

121 **ass-head** This emendation seems necessary because (*a*) the article 'a' was required before consonants other than *h*,
and (*b*) the *an/Anne* homophone is indis-
pensable to the jest (which F emphasizes
by spelling Anne's name as *An* on its

other two occurrences in this speech: elsewhere it is never *An* except in 1.1.204–5,
in a line cramped for space, which is not
the case here). Both 'an ass-head of your
own' and 'a fool's head of your own'
(Tilley A388, F519) were proverbial,
the former first recorded in *Dream*
3.1.111–12. Why, if *ass-head* is required,
F has 'fooles head' is hard to explain. A
misreading is surely impossible; so is the
substitution of a synonym, in view of the
juxtaposition with '*An*—'; and an omission (from 'ass-head, a fool's head') is
unlikely, since both phrases would hardly
be used in view of the familiarity of each.

121–2 **for that** on that subject

126 **I trow** I wonder; as in 2.1.59 (with the
same unusual spelling in F). An idiomatic
use found also (in abbreviated form) in
Much Ado 3.4.54 ('What means the fool,
trow?') and *Cymbeline* 1.6.48 ('What is
the matter, trow?').

126–7 **Come near the house** come into the
house. Compare 3.3.141. Hart cites the
phrase 'come near house', in this sense,
from Thomas Heywood's *1 Edward IV*
(before 1600).

127.1 *Enter Fenton* In Q Fenton does not

FENTON How now, good woman, how dost thou?

MISTRESS QUICKLY The better that it pleases your good
worship to ask.   130

FENTON What news? How does pretty Mistress Anne?

MISTRESS QUICKLY In truth, sir, and she is pretty, and
honest, and gentle, and one that is your friend—I can
tell you that by the way, I praise heaven for it.

FENTON Shall I do any good, think'st thou? Shall I not lose
my suit?

MISTRESS QUICKLY Troth, sir, all is in His hands above. But
notwithstanding, Master Fenton, I'll be sworn on a
book she loves you. Have not your worship a wart
above your eye?   140

FENTON Yes, marry, have I. What of that?

MISTRESS QUICKLY Well, thereby hangs a tale. Good faith, it
is such another Nan!—but, I detest, an honest maid as
ever broke bread. We had an hour's talk of that wart. I
shall never laugh but in that maid's company. But,
indeed, she is given too much to allicholy and musing.
But for you—well—go to—

FENTON Well, I shall see her today. Hold, there's money
for thee; let me have thy voice in my behalf. If thou seest
her before me, commend me—   150

---

appear in this scene. Caius gives Simple
the letter and a threatening message for
Evans, and leaves with Rugby. Mistress
Quickly bids Simple farewell, telling him
that she will do what she can for Slender.

129–30 **The better ... ask** a conversational
cliché (Dent B332.1)

132 **and she** The 'and', which is redundant,
helps to throw the stress on 'is'.

133 **honest** virtuous
gentle mild-mannered (*OED gentle a.* 8)
your friend well disposed towards you

138–9 **on a book** on the Bible. This elliptical
use (*OED book sb.* 4a), with the indefinite
article, is recorded in *c*.1450.

139 **Have** The pronoun 'you' is understood
in the deferential phrase *your worship*.

139–40 **a wart ... eye** Hart compares the
reported jesting about a white hair on
Troilus's chin (*Troilus* 1.2.135–65). For
the idea that a blemish can add to beauty,
compare Lyly, *Euphues* (Lyly, i.185):

'Venus had her mole in her cheek which
made her more amiable, Helen her scar in
her chin which Paris called *cos amoris* the
whetstone of love, Aristippus his wart,
Lycurgus his wen.'

142 **thereby hangs a tale** A cliché (Tilley
T48), several times used by Shakespeare,
once with a pun on 'tail' (*Othello* 3.1.8),
though not here.

142–3 **it is such another Nan** she is such an
extraordinary Nan. A conventional
idiom (Tilley A250).

143 **detest** An error for 'protest', also made
by Elbow in *Measure* 2.1.66 (unless he
means 'attest').

143–4 **an honest ... bread** Proverbial (Tilley
M68). Dogberry refers to Verges in a
similar way, *Much Ado* 3.5.36–7.

146 **allicholy** An error for 'melancholy',
made also by the Host in *Two Gentlemen*,
4.2.26.

147 **go to** enough of that

MISTRESS QUICKLY Will I? I'faith, that I will. And I will tell
your worship more of the wart the next time we have
confidence, and of other wooers.

FENTON Well, farewell; I am in great haste now.

MISTRESS QUICKLY Farewell to your worship.

Exit Fenton

Truly, an honest gentleman. But Anne loves him not,
for I know Anne's mind as well as another does.—Out
upon't! What have I forgot!   *Exit*

2.1   *Enter Mistress Page, with a letter*

MISTRESS PAGE What, have I 'scaped love-letters in the
holiday time of my beauty, and am I now a subject for
them? Let me see.

She reads

'Ask me no reason why I love you, for though Love use
Reason for his precisian, he admits him not for his

---

151 I] HANMER; wee F   155.1 *Exit Fenton*] ROWE (*after* 154); *not in* F
   2.1 F (*Actus Secundus. Scœna Prima.*)   0.1] ROWE; *Enter Mistris Page, Mistris Ford, Master*
Page, *Master Ford, Pistoll, Nim, Quickly, Host, Shallow.* F; *Enter Mistresse Page, reading of a*
Letter. Q   I have I] Q3; haue F   3.1] CAPELL; *not in* F   5 precisian] F; physician COLLIER
1853 (*conj.* Johnson)

---

151 **that I will**] HANMER; that wee will F.
   justified because Mistress Quickly does
   not confuse 'I' and 'we'; F's reading may
   result from the fact that 'we' occurs in F's
   following line (Jowett).
   that Anne does not love Fenton, which
   presumably is just her way of laying
   claim to a special understanding of
   Anne's feelings.
157–8 **Out … forgot** Shakespeare's device
   to get Mistress Quickly off-stage.
2.1 Pope and all later editors who localize
   the scene place it 'before Page's house',
   but it is inconvenient to imagine it con-
   tinuously there. Mistress Page and Mistress Ford meet somewhere in town between their houses (ll. 30–2), where they
   later observe their husbands talking to
   Pistol and Nim, and accost them:
   'Whither go you, George?' would be odd
   if the Pages were both before their own
   house, and Mistress Ford's 'Will you go,
   Mistress Page?' (i.e. shall we be going),
   and the reply, would be equally odd.

1–2 **the holiday time** the best time.
   Shakespeare contrasts 'holiday' with
   'working-day' (i.e. ordinary, everyday) in
   As You Like It 1.3.11–14.
3 **Let me see** 'Let me look it over again.'
   Mistress Page's reference to *love-letters*
   shows that she has already read it, and
   l. 32 shows that she is on her way to tell
   Mistress Ford.
5 **Reason** Falstaff's letter 'begins with an
   affected pseudo-Petrarchan personifica-
   tion' (Vickers, p. 149). Reason and Love
   are personified in conflict in one of Sidney's sonnets (*Astrophil and Stella*, no.
   10). See 3.3.40, where Falstaff quotes
   from one of Sidney's songs.
   precisian *OED* notes that the word was
   synonymous with 'puritan' in the 16th
   and 17th cc., and cites the present passage as using the word in a related
   general sense. In the context it seems to
   mean 'strict spiritual guide'. But there
   are 'difficulties: the word is not used
   elsewhere by Shakespeare; and the parallel between *his precisian* and *his counsel-*
   lor suggests that it denotes a paid or

counsellor. You are not young, no more am I. Go to,
then, there's sympathy. You are merry, so am I. Ha, ha,
then there's more sympathy. You love sack, and so do I.
Would you desire better sympathy? Let it suffice thee,
Mistress Page—at the least if the love of soldier can   10
suffice—that I love thee I will not say, pity me—'tis not
a soldier-like phrase—but I say, love me. By me,

> Thine own true knight,
> By day or night,
> Or any kind of light,
> With all his might
> For thee to fight,

John Falstaff.'

What a Herod of Jewry is this! O, wicked, wicked world!
One that is well-nigh worn to pieces with age to show   20
himself a young gallant! What unweighed behaviour

---

10 soldier] F; a soldier F3   21 What] F3; What an F

unpaid employment (*his counsellor* can be
paraphrased as 'him who counsels him',
but *his precisian* cannot be similarly paraphrased). Therefore Johnson's emendation deserves consideration, even though
precisian is an unlikely misreading of the
more common word *physician*. Compare
'I care not if I do become your physician'
(the Lord Chief Justice, speaking figuratively to Falstaff, *2 Henry IV* 1.2.126–7).

6 **counsellor** confidant (Hart, comparing
Romeo 1.1.144, 'his own affection's
counsellor'). Juliet apostrophizes the
Nurse as 'counsellor' with reference to
their former relationship as well as to the
unacceptable counsel that the Nurse has
just given her (*Romeo* 3.5.239).

7 **sympathy** resemblance, as in *Titus*
3.1.148, 'what a sympathy of woe' (i.e.
likeness in suffering). Compare Lyly, *Euphues* (Lyly, i. 197): 'Doth not the sympathy of manners make the conjunction of
minds?'
   Ha, ha An incongruous interjection in a
letter. Performers of Mistress Page's role
usually bring out this point in their
reading-out of the letter, e.g. by pro-
nouncing it with a deliberate absence of
expression.

8 **sack** wine (usually white wine) from
Spain or the Canaries

13–17 **Thine own … fight** Hart aptly compares Nashe, *A Countercuff given to Mart-
in Junior* (1589), *Works*, i. 64: 'To come
to a close | In rhyme or in prose, | In spite
of thy nose | Thine for these seven years:
| Pasquil of England.' Falstaff's own
rhymes may be a recollection of Malory's
peroration in *Morte D'Arthur* (printed by
William Caxton, 1485): 'For this book
was ended the ninth year of the reign of
King Edward the Fourth, by Sir Thomas
Malory, Knight, as Jesu help him for his
great might, as he is the servant of Jesu
both day and night.'

19 **Herod of Jewry** ranting villain. Compare
Hamlet's allusion to the Herod of the
miracle plays as a type of the exaggerat-
ing actor, *Hamlet* 3.2.14.

21 **What unweighed behaviour** F's reading
gives the sense 'How unweighed a behaviour' and is exclamatory; F3's reading
gives the sense 'What behaviour of an
unweighed kind' and is interrogative.
Whether *unweighed* means 'unconsi-
dered' (*OED weigh v.*[1] II. 11) or 'light'
(*OED weigh v.*[1] III) is debatable: this is
Shakespeare's only use of it, and his only
use of 'unweighing' (by Lucio of the Duke
in *Measure* 3.1.401) may mean either 'of
no weight' or 'unreflecting'. Whatever
the meaning, F3's reading seems preferable, since Mistress Page is quite unable to

hath this Flemish drunkard picked—with the devil's
name!—out of my conversation, that he dares in this
manner assay me? Why, he hath not been thrice in my
company. What should I say to him? I was then frugal
of my mirth. Heaven forgive me! Why, I'll exhibit a bill
in the parliament for the putting down of men. How
shall I be revenged on him? For revenged I will be, as
sure as his guts are made of puddings.

> *Enter Mistress Ford.*
> ⌈*Mistress Page conceals the letter*⌉

MISTRESS FORD Mistress Page! Trust me, I was going to   30
your house.

MISTRESS PAGE And, trust me, I was coming to you. You
look very ill.

MISTRESS FORD Nay, I'll ne'er believe that: I have to show
to the contrary.

---

22 with the] F (with | The); i'th' F3   29.1 *Enter Mistress Ford*] Q; *not in* F   29.2 *Mistress
. . . letter*] This edition; *not in* F

specify the behaviour of hers that Falstaff
has apparently taken encouragement
from, but concludes that she must have
involuntarily said or done something
unseemly (ll. 25–6). F's insertion of 'an'
might result accidentally from the immediately following 'vn' of 'vnwaied', or it
might be a scribal alteration, conscious
or unconscious, to correspond to 'What a
Herod of Jewry'.

22 **Flemish drunkard** The reference is to
Falstaff's bulk; compare 'swag-bellied
Hollander', *Othello* 2.3.72.

22–3 **with the devil's name** F1's abusive
interjection is confirmed by Nashe, *The
Unfortunate Traveller* (1594), *Works*, ii.
212: a host tells his tapster to 'look to the
bar, and come when he is called, with a
devil's name'.

23 **conversation** conduct

25 **should I say** can I have said (Abbott 325)

26 **exhibit** submit (*OED exhibit v.* 5a); the
technical term for the process. The word
occurs in the passage in Holinshed's
Chronicles that was the source for Act 1,
Scene 1 of *Henry V*. The humorous idea
may derive from Nashe, who quotes
Gabriel Harvey's phrase 'some tools are
false prophets' and comments 'That's the
cause we have so many bad workmen

nowadays: put up a bill against them
next parliament' (*Have with you to Saffron-
Walden*, 1596, *Works*, iii. 48). See also
notes to 3.3.23 and 4.5.29–31.

27 **putting down** abolition

29 **puddings** The pudding of the 16th c. was
like the haggis of today, i.e. a mixture of
minced meat, meal, herbs, etc., stuffed
into a skin, usually the stomach or
intestine of a pig or sheep (*OED*).

29.2 In Q it is Mistress Ford's sight of
Mistress Page reading that initiates their
conversation. Mistress Page shows her
letter, and Mistress Ford produces her
own, which is a duplicate ('Only the
name | Of misteris *Page*, and misteris
Foord disagrees'). The rest of the scene
follows the same course as that in F,
except that at the end Page and Ford go
off to dinner together and Ford has no
soliloquy.

33 **ill** Mistress Ford is probably looking pale
with anger. In *Much Ado* 1.1.232 Bene-
dick says that he may come to look pale
'with anger, with sickness, or with hun-
ger'. Mistress Page thinks that she looks
sick. Mistress Ford's reply is a denial that
she looks ill, i.e. ugly.

34 **have to show** have something (i.e. her
letter from Falstaff) to show

MISTRESS PAGE Faith, but you do, in my mind.

MISTRESS FORD Well, I do, then. Yet I say I could show you
to the contrary. O Mistress Page, give me some counsel!

MISTRESS PAGE What's the matter, woman?

MISTRESS FORD O woman, if it were not for one trifling   40
respect, I could come to such honour!

MISTRESS PAGE Hang the trifle, woman, take the honour.
What is it? Dispense with trifles. What is it?

MISTRESS FORD If I would but go to hell for an eternal
moment or so, I could be knighted.

MISTRESS PAGE What? Thou liest! Sir Alice Ford? These
knights will hack, and so thou shouldst not alter the
article of thy gentry.

MISTRESS FORD We burn daylight. Here, read, read. Perceive how I might be knighted.   50

> *She produces a letter and gives it to Mistress Page, who
> reads it*

I shall think the worse of fat men as long as I have an
eye to make difference of men's liking. And yet he would

---

46 What? Thou liest!] JOHNSON; What thou liest? F   50.1-2] This edition; *not in* F

---

42 **Hang** This imprecation is specially frequent in this play.

46 **Thou liest** Hart shows that the expression
was 'often used jocularly, or merely in
repartee, as it is here'.

46-7 **These knights** The derogatory gener-
alization would amuse the original audience if the first performance of the play
was at a Garter Feast (Introduction,
pp. 1-6).

47 **hack** Not positively explained. It may
here be used in the same sense (equally
doubtful) as in 4.1.60, where the context
suggests sexual misconduct. In both
places the verb seems to be used intransi-
tively, so that *OED hack v.*[1] 8 ('to make
rough cuts, to deal cutting blows') is the
probable primary sense; 'hack our English', 3.1.72, and every other Shakespearian use of 'hack' as verb or noun, has
a related sense, so *OED hack v.*[3] 1 ('to put
to indiscriminate or promiscuous use',
i.e. to hackney; no instances before 18th
c.), adduced by Oliver, seems inapplica-
ble. *OED striker sb.* 2d ('a fornicator';
instances from 1593 and 1596) perhaps
offers an analogy, though Shakespeare's

only sexual use of 'strike', *Titus* 2.1.119,
130, turns on a bow-and-arrow metaphor, not a sword one.

47-8 **and so ... gentry** This seems an unnecessarily elaborate way of saying 'and
therefore you ought not to change your
station' (*OED article sb.* 10b, with
'of' = 'the matter of'; *gentry sb.* 1, 'rank
by birth; rarely, in neutral sense'). Perhaps there is some innuendo connected
with the primary sense of *article* (*OED sb.*
1, 'a joint connecting two parts of the
body'), as in Holofernes's statement,
'This swain, because of his great limb or
joint, shall pass Pompey the Great' (*LLL*
5.1.121-2), which sounds suggestive. Is
there an innuendo about Mistress Ford's
acquiring, by being knighted, the sexual
organs of a man? Clearly, any innuendo
of Mistress Page's must not anticipate
Mistress Ford's explanation.

49 **burn daylight** waste time. Proverbial
(Tilley D123).

52 **make difference of men's liking** differenti-
ate between men's physical condition
(*OED liking sb.* 6)

not swear, praised women's modesty, and gave such
orderly and well-behaved reproof to all uncomeliness
that I would have sworn his disposition would have
gone to the truth of his words. But they do no more
adhere and keep place together than the Hundredth
Psalm to the tune of 'Greensleeves'. What tempest, I
trow, threw this whale, with so many tuns of oil in his
belly, ashore at Windsor? How shall I be revenged on   60
him? I think the best way were to entertain him with
hope till the wicked fire of lust have melted him in his
own grease.—Did you ever hear the like?

MISTRESS PAGE Letter for letter, but that the name of Page
and Ford differs.

⌈*She holds up the first letter*⌉

To thy great comfort in this mystery of ill opinions,
here's the twin-brother of thy letter. But let thine inherit
first, for I protest mine never shall.

⌈*She gives the two letters to Mistress Ford, who
compares them*⌉

I warrant he hath a thousand of these letters, writ with

53 praised] THEOBALD; praise F   57 place] F; pace RANN (*conj.* Capell)   57–8 Hundredth
Psalm] ROWE; hundred Psalms F; hundred and fifty psalms OXFORD   59 trow] ROWE; troa F
65.1] This edition; *holding the two letters side by side* NCS; *She gives Mistress Ford her letter*
OXFORD; *not in* F   68.1–2] This edition; *not in* F

54 **uncomeliness** unseemly behaviour
56 **gone to the truth of** truly accorded with
57 **adhere and keep place together** correspond and fit together
57–8 **Hundredth Psalm** The metrical version
of Psalm 100 ('All people that on earth do
dwell, | Sing to the Lord with cheerful
voice', etc.) must always have been one of
the best-known psalms. The point of the
comparison is the incongruity between
the rhythm of a very well-known psalm
and that of a very well-known secular
tune. In F's reading this point is lost. Since
there are 150 psalms, not 100, F's reading
is particularly open to objection. To account for F's error it is not necessary to
suppose that Shakespeare used the archaic form 'hundred' when he meant
'hundredth'; it is only necessary to suppose that the scribe or the compositor misread 'hundredth' as 'hundreth' (a widely-
current spelling of 'hundred') and regular-
ized accordingly, at the same time altering
'psalm' to 'psalms' to correct the sense.

58 **Greensleeves** This tune, which is still well
known, was entered to Richard Jones in
the Stationers' Register in Sept. 1580 as
'a new northern ditty of the Lady Greensleeves'.
58–9 **I trow** I wonder (see 1.4.126)
59 **tuns** barrels
61 **entertain him** keep his thoughts occupied
(*OED* 9: first example)
62–3 **till the wicked . . . grease** The
proverbial 'to fry in one's own grease'
(Tilley G433) is still current in the form
'to stew in one's own juice'.
66 **mystery of ill opinions** 'puzzle about the
bad characters or reputations we seem to
have' (Hart)
67–8 **inherit first** i.e. as the elder twin
69–70 **a thousand . . . names** Hyperbolical
fantasy. Hibbard sees an allusion to the
practice of hack-writers of dedicating
copies of the same published work to
several different persons, an unconvincing suggestion because print has not yet
been mentioned.

blank space for different names—sure, more, and these   70
are of the second edition. He will print them, out of
doubt; for he cares not what he puts into the press,
when he would put us two. I had rather be a giantess
and lie under Mount Pelion. Well, I will find you twenty
lascivious turtles ere one chaste man.

MISTRESS FORD   Why, this is the very same: the very hand,
the very words. What doth he think of us?

MISTRESS PAGE   Nay, I know not. It makes me almost ready
to wrangle with mine own honesty. I'll entertain myself
like one that I am not acquainted withal; for, sure,   80
unless he know some strain in me that I know not
myself, he would never have boarded me in this fury.

MISTRESS FORD   'Boarding' call you it? I'll be sure to keep
him above deck.

MISTRESS PAGE   So will I. If he come under my hatches, I'll
never to sea again. Let's be revenged on him. Let's
appoint him a meeting, give him a show of comfort in
his suit, and lead him on with a fine-baited delay till he
hath pawned his horses to mine host of the Garter.

MISTRESS FORD   Nay, I will consent to act any villainy   90
against him that may not sully the chariness of our
honesty. O that my husband saw this letter! It would
give eternal food to his jealousy.

    Enter Ford with Pistol, and Page with Nim

93.1] ROWE; *Enter Ford, Page, Pistoll and Nym.* Q; *not in* F

71 **of the second edition** two of the second
thousand copies
print them Further fantasy, introducing
the quibble on 'press'.

73–4 **I had rather . . . Pelion** According to
Greek mythology, the giants, in their war
with the gods, piled Pelion (a mountain in
Thessaly) on the neighbouring Ossa in
order to scale Olympus. In retaliation Zeus
imprisoned them under the mountains.
Giantesses were not, of course, involved in
the war; this is Mistress Page's adaptation
of the myth to the present occasion.

75 **turtles** turtle-doves, proverbially true to
their mates (Tilley T624)

79 **wrangle with mine own honesty** quarrel
with my own virtue (i.e. for not being so
perfect that Falstaff would never have
dared to assail it)

79 **entertain** treat

81 **strain** tendency, disposition

82 **boarded** assailed. The metaphor is from
one ship's coming alongside another.
'Board' in this sense (of courtship) is
common in the period, e.g. *Twelfth Night*
1.3.53–4 '"Accost" is front her, board
her, woo her, assail her.' The following
two speeches develop the sexual innuendo.
fury violent manner

87–8 **show . . . suit** deceitful appearance
(*OED show sb.* 7) of encouragement (*OED
comfort, sb.* 1) in his courtship

88 **fine-baited** finely (i.e. skilfully) baited

89 **pawned his horses** i.e. to pay for the
expenses of his courtship

91–2 **sully . . . honesty** blemish the chastity
that we have so carefully preserved

MISTRESS PAGE Why, look where he comes, and my goodman too. He's as far from jealousy as I am from giving
him cause, and that, I hope, is an unmeasurable
distance.

MISTRESS FORD You are the happier woman.

MISTRESS PAGE Let's consult together against this greasy
knight. Come hither.   100

          ⌈*They withdraw*⌉

FORD Well, I hope it be not so.

PISTOL

Hope is a curtal dog in some affairs.
Sir John affects thy wife.

FORD Why, sir, my wife is not young.

PISTOL

He woos both high and low, both rich and poor,
Both young and old, one with another, Ford.
He loves the gallimaufry. Ford, perpend.

FORD Love my wife?

PISTOL

With liver burning hot. Prevent, or go thou
Like Sir Actaeon he, with Ringwood at thy heels.   110

94–5 goodman] BOWERS; good man F   100.1] *as* THEOBALD; *not in* F   107 gallimaufry.
Ford, perpend.] CAPELL; Gally-mawfry (*Ford*) perpend. F

94–5 **goodman** husband

102 **curtal dog** dog whose tail has been
docked. In *Errors* a turnspit (3.2.151–2).
Pistol's grotesque metaphor—surely
original and not a quotation—has no
specific meaning, and editors' attempts to
give it one are unconvincing.

103 **affects** loves

106 **Both ... another** Fripp, i. 86–7, notes
the allusion to Psalm 49:2 in the Book of
Common Prayer (1559) version: 'High
and low, rich and poor; one with
another'; compare 1.3.82.

107 **gallimaufry** 'whole lot' (Hibbard). A
gallimaufry is a stew in which any available materials are combined (*OED*).
perpend consider; weigh my words.
Shakespeare reserves this word for Pistol
(here and in *Henry V* 4.4.8), Feste,
Touchstone, and Polonius. Hart cites
'perpend in heart my dolours great' from
a poem of 1568, which is very much the
archaic kind of context that it seems to
have had for Shakespeare. For its use
after a vocative compare Thomas Pres-

ton's *Cambises* (c.1570), l. 1018: 'My
queen, perpend. What I pronounce I will
not violate'.

109 **liver** The liver was supposed to be the
seat of love, and is frequently mentioned
as such by Shakespeare.
Prevent This absolute use of the imperative, but without Pistol's affected style,
occurs again in *Caesar* 2.1.28: 'Then lest
he may, prevent.'

110 **Sir Actaeon he** Pistol uses an archaic
formula found, e.g., in the anonymous
play *Clyomon and Clamydes* (Malone Soc.,
1913, ll. 778, 827, and many other
times). Actaeon was killed by his own
hounds when he had come upon Diana
bathing and had been changed into a
stag by her.
Ringwood Golding, transl. Ovid's *Metamorphoses*, 3.270, names one of Actaeon's 35 hounds as Ringwood, which was
a common English name for a hound and
is the name of a town to the west of the
New Forest in Hampshire.

O, odious is the name!

FORD What name, sir?

PISTOL

The horn, I say. Farewell.

Take heed, have open eye, for thieves do foot by night.

Take heed, ere summer comes, or cuckoo-birds do sing.

Away, Sir Corporal Nim!

Believe it, Page; he speaks sense.   *Exit*

FORD (*aside*)

I will be patient. I will find out this.

NIM (*to Page*) And this is true. I like not the humour of
lying. He hath wronged me in some humours. I should   120
have borne the humoured letter to her, but I have a
sword and it shall bite upon my necessity. He loves your
wife. There's the short and the long. My name is
Corporal Nim. I speak, and I avouch 'tis true. My name
is Nim, and Falstaff loves your wife. Adieu. I love not the
humour of bread and cheese. Adieu.   *Exit*

---

117 *Exit*] Q (*Exit Pistoll.*); *not in* F   124 avouch 'tis true.] Q (auouch tis true:); auouch; 'tis
true: F1; auouch, tis true: F3   126 cheese. Adieu.] F (cheese: adieu.); cheese: | And theres
the humor of it. Q   *Exit*] Q (*Exit Nym.*); *not in* F

111 **the name** not the name Actaeon (as
Ford's question shows), but the unmen-
tionable name of cuckold. Pistol, in his
reply, alludes to it obliquely.

113 **The horn** 'Cuckolds were fancifully said
to wear horns on the brow' (*OED horn sb.*
7)

114 **foot** walk

115 **cuckoo-birds** Cuckoos arrive in late
spring, and lay their eggs in other birds'
nests. Their song, from which their name
is derived, was treated as a reproach to
the cuckold (which word is derived from
the name of the cuckoo).

118 **find out** find out the truth of

122 **upon my necessity** at my need. The
expression, which is affected and without parallel in Shakespeare, suggests
that Nim's sword will accidentally
bite upon some necessary part of his
person.

123 **the short and the long** the whole truth
of the matter. Proverbial (Tilley L419)
both in this order and in the modern form
'the long and the short of it'.

124 **avouch 'tis true** Q's punctuation; F has
14 colons and semicolons in this speech.

Shakespeare nowhere else uses the verb
avouch absolutely. Nim might. If he did,
the hexameters 'My name ... avouch;
| 'Tis true ... wife' would be effective, but
would be rather in Pistol's style than in
his own.

126 **bread and cheese** i.e. the bare necessi-
ties of life, in Falstaff's service or out of it.
In the old play of *King Leir* Gonorill says of
Leir, whom she is about to expel from her
house, 'I'll provide him a piece of bread
and cheese' (Bullough, vii. 357, Sc.10,
834). NCS suggests that Nim refers to
'the cuckoo-bread flower' and thereby
alludes to Falstaff's designs. This is
strained: *OED* (*bread sb.*[1] 2d) gives 'bread
and cheese' as 'a child's name for the
young leaves of the Hawthorn, the
Wood-Sorrel or "Cuckoo-bread", and
one or two other plants', so there is no
unmistakable allusion (contrast 'lords
and ladies', 1.1.216, where only one
plant can be meant). Nim means Page
to understand that he is a respectable
man, a corporal, not a needy or cast-off
serving-man.

PAGE (*aside*) The humour of it, quoth 'a! Here's a fellow frights English out of his wits.

FORD (*aside*) I will seek out Falstaff.

PAGE (*aside*) I never heard such a drawling, affecting rogue.   130

FORD (*aside*) If I do find it—well.

PAGE (*aside*) I will not believe such a Cathayan, though the priest o'th' town commended him for a true man.

FORD (*aside*) 'Twas a good sensible fellow—well.

    Mistress Page and Mistress Ford come forward

PAGE How now, Meg?

MISTRESS PAGE Whither go you, George? Hark you.

    ⌈*They withdraw and talk*⌉

MISTRESS FORD How now, sweet Frank, why art thou melancholy?

FORD I melancholy? I am not melancholy. Get you home, go.   140

MISTRESS FORD Faith, thou hast some crotchets in thy head now.—Will you go, Mistress Page?

MISTRESS PAGE Have with you.—You'll come home to dinner, George?

127–34 *aside*] OXFORD; *not in* F   128 English] F; humor Q   132 Cathayan] F (*Cataian*)
134.1] THEOBALD; *not in* F   136.1] *as* HIBBARD; *not in* F   141–2 head now.—Will]
HANMER; head, | Now: will F   143 come home] This edition; come F

127 **The humour of it** As Oliver says, this phrase need not be a repetition of Nim's Q phrase 'the humor of it': Page's *of it* means *of bread and cheese*. It is not likely that F has accidentally omitted Q's phrase. On the incidence of 'there's the humour of it' in Q see Introduction, p. 50.

128 **frights ... wits** *his* means 'its'. A similar idea is in *Much Ado* 5.2.50–1: 'Thou hast frighted the word out of his right sense, so forcible is thy wit.'

130 **drawling, affecting** Oliver compares *Romeo* 2.3.26–7, where Mercutio abuses 'such antic, lisping, affecting phantasims' as Tybalt. *OED* (*drawl v.* 2: the earliest citation) takes Nim to have been speaking slowly, 'prolonging the words', but this is not the impression that Nim's clipped style gives. Perhaps Page rather means that Nim has been prolonging the word out of his right sense, so saying the same thing over and over again.

132 **Cathayan** Literally, an inhabitant of China (Cathay). The figurative sense is obscure. Page is quite sure that Nim is a liar, and William Waterman's *Fardle of Fashions* (1555, quoted by Hart) states that the Cathayans 'know not what we mean when we speak of faithfulness or trustiness', but Page need mean no more by calling Nim a Cathayan than that he is a rogue, which is what the word is generally used to mean (*OED Cataian sb.*); compare l. 160, 'very rogues'. The word occurs again in *Twelfth Night* 2.3.72.

136 **Whither go you, George?** Not an indication that Page is moving towards an exit. The situation is that both wives have met their husbands in the street. Mistress Page is asking her husband where he is going because she wants to know whether he is coming home to dinner, ll. 143–4.

141 **crotchets** fancies. The phrase is proverbial (Tilley C843).

143 **Have with you** I'll go along with you; i.e. let us go. Compare 3.2.82.
    come home Though never previously emended, F's reading is inappropriate

Enter Mistress Quickly

(*Aside to Mistress Ford*) Look who comes yonder. She shall be our messenger to this paltry knight.

MISTRESS FORD (*aside to Mistress Page*) Trust me, I thought on her. She'll fit it.

MISTRESS PAGE You are come to see my daughter Anne?

MISTRESS QUICKLY Ay, forsooth; and I pray how does good   150
Mistress Anne?

MISTRESS PAGE Go in with us and see. We have an hour's talk with you.

Exeunt Mistress Page, Mistress Ford, and Mistress Quickly

PAGE How now, Master Ford?

FORD You heard what this knave told me, did you not?

PAGE Yes, and you heard what the other told me?

FORD Do you think there is truth in them?

PAGE Hang 'em, slaves! I do not think the knight would offer it. But these that accuse him in his intent towards our wives are a yoke of his discarded men—very rogues,   160
now they be out of service.

FORD Were they his men?

PAGE Marry, were they.

FORD I like it never the better for that. Does he lie at the Garter?

PAGE Ay, marry, does he. If he should intend this voyage

144.1] ROWE; *at line corresponding to* 136 Q; *not in* F   152 we have] F; we would have WALKER *conj.*   153.1 Exeunt ... Quickly] Q (*Exit Mistresse* Ford, Mis. Page, *and* Quickly.); *not in* F

to its context: a guest would 'come to dinner' but not a resident. The contrast is illustrated by *Othello* 4.1.156, 'An you'll come to supper tonight, you may' (Bianca to Cassio), and *Errors* 1.2.89–90, 'She that doth fast till you come home to dinner, | And prays that you will hie you home to dinner' (Adriana's message delivered by Dromio to her supposed husband: also 2.1.59, 'When I desired him to come home to dinner'). A scribal or compositorial error caused by the similar endings of 'come' and 'home' would be easy: compare *Errors* 2.1.63, where F, in a passage of strictly regular verse, reads 'Will you come, quoth I: my gold, quoth he'

('come home', Theobald, 1740, and later editors).

147 **paltry** despicable, contemptible

152–3 **We have ... with you** For the idiom cf. Beaumont and Fletcher, *The Maid's Tragedy* 3.1.147, 'I have some speech with you'. In both cases the speaker intends to do most of the talking. Cf. also Caesar to Trebonius, 'I have an hour's talk in store for you', *Caesar* 2.2.121.

159 **offer it** attempt it

160 **yoke** pair

166 **voyage** Often used figuratively by Shakespeare, so there is no need to suppose that 'Nim may have quoted Falstaff's remarks' about the East and West Indies in 1.3.65–6 to Page (as Hart

toward my wife, I would turn her loose to him; and
what he gets more of her than sharp words, let it lie on
my head.

FORD I do not misdoubt my wife, but I would be loath to   170
turn them together. A man may be too confident. I
would have nothing lie on my head. I cannot be thus
satisfied.

    Enter Host

PAGE Look where my ranting host of the Garter comes.
There is either liquor in his pate or money in his purse
when he looks so merrily.—How now, mine host?

HOST How now, bully rook? Thou'rt a gentleman.

    ⌈*He turns and calls*⌉

Cavaliero justice, I say!

    Enter Shallow

SHALLOW I follow, mine host, I follow.—Good even and
twenty, good Master Page. Master Page, will you go   180
with us? We have sport in hand.

HOST Tell him, cavaliero justice; tell him, bully rook.

SHALLOW Sir, there is a fray to be fought between Sir
Hugh the Welsh priest and Caius the French doctor.

FORD Good mine host o'th' Garter, a word with you.

HOST What sayst thou, my bully rook?

    They withdraw and talk

SHALLOW (*to Page*) Will you go with us to behold it? My
merry host hath had the measuring of their weapons,
and, I think, hath appointed them contrary places; for,

173.1] DYCE; *Enter Host and Shallow.* Q; *not in* F   174 ranting] F; ramping Q   177.1]
NCS; *not in* F   178.1] DYCE; *not in* F   186.1] *as* Q (Ford *and the Host talkes.*); *not in* F

suggests), though the audience may recall them.

167 **turn her loose to him** i.e. let her receive
his visit of courtship: 'a farmyard reference to the turning loose of a cow and a
bull in the same pasture' (Hibbard).

168–9 **lie on my head** be upon my head (i.e.
be my action's consequence to me).
Ford's rejoinder alludes to the cuckold's
horns.

174 **ranting** bombastic (*OED*'s first citation)

178 **Cavaliero** courtly gentleman (*OED* 2).
Here a fanciful title bestowed by the Host
(as at ll. 182, 193, and 2.3.67); also
applied, as 'Cavaliery', by Bottom to

Peaseblossom (*Dream* 4.1.22). The word
apparently came into English use at the
time of the Armada (Hart, who points out
that *OED*'s first citation is from 1589).
Spanish *caballero*, Italian *cavaliere*, *cavaliero*.

179–80 **Good even and twenty** 'Good after-
noon, many times over.' Oliver points out
that though 'even' could mean any time
after noon, several subsequent events
happen before Falstaff's first assignation
which is fixed between 10 and 11 a.m.
Hibbard adds that 'dinner' (mentioned as
being in the future, l. 144) was a midday
meal. On the handling of time in the play
see Introduction, pp. 54–5.

believe me, I hear the parson is no jester. Hark, I will tell   190
you what our sport shall be.
> *They withdraw and talk.*
> *Ford and Host come forward*

HOST Hast thou no suit against my knight, my guest-
cavaliero?

FORD None, I protest. But I'll give you a pottle of burnt
sack to give me recourse to him and tell him my name is
Brook—only for a jest.

HOST My hand, bully. Thou shalt have egress and regress—said I well?—and thy name shall be Brook. It is a
merry knight. (*To Shallow and Page*) Will you go,
mynheers?   200

SHALLOW Have with you, mine host.

PAGE I have heard the Frenchman hath good skill in his
rapier.

SHALLOW Tut, sir, I could have told you more. In these
times you stand on distance, your passes, stoccadoes,
and I know not what. 'Tis the heart, Master Page; 'tis

191.1] *as* CAPELL; *not in* F   191.2] This edition; *not in* F   192–3 my guest-cavaliero]
KITTREDGE; my guest-Caualeire F; My guest, my cauellira Q   194 FORD] Q; Shal⟨low⟩. F
196 Brook] *as* Q (*Rrooke; thereafter Brooke*); Broome F (*and so thereafter*)   199 To … Page]
OXFORD; *not in* F   200 mynheers] HANMER, *conj.* Theobald; An-heires F; Ameers NCS, *conj.*
Hart; mijnheers OXFORD   205 distance] F; your distance This edition *conj.*

192–3 **my guest-cavaliero** i.e. Falstaff. F's
spelling, inconsistent with the Host's
other uses of the word 'cavaliero', is
probably an error caused by misreading.

194 **pottle** vessel containing half a gallon,
four pints (as at 3.5.27)

194–5 **burnt sack** 'mulled sack, white wine
heated over a fire' (Hibbard)

196 **Brook** Q preserves the correct name
adopted by Ford. See 2.2.143, and Introduction, pp. 10–11, 56–8.

197–8 **egress and regress** The phrase was in
legal use, but the Host merely plays with
it, as with 'the potions and the motions',
3.1.94.

200 **mynheers** (Dutch) sirs, gentlemen
(*OED*, first occurrence 1652). F's reading
is unintelligible, and the later Folios'
failure to emend may mean no more than
that they were prepared to print a non-
sense-word in a speech by the Host. The
unintelligible 'An-heires' may be related
to the unintelligible 'Oneyers' (variant
'Oneyres') of 1 *Henry IV* 2.1.76, but
discussion of the point has been inconclu-

sive. 'Ameers', an alternative spelling of
'emirs' (independent chieftains in the
East and in North Africa), is too incongruous, even for the Host, as an address
to the present company: editors who
conjecture or adopt it (Hart, NCS, Hibbard) also interpret F's 'Pheazar' (1.3.9)
in an oriental sense as meaning 'vizier'.

204 **I could have told you more** Shallow's
retort is an impatient taking-up of Page's
'I have heard'. The implication is 'You
may have heard that, but let me tell you
that all this fighting with rapiers is a silly
modern fashion.'

205 **you stand on** you insist on, you attach
great importance to. Hibbard notes that
'you' and 'your' are used 'indefinitely,
not with reference to persons present'.
This is true, but Shallow's querulous tone
is addressed to Page personally.
distance space between duellists
passes, stoccadoes kinds of thrust

206–7 **'tis here** Shallow here surely taps his
chest.

here, 'tis here. I have seen the time, with my long
sword, I would have made you four tall fellows skip like
rats.

HOST Here, boys, here, here! Shall we wag?   210

PAGE Have with you. I had rather hear them scold than
fight.   *Exeunt Host, Shallow, and Page*

FORD Though Page be a secure fool and stands so firmly
on his wife's frailty, yet I cannot put off my opinion so
easily. She was in his company at Page's house, and
what they made there I know not. Well, I will look
further into't, and I have a disguise to sound Falstaff. If I
find her honest, I lose not my labour. If she be otherwise, 'tis labour well bestowed.   *Exit*

2.2   *Enter Falstaff and Pistol*

FALSTAFF I will not lend thee a penny.

PISTOL

Why then, the world's mine oyster,
Which I with sword will open.

211 hear] F; have HANMER   than] F (then); than see them COLLIER 1853   212] ROWE;
Exit Host and Shallow. Q; *not in* F   219 *Exit*] ROWE; *Exeunt.* F; *Exit omnes.* Q
    2.2] F (*Scœna Secunda.*)   0.1] Q (*Enter Syr Iohn, and Pistoll.*); *Enter* Falstaffe, Pistoll, Robin,
Quickly, Bardolffe, Ford. F   1–3] *as* F; *Fal⟨staff⟩*. Ile not lend thee a peny. | *Pis⟨tol⟩*. I will
retort the sum in equipage. Q; *Fal⟨staff⟩*. I will not lend thee a penny. | *Pist⟨ol⟩*. Why, then the
world's mine oyster, which I with sword will open.—I will retort the sum in equipage.
THEOBALD; *Pistol*. I will retort the sum in equipage. | *Falstaff*. I will not lend thee a penny. | *Pistol*.
Why, then the world's mine oyster, | Which I with sword will open. NCS; *Fal⟨staff⟩*. I will not
lend thee a penny. | *Pist⟨ol⟩*. I will retort the sum in equipage. | *Fal⟨staff⟩*. Not a penny. | *Pist⟨ol⟩*.
Why then the world's mine oyster, which I with sword will open. ALEXANDER

207–8 **long sword** the 'two hand sword' of
  Q, as contrasted with the lightweight
  rapier. In *Romeo* 1.1.72 Capulet calls for
  his long sword.
208 **made ... skip** 'made four lusty fellows
  skip, I can tell you' (Hibbard); on 'you'
  see Abbott 220.
210 **wag** go (as in 1.3.6)
213 **secure** over-confident
213–14 **stands so firmly on** relies so completely on
214 **frailty** moral weakness (i.e. which Page
  wrongly supposes to be strength)
216 **made** 'did, got up to' (Hibbard)
217 **disguise** i.e. his assumed identity as
  Brook, in which he has just arranged to be
  presented to Falstaff. Perhaps also an actual disguise: compare 2.2.145.1 and n.
  sound (figuratively) measure the depth of
  (as with a sounding-line in water)

2.2.2–3 **Why then ... will open** Q's substitute for this speech looks like a reporter's
  attempt to improve upon the original
  rather than to recall it. It is probably
  influenced by Pistol's 'I do retort the solus
  in thy bowels' (*Henry V* 2.1.49) and
  Pistol perhaps means that he will repay in
  goods (Hart) or with equity (Greg).
  Shakespeare uses 'equipage' only in Sonnets 32.12 ('of better equipage', i.e. more
  richly equipped). There is no reason why
  F should have omitted it if it continued
  Pistol's speech in the copy. Alexander's
  reconstruction requires Falstaff to say
  'Not a penny' in answer to two successive
  speeches by Pistol; this seems dramatically weak, whereas in F's dialogue the
  single 'Not a penny' is concise, conclu-
  sive, and dramatically strong.
  2 **the world's mine oyster** i.e. from which I

FALSTAFF Not a penny. I have been content, sir, you
    should lay my countenance to pawn. I have grated
    upon my good friends for three reprieves for you and
    your coach-fellow Nim, or else you had looked through
    the grate, like a gemini of baboons. I am damned in hell
    for swearing to gentlemen my friends you were good
    soldiers and tall fellows. And when Mistress Bridget lost   10
    the handle of her fan, I took't upon mine honour thou
    hadst it not.

PISTOL
    Didst not thou share? Hadst thou not fifteen pence?

FALSTAFF Reason, you rogue, reason. Think'st thou I'll
    endanger my soul gratis? At a word, hang no more
    about me; I am no gibbet for you. Go—a short knife and
    a throng—to your manor of Picked-hatch, go. You'll

17 Picked-hatch] F (*Pickt-hatch*)

will extract the pearl. Oliver's interpretation, that Pistol means 'an unwilling—
and rotten—world' and is 'adapting the
proverbial "open an oyster with a dagger"' (Tilley M777), where the dagger
implies keeping one's distance because of
the smell', is strained. Pistol is merely
reiterating his determination to survive
his dismissal; compare 1.3.83–4.

  5 **lay my countenance to pawn** pawn my
    patronage; i.e. borrow money from oth-
    ers on the strength of being in my service
5–6 **grated upon** harassingly importuned
    (*OED v.*[1] 4)
  7 **coach-fellow** horse yoked with another to
    draw a coach
7–8 **looked through the grate** looked out
    through the prison-bars (and begged for
    alms)
  8 **gemini** pair of twins. Alluding to the
    zodiacal sign as portrayed, in almanacs,
    as a pair of naked boys. *OED*'s first
    instance of 'a gemini'.
    baboons Falstaff uses 'baboon' of Poins,
    whose wit he is disparaging, in *2 Henry
    IV* 2.4.242. Here the allusion is rather to
    the ugly dog-faced appearance of Pistol
    and Nim.
 10 **Mistress Bridget** The name Bridget occurs
    twice elsewhere in Shakespeare: *Errors*
    3.1.31 (in a list of servants) and *Measure*
    3.1.345 ('Does Bridget paint still, Pom-
    pey, ha?', where Lucio must mean one of
    Mistress Overdone's whores). Falstaff's

single mention of 'old Mistress Ursula',
whom he says he has long promised to
marry, in *2 Henry IV* 1.2.241–3, may be
compared with this single mention of
Mistress Bridget.
 11 **handle of her fan** Fan-handles were often
    made of valuable materials, especially
    silver, which Hart suggests was the case
    here, in view of the second-hand value of
    the handle, 30*d.*, or half a crown.
    took't upon mine honour swore by my
    honour
 13 **share** have an equal share
 14 **Reason** i.e. and with good reason. Fifteen
    pence, Falstaff says, was the least he
    could receive for endangering his soul.
15–16 **hang no more about me** be no longer
    a burden to me. The 'gibbet' metaphor
    implies a quibble on 'hang'.
16–17 **a short ... throng** i.e. ply your trade
    as a cutpurse. Falstaff tells Pistol to find a
    crowd and there cut holes in purses to
    steal money.
 17 **manor** Used ironically, i.e. country house
    with the adjoining land (*OED* 2).
    Picked-hatch The literal meaning is 'A
    hatch or half-door, surmounted by a row
    of pikes or spikes, to prevent climbing
    over' (*OED*). Contemporary references in
    Marston's *Scourge of Villainy* and Jon-
    son's *Every Man in his Humour* (quoted in
    OED) suggest that it may have originally
    been the popular name of some particular
    brothel so equipped. Later (*OED* quota-
    tion from Randolph, 1634, augmented

not bear a letter for me, you rogue? You stand upon
your honour! Why, thou unconfinable baseness, it is as
much as I can do to keep the terms of my honour   20
precise. I, I, I myself sometimes, leaving the fear of God
on the left hand and hiding mine honour in my
necessity, am fain to shuffle, to hedge, and to lurch; and
yet you, you rogue, will ensconce your rags, your cat-a-
mountain looks, your red-lattice phrases, and your bull-

21 I, I, I] F; I, I Q; I POPE; I, ay, I WHITE; Ay, ay, I NCS   God] Q; heauen F   24 yet you,
you rogue, will] COLLIER 1853; yet, you Rogue, will F; yet you, rogue, will POPE   25–6 bull-
baiting oaths] HANMER; bold-beating-oathes F; bowl-beating oaths NCS *conj.*

by Hart) its name is used along with
Clerkenwell and Shoreditch to imply a
disreputable part of London, but its exact
location is not known (Hart records two
19th-c. suggestions, both relating to the
Clerkenwell district).

19 **unconfinable** infinite
21 **precise** pure
     I, I, I myself A threefold iteration of the
     pronoun, with increasing vehemence, is
     both easy to speak and theatrically effec-
     tive, whereas it would be difficult to
     convey the distinct senses in 'Ay, ay, I'
     (and if Falstaff meant an affirmative, the
     emphatic 'yea' would be more appropri-
     ate, besides being easier to understand in
     the hearing).
21–2 **leaving ... hand** disregarding the fear
     of God
23 **to shuffle ... lurch** These verbs are 'more
     or less synonymous' (Oliver) and all
     imply acting dishonestly: though *lurch*
     could mean 'pilfer, steal' (*OED v.*[1] 3) as
     well as 'lurk' (*OED v.*[1] I, citing this
     passage), it is improbable that Falstaff, a
     confidence-trickster, ever actually steals
     as Pistol, Nim, and Bardolph do.
24 **you, you rogue, will** Collier's emendation
     is supported by Shakespeare's use of 'you
     rogue' twice before in this speech and by
     his practice elsewhere. Q's passage
     corresponding to F's ll. 23–7 also sup-
     ports it: 'And yet you stand vpon your
     honor, you rogue. You, you.'
     ensconce hide; a sconce is a fortification
24–5 **cat-a-mountain** The word was used in
     Shakespeare's time both for the leopard
     and for the wild cat (*OED*, and supple-
     mentary references by Hart); in *Tempest*
     4.1.259 both 'pard' and 'cat o' moun-
     tain' are types of spottedness; there
     are three references to the wild cat (*Mer-*

chant 2.5.47; *Shrew* 1.2.195; *Othello*
2.1.113), but all relate to its behaviour,
not to its appearance; in *As You Like It*
2.7.150 the soldier is described as
'bearded like the pard'. The present reference may be either to savage facial
expressions or to extravagant whiskers or
to both.

25 **red-lattice** tavern-like. Wooden lattices
     painted red (occasionally green) were
     used instead of glass windows and also
     served as a sign; one is compared in
     colour with Bardolph's face in *2 Henry IV*
     2.2.72–3.
25–6 **your bull-baiting oaths** F's hyphens
     may be merely the scribe Crane's man-
     nerism, but even if they are discounted its
     phrase is dubious. The difficulty of taking
     'bold' and 'beating' as two adjectives, the
     latter synonymous with 'swingeing', is
     that 'beating' does not seem ever to have
     been current in this sense. Both the two
     parallel adjectives, 'cat-a-mountain' and
     'red-lattice', are vivid and are formed
     from nouns; 'bold beating' is neither.
     NCS emends to 'bowl-beating' (i.e. pot-
     thumping), assuming a 'boule'/'bould'
     misreading. The resulting word is tolera-
     bly vivid and is partly composed of a
     noun, but the supporting argument
     ('drinking bowls were, of course, made of
     pewter, and Cloten broke a man's pate
     with one') is poor, for drinking-bowls
     were made of wood as well, and Cloten's
     opponent was playing bowls with him
     (*Cymbeline* 2.1.1–7). Hanmer's emenda-
     tion 'bull-baiting' is adopted here, a mis-
     reading of 'bull'/'bold' being possible (as
     Sisson, *New Readings*, i. 69, explains) and
     one of 'baiting'/'beating' easy, and the
     phrase meaning 'fit for a bull-baiting
     ring'. Joris Hofnagel's map of London
     (1572) shows the 'Bowll-bayting' (i.e.

baiting oaths, under the shelter of your honour! You
will not do it! You!

PISTOL

I do relent. What wouldst thou more of man?

Enter Robin

ROBIN Sir, here's a woman would speak with you.

FALSTAFF Let her approach.   30

Enter Mistress Quickly

MISTRESS QUICKLY Give your worship good morrow.

FALSTAFF Good morrow, good wife.

MISTRESS QUICKLY Not so, an't please your worship.

FALSTAFF Good maid, then.

MISTRESS QUICKLY

That I am, I'll be sworn,

As my mother was the first hour I was born.

FALSTAFF

I do believe the swearer. What with me?

MISTRESS QUICKLY Shall I vouchsafe your worship a word
  or two?

FALSTAFF Two thousand, fair woman, and I'll vouchsafe   40
thee the hearing.

---

28 relent] F; recant Q   wouldst] Q; would F   28.1] ROWE; *not in* F   30.1] Q; *not in* F
32 good wife] F4; good-wife F1; faire wife Q   35 That I am, I'll] Q; Ile F

bull-baiting house) as a circular building
in Southwark on the south bank of the
Thames.

28 **relent** repent (*OED v.*[1] 5, citing only
Spenser, *Faerie Queene* III.vi.25). Pistol is
apologizing. In Q (which reads 'recant')
Falstaff replies 'Well go too, away, no
more', indicating that the apology is
accepted and Pistol reinstated; F's 'Mine
own people, mine own people' (l. 49) and
Q's corresponding 'heeres none but my
owne household' confirm the dramatic
point. Pistol remains on stage, like Robin,
throughout Mistress Quickly's visit in F.
In Q Robin does not appear in the scene,
and Pistol has no further speeches and no
marked exit.

35 **That I am** so I am. F omits these words,
but they seem necessary to the sense,
which is much harder to convey without
them, since *I'll be sworn* (frequent in
Shakespeare) normally either follows or
introduces a statement by the speaker;

the only exception is Paulina's 'I dare be
sworn', *Winter's Tale* 2.2.32. They also
put the necessary metrical stress on
sworn, thereby introducing the rhyming
line which follows.

36 **As ... born** The rhyme, and the doggerel
metre (frequent in Shakespeare), show
that F is correct in printing verse here. As
Oliver says, Mistress Quickly conflates
two proverbs, 'as good a maid as her
mother' (i.e. as her mother was before
conceiving her; Tilley M14) and 'as
innocent as a new-born babe' (Tilley B4).
Falstaff's reply makes it clear to the
audience (*a*) that she has not said what
she meant, and (*b*) that he believes that
what she said, not what she meant, is
true.

38 **vouchsafe** Mistress Quickly's error for
'beseech' or 'entreat'. Like the names of
the humours (1.3.70, 86), all these
words are in her vocabulary but she
misapplies them.

MISTRESS QUICKLY There is one Mistress Ford, sir—I pray,
come a little nearer this ways. I myself dwell with
Master Doctor Caius.

FALSTAFF Well, on. Mistress Ford, you say—

MISTRESS QUICKLY Your worship says very true. I pray
your worship, come a little nearer this ways.

FALSTAFF I warrant thee nobody hears—(*indicating Pistol
and Robin*) mine own people, mine own people.

MISTRESS QUICKLY Are they so? God bless them and make   50
them His servants!

FALSTAFF Well, Mistress Ford—what of her?

MISTRESS QUICKLY Why, sir, she's a good creature. Lord,
Lord, your worship's a wanton! Well, heaven forgive
you, and all of us, I pray!

FALSTAFF Mistress Ford—come, Mistress Ford—

MISTRESS QUICKLY Marry, this is the short and the long of
it: you have brought her into such a canaries as 'tis
wonderful. The best courtier of them all, when the court
lay at Windsor, could never have brought her to such a   60
canary; yet there has been knights, and lords, and
gentlemen, with their coaches, I warrant you, coach
after coach, letter after letter, gift after gift, smelling so

45 Well, on. Mistress] F (Well, on; Mistresse); Well, one Mistress HALLIWELL (*conj.* Douce)
48–9 *indicating ... Robin*] *as* NCS; *not in* F   50 God bless] *as* Q (Now God blesse); heauen-
blesse F   55 pray!] CAMBRIDGE; pray—F   56] CAMBRIDGE; Mistresse *Ford*: come, Mistresse
Ford. F   58 canaries] F (Canaries); canary This edition *conj.*   61 canary] F (Canarie)

43 **this ways** a dialectal form of 'this way',
influenced by the expressions 'come your
ways' and 'go your ways'.
45 **on** go on. F's reading (as against Halliwell's emendation) is confirmed by Q's
loosely reported version of this dialogue:
'Say on I prethy . . . So from Mistresse
Foord. Goe on.'
50–1 **God . . . servants** See Introduction,
p. 59.
57 **short and the long** see 2.1.123.
58 **canaries** Since F reads 'Canaries' here but
'Canarie' in the repetition two lines below, and since the use of the indefinite
article with a plural noun is characteristic of Evans (e.g. 1.1.48) but not of
Mistress Quickly, one is tempted to
emend. But perhaps the plural is used to
make it clear to the audience that Mistress Quickly is committing a malapro-
pism. She means 'quandary' (Steevens),

a word of unknown origin which came
into general use from *c.*1580 and was
accented on the second syllable until
much later (*OED*), meaning 'a state of
mental agitation'. It is a favourite word of
Lyly's, who uses it in the first sentence of
his preface to *Euphues*, 'To the gentlemen
readers', and later has 'The gentlewomen
were struck into such a quandary with
this sudden change that they all changed
colour' (Lyly, i. 204–5). *OED* gives two
16th-c. meanings of 'canary', 'a lively
Spanish dance' (*sb.* 1) and 'a light sweet
wine from the Canary Islands' (*sb.* 2); in
both senses the word could be in either
the singular or the plural form.
59–60 **when ... Windsor** This does not
necessarily mean that the court is not at
Windsor now; it may equally mean 'on
previous occasions when the court has
been at Windsor'.

sweetly, all musk, and so rushling, I warrant you, in silk
and gold, and in such alligant terms, and in such wine
and sugar of the best and the fairest, that would have
won any woman's heart, and, I warrant you, they
could never get an eye-wink of her. I had myself twenty
angels given me this morning, but I defy all angels in
any such sort, as they say, but in the way of honesty.   70
And, I warrant you, they could never get her so much
as sip on a cup with the proudest of them all, and yet
there has been earls—nay, which is more, pensioners—
but, I warrant you, all is one with her.

FALSTAFF But what says she to me? Be brief, my good she-
Mercury.

MISTRESS QUICKLY Marry, she hath received your letter, for
the which she thanks you a thousand times, and she
gives you to notify that her husband will be absence
from his house between ten and eleven.   80

FALSTAFF Ten and eleven.

64 rushling] F; rustling OXFORD

64 **rushling** Though 'rushle' is a variant
spelling recorded in OED it is one which
was archaic in the 16th c., and the
spelling of the three other instances of
'rustle' and 'rustling' in F gives no reason
for supposing that they were pronounced
with the 'sh' sound, which is therefore
retained here as an idiosyncratic pronunciation of Mistress Quickly's.

65 **alligant** OED defines this as (1) an obsolete form of 'alicant' (a kind of white wine
made at Alicante in Spain) and (2) a
catachresis for 'elegant', and (*alicant sb.*)
compares the present passage with one in
Beaumont and Fletcher mentioning 'Butter'd beer coloured with Alligant'. In the
16th and 17th cc. the form 'alligant/ali-
gant' was as common as 'alicant'. The
error for 'elegant' is apparently peculiar
to Mistress Quickly, and her immediately
following mention of *wine and sugar* ensures that it does not go unnoticed.

68 **eye-wink** OED gives only Shakespeare's
use (this passage) of this word before the
19th c. It seems to be his coinage designed to suit Mistress Quickly's style;
wink (OED 2) is here 'a glance or significant movement of the eye'.

69 **defy** reject. Edgar's 'defy the foul fiend'

(*Lear* 3.4.91) shows the incongruity of
Mistress Quickly's phrase.

70 **sort** manner. The commonest sense in
Shakespeare.

72 **sip** to sip (Abbott 349)

73 **which is more** moreover. Used similarly
by Dogberry in a context which comically
suggests, as here, that *more* means
'of more importance' (*Much Ado*
4.2.77–80).
pensioners 'a body of gentlemen, insti-
tuted by Henry VIII in 1509, as a body-
guard to the sovereign within the royal
palace' (OED *sb.* 2). Hart quotes the
phrase 'as brave as any pensioner or
nobleman' from Nashe, *Piers Penniless*
(1592).

75–6 **she-Mercury** Mercury was the messenger of the gods.

78–9 **gives you to notify** i.e. gives you to
understand (which is a frequent expression, e.g. *1 Henry IV* 4.4.11). The present
expression is peculiar to Mistress Quickly.
The only other Shakespearian use of
'notify' is by the Clown in *Othello*
3.1.27–8: 'I shall seem to notify unto
her.'

79 **absence** Evans has the same misuse (for
'absent'), 1.1.242.

MISTRESS QUICKLY Ay, forsooth; and then you may come
and see the picture, she says, that you wot of. Master
Ford, her husband, will be from home. Alas, the sweet
woman leads an ill life with him; he's a very jealousy
man; she leads a very frampold life with him, good
heart.

FALSTAFF Ten and eleven. Woman, commend me to her. I
will not fail her.

MISTRESS QUICKLY Why, you say well. But I have another   90
messenger to your worship. Mistress Page hath her
hearty commendations to you too; and let me tell you in
your ear, she's as fartuous a civil modest wife, and one,
I tell you, that will not miss you morning nor evening
prayer, as any is in Windsor, whoe'er be the other. And
she bade me tell your worship that her husband is
seldom from home, but she hopes there will come a
time. I never knew a woman so dote upon a man.
Surely, I think you have charms, la! Yes, in truth.

FALSTAFF Not I, I assure thee. Setting the attraction of my   100
good parts aside, I have no other charms.

MISTRESS QUICKLY Blessing on your heart for't!

FALSTAFF But I pray thee tell me this: has Ford's wife and
Page's wife acquainted each other how they love me?

MISTRESS QUICKLY That were a jest indeed! They have not
so little grace, I hope. That were a trick indeed! But

---

105 That were a jest indeed] F; O God no sir: there were a iest indeed Q

85-6 **a very jealousy man** Evans has a
  similar misuse ('a very simplicity
  'oman'), at 4.1.27.
86 **frampold** peevish. The adjective, transferred from Ford to Mistress Ford's life
  with him, has the sense here of 'troublesome'.
86-7 **good heart** i.e. poor creature
91 **messenger** in error for 'message'
  hath i.e. 'has (for me to deliver)'. Similar
  elliptical uses of the verb 'have' are
  common in Shakespeare (Onions, 'have',
  3).
93 **fartuous** in error for 'virtuous'. Though
  OED does not give 'vartuous' as a form of
  'virtuous', it does give 'vartue' as a form
  of 'virtue', of which it was a common
  pronunciation (Cercignani, p. 66).
94 **miss you** The pronoun is redundant,

equivalent to 'look you' (Abbott 220).
99 **charms** enchantments, magic spells
101 **good parts** (a) personal merits, (b) physical attributes. The ambiguity is stressed
  in the repetitions of 'excellent good parts'
  in Jonson, *Every Man in his Humour*,
  3.4.192-6 (1601), 4.3.32-9 (1616).
102 **Blessing** F is perhaps expurgated here.
  In *2 Henry IV* 2.4.307 Mistress Quickly's
  'God's blessing of your good heart' (Q) is
  expurgated as 'Blessing on your good
  heart' (F). The line 'Yet blessing on his
  heart that gives it me' (*Richard II* 5.5.64)
  shows that the present phrase was ac-
  ceptably idiomatic.
105 **That were a jest indeed** A common
  expression. Q's prefixed 'O God no sir:'
  may be an interpolation of the reporter
  rather than an original phrase expur-

Mistress Page would desire you to send her your little
page, of all loves. Her husband has a marvellous
infection to the little page; and truly, Master Page is an
honest man. Never a wife in Windsor leads a better life   110
than she does. Do what she will, say what she will, take
all, pay all, go to bed when she list, rise when she list, all
is as she will. And, truly, she deserves it; for if there be a
kind woman in Windsor, she is one. You must send her
your page, no remedy.

FALSTAFF Why, I will.

MISTRESS QUICKLY Nay, but do so, then; and, look you, he
may come and go between you both. And in any case
have a nay-word, that you may know one another's
mind, and the boy never need to understand anything;   120
for 'tis not good that children should know any
wickedness. Old folks, you know, have discretion, as
they say, and know the world.

FALSTAFF Fare thee well; commend me to them both.
There's my purse; I am yet thy debtor.—Boy, go along
with this woman.   *Exeunt Mistress Quickly and Robin*
(*Aside*) This news distracts me.

PISTOL (*aside*)
This punk is one of Cupid's carriers.

126 *Exeunt ... Robin*] ROWE; *Exit Mistress Quickly.* Q; *not in* F   127 *Aside*] OXFORD; *not in* F
128 punk] F (Puncke); pink WARBURTON

gated in F, for it corresponds in sentiment
to F's 'They have not so little grace, I
hope' (not in Q). See Introduction,
pp. 60–1.

108 **of all loves** 'A phrase of strong adjura-
tion or entreaty' (Onions), as in *Dream*
2.2.160.

109 **infection** in error for 'affection' in the
sense 'inclination' (*OED sb.* 5). Similarly
misused by Old Gobbo, *Merchant*
2.2.119, though without Mistress Quickly's unconscious sexual innuendo.

111–12 **take all, pay all** This 'ready-made
phrase' (Oliver: Tilley A203) seems to
mean that Mistress Page has unlimited
housekeeping money to spend as she
likes.

115 **no remedy** Another common phrase,
here equivalent to 'that's certain'; in
1.3.30 the sense was 'there's no alternative'.

119 **nay-word** password, word of private
significance. The word is of obscure origin (*OED*).

121–2 **'tis not good ... wickedness** Compare
her rebuke to Evans for teaching William
improper words, 4.1.59–62.

128–30 This speech is Shakespeare's device
for getting Pistol off stage; see note on
relent (l. 28) for the reason for his presence hitherto. Instead of being seen to
pursue his plan, Pistol here disappears
from the play, apart from 5.5, in which
his appearance may not be in his own
character. In *Henry V* he has married
Mistress Quickly. For discussion of the
implications of this see Introduction,
p. 12.

128 **punk** prostitute (*OED*'s first citation,
from Lodge, is dated 1596). Warburton's
emendation 'pink' (i.e. small coasting
and fishing vessel: *OED pink sb.*¹, first
citation 1471), though superficially

Clap on more sails; pursue; up with your fights;
Give fire! She is my prize, or ocean whelm them all!   130
                             Exit

FALSTAFF   Sayst thou so, old Jack? Go thy ways. I'll make
more of thy old body than I have done. Will they yet
look after thee? Wilt thou, after the expense of so much
money, be now a gainer? Good body, I thank thee. Let
them say 'tis grossly done, so it be fairly done, no
matter.

     Enter Bardolph with a goblet of sack

BARDOLPH   Sir John, there's one Master Brook below would
fain speak with you, and be acquainted with you, and
hath sent your worship a morning's draught of sack.

FALSTAFF   Brook is his name?   140

BARDOLPH   Ay, sir.

FALSTAFF   Call him in.   *Exit Bardolph*
Such Brooks are welcome to me, that o'erflows such
liquor. ⌈*He drinks*⌉ Aha! Mistress Ford and Mistress
Page, have I encompassed you? Go to; *via!*

     Enter Bardolph, with Ford disguised as Brook

130.1] ROWE; *not in* F   136.1] *as* OXFORD; *Enter Bardolfe.* Q; *not in* F   142 *Exit Bardolph*]
THEOBALD; *after* 'liquor', 144 OXFORD; *not in* F   144 *He drinks*] This edition; *after* 'in', 142,
and 'you', 145 OXFORD; *not in* F   145.1] *as* THEOBALD; *Enter Foord disguised like Brooke.*
Q; *not in* F

---

attractive because of the nautical metaphor in the next two lines, is less appropriate than *punk* to the present line, in
which a literal word, not a figurative one,
is needed.

128 **carriers** messengers

129 **fights** low canvas screens used to pro-
tect men on deck during a sea-fight

130 **Give fire** discharge a volley. Compare
Pistol's 'Fear we broadsides? No; let the
fiend give fire!' (*2 Henry IV* 2.4.179).
ocean whelm them all! let the ocean
submerge them all. The only Shakespearian instance of *whelm*. As *them* has no
antecedent noun, the phrase seems to be
one of Pistol's theatrical imprecations,
used without any precise reference.

131 **Sayst thou so** equivalent to the frequent
'Is it even so?', i.e. 'Is that how matters
stand?'

131–2 **make more of** think better of

133 **look after thee** i.e. 'think you (my body)

worth turning their heads to gaze desir-
ingly upon.'

133–4 **the expense of so much money** i.e. in
food and drink

135 **grossly** clumsily (*OED adv.* 6b)
fairly handsomely, i.e. completely (*OED
adv.* 7). Falstaff also uses both *grossly* and
fairly in allusion to his body, which is
'gross' (fat) and yet 'fair' (handsome).

143 **o'erflows** overflow with (the third person plural in -*s*, Abbott 333)

145 **encompassed** come by, got possession of
(Schmidt), as in *Two Gentlemen* 2.4.212:
'If not, to compass her I'll use my skill'.
Falstaff declares that he has already won
the two wives' hearts. This interpretation
is preferable to *OED*'s 'outwit, take advantage of, "get round" a person' (*en-
compass v.* 5, this citation only).
via! (Italian) an exclamation of encouragement, used five other times by
Shakespeare.

145.1 **disguised as Brook** Though Ford did

FORD God bless you, sir.

FALSTAFF And you, sir. Would you speak with me?

FORD I make bold to press with so little preparation upon you.

FALSTAFF You're welcome. What's your will? (*To Bar-*   150
dolph) Give us leave, drawer.   *Exit Bardolph*

FORD Sir, I am a gentleman that have spent much. My name is Brook.

FALSTAFF Good Master Brook, I desire more acquaintance of you.

FORD Good Sir John, I sue for yours; not to charge you, for I must let you understand I think myself in better plight for a lender than you are, the which hath something emboldened me to this unseasoned intrusion; for they say if money go before, all ways do lie open.   160

FALSTAFF Money is a good soldier, sir, and will on.

FORD Troth, and I have a bag of money here troubles me.
⌈*He sets it down*⌉
If you will help to bear it, Sir John, take half, or all, for easing me of the carriage.

FALSTAFF Sir, I know not how I may deserve to be your porter.

FORD I will tell you, sir, if you will give me the hearing.

FALSTAFF Speak, good Master Brook. I shall be glad to be your servant.

146 God bless] OXFORD; 'Blesse F; God saue Q   151 *Exit Bardolph*] THEOBALD; *not in* F
162.1] This edition; *not in* F   163 half, or all] COLLIER 1853; all, or halfe F

not tell the Host in 2.1 that he would assume a disguise as well as a false name, Q's stage direction is dramatically appropriate to Ford's new identity. A false beard is the obvious form for his disguise to take (compare *Othello* 1.3.340, *Twelfth Night* 4.2.1), and if he tears it off before his soliloquy at the end of the scene the gesture makes a good theatrical effect.

146 **God bless you** F's ''Bless you' is probably an expurgation.
148 **make bold** am unmannerly
150 **What's your will?** 'What can I do for you?'
151 **Give us leave** A formula of dismissal, as in *John* 1.1.230.
drawer That Falstaff affects not to know

Bardolph's name is a neat touch of characterization. When he is not in company he uses it (3.5.1).
156 **charge you** put you to expense (literally, load you).
159 **unseasoned** unseasonable, untimely (*OED a.* 3)
160 **if money . . . open** Proverbial (Tilley M1050).
161 **will on** will go forward
163 **half, or all** F's reading must be an accidental transposition, as Ford is making neither a joke nor (like Evans at 3.3.208–9) a mistake. His polite offer represents himself as being twice as obliged to Falstaff for taking the weight of all the money.

FORD Sir, I hear you are a scholar—I will be brief with   170
you—and you have been a man long known to me,
though I had never so good means as desire to make
myself acquainted with you. I shall discover a thing to
you wherein I must very much lay open mine own
imperfection. But, good Sir John, as you have one eye
upon my follies as you hear them unfolded, turn
another into the register of your own, that I may pass
with a reproof the easier, sith you yourself know how
easy it is to be such an offender.

FALSTAFF Very well, sir. Proceed.   180

FORD There is a gentlewoman in this town—her husband's name is Ford.

FALSTAFF Well, sir.

FORD I have long loved her, and, I protest to you, bestowed much on her, followed her with a doting
observance, engrossed opportunities to meet her, fee'd
every slight occasion that could but niggardly give me
sight of her, not only bought many presents to give her
but have given largely to many to know what she
would have given. Briefly, I have pursued her as love   190
hath pursued me, which hath been on the wing of all
occasions. But whatsoever I have merited, either in my
mind or in my means, meed I am sure I have received
none, unless experience be a jewel, that I have pur-
chased at an infinite rate, and that hath taught me to
say this:
'Love like a shadow flies when substance love pursues,
Pursuing that that flies, and flying what pursues.'

194 jewel, that] F; jewel; that THEOBALD

173 **discover** reveal; synonymous with 'lay
open', l. 174.
177 **register** record
177–8 **pass with a reproof the easier** get off
with an easier reproof
178 **sith** since
186 **observance** obsequiousness
engrossed accumulated, in the figurative
sense (*OED v.* 4b) associated with a
greedy 'engrosser' (*OED sb.* 1), one who
buys up materials, lands, or houses for
his own gain.
186–7 **fee'd ... occasion** employed (as if
paying a servant) the smallest opportunity

190 **have given** have me give her
194 **that** which (like the following *that*).
Theobald's repunctuation changes the
word from a relative pronoun to a
demonstrative pronoun (i.e. 'that thing
experience'), so that the second *that* must
either be read (unidiomatically) as
another pronoun or changed to 'it'.
197–8 This couplet, fittingly rounding off
Ford's studied speech, is presumably
original. The quotation marks are a common device for emphasizing such sententious statements as this (Oliver, who
compares Tilley L518: 'Love, like a

FALSTAFF Have you received no promise of satisfaction at
    her hands?   200
FORD Never.
FALSTAFF Have you importuned her to such a purpose?
FORD Never.
FALSTAFF Of what quality was your love, then?
FORD Like a fair house built on another man's ground, so
    that I have lost my edifice by mistaking the place where
    I erected it.
FALSTAFF To what purpose have you unfolded this to me?
FORD When I have told you that, I have told you all. Some
    say that though she appear honest to me, yet in other   210
    places she enlargeth her mirth so far that there is
    shrewd construction made of her. Now, Sir John, here is
    the heart of my purpose: you are a gentleman of
    excellent breeding, admirable discourse, of great admit-
    tance, authentic in your place and person, generally
    allowed for your many warlike, courtlike, and learned
    preparations.
FALSTAFF O, sir!
FORD Believe it, for you know it. ⌜*Pointing to the bag*⌝
    There is money. Spend it, spend it; spend more; spend   220
    all I have. Only give me so much of your time in
    exchange of it as to lay an amiable siege to the honesty

219 *Pointing ... bag*] This edition; *he places the bag on the table* NCS; *He offers money* OXFORD;
not in F

shadow, flies one following and pursues
one fleeing').
197 **substance** wealth. There is also a quibble
on *substance* as opposed to *shadow*.

204 **quality** kind
205-7 **Like . . . erected it** An accurate
statement as to the law. The image was
proverbial (Tilley G470: 'Who builds
upon another's ground loses both mortar
and stones').
210 **appear honest to me** puts on a chaste
behaviour in her dealings with me
211 **enlargeth her mirth so far** is so free in
her merriment. Compare *Macbeth*
3.4.10, 'Be large in mirth.' Here with a
suggestion of indelicate behaviour; compare *Much Ado* 4.1.52, 'I never tempted
her with word too large'.
211-12 **there is ... her** people interpret her
(i.e. her conduct) critically

214-15 **of great admittance** i.e. admitted to
the houses of the greatest people. *OED* (2)
defines the word (this citation only) as
'the habit or faculty of being admitted;
admissibility'.
215 **authentic** respectable (*OED a.* 1)
215-16 **generally allowed** universally approved
216 **warlike, courtlike, and learned** This
anticipates Ophelia's praise of Hamlet
(3.1.154: 'The courtier's, soldier's,
scholar's eye, tongue, sword'). Ford compliments Falstaff on being the 'complete
man' of the Renaissance.
217 **preparations** accomplishments (*OED sb.*
4: this citation only). The unusual sense
of the word suits the exaggeratedly complimentary style used by Ford as Brook.
222 **amiable** amorous. Literally 'friendly'
(*OED a.* 1c), but 'friend' can be synonymous with 'lover' (as in 3.3.111), and

of this Ford's wife. Use your art of wooing, win her to
consent to you. If any man may, you may as soon as
any.

FALSTAFF Would it apply well to the vehemency of your
affection that I should win what you would enjoy?
Methinks you prescribe to yourself very preposterously.

FORD O, understand my drift. She dwells so securely on
the excellency of her honour that the folly of my soul   230
dares not present itself. She is too bright to be looked
against. Now, could I come to her with any detection in
my hand, my desires had instance and argument to
commend themselves. I could drive her then from the
ward of her purity, her reputation, her marriage-vow,
and a thousand other her defences, which now are too
too strongly embattled against me. What say you to't,
Sir John?

FALSTAFF Master Brook, I will first make bold with your
money; ⌈*he takes the bag*⌉ next, give me your hand;   240
⌈*he grasps Ford's hand*⌉ and last, as I am a gentleman,
you shall, if you will, enjoy Ford's wife.

FORD O good sir!

FALSTAFF I say you shall.

FORD Want no money, Sir John; you shall want none.

FALSTAFF Want no Mistress Ford, Master Brook; you shall
want none. I shall be with her, I may tell you, by her

240 *he ... bag*] *as* OXFORD; *not in* F   241 *he ... hand*] *as* OXFORD; *not in* F

Ford's style is consistent with this sense of
the adjective. Compare *Much Ado*
3.3.145, 'this amiable encounter'.

223 **your art of wooing** your skill as a lover;
with an indirect allusion to Ovid's *Ars
Amatoria*, the handbook of the polished
seducer.
226–8 **Would it ... preposterously** Falstaff
replies in Ford's style.
226 **apply well to** be appropriate to
228 **preposterously** unnaturally; literally,
inverting the proper order of things
229 **drift** aim
  dwells so securely on takes her stand so
  confidently upon
230 **folly of my soul** wantonness that is
  hidden in my heart
231–2 **looked against** looked directly at. The
  implied image is that of the sun.

232 **detection** accusation, specifically by exposure of what was concealed (*OED sb.* 1)
233 **had** would have (subjunctive)
  instance and argument Both these are
  terms used in scholastic logic. An *instance*
  (*OED sb.* 5) is 'a case adduced in objection
  to or disproof of a universal assertion',
  the assertion in this case being that
  Mistress Ford is always chaste. An *argument* (*OED sb.* 3) is 'a reason produced in
  support of a proposition'.
235 **ward** defence (a fencing image, as in
  'He's beat from his best ward', *Winter's
  Tale* 1.2.33)
236 **other her defences** other defences of
  hers (Abbott 13, transposed possessive
  adjectives)
236–7 **too too** much too (emphatic)
237 **embattled** drawn up in battle array

own appointment. Even as you came in to me, her
spokesmate or go-between parted from me. I say I shall
be with her between ten and eleven, for at that time the   250
jealous rascally knave her husband will be forth. Come
you to me at night, you shall know how I speed.

FORD I am blest in your acquaintance. Do you know Ford,
sir?

FALSTAFF Hang him, poor cuckoldly knave! I know him
not. Yet I wrong him to call him poor. They say the
jealous wittolly knave hath masses of money, for the
which his wife seems to me well-favoured. I will use her
as the key of the cuckoldly rogue's coffer, and there's
my harvest-home.   260

FORD I would you knew Ford, sir, that you might avoid
him if you saw him.

FALSTAFF Hang him, mechanical salt-butter rogue! I will
stare him out of his wits. I will awe him with my cudgel;
it shall hang like a meteor o'er the cuckold's horns.
Master Brook, thou shalt know I will predominate over
the peasant, and thou shalt lie with his wife. Come to

---

249 spokesmate] Q; assistant F

249 **spokesmate** mouthpiece. 'Q has a
strong claim to be authorial on the basis
of the word's appropriateness and rarity'
(Jowett, who points out that OED cites
one prior instance, Stanyhurst's lines 'O
sacred Trojan . . . Of gods the spokesmate,
the truchman [i.e. interpreter] of hallowed Apollo' (*Aeneis* (1582), 2nd edn.
1583, iii. 52: 'spooks make' in 1st edn.).

257 **wittolly** A wittol is strictly a complai-
sant, as distinct from an involuntary,
cuckold; but Shakespeare, who except in
this play uses only 'cuckold' and 'cuckoldly', uses 'wittol' and 'wittolly' (OED's
first citation for this adjective) as their
synonyms in order to amplify Falstaff's
abuse of Ford.

259–60 **there's my harvest-home** therein
(i.e. in having ransacked Ford's money-
chest) my harvest is gathered in.
Shakespeare uses *harvest-home* in 1 *Henry
IV* 1.3.34, as here, to mean the completion of the harvesting, not the celebration
that marked it.

263 **mechanical** base (compare 'most mechanical and dirty hand', 2 *Henry IV*

5.5.36); derived from the noun (i.e.
manual workman), as in *Dream* 3.2.9.

263 **salt-butter** Hart quotes Nashe, *Piers
Penniless* (1592), who describes a penuri-
ous man living 'all the year long with [i.e.
on] salt butter and Holland cheese in his
chamber'.

264 **stare him out of his wits** Compare
Marlowe, *Jew of Malta* 4.2.14–16 ('and
so I left him, being driven to a non-plus at
the critical aspect of my terrible countenance'), and *Lear* 4.5.108 ('When I do
stare, see how the subject quakes').

265 **like a meteor** i.e. ready to fall, and also
as a portentous sign. Compare *predominate* (l. 266), used in the astrological
sense of 'have ascendancy (like a planet)'.

266 **thou shalt** Hitherto Falstaff has addressed 'Master Brook' as *you*. The repeated use of *thou shalt* displays his
familiarity and self-confidence.

267 **peasant** rascal. Frequent in such contexts, e.g. *Arden of Faversham* Sc. 2, 105:
'My fingers itches to be at the peasant.'
Pistol uses it to address his French
prisoner, *Henry V* 4.4.37.

me soon at night. Ford's a knave, and I will aggravate
his style: thou, Master Brook, shalt know him for knave
and cuckold. Come to me soon at night.   *Exit*   270
FORD What a damned epicurean rascal is this! My heart is
ready to crack with impatience. Who says this is
improvident jealousy? My wife hath sent to him, the
hour is fixed, the match is made. Would any man
have thought this? See the hell of having a false
woman! My bed shall be abused, my coffers ransacked,
my reputation gnawn at; and I shall not only receive
this villainous wrong, but stand under the adoption of
abominable terms, and by him that does me this wrong.
Terms! Names! Amaimon sounds well; Lucifer, well;   280
Barbason, well; yet they are devils' additions, the
names of fiends. But cuckold! Wittol! Cuckold! The devil
himself hath not such a name. Page is an ass, a secure
ass. He will trust his wife, he will not be jealous. I will
rather trust a Fleming with my butter, Parson Hugh the
Welshman with my cheese, an Irishman with my aqua-
vitae bottle, or a thief to walk my ambling gelding, than
my wife with herself. Then she plots, then she rumi-

270 *Exit*] Q (*Exit Falstaffe.*); *not in* F

268–9 **aggravate his style** i.e. add the title of
   cuckold to the title of *knave*
271 **epicurean** sensual (as always in
   Shakespeare's use of 'epicurean', 'epicu-
   rism', and 'epicure')
273 **improvident** rash
278–9 **stand ... terms** 'suffer being called
   detestable names' (Hibbard). Hart refers
   to *Measure* 1.4.46 'Adoptedly, as school-
   maids change their names' (with reference to Juliet and Isabella calling themselves each other's cousin).
280 **Amaimon** This name (variously spelled
   on its several appearances) occurs in
   Reginald Scot's *Discovery of Witchcraft*
   (1584), as does 'Marbas, alias Barbas',
   which must have been the ultimate
   source of Shakespeare's *Barbason*. Amaimon and Lucifer are mentioned together
   in Falstaff's speech ridiculing Glendower
   in *1 Henry IV* 2.5.339–40; Barbason is
   mentioned by Nim when quarrelling
   with Pistol in *Henry V* 2.1.52. In his note
   on this last passage J. H. Walter convincingly derives Barbason from the French
   knight of that name who encountered

Henry V in single combat at the siege of
Melun (Holinshed, iii. 577); he ascribes it
to confusion, but Shakespeare may have
deliberately lengthened the name Barbas
in his *Merry Wives* passage, to match the
trisyllabic *Amaimon* and *Lucifer* (remembering the name *Barbason* from his reading of Holinshed), and then used the
name in the same form in *Henry V*.
281 **additions** titles
285 **Fleming** Flemings and Dutchmen were
   traditionally great eaters of butter (cf.
   3.5.110), as Welshmen were eaters of
   cheese (see 1.2.13, 5.5.80–1), and
   Irishmen drinkers of spirits. Hart quotes
   passages confirming this.
286–7 **aqua-vitae** (Lat. 'water of life') strong
   spirits in any form (*OED*), perhaps here
   implying whiskey because of the association with Irishmen
287 **walk** exercise gently, either by leading
   or riding
   ambling gelding a gelding that 'goes
   easily' (*Much Ado* 5.1.156), i.e. a good
   riding horse

nates, then she devises; and what they think in their
hearts they may effect, they will break their hearts but   290
they will effect. God be praised for my jealousy! Eleven
o'clock the hour. I will prevent this, detect my wife, be
revenged on Falstaff, and laugh at Page. I will about it.
Better three hours too soon than a minute too late. Fie,
fie, fie! Cuckold, cuckold, cuckold!   *Exit*

2.3   *Enter Caius and Rugby, with rapiers*

CAIUS Jack Rugby!

RUGBY Sir?

CAIUS Vat is the clock, Jack?

RUGBY 'Tis past the hour, sir, that Sir Hugh promised to
meet.

CAIUS By gar, he has save his soul dat he is no come. He
has pray his Pible well dat he is no come. By gar, Jack
Rugby, he is dead already if he be come.

RUGBY He is wise, sir. He knew your worship would kill
him if he came.   10

CAIUS By gar, de herring is no dead so as I vill kill him.
⌈*He draws his rapier*⌉ Take your rapier, Jack. I vill tell
you how I vill kill him.

RUGBY Alas, sir, I cannot fence.

CAIUS Villainy, take your rapier.

RUGBY Forbear. Here's company.
          ⌈*Caius sheathes his rapier.*⌉
          Enter Host, Shallow, Slender, and Page

291 God] Q; Heauen F   294–5 Fie, fie, fie] F; Gods my life Q
  2.3] F (*Scena Tertia.*)   0.1] OXFORD; *Enter the Doctor and his man.* Q; *Enter Caius, Rugby,
Page, Shallow, Slender, Host.* F   12 *He ... rapier*] This edition; *at beginning of Caius's speech,*
OXFORD; *not in* F   15 Villainy] F (Villanie); Villan-a JOHNSON; Villain DYCE 1866   16.1
Caius ... rapier] OXFORD; *not in* F   16.2] Q (*Enter Shallow, Page, my Host, and Slender.*); *not in* F

291 **God** F's 'Heauen', not found elsewhere
     in Shakespeare in connection with
     praise, is probably an expurgation.
292 **the hour** i.e. of Falstaff's assignation
     with Mistress Ford
294 **Better ... late** Proverbial (Tilley H745).
294–5 **Fie, fie, fie!** F's exclamation, express-
     ing disgust and indignation, is wholly
     appropriate here. Q's exclamation, though
     paralleled in *Dream* 4.1.201 and *Much
     Ado* 4.2.68, there expresses astonish-
     ment, is inappropriate here, and must be
     a substitution.

2.3.11 **de herring ... kill him** i.e. 'I should
     have killed him deader than a herring.'
     'Dead as a herring' became proverbial
     (Tilley H446), but may have originated
     here. The expression 'kill her dead' oc-
     curs in *Dream* 3.2.270.
12–13 **tell you** i.e. 'show you'. Caius's ec-
     centric diction draws attention to Rug-
     by's comic danger. The incident is not in
     Q.
15 **Villainy** i.e. 'villain'; compare 1.4.62.
     Caius's sudden rage is thrown into relief
     by the fact that in this scene he has been

HOST Bless thee, bully doctor!

SHALLOW Save you, Master Doctor Caius!

PAGE Now, good Master Doctor!

SLENDER Give you good morrow, sir.   20

CAIUS Vat be all you, one, two, tree, four, come for?

HOST To see thee fight, to see thee foin, to see thee
    traverse; to see thee here, to see thee there; to see thy
    pass, thy punto, thy stock, thy reverse, thy distance, thy
    montant. ~~Is he dead, my Ethiopian? Is he dead, my~~
    ~~Francisco? Ha, bully? What says my Aesculapius, my~~
    ~~Galen, my heart of elder, ha? Is he dead, bully stale? Is~~
    ~~he dead?~~

17 Bless] F ('Blesse'); God blesse Q   18 SHALLOW. Save you] F; Pa⟨ge⟩. God saue you Q   20
Give] F; God give OXFORD *conj.*   23–4 thy pass, thy punto] This edition; thee passe thy
puncto F; thee passe the punto Q   26 Francisco] F; francoyes Q   27 Galen] ROWE; *Galien*
F; gallon Q

calling his servant 'Jack', not 'Rugby' as
he did throughout 1.4.

22 **foin** thrust (as in *2 Henry IV* 2.1.17,
    2.4.233)
23 **traverse** 'To traverse one's ground, to
    move from side to side, in fencing or
    fighting' (*OED*)
23–4 **thy pass** thy thrust (*OED pass sb.²* 9);
    compare 2.1.207, 'your passes'. Though
    Q and F both have 'thee passe', the
    emendation is not ruled out by their
    agreement, since the phrase 'to see thee',
    five times repeated in both, may probably
    have influenced their reading here. The
    verb *pass* in fencing is intransitive (*OED v.*
    24). *OED* gives only one example (this
    passage) of *pass* used transitively in fenc-
    ing to mean 'to make or execute (a
    thrust)' (*pass v.* 53); even if this meaning
    is accepted, *pass* can hardly govern *thy
    distance*, which is not a thrust. Moreover,
    of the preceding five phrases, the first
    three relate to verbs (*fight*, *foin*, *traverse*),
    and the next two to adverbs (*here*, *there*);
    a return to another verb is less likely than
    a string of nouns.
24 **punto** another thrust. 'The foin, the
    venue, the stoccata (or stock), and the
    punto,—all nearly synonymous,—to-
    gether with the punto reverso . . . or back-
    handed thrust, and the montanto, ex-
    haust the list of Shakespeare's hits. Other
    terms, common enough with his contem-
    poraries, . . . are absent from his works'

(*Shakespeare's England*, ii. 401).
24 **stock** see preceding note
    reverse back-handed thrust, the punto
    reverso (*Romeo* 2.3.24); also back-
    handed cut
    distance i.e. from the opponent
25 **montant** upward cut or thrust. 'Signor
    Mountanto' is Beatrice's satirical name
    for Benedick, *Much Ado* 1.1.29.
    Ethiopian i.e. ugly swarthy fellow.
    Shakespeare has several *Ethiop* refer-
    ences, nearly all of them in antithesis
    with beauty, e.g. *Two Gentlemen* 2.6.26,
    Much Ado 5.4.38, *Dream* 3.2.258.
26 **Francisco** i.e. Frenchman (the Host's
    coinage)
    Aesculapius the classical god of medicine
27 **Galen** Greek physician (2nd c. AD)
    heart of elder 'Heart of oak' was a
    common expression in the literal sense
    (*OED heart sb.* 19: first citation 1523),
    meaning the hard central wood of the
    tree; *OED*'s first recorded figurative use,
    as a type of sturdy manliness, is dated
    1609. 'Heart of elder' implies just the
    opposite, for an 'elder-gun' (*Henry V*
    4.1.197) was made by extracting the soft
    pith from a straight piece of elder branch.
    Compare Lyly, *Euphues* (Lyly, i. 194):
    'the elder tree, though he be fullest of
    pith, is farthest from strength'.
    stale urine (*OED sb.³*); i.e. doctor (refer-
    ring to the method of diagnosis by in-
    specting the patient's urine, as in *2 Henry
    IV* 1.2.1–5)

CAIUS By gar, he is de coward jack priest of de vorld. He is
not show his face.   30

HOST Thou art a Castalion King Urinal Hector of Greece,
my boy!

CAIUS I pray you bear witness that me have stay six or
seven, two, tree hours for him, and he is no come.

SHALLOW He is the wiser man, Master Doctor. He is a
curer of souls, and you a curer of bodies. If you should
fight, you go against the hair of your professions. Is it
not true, Master Page?

PAGE Master Shallow, you have yourself been a great
fighter, though now a man of peace.   40

SHALLOW Bodykins, Master Page, though I now be old and
of the peace, if I see a sword out, my finger itches to
make one. Though we are justices and doctors and
churchmen, Master Page, we have some salt of our
youth in us. We are the sons of women, Master Page.

PAGE 'Tis true, Master Shallow.

SHALLOW It will be found so, Master Page.—Master Doctor

31–2 Castalion King Urinal Hector of Greece, my boy!] This edition; Castalion-king-Vrinall:
Hector of Greece (my Boy)∧ F; castallian king vrinall. *Hector of Greece* my boy. Q; *Castillian,
king urinal; Hector of Greece, my boy.* CAPELL

29 **he is . . . vorld** i.e. 'he is the most
cowardly knave of a priest in the world'
31 **Castalion King Urinal** a phrase of doubtful meaning, probably adjectival in relation to *Hector of Greece*. F's *Castalion* is a
contemporary spelling of Castiglione, e.g.
in Nashe, *The Anatomy of Absurdity*
(1589), *Works*, i. 7: 'Castalion's Courtier'. Baldassare Castiglione's *Il cortegiano*
(1528, translated 1561) presents a picture of the 'complete man' of the Renaissance. It would be appropriate for the
Host to apply the name to Caius as
gentleman, scholar, and swordsman. F's
spelling is more likely to be correct than
Q's 'castallian' because the -ian ending is
the more common, in adjectives of na-
tionality, etc., though 'Castalian' might
be defended as a reference to Castalia, the
Muses' sacred spring on Mount Parnas-
sus, and as having ironical connections
with *stale* (l. 27) and *urinal*. The agreement of Q and F about the middle vowel
makes it unlikely that both print incorrect versions of 'Castilian'.
Hector of Greece Not the Host's error but

his jest. Hector (of Troy) was traditionally
numbered among the Nine Worthies;
compare *LLL* 5.2.530–1.
33 **I pray you** Caius's courteous style shows
that he is addressing the four newcomers,
not Jack Rugby, who is the only person
on stage qualified to bear witness.
37 **against the hair** of contrary to. Proverbial
(Tilley H18), from rubbing an animal's
fur the wrong way.
41 **Bodykins** a euphemistic form of the oath
'by God's body'
42–3 **if I . . . make one** Such expressions
usually contain sexual innuendo in
Shakespeare, e.g. *Romeo* 2.3. 147–50, *2
Henry IV* 2.1. 14–18. Shallow's *my finger
itches* draws attention to the innuendo by
not being in the usual plural (contrast
Romeo 3.5.164), and *some salt of our
youth* serves the same purpose.
43 **make one** join in
44 **salt** 'that which gives liveliness, piquancy, or freshness to a person's character, life, etc.' (*OED sb.*¹ 3b); but also
suggesting *salt a.*² b, 'lecherous, sala-
cious' (as frequently in Shakespeare)

Caius, I am come to fetch you home. I am sworn of the
peace. You have showed yourself a wise physician, and
Sir Hugh hath shown himself a wise and patient   50
churchman. You must go with me, Master Doctor.

HOST Pardon, guest Justice.—(*To Caius*) A word, Monsieur
Mockwater.

CAIUS Mockvater? Vat is dat?

HOST Mockwater, in our English tongue, is valour, bully.

CAIUS By gar, then I have as much mockvater as de
Englishman. Scurvy jack-dog priest! By gar, me vill cut
his ears.

HOST He will clapper-claw thee tightly, bully.

CAIUS Clapper-de-claw? Vat is dat? ·   60

HOST That is, he will make thee amends.

CAIUS By gar, me do look he shall clapper-de-claw me, for,
by gar, me vill have it.

HOST And I will provoke him to't, or let him wag.

CAIUS Me tank you for dat.

HOST And moreover, bully—but first, Master guest, and

52–3 A word, Monsieur Mockwater] Q (A word monsire mockwater); a Mounseur Mocke-
|water F; A word, Monsire Make-water SISSON (*conj.* Cartwright)

52 **guest Justice** Shallow, like Falstaff, is
lodging at the Garter inn; compare
Master guest (l. 66).

53 **Mockwater** Not found except in this
passage, this apparently invented word is
used, like *clapper-claw* (l. 59), as the opposite of the definition that the Host gives
Caius. Q and F both have the word, so it is
probably right. The objections to the
emendation 'Make-water' (with an allusion to urinating because of fear) are that
its derogatory sense would be obvious
even to Caius and that its actual and
pretended senses are grammatically in-
harmonious, the former indicating the
act and the latter the product (as is not
the case with *clapper-claw*, l. 59); the
emendation 'Muck-water' (i.e. liquid
manure) escapes at least the second objection, but Shakespeare's only use of
'muck' is in *Coriolanus* 2.2.126, 'the
common muck of the world'.

56–7 **de Englishman** i.e. any valiant Englishman

57 **jack-dog** male dog. OED (*jack sb.*[1] 37)
gives examples of 'jack' prefixed to ani-
mals' names and signifying the male. The

absurdity of Caius's expression lies in his
unawareness that 'dog' (in 16th-c. English) is by definition male. The word has
also been glossed as a compound of 'jack'
(i.e. knave) and 'dog'. Compare 3.1.77
'de Jack dog, John ape'.

57–8 **cut his ears** i.e. cut off his ears (compare 1.4.106). The NCS editors, who
annotate 'Referring to "jack-dog" =
mongrel' (a definition not supported by
OED), seem to understand it to mean
'crop his ears'.

59 **clapper-claw** maul. 'Formed by some
process from clap (strike) and claw
(scratch)' (Hart). Used by Nashe (1590:
OED's first citation) and in *Troilus* 5.4.1.

64 **wag** i.e. go to the devil; literally, depart
(as in 1.3.6)

66 **And moreover, bully** It is dramatically
awkward if the Host, having engaged
Caius's attention by these words, immediately deserts him and begins whisper-
ing to the others. It is more natural for
him to pretend to recollect that he has a
little business to do with the others, and
not to lower his voice till he has begun to
address them.

Master Page, and eke Cavaliero Slender, ⌜*aside*⌝ go you
through the town to Frogmore.

PAGE ⌜*aside to Host*⌝ Sir Hugh is there, is he?

HOST ⌜*aside to Page*⌝ He is there. See what humour he is   70
in; and I will bring the doctor about by the fields. Will it
do well?

SHALLOW ⌜*aside to Host*⌝ We will do it.

⌜PAGE, SHALLOW, *and* SLENDER⌝ Adieu, good Master
Doctor.   *Exeunt Page, Shallow, and Slender*

CAIUS By gar, me vill kill de priest, for he speak for a
jackanape to Anne Page.

HOST Let him die. Sheathe thy impatience; throw cold
water on thy choler. Go about the fields with me
through Frogmore. I will bring thee where Mistress   80
Anne Page is, at a farmhouse a-feasting; and thou shalt
woo her. ~~Cried game! Said I well?~~   *KISSING*

CAIUS By gar, me dank you vor dat. By gar, I love you,
and I shall procure-a you de good guest—de earl, de
knight, de lords, de gentlemen, my patiences.

HOST For the which I will be thy adversary toward Anne
Page. Said I well?

67 aside] CLARKE; *after* 'bully', 66 CAPELL; *not in* F   69 aside to Host] This edition; *not
in* F   70 aside to Page] This edition; *not in* F   73 aside to Host] This edition; *not in* F   74
PAGE, SHALLOW, *and* SLENDER] MALONE; *All.* F   75 Exeunt ... Slender] ROWE; *Exit all but the
Host and Doctor.*] Q; *not in* F   78 die. Sheathe thy] F (die: sheath thy); die, but first sheth
your Q   80 Frogmore.] HIBBARD; *Frogmore*, F; *Frogmore, and* Q   82 her. Cried game!] F
(her: Cride-game,); hir cried game: Q; her. Cried I aim? HALLIWELL (*conj.* Douce); her. Cried
game? SISSON   85 my patiences] OXFORD; my patients F; mon patinces Q

77 **jackanape** Slender, who is hardly out of
earshot

78 **Let him die** Either literally (i.e.'kill him by
all means; but for the present, ... ') or
figuratively (i.e. 'forget him'; compare
'die in oblivion', *Shrew* 4.1.74).

81 **at ... a-feasting** 'Excursions to the farms
in the suburbs of London are frequently
referred to' (McKerrow, in Nashe, *Works*,
iv. 262, with reference to the phrase 'go
to Islington and eat a mess of cream', i.e.
some form of curds and whey, or junket).

82 **Cried game!** Not positively explained,
and not in OED. 'Possibly sporting slang,
now lost' (NCS). F and Q agree as to the
words, though not as to the punctuation.
Hart explains it as the Host's announcement 'that the sport is arranged or pro-
claimed', and cites a reference in Jonson's
Epicene to a bearward who 'cried his

games under Master Morose's window'
(1.1.173–6). Others (NCS, Oliver, Hibbard) suggest that it means that the
quarry has been sighted. NCS interprets it
as a vocative addressed to Caius as 'an
insult (the Host's parting shot)', meaning
that he is the quarry pursued by the
Host's ridicule; but the fact that Caius
does not ask for an explanation, as he did
of 'Mockwater' and 'clapper-claw', is
against this interpretation. Oliver points
out that in Dennis's version of 1702 the
phrase is omitted, perhaps because no
longer understood.

85 **patiences** Q's word, though misprinted,
seems to preserve a characteristic error of
Caius's which F unnecessarily corrects.

86 **adversary** The Host invites Caius to
understand this in the sense of 'advocate'
while enjoying his private joke.

CAIUS By gar, 'tis good. Vell said.

HOST Let us wag, then.

CAIUS Come at my heels, Jack Rugby.   *Exeunt*   90

3.1   *Enter Evans ⌈with a Bible in one hand and a drawn*
      rapier in the other⌉ and Simple ⌈carrying Evans's
      gown⌉

EVANS I pray you now, good Master Slender's serving-
      man, and friend Simple by your name, which way have
      you looked for Master Caius, that calls himself Doctor of
      Physic?

SIMPLE Marry, sir, the Petty-ward, the Park-ward, every
      way; Old Windsor way, and every way but the town
      way.

EVANS I most fehemently desire you you will also look that
      way.

SIMPLE I will, sir.   ⌈*He walks aside*⌉   10

EVANS Pless my soul, how full of cholers I am, and

3.1] F (*Actus Tertius. Scœna Prima.*)   0.1–3] *as* OXFORD; *Enter Euans, Simple, Page, Shallow,
Slender, Host, Caius, Rugby.* F; *Enter Syr Hugh and Simple.* Q   5 Petty-ward] COLLIER (petty-
ward); pittie-ward F   Park-ward] F (Parke-ward)   5–6 every way; Old Windsor way] F
(euery way: olde *Windsor* way); Old Windsor way This edition *conj.*   10 He walks aside] *as*
OLIVER; *Exit* CAMBRIDGE; *not in* F   11 Pless my soul] F ('Plesse); Ieshu ples mee Q; Jeshu
pless my soul RIVERSIDE

90 **Come ... Rugby** Rugby has not uttered a
    word, or been taken notice of, since his
    opening dialogue with Caius.
3.1 It is unlikely that an interval separated
    this scene from the one before, to which
    it is so closely connected. If the scribe's
    copy was Shakespeare's manuscript no
    act-divisions may have been indicated
    in it. Act 3 is the longest in the play, Act 5
    being only half its length and the other
    three acts about four-fifths as long as it
    and of equal length with each other.
0.1 **Bible** Shallow indicates that Evans is
    holding a book (l. 37) which is the Bible
    (l. 41); NCS's suggestion that he has been
    reading his 'songs' out of it is whimsical.
1–2 **good Master Slender's serving-man** The
    adjective *good* governs the rest of the
    phrase, and is applied to Simple, not to
    Slender. The expression *friend Simple by
    your name* (as if *friend* were part of the
    name) is equally eccentric.
3 **calls himself** Evans suggests that Caius is
    not entitled to his title. This prepares for
    the humour of ll. 56–7, where Page gives

it with full honours, to Evans's annoy-
ance.
5 **the Petty-ward** presumably towards
    Windsor Little Park; *petty* (French *petit*,
    little) was probably pronounced as F's
    spelling indicates.
    the Park-ward towards Windsor Great
    Park .
6 **Old Windsor** a village south of Frogmore
10 **He walks aside** Since Simple can see
    people coming from another direction
    without leaving the stage (ll. 30–2), it is
    better for him to stand and look through
    an open doorway now than to leave the
    stage altogether. The stage action re-
    quired when Rugby looks through an off-
    stage casement for Caius's return in 1.4 is
    different.
11 **Pless my soul** Though *my soul* does not
    occur elsewhere in Shakespeare as the
    object of *bless* (Jowett), Shakespeare no-
    where else has a parson in a comparable
    situation, so F's reading may stand, as at
    l. 15.
    cholers The association of this word with

trempling of mind! I shall be glad if he have deceived
me. How melancholies I am! I will knog his urinals
about his knave's costard when I have good opportunities for the 'ork. Pless my soul!

> (*Sings*) To shallow rivers, to whose falls
> Melodious birds sings madrigals.
> There will we make our peds of roses,
> And a thousand fragrant posies.
> To shallow—   20

Mercy on me! I have a great dispositions to cry.

> (*Sings*) Melodious birds sing madrigals—
> Whenas I sat in Pabylon—
> And a thousand vagrom posies.
> To shallow (*etc.*)

16, 22, 28 *Sings*] *as* POPE; *not in* F   25] F; CAMBRIDGE *adds* '*Enter Simple.*'

trempling of mind shows that Evans means
to say 'melancholies' (with his characteristic plural). Mistress Quickly confused
the words the opposite way in 1.4.86.

13 **melancholies** Evans now either gets the
right word at last, or means to say
'choleric' and gets the wrong word again.
The following sentence, assuming that it
follows from this one, supports the latter
interpretation.
   urinals The physician's urinal was a
spherical glass vessel with a long neck by
which to hold it. Evans of course means
one urinal, not several.

14 **costard** head (from 'costard', a large kind
of apple)

14–15 **good opportunities** good opportunity. Shakespeare always uses 'opportunity' without qualification except here and
in *Henry V* 3.3.80–1 ('whèn there is
more better opportunity to be required'),
where the speaker is another Welshman,
Fluellen.

16 *Sings* By italicizing the words of the
poem, F differentiates them from the rest
of Evans's speeches. He sings to cheer
himself up, unsuccessfully.

16–19 Part of two consecutive stanzas from
Marlowe's poem beginning 'Come live
with me and be my love': 'And we will sit
upon the rocks, | Seeing the shepherds
feed their flocks | By shallow rivers, to
whose falls | Melodious birds sing madri-
gals. || And I will make thee beds of
roses, | And a thousand fragrant posies
... ' (text from *England's Helicon*, 1600;

that in *The Passionate Pilgrim*, 1599, is
less close to Evans's version). Marlowe's
lyric was well known in his lifetime, for
he adapts it comically in his *Jew of Malta*
4.3.103–4. For a perhaps contemporary
tune, published in 1612, see Appendix B.

16 **falls** cascades (*OED sb.*[1] 7). Birds' song
and waterfalls are similarly in harmony
in Spenser, *Faerie Queene* II.xii.71.

23 **Whenas ... Pabylon** From the opening of
Psalm 137 in the metrical version: 'Whenas we sat in Babylon the rivers round
about, | And in remembrance of Sion the
tears for grief burst out, | We hanged our
harps and instruments the willow-trees
upon, | For in that place men for their use
had planted many one.' The melancholy
phrase shows Evans's melancholy mood
breaking in. The connecting word in his
mental process is 'rivers'. It may be
assumed that he sings this phrase to the
tune of the line for which he has substituted it ('There will we make our beds of
roses'). That he should sing two lines of
Marlowe's poem to the tune of the psalm
is impossible, for the poem is in iambic
tetrameters throughout and the psalm in
iambic fourteeners (i.e. tetrameters alternating with trimeters).

24 **vagrom** vagrant. OED defines 'vagrom'
(first citation from *Much Ado* 3.3.24,
spoken by Dogberry) as an 'illiterate
alteration of "vagrant"'. Here used by
phonetic confusion with 'fragrant'.

25 *etc.* Evans continues to sing, perhaps
with diminishing volume.

SIMPLE Yonder he is coming, this way, Sir Hugh.

EVANS He's welcome.

    (*Sings*) To shallow rivers, to whose falls—
Heaven prosper the right! What weapons is he?

SIMPLE No weapons, sir. There comes my master, Master   30
Shallow, and another gentleman, from Frogmore, over
the stile, this way.

EVANS Pray you, give me my gown—or else keep it in
your arms.

    ⌈*He opens the Bible and reads it.*⌉
    Enter Page, Shallow, and Slender

SHALLOW How now, Master Parson? Good morrow, good
Sir Hugh. Keep a gamester from the dice, and a good
student from his book, and it is wonderful.

SLENDER (*aside*) Ah, sweet Anne Page!

PAGE Save you, good Sir Hugh!

EVANS Pless you from his mercy sake, all of you!   40

SHALLOW What, the sword and the word? Do you study
them both, Master Parson?

---

29 Heaven] F; God OXFORD 34.1] This edition; *Reads in a book.* DYCE (*conj.* Collier); *not in* F
34.2] Q; *not in* F 39 Save you, good Sir Hugh!] F ('Saue); God saue you Sir *Hugh.* Q
40 Pless you from his mercy sake, all of you!] F ('Plesse): God plesse you all from his mercies sake
now. Q

26 **Yonder he is coming, this way** This must
refer to Caius because Simple was asked
to look out for him. According to the
Host's plan, the others, approaching
from the other direction, still arrive first.

29 **Heaven** Possibly an expurgation (as in
2 Henry IV 3.2.289–90, where Q has
'The Lord bless you; God prosper your
affairs! God send us peace!' and F has
'Heaven . . . and prosper . . . and send
. . .'); alternatively, an expression in
keeping with the speaker.

30 **No weapons** Presumably Simple means
that Caius has not a drawn sword in his
hand. The Host bids the others lay the
duellists' swords to pawn, ll. 101–2.
    There comes Not synonymous with 'here
comes' (which is very common in
Shakespeare), nor with 'yonder comes',
but an impersonal construction (as in *2
Henry IV* 2.4.78–9, 'There comes no
swaggerers here'). F's semicolon after
'gentleman' therefore needs replacing by

a comma.

33 **or else** i.e. or rather, on second thoughts.
Evans sees that it is too late to put it on
and thereby hide his sword.

36–7 **Keep ... wonderful** Oliver compares
such proverbs as 'Keep flax from fire and
youth from gaming' (Tilley F351),
though Dent points out that this particular proverb is not known to have been
current in Shakespeare's time.

40 **Pless you from his mercy sake** The implied 'God' need not be supplied from Q,
since 'Bless you' is an idiomatic construction, and its relation to the rest of the
phrase (with the incongruous substitution of 'from' for 'for') is characteristic of
Evans, who is imperfectly recollecting
Psalm 6: 4, 'O save me for thy mercies'
sake'.

41 **the word** the scripture. In *2 Henry IV*
4.1.236 Prince John accuses the Arch-
bishop of York of 'Turning the word to
sword, and life to death'.

PAGE And youthful still—in your doublet and hose this raw rheumatic day?

EVANS There is reasons and causes for it.

PAGE We are come to you to do a good office, Master Parson.

EVANS Fery well. What is it?

PAGE Yonder is a most reverend gentleman, who, belike, having received wrong by some person, is at most odds   50
with his own gravity and patience that ever you saw.

SHALLOW I have lived fourscore years and upward. I never heard a man of his place, gravity, and learning so wide of his own respect.

EVANS What is he?

PAGE I think you know him: Master Doctor Caius, the renowned French physician.

EVANS Got's will and his passion of my heart! I had as lief you would tell me of a mess of porridge.

PAGE Why?   60

EVANS He has no more knowledge in Hibbocrates and Galen—and he is a knave besides, a cowardly knave as you would desires to be acquainted withal.

PAGE ⌜*to Shallow*⌝ I warrant you, he's the man should fight with him.

43 still—] HIBBARD; still, F   59 porridge] FQ; pottage OXFORD   61 Hibbocrates] F (*Hibocrates*)   62 Galen—] HIBBARD; *Galen,* F   64 *to Shallow*] OXFORD; *not in* F

44 **rheumatic** Accented on the first syllable, as in Shakespeare's verse, e.g. *Dream* 2.1.105.

49 **reverend** respectable

53–4 **wide of his own respect** far from his proper reasonableness (*OED respect sb.* 13, 'regard, consideration'). Shakespeare associates 'respect and reason' (*Lucrece* 275), 'reason and respect' (*Troilus* 2.2.48).

58 **Got's ... heart** A triple conflation of oaths (God's will! God's passion! Passion of my heart!), notable for its inclusion in the frequently expurgated text of F.

59 **mess of porridge** dish of stew (the only meaning of *porridge* in the 16th c.). Shakespeare has both 'porridge' (frequently) and the synonymous 'pottage' (once, in *Lear* 3.4.52 in Q, where F has 'porridge'). Evans, being a parson, may be thinking of the 'mess of pottage' for which Esau sold his birthright (Genesis

25: chapter-heading) according to the text of the Geneva Bible (1560). But his figurative point seems to be the contrast between porridge (as the first course of a meal) and meat (the more substantial joint that followed it); compare *Troilus* 1.2.239, 'porridge after meat!' (said in scorn of the common soldiers following their heroic leaders), and Jonson's *Poetaster* 3.4.280–1, 'He will eat a leg of mutton while I am in my porridge.'

61–2 **He has ... Galen** A sentence which, if Evans's indignation had allowed him to complete it, might have run 'than is a puppy dog', as in Fluellen's similar criticism of Macmorris's ignorance of the Roman disciplines of war, *Henry V* 3.2.18.

61 **Hibbocrates** Hippocrates, Greek physician (5th c. BC)

64–5 **he's the man should fight with him** this is the man who is to fight with Caius.

SLENDER *(aside)* O sweet Anne Page!

SHALLOW It appears so by his weapons.

Enter Host, Caius, and Rugby

Keep them asunder; here comes Doctor Caius.

Evans and Caius offer to fight

PAGE Nay, good Master Parson, keep in your weapon.

SHALLOW So do you, good Master Doctor.   70

HOST Disarm them, and let them question. Let them keep
their limbs whole and hack our English.

Shallow and Page take Caius's and Evans's rapiers

CAIUS I pray you let-a me speak a word with your ear.
Verefore vill you not meet-a me?

EVANS *(aside to Caius)* Pray you, use your patience. *(Aloud)*
In good time.

CAIUS By gar, you are de coward, de Jack dog, John ape.

EVANS *(aside to Caius)* Pray you, let us not be laughing-
stocks to other men's humours. I desire you in
friendship, and I will one way or other make you   80
amends. *(Aloud)* I will knog your urinal about your
knave's cogscomb.

CAIUS *Diable!* Jack Rugby, mine host de Jarteer, have I not
stay for him to kill him? Have I not, at de place I did
appoint?

EVANS As I am a Christians soul, now, look you, this is the
place appointed. I'll be judgement by mine host of the
Garter.

67.1] ROWE; *Enter Doctor and the Host, they offer to fight.* Q; *not in* F   68.1] *as* Q (67.1); *not in* F
71–2] F; *Host. Disarme, let them question. | Shal⟨low⟩. Let them keep their limbs hole, and
hack our English.* Q   72.1] OXFORD; *not in* F   75 *aside to Caius*] CAMBRIDGE; *not in* F   75–6
patience. In] JOHNSON; patience in F   75 *Aloud*] BOWERS; *not in* F   78 *aside to Caius*]
STAUNTON; *not in* F   81 *Aloud*] STAUNTON; *not in* F   I will] F; By Ieshu I will Q   urinal]
F; vrinalls Q   82 cogscomb] F; cockcomes, for missing your meetings and appointments Q

Page and Shallow pretend not to have
been told this.

71 **question** ask questions (*OED v.* 3), i.e. of
each other
76 **In good time** Very well. This may be said
either in acquiescence (e.g. *Measure*
3.1.181) or in indignation (e.g. *Shrew*
2.1.195), according to whether Evans
means 'I will meet you here and now' or
'How dare you ask why I will not meet you
when I have been waiting for you here?'
77 **John ape** Caius has noted (1.4.53) that

Jack and John are synonymous, and now
applies that knowledge.
81 **urinal** This word and *cogscomb* are both
singular in F and both plural in Q (which
includes two more plurals in its additional phrase). Probably F is correct:
Evans's speech has already included
three genuine plurals, so these singular
forms avoid an overdone effect and also
make for clarity of sense. Earlier
(ll. 13–14) F had 'urinals' and 'costard'.
82 **cogscomb** coxcomb (i.e. head)
86–7 **this is the place appointed** With a

HOST Peace, I say, Gallia and Gaul, French and Welsh,
   soul-curer and body-curer.   90
CAIUS Ay, dat is very good, *excellent.*
HOST Peace, I say. Hear mine host of the Garter. Am I
   politic? Am I subtle? Am I a Machiavel? Shall I lose my
   doctor? No; he gives me the potions and the motions.
   Shall I lose my parson, my priest, my Sir Hugh? No; he
   gives me the proverbs and the no-verbs. (*To Caius*) Give
   me thy hand, terrestrial; so. (*To Evans*) Give me thy
   hand, celestial; so. Boys of art, I have deceived you
   both. I have directed you to wrong places. Your hearts
   are mighty, your skins are whole, and let burnt sack be   100
   the issue. (*To Shallow and Page*) Come, lay their swords
   to pawn. (*To Caius and Evans*) Follow me, lads of peace;
   follow, follow, follow.   *Exit*

89 Gallia and Gaul] F (*Gallia* and *Gaule*); gawle and gawlia Q; Gallia and Wallia HAN-
MER; Gwallia and Gaul RANN, *conj.* Farmer   91 *excellent*] F (excellant)   93 a Machiavel] F (a
Machiuell); Matchauil Q   96 *To Caius*] OXFORD; *not in* F   96–8 Give me thy hand,
terrestrial ... Boys] THEOBALD; Giue me thy hand (Celestiall) so: Boyes F; Giue me thy hand
terestiall, | So giue me thy hand celestiall: | So boyes Q   97 *To Evans*] OXFORD; *not in* F   101 *To
Shallow and Page*] *as* NCS; *not in* F   102 *To Caius and Evans*] OXFORD; *not in* F   lads] Q; Lad F
103 follow, follow, follow] F; follow me. Ha, ra, la. Follow Q   *Exit*] Q (*Exit Host.*); *not in* F

heavy emphasis on *this*. Q's addition to
his previous speech robs the present
speech of its indignant tone of surprise, is
not necessary to prompt Caius's reply,
and unprofitably anticipates 'appoint'
and 'appointed' in the speeches of Caius
and Evans.

89 **Gallia and Gaul** A difficult phrase,
though it obviously means the antag-
onists' two nations. *Gallia* and *Gaul* can
both mean France, and neither apparently can mean Wales; hence the emendations, none of which is satisfactory.
Shakespeare uses *Gallia* (and its adjective
Gallian), always with reference to France,
in *1 Henry VI*, *3 Henry VI*, *Henry V*
(1.2.216, 5.1.85), and *Cymbeline* (eight
times, and in a play where much of the
action is set in Wales). He uses *Gaul* only
on this occasion. *Gallia* must therefore
mean France, and *Gaul* (or the word for
which it may be an error) Wales. Q's
reading 'gawle and gawlia' does not
throw light on the problem. Possibly the
copy for the F text read 'Gwal' or 'Gual'
(though neither of these is the correct
form of Gwalia, a pseudo-Welsh name for

Wales), or 'Gall' if Shakespeare had in
mind the Fr. name for Wales, le Pays de
Galles).

91 **Ay ... *excellent*** An angrily ironical reply
to Evans's speech (not an appreciative
comment on the Host's), as the Host's
reiterated *Peace* shows. The F spelling
'excellant' is unusual enough to suggest
that the French equivalent is meant.

93 **a Machiavel** a complete intriguer. With
reference to the political practices recom-
mended in Machiavelli's *The Prince*
(1532); compare *politic* and *subtle*. Here
used without the usual sinister significance, or perhaps with a jocular allusion
to it. The F and Q spellings indicate the
pronunciation, the usual Elizabethan
one.

94 **motions** bowel movements (after purga-
tive *potions*). OED *motion* sb. 11 (first
citation).

96 **no-verbs** non-words (i.e. Evans's eccentric language): a nonce-word

98 **art** learning

100 **burnt sack** See 2.1.194–5.

101–2 **lay their swords to pawn** The Host's
figurative way of saying that they no
longer need their swords.

SHALLOW Trust me, a mad host. Follow, gentlemen, follow.

SLENDER (*aside*) O sweet Anne Page!

Exeunt Shallow, Slender, and Page

CAIUS Ha, do I perceive dat? Have you make-a de sot of us, ha, ha?

EVANS This is well. He has made us his vlouting-stog. I desire you that we may be friends, and let us knog our   110
prains together to be revenge on this same scall, scurvy, cogging companion, the host of the Garter.

CAIUS By gar, with all my heart. He promise to bring me where is Anne Page. By gar, he deceive me too.

EVANS Well, I will smite his noddles. Pray you follow.

Exeunt

3.2   *Enter Robin, followed by Mistress Page*

MISTRESS PAGE Nay, keep your way, little gallant. You were wont to be a follower, but now you are a leader. Whether had you rather, lead mine eyes, or eye your master's heels?

ROBIN I had rather, forsooth, go before you like a man than follow him like a dwarf.

MISTRESS PAGE O, you are a flattering boy: now I see you'll be a courtier.

Enter Ford

FORD Well met, Mistress Page. Whither go you?

MISTRESS PAGE Truly, sir, to see your wife. Is she at home?   10

FORD Ay, and as idle as she may hang together, for want

104–5 Trust me ... follow] F; Afore God a mad host, come let vs goe Q   106.1] NEILSON; *not in* F   115.1] POPE; *Exit omnes* Q; *not in* F

3.2] F (*Scena Secunda.*)   0.1] OXFORD; *Mist. Page, Robin, Ford, Page, Shallow, Slender, Host, Euans, Caius.* F: *Enter M. Foord.* Q   8.1] Q: *not in* F

---

107 **sot** fool. The French word was established in English, and Caius uses the English pronunciation.

109 **vlouting-stog** flouting-stock, butt of mockery. *OED* gives an instance from Gabriel Harvey (1592).

111 **scall** scalled (affected with scall, a scabby disease of the scalp), i.e. contemptible. Fluellen uses 'scalled' repeatedly of Pistol in *Henry V* 5.2.5, 29, 31, 50.

112 **cogging companion** deceitful rogue

115 **noddles** for 'noddle', head

3.2 Q omits the opening of this scene and begins with a soliloquy by Ford ('The time drawes on he should come to my house', etc.).

1 **keep your way** go on (ahead)

11 **as idle ... together** 'as bored as she can be without falling completely to pieces' (Hibbard). A similar expression is used in *Winter's Tale* 2.2.25–6.

of company. I think if your husbands were dead you two
would marry.

MISTRESS PAGE Be sure of that—two other husbands.

FORD Where had you this pretty weathercock?

MISTRESS PAGE I cannot tell what the dickens his name is
my husband had him of. What do you call your knight's
name, sirrah?

ROBIN Sir John Falstaff.

FORD (*aside*) Sir John Falstaff!   20

MISTRESS PAGE He, he. I can never hit on's name. There is
such a league between my goodman and he! Is your
wife at home indeed?

FORD Indeed she is.

MISTRESS PAGE By your leave, sir. I am sick till I see her.

Exeunt Robin and Mistress Page

FORD Has Page any brains? Hath he any eyes? Hath he
any thinking? Sure, they sleep; he hath no use of them.
Why, this boy will carry a letter twenty mile as easy as a
cannon will shoot point-blank twelve score. He pieces
out his wife's inclination. He gives her folly motion and   30
advantage. And now she's going to my wife, and
Falstaff's boy with her. A man may hear this shower
sing in the wind. And Falstaff's boy with her! Good plots

20 *aside*] This edition; *not in* F   22 goodman] F1; good man F4   25.1] OXFORD; *not in* F
33–4 Good ... laid,] F (good plots, they are laide,); Good plots! They are laid; OLIVER

15 **weathercock** The sense of the metaphor
is not certain, and Shakespeare's two
other uses of *weathercock* do not establish
it; in *Two Gentlemen* 2.1.128, 'a weathercock on a steeple' implies conspicuous-
ness; in *LLL* 4.1.93–4, a weathercock is
one of three images for a giddy brain (the
others being a plume of feathers and a
vane). Robin's costume appeared to be a
skirted coat in 1.3.80, and that it is gaudy
or includes a feathered hat is only editorial conjecture.

16–21 **I cannot ... hit on's name** Mistress
Page knows Falstaff's name very well, so
there seems to be a topical joke, on
Shakespeare's part, about the fact that
the Falstaff of the history plays was called
Oldcastle before objections from the
Brooke family forced a change. (See Introduction, pp. 9–10.) The dialogue also
draws attention to Ford's response when
he learns the name.

16 **what the dickens** i.e. what the devil. A
euphemistic form of an emphatic expression (compare 'I' fackins' for 'I' faith').
OED's first citation.

22 **league** bond of friendship

29 **point-blank twelve score** with direct aim
(in a horizontal line) at 240 yards or
paces: 'as contrasted with shooting an
arrow accurately at this distance, the
usual phrase for an exceptional feat (as in
2 Henry IV 3.2.45)' (Oliver).

29–30 **pieces out** adds to. The image is from
the tailor's craft, i.e. 'letting in' an extra
piece of material (*OED piece v.* 6).

30 **motion** instigation (*OED sb.* 9)

31 **advantage** opportunity (*OED sb.* 4)

32–3 **hear ... wind** i.e. foresee trouble here.
The expression is used literally in *Tempest*
2.2.19–20.

33–4 **Good plots they are laid** Compare
'Plots have I laid, inductions dangerous',
Richard III 1.1.32.

they are laid, and our revolted wives share damnation
together. Well, I will take him, then torture my wife,
pluck the borrowed veil of modesty from the so-seeming
Mistress Page, divulge Page himself for a secure and
wilful Actaeon; and to these violent proceedings all my
neighbours shall cry aim.

Clock strikes

The clock gives me my cue, and my assurance bids me   40
search. There I shall find Falstaff. I shall be rather
praised for this than mocked, for it is as positive as the
earth is firm that Falstaff is there. I will go.

Enter Page, Shallow, Slender, Host, Evans, Caius, and
Rugby

SHALLOW, PAGE, *etc.* Well met, Master Ford.

FORD Trust me, a good knot. I have good cheer at home,
and I pray you all go with me.

SHALLOW I must excuse myself, Master Ford.

SLENDER And so must I, sir. We have appointed to dine
with Mistress Anne, and I would not break with her for
more money than I'll speak of.   50

SHALLOW We have lingered about a match between Anne

39.1] *as* CAPELL; *not in* F   40 cue] F (Qu)   43.1–2] CAPELL; *Enter Shallow, Page, host,*
Slender, Doctor, and sir Hugh. Q; *not in* F   44 SHALLOW, PAGE, *etc.*] F (*Shal. Page, &c.*)   45
FORD ... knot] F; *Ford (aside)* ... knot OLIVER   Trust me] F; By my faith Q

34 **revolted** i.e. from their marital duty, as in
    Winter's Tale 1.2.200.
35 **take** catch
    torture my wife make my wife suffer.
    Compare *Merchant* 3.2.110–11 (Shy-
    lock, of Antonio), 'I'll plague him, I'll
    torture him.'
36 **so-seeming** modest-seeming (but really
    immodest)
37 **divulge** proclaim (*OED v.* 1 b)
39 **cry aim** be spectators. The expression
    seems to have originated in the encour-
    aging of archery contestants (*OED aim sb.*
    3c). Shakespeare's other instance is in
    John 2.1.196–7, 'It ill beseems this pres-
    ence to cry aim | To these ill-tunèd repeti-
    tions', where there is no question of
    encouragement.
39.1 *Clock strikes* Shakespeare has this
    stage-effect again in *Caesar* 2.1.191.1
    and *Twelfth Night* 3.1.128.1, both in
    outdoor scenes.
45 **a good knot** Ford's use of *knot* in a

derogatory context at 4.2.107, and similar uses of it elsewhere in Shakespeare, do
not justify Oliver's taking it thus here and
treating the remark as an aside. Ford has
nothing against any of these persons, and
intends to involve them in his detection of
Falstaff. His reply to Page's remark is
therefore a friendly equivalent to it; Q
conflates them, showing that this is the
sense.

49 **break with her** break my promise to her.
This is obviously Slender's meaning, but
there is no comparable expression in
Shakespeare (*Coriolanus* 4.6.48–9 refers
to breaking a truce). The usual, very
frequent, sense of *break with* is to make a
revelation, disclosure, or proposal (e.g.
Much Ado 1.1.292, 309, 1.2.13–14,
2.1.280, 3.2.68), and this is precisely
what Slender does not do in 3.4, so that
he here speaks more truly than he knows.

51 **lingered** Though *OED* gives this passage
as an example of *linger v.* 4 ('to be tardy in

Page and my cousin Slender, and this day we shall have
our answer.

SLENDER I hope I have your good will, father Page.

PAGE You have, son Slender—I stand wholly for you. (*To
Caius*) But my wife, Master Doctor, is for you altogether.

CAIUS Ay, by gar, and de maid is love-a me; my nursh-a
Quickly tell me so mush.

HOST (*to Page*) What say you to young Master Fenton? He
capers, he dances, he has eyes of youth, he writes   60
verses, he speaks holiday, he smells April and May. He
will carry't, he will carry't; 'tis in his buttons he will
carry't.

PAGE Not by my consent, I promise you. The gentleman is
of no having. He kept company with the wild Prince and ⸲
Poins. He is of too high a region; he knows too much.

---

55 son] Q; Mr F   59 *to Page*] OXFORD; *not in* F   61 smells April] F; smelles | All April Q
62 buttons he] OLIVER; buttons, he F; betmes he Q; talons—he NCS *conj.*; fortunes, he SISSON

doing or beginning anything') it is more
probably used in OED's primary sense (*v.*
1), 'to tarry'. Shallow is explaining why
he and Slender are still at Windsor and
have not returned home to Gloucestershire.

55 **son Slender** Q's reading is preferable to
F's because Page addresses Slender in the
same way at 3.4.73 (in a line of verse),
and his reply to Slender in the present
passage is an encouragement and not a
snub (as the use of 'Master' in reply to
Slender's *father* would have been). F's 'Mr
Slender' seems to have been caught from
'Mr Doctor' in the line below.
stand wholly for wholly support

61 **speaks holiday** speaks in refined language. The context (reminiscent of Chaucer's description of the Squire in the
General Prologue to the *Canterbury Tales*,
I(A).79–100) excludes any suggestion of
affectation; contrast 'holiday and lady
terms' in *1 Henry IV* 1.3.45 (Hotspur, of
the 'popinjay').

62 **carry't** prevail, 'carry it away'
'tis in his buttons Never satisfactorily
explained, though obviously a confident
statement, either complete in itself or (as
Q's lack of punctuation may suggest)
connected to *he will carry't* by an implied
'that'. Q's 'betmes' is meaningless, and is
an extraordinary error if *buttons* was the

reporter's word: conceivably *buttons* was
written down, then misread as *betimes*,
and then misprinted. At least it casts
doubt on the emendations *talons* and
fortunes, which do not begin with the
letter b and which postulate misreading
errors in both Q and F. *Buttons* (assuming
that it is the right reading) can mean
either ordinary buttons (e.g. of a doublet)
or flower-buds (Fr. *boutons*: compare
Hamlet 1.3.40 and, in association with
May as in l. 61, *Kinsmen* 3.1.4–6). In the
former case, the sense is 'He has it in him,
buttoned up, as it were, inside' (Hart); in
the latter, 'the image is of the flower that
is yet to open but whose colour and
character are already determined'
(Oliver).

65 **having** wealth

65–6 **He kept ... Poins** See Introduction,
p. 11.

65 **region** social station. OED's only figurative example of *region sb.* 4a ('one of the
successive portions into which the air or
atmosphere is theoretically divided according to height').
he knows too much The precise meaning
of this charge is not clear. Fenton is
not represented in the play as a scholar
but as a courtier, so Page probably
means 'he knows too much of fashionable society'.

153

No, he shall not knit a knot in his fortunes with the
finger of my substance. If he take her, let him take her
simply. The wealth I have waits on my consent, and my
consent goes not that way.   70

FORD I beseech you heartily, some of you go home with
me to dinner. Besides your cheer, you shall have sport: I
will show you a monster. Master Doctor, you shall go.
So shall you, Master Page, and you, Sir Hugh.

SHALLOW Well, fare you well. ⌈*Aside to Slender*⌉ We shall
have the freer wooing at Master Page's.

Exeunt Shallow and Slender

CAIUS Go home, John Rugby. I come anon.   *Exit Rugby*

HOST Farewell, my hearts. I will to my honest knight
Falstaff, and drink canary with him.   *Exit*

FORD (*aside*) I think I shall drink in pipe-wine first with   80
him; I'll make him dance.—Will you go, gentles?

⌈PAGE, CAIUS, *and* EVANS⌉ Have with you to see this
monster.   *Exeunt*

3.3   *Enter Mistress Ford and Mistress Page*

MISTRESS FORD What, John! What, Robert!

75–6 Well, fare you well. We ... Page's] F; Wel, wel, God be with you, we shall haue the
fairer | Wooing at Maister Pages Q   75 Aside to Slender] OXFORD; *not in* F   76.1 Exeunt ...
Slender] Q; *not in* F   77 Exit Rugby] CAPELL; *not in* F   79 Exit] Q (*Exit host.*); *not in* F
82 ⌈PAGE, CAIUS, *and* EVANS⌉] *All.* F

    3.3] F (*Scena Tertia.*)   0.1] CAPELL; *Enter M. Ford, M. Page, Seruants, Robin, Falstaffe,
Ford, Page, Caius, Euans.* F; *Enter Mistresse Ford, with two of her men, and a great buck basket.* Q

67–8 **he shall not ... substance** The sense is
    clear—'he shall not secure his prosperity
    by means of my wealth'—but the implica-
    tion of the imagery is obscure. Oliver sug-
    gests 'as one ties a knot in a rope or a piece
    of string to prevent its fraying further'.
    More probably, however, the reference is
    to Fenton's future prosperous fortune
    rather than to his present decayed one.
    The image is of a double knot; one ties the
    first knot with one's two hands, and then
    a friend puts his finger on it to hold it
    secure while one ties the second knot.

69 **simply** as she is, i.e. without a dowry

73 **monster** 'an animal or plant deviating in
    one or more of its parts from the normal
    type' (*OED sb.* 2)

75–6 **We ... Page's** Given as an aside in this
    edition because Caius, who has the next
    speech, takes no notice of the remark,
    which he might be expected to do if he

heard it, being himself a suitor to Anne
Page.

80–1 **I shall ... dance** The first *I* is emphasized: Ford expects to meet Falstaff before
the Host does. The expression *drink in*
(followed by the thing drunk) is not found
elsewhere in Shakespeare, nor in *OED*
(except, *v.* 3, with reference to absorp-
tion, or, *v.* 4, figuratively), but the agreement of F and Q supports it: it may mean
'drink some'. The quibble in *pipe-wine*
seems to be on *pipe* (a cask holding four
barrels' quantity) and *pipe* (a musical
instrument), the latter associated with
dance in many familiar sayings, of which
Hart gives a number. The fact that *canary*
means both a wine and a dance (2.2.58
and n.) reinforces the quibble. By *make him
dance* Ford means 'beat him'. NCS makes
the quibbling more elaborate than it is.

MISTRESS PAGE Quickly, quickly! Is the buck-basket—

MISTRESS FORD I warrant. What, Robert, I say!

    Enter John and Robert with a great buck-basket

MISTRESS PAGE Come, come, come.

MISTRESS FORD Here, set it down.

MISTRESS PAGE Give your men the charge. We must be
brief.

MISTRESS FORD Marry, as I told you before, John and
Robert, be ready here hard by in the brew-house, and
when I suddenly call you, come forth, and without any   10
pause or staggering take this basket on your shoulders.
That done, trudge with it in all haste, and carry it
among the whitsters in Datchet Mead, and there empty
it in the muddy ditch close by the Thames side.

MISTRESS PAGE *(to John and Robert)* You will do it?

MISTRESS FORD I ha' told them over and over, they lack no
direction.—Be gone, and come when you are called.

                         Exeunt John and Robert

    Enter Robin

MISTRESS PAGE Here comes little Robin.

MISTRESS FORD How now, my eyas-musket, what news
with you?   20

ROBIN My master, Sir John, is come in at your back door,
Mistress Ford, and requests your company.

MISTRESS PAGE You little Jack-a-Lent, have you been true
to us?

---

3 Robert] BOWERS; *Robin* F   3.1] *as* OLIVER *(after* Q *at* 3.3.0.1)   13 Datchet] ROWE; *Dotchet* F
15 *to John and Robert*] OXFORD; *not in* F   17.1] *as* JOHNSON; *Exit seruant.* Q; *not in* F
17.2] ROWE; *not in* F

3.3.2 **buck-basket** basket for clothes going
   to be washed. To *buck* clothes is to wash
   them, sometimes in the specific sense to
   bleach them in an alkaline solution (e.g.
   of ashes and water). The word's origin is
   obscure: perhaps the bleaching-tub was
   so called. The noun *buck* came to be used
   of the clothes themselves (*OED buck v.*[1],
   sb.[3] 3).

3 **Robert** F's '*Robin*' is an error caused by
   the proximity of Robin's name in the
   'massed entry'.

9 **brew-house** outhouse where the household's liquor was brewed

11 **staggering** In conjunction with *pause*, the
   sense is primarily figurative (*OED vbl. sb.*
   1c: 'wavering, vacillating'), though *OED*

gives this passage under 1a: 'reeling'.
The literal sense is of course humorously
included because of the weight that will
be in the basket, as the audience immediately guesses.

12 **trudge** walk resolutely

13 **whitsters** bleachers (i.e. whiteners) of
   clothes
   Datchet Mead the meadow between
   Windsor Little Park and the Thames

19 **eyas-musket** young male sparrow-hawk
   taken from the nest to be trained for
   hawking; figuratively, sprightly child. A
   musket is a male sparrow-hawk; 'an eyas'
   derives from 'a nyas', which is from Latin
   nidus, a nest.

23 **Jack-a-Lent** puppet (here figurative and

ROBIN Ay, I'll be sworn. My master knows not of your
being here, and hath threatened to put me into everlasting liberty if I tell you of it; for he swears he'll turn me
away.

MISTRESS PAGE Thou'rt a good boy. This secrecy of thine
shall be a tailor to thee and shall make thee a new   30
doublet and hose.—I'll go hide me.

MISTRESS FORD Do so.   ⌈*Exit Mistress Page*⌉
(*To Robin*) Go tell thy master I am alone.   *Exit Robin*
Mistress Page, remember you your cue.

MISTRESS PAGE ⌈*within*⌉ I warrant thee. If I do not act it,
hiss me.

MISTRESS FORD Go to, then.—We'll use this unwholesome
humidity, this gross watery pumpkin. We'll teach him
to know turtles from jays.

     Enter Falstaff

FALSTAFF Have I caught thee, my heavenly jewel? Why,   40

32 *Exit Mistress Page*] This edition; ROWE (*after* 36); NCS (*after* 39); *not in* F   33 *Exit Robin*]
NCS; ROWE (*after* 34); *not in* F   34 cue] F (*Qu*)   35 *within*] This edition; *not in* F   38
pumpkin] F (Pumpion)   39.1] Q (*Enter Sir John.*); *not in* F   40 caught thee,] F; caught Q

affectionate). A Jack-a-Lent was a dummy
figure set up to be pelted as a sport during
Lent. Nashe writes of Gabriel Harvey,
'For his stature, he is such another pretty
Jack-a-Lent as boys throw at in the street'
(*Have with you to Saffron-Walden*, 1596,
Works, iii. 94). Shakespeare may echo
Nashe here and in Ford's phrase (also
describing Robin) *this pretty weathercock*,
3.2.15.

26-7 **put me into everlasting liberty** This
looks like one of the ridiculous mistakes of
Shakespeare's clowns (compare Dogberry's 'everlasting redemption', *Much
Ado* 4.2.54-5), so Robin's witty explanation comes as a surprise.

34 **Mistress Page ... cue** The fact that Mistress Ford addresses Mistress Page by
name indicates that the latter is off-
stage.

37 **use** treat (*OED v.* 17a). The verb in this
sense is always followed by an adverb or
adverbial clause; *OED* offers no parallel
to this passage. Some such words as 'as
he deserves' have to be understood, unless the punctuation is changed to indicate an unfinished statement.

38 **pumpkin** F's form of the word, 'Pum-

pion', reappears in another of its forms in
the phrase '*Pompion* the great' (*LLL*
5.2.502), where it is Costard's mistake
for 'Pompey the Great'. In the present
context the capital P is without significance.

39 **turtles   from   jays** turtle-doves
(proverbially faithful) from jays (brightly
coloured, and hence morally suspect;
compare *Cymbeline* 3.4.49-50 'some jay
of Italy, | Whose mother was her paint-
ing').

40 **Have ... jewel?** An adapted quotation, of
the opening line of the Second Song in
Sidney's *Astrophil and Stella*: 'Have I
caught my heavenly jewel | Teaching
sleep more fair to be? | Now will I teach
her that she, | When she wakes, is too too
cruel.' The remainder of the song describes stealing a kiss. Q, and some editors, give the phrase as in the poem, but
this unprofitably draws attention to the
incompleteness of the sense, whereas F's
adaptation creates a different sense (as in
Lear's words to Cordelia, 'Have I caught
thee?' *Lear* 5.3.21). 'My heavenly jewel'
means 'my star' (i.e. in the original,
Stella).

now let me die, for I have lived long enough. This is the
period of my ambition. O this blessèd hour!

MISTRESS FORD O sweet Sir John!

FALSTAFF Mistress Ford, I cannot cog, I cannot prate,
Mistress Ford. Now shall I sin in my wish: I would thy
husband were dead. I'll speak it before the best lord, I
would make thee my lady.

MISTRESS FORD I your lady, Sir John? Alas, I should be a
pitiful lady.

FALSTAFF Let the court of France show me such another. I   50
see how thine eye would emulate the diamond. Thou
hast the right arched beauty of the brow that becomes
the ship-tire, the tire-valiant, or any tire of Venetian
admittance.

MISTRESS FORD A plain kerchief, Sir John. My brows
become nothing else, nor that well neither.

FALSTAFF By the Lord, thou art a tyrant to say so. Thou
wouldst make an absolute courtier, and the firm fixture
of thy foot would give an excellent motion to thy gait in
a semicircled farthingale. I see what thou wert if   60

53 tire-valiant] F (Tyre-valiant); tire vellet Q; tire-volant STEEVENS 1773 *conj.*   57 By the
Lord, thou art a tyrant] COLLIER; Thou art a tyrant F; By the Lord thou art a traitor Q   60–1
if Fortune … friend] This edition; if Fortune thy foe, were not Nature thy friend F1; if Fortune
thy foe were not, Nature thy friend F2; if fortune thy foe, were but nature thy friend STAUNTON
conj.; if Fortune thy foe were, not Nature, thy friend ALEXANDER; if fortune, thy foe, were, with
nature, thy friend OXFORD

42 **period** conclusion (literally, full stop)

44 **Cog** fawn, wheedle (*OED*) *v.*¹ 5)

52 **becomes** suits

53 **ship-tire** A *tire* (*OED sb.*¹ 3, derived from
'attire') was an ornamental head-dress
worn by women. Bartholomew Young's
translation (1598) of Montemayor's
Diana describes one composed of 'two
little ships made of emeralds, with all the
shrouds and tackling of clear sapphires'
(Wheatley).

tire-valiant Not in *OED*, nor elsewhere in
Shakespeare, who always uses *valiant* in
the usual sense. Onions glosses 'fanciful
headdress', the generally accepted meaning.

53–4 **of Venetian admittance** accepted (as
fashionable) in Venice. 'Italian fashions
were the rage at court at the close of
Elizabeth's reign' (Hart, with supporting
quotations).

57 **By the Lord** The oath, characteristic of

Falstaff in *1 Henry IV* (six times) and *2
Henry IV* (twice), is in Q but not in F
(where it was probably expurgated).

57 **a tyrant** i.e. cruel. Shakespeare has many
such figurative uses of *tyrant*. Q's reading
'traitor' may derive from Falstaff's 'By
the Lord, I'll be a traitor, then, when thou
art king' in *1 Henry IV* 1.2.144–5. NCS
unnecessarily suggests a pun on 'tire'.

58 **absolute** perfect
courtier The word was used of either sex
(*OED*).

58–9 **the firm fixture of thy foot** i.e. the
confident way in which you tread. This
use of *fixture* (in Falstaff's affected style) is
unique in Shakespeare, and *OED* offers
no parallel.

60 **semicircled farthingale** A farthingale (skirt
made to project by a framework of hoops
beneath it) could be either circular or
semicircular (i.e. hooped at the back only).

60–1 **if Fortune … friend** if Fortune were

Fortune thy foe were Nature thy friend. Come, thou
canst not hide it.

MISTRESS FORD Believe me, there's no such thing in me.

FALSTAFF What made me love thee? Let that persuade
thee there's something extraordinary in thee. Come, I
cannot cog and say thou art this and that, like a many
of these lisping hawthorn-buds that come like women in
men's apparel and smell like Bucklersbury in simple-
time; I cannot. But I love thee, none but thee; and thou
deserv'st it.   70

MISTRESS FORD Do not betray me, sir. I fear you love
Mistress Page.

FALSTAFF Thou mightst as well say I love to walk by the
Counter gate, which is as hateful to me as the reek of a
lime-kiln.

MISTRESS FORD Well, heaven knows how I love you, and
you shall one day find it.

FALSTAFF Keep in that mind; I'll deserve it.

---

65 thee there's] Q (thee | Ther's); thee. Ther's F   75 lime-kiln] F (Lime-kill), Q (lime kill)

Nature, and therefore not your foe but
your friend. 'Fortune my foe, why dost
thou frown on me?' was the first line of a
popular song, the tune of which came to
be known by the first three words; many
ballads were sung to it. Compare the
allusion in *Henry V* 3.6.37, 'Fortune is
Bardolph's foe, and frowns on him.' The
'not' of F is taken in this edition to be an
erroneous insertion made either because
the next word is 'nature' or because 'not'
occurs in the next sentence. Previous
editorial attempts to justify its retention
involve understanding 'not', unjustifi-
ably, as 'as well as'. Fortune is called
Mistress Ford's foe because she is only a
citizen's wife, Nature her friend because
she is handsome. Compare the opening
sentence of Lyly's *Euphues*: 'There dwelt
in Athens a young gentleman of great
patrimony and of so comely a personage
that it was doubted whether he were
more bound to Nature for the lineaments
of his person or to Fortune for the increase of his possessions.'

67 **lisping** Always used by Shakespeare in

contexts implying the affectation (specially by lovers) of this defect of speech. The
idea may originate in Chaucer's Friar
(*Canterbury Tales*, General Prologue, I(A).
264–5);

67 **hawthorn-buds** i.e. young perfumed fops.
The hawthorn blossom, a sign of spring
(*Dream* 1.1.185), was traditionally gath-
ered on May Day.

68 **Bucklersbury** a street off Cheapside in the
City of London, inhabited by grocers and
apothecaries who sold *simples* (medicinal
herbs and the medicaments made from
them); supplies would be at their height
at midsummer.

71 **betray** deceive

74 **Counter gate** the gate of the Counter or
Compter, a debtor's prison in Southwark,
on the south side of the Thames: probably specific here, though *counter* was
also generally used as a synonym for
'prison', and there were other prisons so
called (in the Poultry, in Bread Street,
and in Wood Street) in the City. Prisons
were notoriously ill-smelling.
reek smoke

MISTRESS FORD Nay, I must tell you, so you do, or else I
could not be in that mind.   80
    Enter Robin
ROBIN Mistress Ford, Mistress Ford! Here's Mistress Page
at the door, sweating and blowing and looking wildly,
and would needs speak with you presently.
FALSTAFF She shall not see me. I will ensconce me behind
the arras.
MISTRESS FORD Pray you, do so; she's a very tattling
woman.
    Falstaff hides himself behind the arras.
    Enter Mistress Page
What's the matter? How now?
MISTRESS PAGE O Mistress Ford, what have you done?
You're shamed, you're overthrown, you're undone for   90
ever.
MISTRESS FORD What's the matter, good Mistress Page?
MISTRESS PAGE O well-a-day, Mistress Ford, having an
honest man to your husband, to give him such cause of
suspicion!
MISTRESS FORD What cause of suspicion?
MISTRESS PAGE What cause of suspicion! Out upon you!
How am I mistook in you!
MISTRESS FORD Why, alas, what's the matter?
MISTRESS PAGE Your husband's coming hither, woman,   100
with all the officers in Windsor, to search for a gentleman that he says is here now in the house, by your
consent, to take an ill advantage of his absence. You are
undone.
MISTRESS FORD 'Tis not so, I hope.
MISTRESS PAGE Pray heaven it be not so that you have
such a man here! But 'tis most certain your husband's
coming, with half Windsor at his heels, to search for
such a one. I come before to tell you. If you know

80.1] CAPELL; *not in* F   87.1] *as* Q (*Falstaffe stands behind the aras.*); *not in* F   87.2] Q (*placed
before* 87.1); *not in* F   102–3 house, by your consent, to] POPE; house; by your consent to F

83 **presently** immediately
84 **ensconce me** hide myself, take shelter
85 **arras** tapestry, woven with scenes and
    figures, and hung as a screen in front of

the wall and at some distance from it.
Falstaff hides behind the arras, and falls
asleep there, in *1 Henry IV* 2.4.506, 534.

yourself clear, why, I am glad of it; but if you have a   110
friend here, convey, convey him out. Be not amazed,
call all your senses to you, defend your reputation, or
bid farewell to your good life for ever.

MISTRESS FORD What shall I do? There is a gentleman, my
dear friend; and I fear not mine own shame so much as
his peril. I had rather than a thousand pound he were
out of the house.

MISTRESS PAGE For shame, never stand 'you had rather'
and 'you had rather'! Your husband's here at hand.
Bethink you of some conveyance. In the house you   120
cannot hide him.—O, how have you deceived me!—
Look, here is a basket. If he be of any reasonable stature,
he may creep in here; and throw foul linen upon him,
as if it were going to bucking. Or it is whiting-time—
send him by your two men to Datchet Mead.

MISTRESS FORD He's too big to go in there. What shall I do?
        Falstaff rushes out of hiding

FALSTAFF Let me see't, let me see't. O, let me see't! I'll in,
I'll in. Follow your friend's counsel. I'll in.

MISTRESS PAGE What, Sir John Falstaff! (*Aside to him*) Are
these your letters, knight?   130

FALSTAFF (*aside to Mistress Page*) I love thee, and none but
thee. Help me away. Let me creep in here. I'll never—
        He gets into the basket; they cover him with dirty linen

MISTRESS PAGE (*to Robin*) Help to cover your master,

126.1] *as* CAPELL.; *not in* F   129 *Aside to him*] Q (*Aside.*); *not in* F   131 *aside to Mistress Page*]
HIBBARD, *conj.* Malone; *not in* F   131–2 thee, and none but thee] Q; thee F   132.1] *as* Q
(*Sir Iohn goes into the basket, they put cloathes ouer him, the two men carries it away: Foord meetes it,
and all the rest, Page, Doctor, Priest, Slender, Shallow.*); *not in* F   133 *to Robin*] HIBBARD;
not in F

110 **clear** innocent
111 **friend** lover (*OED sb.* 4)
      amazed bewildered
113 **good life** good name
118 **stand** 'lose time (saying)'; literally 're-
      main or stay (to do something)', and
      always used with an infinitive elsewhere,
      e.g. *Two Gentlemen* 5.2.42, 'stand not to
      discourse'.
124 **whiting-time** bleaching-time
130 **your letters** Not an accusation that he
      has written love-letters to them both, but
      an accusation that he has written a love-
      letter to her and is now here courting

Mistress Ford. The plural is intensive and
expresses indignation.
131–2 **I love ... but thee** Falstaff has already
      told Mistress Ford 'I love thee, none but
      thee' (l. 69). His use of the same words to
      Mistress Page underlines the comedy of
      the situation. Q has the words in both
      places. Oliver suggests that Q's second
      use of them is the result of confusion with
      the first; but more probably F has omitted
      part of them on the second occasion
      because of eye-skip caused by the recur-
      rence of *thee*.

boy.—Call your men, Mistress Ford. (*Aside to Falstaff*)
You dissembling knight!   ⌐*Exit Robin*⌐
MISTRESS FORD What, John! Robert! John!
 Enter John and Robert
Go, take up these clothes here quickly. Where's the
cowl-staff? (*John and Robert fit the cowl-staff*) Look how
you drumble! Carry them to the laundress in Datchet
Mead. Quickly, come!   140
 They lift the basket and start to leave.
 Enter Ford, Page, Caius, and Evans
FORD (*to his companions*) Pray you, come near. If I sus-
pect without cause, why then make sport at me, then let
me be your jest, I deserve it. (*To John and Robert*) How
now? Whither bear you this?
⌐JOHN⌐ To the laundress, forsooth.
MISTRESS FORD Why, what have you to do whither they
bear it? You were best meddle with buck-washing!
FORD Buck? I would I could wash myself of the buck!
Buck, buck, buck! Ay, buck! I warrant you, buck—and
of the season too, it shall appear.   150
  Exeunt John and Robert with the basket
Gentlemen, I have dreamed tonight. I'll tell you my
dream. Here, here; here be my keys. Ascend my

---

134 *Aside to Falstaff*] HIBBARD; *not in* F 135 *Exit Robin*] *as* CAPELL; *at* 150.1 OLIVER; *not in* F
138 *John ... cowlstaff*] *as* NCS; *not in* F 140.1] OXFORD; *not in* F 140.2] ROWE; *not in* F
141 *to his companions*] HIBBARD; *not in* F 143 *To John and Robert*] HIBBARD; *not in* F
145 JOHN] OLIVER; *Ser.* F 150.1] *as* ROWE; *not in* F

---

135 The exit of Robin (who does not appear
 in Q's version of the scene) is better placed
 here than at l. 150.1, which may associate him too obviously with the basket's
 contents.
138 **cowl-staff** wooden pole passed through
 the handles of a *cowl* (tub) or other heavy
 object so that two men could take its
 weight on their shoulders.
139 **drumble** dawdle, move slowly. Only
 here in Shakespeare, but several times in
 Nashe (quoted by Hart).
146 **what have you to do** what business is it
 of yours? *You* is to be stressed in this
 sentence and in the following one.
147 **You were best meddle** A proper thing it
 is for you to meddle (ironical).
148 **Buck** (*a*) washing, (*b*) the male of the
 fallow deer

150 **of the season** in the rutting season, i.e.
 when bucks' antlers, shed and renewed
 every year, have reached their maximum
 growth. Ford means that when his wife's
 lover is discovered, he himself will be a
 manifest cuckold. Attempts to apply the
 passage to Falstaff's fatness or lecherous-
 ness are mistaken.
151 **tonight** this (past) night
152 **Here, here: here be my keys** Ford thinks
 of handing over his keys so that his
 companions can search the upper rooms;
 but when he has locked the door by
 which they entered (and by which Falstaff has just left in the basket) he leads
 the upstairs search, his keys still in his
 hand. In the early 20th-c. productions of
 H. Beerbohm Tree and W. Bridges-
 Adams, Ford tore the keys from Mistress

chambers. Search, seek, find out. I'll warrant we'll unkennel the fox. Let me stop this way first.

He locks the door

So; now escape.

PAGE Good Master Ford, be contented. You wrong your-self too much.

FORD True, Master Page.—Up, gentlemen, you shall see sport anon. Follow me, gentlemen.　　　　*Exit*

EVANS This is fery fantastical humours and jealousies.　　160

CAIUS By gar, 'tis no the fashion of France. It is not jealous in France.

PAGE Nay, follow him, gentlemen; see the issue of his search.　　　*Exeunt Caius and Evans, followed by Page*

154.1] *as* CAPELL; *not in* F　155 escape] DALY; vncape F; uncouple HANMER; uncope NCS; uncase SISSON; uncoop OXFORD　159 *Exit*] CAPELL; *not in* F　164 *Exeunt ... Page*] This edition; *Exit omnes* Q (*after its version of* 160, *having nothing corresponding to* F's 161–4); *Exeunt* F2 (*after* 162); *Exeunt Page, Caius, and Evans* CAPELL; *not in* F1

Ford's belt. 'He was thereby asserting his right to the keys, his house, and his wife' and also 'enacting a symbolic divorce'. After his futile search 'Ford tried to return the keys . . . The first time he offered them Mistress Ford pretended to burst into tears and Mistress Page comforted her. The second time Mistress Page joined her in tears and Ford threw the keys down in anger. The wives were adding discomfort to Ford's failure.' (Peter L. Evans, 'The Stage History of *The Merry Wives Of Windsor*, 1874–1933', University of London (M.Phil.), 1981, p. 246.) This stage action perhaps extracts too much significance from the keys, and may hamper the comic irony of Ford's locking the door and apostrophizing the departed Falstaff with 'So; now escape.'

154 **unkennel** The hunting term for dislodg-ing a fox from cover: *OED v.* 1, citing Turberville (1575).

155 **So** A frequent interjection after perform-ing an action; equivalent in meaning to 'There, that's done.'
　escape i.e. escape if you can. F's 'vncape' has been generally doubted: *OED* has no other example, and glosses it as 'of ob-scure meaning'. In Shakespeare a cape is part of a garment (*OED sb.*² 2), not a synonym for a cloak. Several emenda-tions beginning with *un-* have been pro-posed. Hanmer's 'uncouple' is appropri-

ate to hunting and is Shakespearian (*Dream* 4.1.106), but its sense 'unleash the hounds' is not altogether apt when Ford and his friends are themselves the hounds. Sisson's 'uncase', whether ad-dressed to Falstaff (= disclose, reveal yourself) or to the others (= strip his disguise away), involves in either case a rather strained use of the word. Little can be said in favour of NCS's highly figura-tive nonce-word 'uncope' (= unstitch the lips of a ferret). Oxford's 'uncoop' (assum-ing 'vncope' in the copy) is open to the objection that it is close in meaning to 'unkennel' without being so apt: hens and geese are cooped as a defence against foxes. Hibbard's *escape* (anticipated by Daly) follows very naturally from the action of locking the door, is rich in dramatic irony because Falstaff has that moment left the house, and is explicable if the compositor is supposed to have been led into error by the 'un' of 'unkennel', which he had set at exactly the same place in the immediately preceding line.

156 **be contented** restrain yourself; compare *Lear* 3.4.104.

157 **too much** extremely; compare *Romeo* 1.5.96. For 'wrong yourself', compare l. 195 and 1.1.288–9.

158 **True** Not a meaningful acquiescence in Page's statement, either directly or ironic-ally, but a casual and inattentive acknow-ledgement that Page has spoken to him.

MISTRESS PAGE Is there not a double excellency in this?

MISTRESS FORD I know not which pleases me better—that my husband is deceived, or Sir John.

MISTRESS PAGE What a taking was he in when your husband asked what was in the basket!

MISTRESS FORD I am half afraid he will have need of   170
washing, so throwing him into the water will do him a benefit.

MISTRESS PAGE Hang him, dishonest rascal! I would all of the same strain were in the same distress.

MISTRESS FORD I think my husband hath some special suspicion of Falstaff's being here, for I never saw him so gross in his jealousy till now.

MISTRESS PAGE I will lay a plot to try that, and we will yet have more tricks with Falstaff. His dissolute disease will scarce obey this medicine.   180

MISTRESS FORD Shall we send that foolish carrion Mistress Quickly to him, and excuse his throwing into the water, and give him another hope, to betray him to another punishment?

MISTRESS PAGE We will do it. Let him be sent for tomorrow eight o'clock, to have amends.

Enter Ford, Page, Caius, and Evans

FORD I cannot find him. Maybe the knave bragged of that he could not compass.

MISTRESS PAGE *(aside to Mistress Ford)* Heard you that?

169 what] HARNESS; who F   186.1] CAPELL; *Enter all.* Q; *not in* F

168 **What a taking was he in** what a state (i.e. of agitation) he must have been in (*OED taking*, *vbl. sb.* 4b)

169 **what** Comparison with 3.5.94 confirms Harness's emendation. Common sense must reject F's reading as a natural error caused by the scribe's or compositor's knowledge that Falstaff was in the basket (compare 4.2.180 for a similar error). Ford's question (ll. 143–4) was not strictly this, but amounted to 'What's this basket doing, then?' To have asked what was inside it would have come too close to expressing suspicion about its contents, which might have made the audience wonder why he did not investigate it further.

170–1 **he will have need of washing** he will

have befouled himself in his fright

174 **strain** nature (i.e. dissoluteness)

181 **foolish carrion** *carrion* is not violently pejorative (as used by Capulet to Juliet, *Romeo* 3.5.156) but is humorously adapted from the first verse of Psalm 53 in the Book of Common Prayer (1559): 'The foolish body hath said in his heart, "There is no God."'

185–6 **tomorrow eight o'clock** Shakespeare has no other instance of 'tomorrow' followed directly by an hour, but the idiom is like 'tomorrow midnight' (*Dream* 4.1.87) and 'by tomorrow dinner-time' (*1 Henry IV* 2.5.521).

187 **that** that which

188 **compass** accomplish

MISTRESS FORD You use me well, Master Ford, do you not?   190
FORD Ay, I do so.
MISTRESS FORD Heaven make you better than your thoughts!
FORD Amen!
MISTRESS PAGE You do yourself mighty wrong, Master Ford.
FORD Ay, ay, I must bear it.
EVANS If there be anypody in the house, and in the chambers, and in the coffers, and in the presses, heaven forgive my sins at the day of judgement!   200
CAIUS By gar, nor I too. There is nobodies.
PAGE Fie, fie, Master Ford, are you not ashamed? What spirit, what devil suggests this imagination? I would not ha' your distemper in this kind for the wealth of Windsor Castle.
FORD 'Tis my fault, Master Page. I suffer for it.
EVANS You suffer for a pad conscience. Your wife is as honest a 'omans as I will desires among five thousand, and five hundred too.

190 You use me well, Master Ford, do you not?] This edition; You vse me well, M. *Ford*? Do you? F; You serue me well, do you not? Q (*attaching the line to its version of Evans's speech*, 198–200)   191 Ay, I do so] F (I, I do so); Ay, ay: do, do This edition *conj.*   192 you] F; me OXFORD (*conj.* Capell)

190–1 **You use ... do so** This exchange, as given in F, though never emended, presents difficulty. Mistress Ford's question is obviously indignant, and therefore ironical, so one would expect 'do you not?' instead of 'do you?' (compare *Sir Thomas More* 4.1.290–1: 'Fie, fellow Luggins, you serve us handsomely, do ye not, think you?'). Q gives the line in the form 'You serve [i.e. treat] me well, do you not?' but tacks it on to a speech of Evans's instead of giving it to Mistress Ford. Ford's reply in F (he makes none in Q) also seems to need emending. As it stands, it is either impenitent (and therefore inconsistent with his apologetic expressions at ll. 206 and 213–15) or, if penitent, ironical in expression (and therefore inappropriate as a reply to irony). For 'do, do' (i.e. 'That's right, lay it on!') compare *Troilus* 2.1.55–6 'Do, rudeness! Do, camel, do, do!' (Thersites, being beaten by Ajax), and compare Ford's reply to Mistress Page, l. 197.

192–3 **Heaven ... thoughts!** i.e. May heaven make you a good man and rid you of these evil thoughts of yours! Capell's conjecture 'me' for F's 'you' is open to objection because it makes Mistress Ford admit that she might be made better than she is, and because it makes Ford's reply a criticism of her and not of himself.
197 **bear it** i.e. endure your just reproach
199 **presses** cupboards
199–200 **heaven ... judgement!** As usual with Evans, 'his meaning is good'. Caius's confirmation, 'nor I too', is splendidly independent of syntactical coherence with Evans's speech and with itself.
203 **spirit** here synonymous with *devil*; compare 1 *Henry IV* 2.5.371–2, where both are synonymous with 'fiend'.
     suggests this imagination prompts this delusion; *OED suggest v.* 1 (especially of insinuating or prompting to evil).
206 **fault** weakness; compare *Troilus* 4.5.102: 'it is my vice, my fault.'
208 **as I will desires** Evans means 'as I shall

CAIUS By gar, I see 'tis an honest woman.   210

FORD Well, I promised you a dinner. Come, come walk in
  the Park. I pray you pardon me. I will hereafter make
  known to you why I have done this.—Come, wife,
  come, Mistress Page, I pray you pardon me. Pray
  heartily pardon me.

PAGE (*to Caius and Evans*) Let's go in, gentlemen; but
  trust me, we'll mock him. (*To Ford, Caius, and Evans*) I
  do invite you tomorrow morning to my house to
  breakfast. After, we'll a-birding together. I have a fine
  hawk for the bush. Shall it be so?   220

FORD Anything.

EVANS If there is one, I shall make two in the company.

CAIUS If there be one or two, I shall make-a the turd.

FORD Pray you go, Master Page.

                          Exeunt all but Evans and Caius

EVANS I pray you now, remembrance tomorrow on the
  lousy knave mine host.

CAIUS Dat is good, by gar; with all my heart.

EVANS A lousy knave, to have his gibes and his mockeries!

                                                        Exeunt

---

215 heartily] F (hartly); heartly OLIVER   pardon me] F; NCS *adds stage direction* 'Mistress Ford
and Mistress Page go to prepare dinner.'   216 to Caius and Evans] OXFORD; *not in* F   Let's go
in] F; Let's go This edition *conj.*   216–17 but ... him] F; *as aside* OLIVER   217 To Ford,
Caius, and Evans] OXFORD; *not in* F   224.1] HIBBARD; Exit with Page OLIVER, *as* NCS; *not in* F

desire to find', but in the context he
makes the unintentional suggestion that
he desires Mistress Ford sexually. Compare 4.1.65–6.

211–12 **walk in the Park** i.e. until dinner-
time

213–14 **Come, wife, come, Mistress Page**
Come is here persuasive: compare *Much
Ado* 5.4.84 ('Come, cousin, I am sure you
love the gentleman'). Similarly, in
'Come, come walk in the Park', the sense
of the first 'come' is persuasive.

216 **Let's go in** This proposal, coming immediately after Ford's suggestion that they
walk in the Park before dinner, is unusual. Oliver correctly notes that to leave
the stage was called 'going in'; but
Shakespeare does not incongruously use
the language of stage directions in his
dialogue. His usual meaning in 'go in' is
illustrated in 3.4.91 (i.e. go indoors). The
NCS editors interpret Page's proposal as

'Let's accept the invitation', which is
reasonable in view of the fact that an
embarrassing situation has arisen since
they first agreed to go to dinner at Ford's.
But 'in' may be an error of the scribe or
the compositor, perhaps caused by the
presence of 'invite' in the next line.

219 **a-birding** shooting small birds with a
small gun or 'birding-piece' (4.2.50), as
distinct from shooting wild ducks and
geese with a larger fowling-piece. The
hawk for the bush was employed to drive
the birds into the leafless bushes (birding
was a sport of late winter or early spring)
where they could be shot by the
marksmen. Hart gives illustrative quotations.

222 **make two** 'Evans's attempt to pick up
the English idiom "make one"' (Hart).

225–8 **I pray you ... mockeries** This dialogue serves as a reminder of 3.1.107–15
and a foreshadowing of 4.3 and of
4.5.60–86.

3.4   *Enter Fenton and Anne Page*

FENTON

I see I cannot get thy father's love;

Therefore no more turn me to him, sweet Nan.

ANNE

Alas, how then?

FENTON   Why, thou must be thyself.

He doth object I am too great of birth,

And that, my state being galled with my expense,

I seek to heal it only by his wealth.

Besides, these other bars he lays before me—

My riots past, my wild societies;

And tells me 'tis a thing impossible

I should love thee but as a property.   10

ANNE

Maybe he tells you true.

FENTON

No, heaven so speed me in my time to come!

Albeit I will confess thy father's wealth

Was the first motive that I wooed thee, Anne,

Yet, wooing thee, I found thee of more value

Than stamps in gold or sums in sealèd bags.

And 'tis the very riches of thyself

That now I aim at.

ANNE   Gentle Master Fenton,

Yet seek my father's love, still seek it, sir.

If opportunity and humblest suit   20

3.4] F (*Scæna Quarta.*)   0.1] ROWE;   *Enter Fenton, Anne, Page, Shallow, Slender, Quickly, Page, Mist. Page.* F;   *Enter M. Fenton, Page, and mistresse Quickly.* Q   7 Besides, these other] This edition, *conj.* Walker; Besides these, other F   12 FENTON.] Q3; *not in* F   heaven] F; God OXFORD *conj.*   20 opportunity] F; importunity HANMER

3.4 Q substitutes its version of this scene for F's 4.1, and at this point moves straight on to F's 3.5.

2 **turn** refer

5 **state** estate
   galled made sore with chafing

7 **bars** impediments

8 **societies** companionships

10 **property** mere means to an end (*OED sb.* 4)

12 **heaven** Since there are no comparable

instances in Shakespeare of 'as God' (or 'as heaven') 'shall speed (i.e. prosper) me', there is no strong case for supposing expurgation in F here. The greeting 'God speed you' is not comparable.

16 **stamps in gold** pieces of gold stamped as coin of the realm (*OED stamps sb.* 15)

20 **opportunity and humblest suit** the most humble suit, made at the most favourable opportunity

Cannot attain it, why then—hark you hither.

They talk aside.

Enter Shallow, Slender, and Mistress Quickly

SHALLOW Break their talk, Mistress Quickly. My kinsman shall speak for himself.

SLENDER I'll make a shaft or a bolt on't. 'Slid, 'tis but venturing.

SHALLOW Be not dismayed.

SLENDER No, she shall not dismay me. I care not for that, but that I am afeard.

MISTRESS QUICKLY (*to Anne*) Hark ye, Master Slender would speak a word with you.   30

ANNE

I come to him. (*Aside to Fenton*) This is my father's choice.

O, what a world of vile ill-favoured faults

Looks handsome in three hundred pounds a year!

MISTRESS QUICKLY And how does good Master Fenton? Pray you, a word with you.

She draws Fenton aside

SHALLOW She's coming. To her, coz. O boy, thou hadst a father!

SLENDER I had a father, Mistress Anne. My uncle can tell you good jests of him.—Pray you, uncle, tell Mistress Anne the jest how my father stole two geese out of a   40 pen, good uncle.

SHALLOW Mistress Anne, my cousin loves you.

SLENDER Ay, that I do, as well as I love any woman in Gloucestershire.

21 why then—hark] THEOBALD; why then harke F   21.1] ROWE; *not in* F   21.2] *as* THEOBALD; *Enter M. Page his wife, M. Shallow, and Slender.* Q; *Enter Justice Shallow, Master Slender richly dressed, and Mistress Quickly* OXFORD; *not in* F   31 *Aside to Fenton*] *as* NCS; *Aside* CAPELL; *not in* F   35.1] *as* CAPELL; *not in* F

21 **hark you hither** Anne says this on seeing the approach of Shallow and the rest, who have therefore either entered at some time during her speech or are to be supposed visible to her through the stage doorway (as in 3.1.26–32) and entering as the lovers move to one side of the stage.

24 **I'll make ... on't** I'll do it (i.e. make my proposal of marriage) one way or another. Proverbial (Tilley S264). A *shaft* is the longer and slenderer arrow used in the longbow, a *bolt* the shorter and thicker one used in the crossbow.

24 **'Slid** by God's lid (i.e. eyelid)

26 **dismayed** frightened; hence the absurdity of Slender's reply.

36–7 **thou hadst a father!** an exhortation, which Slender mistakes for a prompt

40–1 **how ... pen** The anecdotes in jestbooks usually have headings beginning with *How* in this manner.

SHALLOW He will maintain you like a gentlewoman.

SLENDER Ay, that I will, come cut and long-tail, under the
degree of a squire.

SHALLOW He will make you a hundred and fifty pounds
jointure.

ANNE Good Master Shallow, let him woo for himself.   50

SHALLOW Marry, I thank you for it; I thank you for that
good comfort.—She calls you, coz. I'll leave you.

    He walks aside

ANNE Now, Master Slender.

SLENDER Now, good Mistress Anne.

ANNE What is your will?

SLENDER My will? 'Od's heartlings, that's a pretty jest
indeed! I ne'er made my will yet, I thank God. I am not
such a sickly creature, I give God praise.

ANNE I mean, Master Slender, what would you with me?

SLENDER Truly, for mine own part, I would little or   60
nothing with you. Your father and my uncle hath made
motions. If it be my luck, so; if not, happy man be his
dole! They can tell you how things go better than I can.

    Enter Page and Mistress Page

You may ask your father; here he comes.

52.1 *He ... aside*] *as* NCS; *not in* F   58, 59 God] OXFORD; Heauen F   63.1] ROWE (*after* 64);
not in F

46–7 **come ... squire** i.e. as well as anyone
else of a squire's rank can do, whoever he
may be. 'Come cut and long-tail' is
proverbial (Tilley C938) for comprehen-
siveness, because every dog and horse
must have either a full-length tail or a
docked one. *Under* (*OED prep.* 16) is 'in
accordance with'.

49 **jointure** The jointure was the part of the
husband's estate which he settled on his
wife in the marriage-contract. It provided
for her income if she were widowed. If
Slender has £300 a year he probably has
capital assets worth about £6,000. The
common-law entitlement of a widow was
one-third of her late husband's total
estate. Slender's widow would be entitled
to an income of £100 a year, so a jointure
bringing in £150 a year is generous.

52 **She calls you** Evidently Slender has wan-
dered away from Anne after urging Shallow to tell the jest about his father.

53 **Now** a greeting. Compare *Caesar*
2.2.120: 'Now, Cinna. Now, Metellus.'
This draws attention to the fact that
though Slender has addressed one speech
directly to her he has not yet entered into
conversation with her.

56 **'Od's heartlings** a euphemistic form of
the oath 'by God's heart'

57, 58 **God** F's 'Heaven' is probably an
expurgation; compare 2.2.291.

62 **motions** proposals

62–3 **happy man be his dole** Proverbial
(Tilley M158), meaning 'May his fortune
(*OED dole sb.*[1] 4) be to be a happy (i.e.
lucky) man.' Used three other times in
Shakespeare (*Shrew* 1.1.138; *Winter's
Tale* 1.2.164; *1 Henry IV* 2.2.74), with a
general sense, i.e. 'Good luck!' Slender
may mean 'Good luck to the man who
wins you' (Hibbard), but may equally
well mean nothing in particular.

PAGE

    Now, Master Slender.—Love him, daughter Anne.—
    Why, how now? What does Master Fenton here?
    You wrong me, sir, thus still to haunt my house.
    I told you, sir, my daughter is disposed of.

FENTON

    Nay, Master Page, be not impatient.

MISTRESS PAGE

    Good Master Fenton, come not to my child.   70

PAGE

    She is no match for you.

FENTON

    Sir, will you hear me?

PAGE   No, good Master Fenton.—
    Come, Master Shallow; come, son Slender, in.—
    Knowing my mind, you wrong me, Master Fenton.
                            Exeunt Page, Shallow, and Slender

MISTRESS QUICKLY (*to Fenton*) Speak to Mistress Page.

FENTON

    Good Mistress Page, for that I love your daughter
    In such a righteous fashion as I do,
    Perforce against all checks, rebukes, and manners
    I must advance the colours of my love
    And not retire. Let me have your good will.   80

ANNE

    Good mother, do not marry me to yon fool.

MISTRESS PAGE

    I mean it not: I seek you a better husband.

MISTRESS QUICKLY (*aside to Anne*) That's my master, Master
    Doctor.

ANNE (*aside*)

    Alas, I had rather be set quick i'th' earth,
    And bowled to death with turnips.

74.1] ROWE; *not in* F   83 *aside to Anne*] *as* BOWERS; *not in* F   85 *aside*] This edition; *not in* F

78 **against ... manners** The word *against*, oddly, does double duty here, meaning 'in resistance to' (as applied to *checks*, i.e. obstacles, and *rebukes*) and also 'contrary to' (as applied to *manners*).

79 **advance ... retire** A metaphor from warfare: compare *LLL* 4.3.343, where, however, there is a sexual innuendo absent from Fenton's speech.

85 **set quick i'th' earth** buried alive (*quick*) in the ground up to the neck. Compare *Titus* 5.3.178: 'Set him [i.e. Aaron] breast-deep in earth and famish him.'

MISTRESS PAGE
  Come, trouble not yourself, good Master Fenton;
  I will not be your friend nor enemy.
  My daughter will I question how she loves you,
  And as I find her, so am I affected.　　　　　　　　　90
  Till then, farewell, sir. She must needs go in;
  Her father will be angry.

FENTON
  Farewell, gentle mistress.—Farewell, Nan.

              Exeunt Mistress Page and Anne

MISTRESS QUICKLY This is my doing now. 'Nay', said I, 'will
you cast away your child on a fool and a physician?
Look on Master Fenton.' This is my doing.

FENTON
  I thank thee, and I pray thee once tonight
  Give my sweet Nan this ring. There's for thy pains.

        He gives her a ring and money

MISTRESS QUICKLY Now heaven send thee good fortune!

                   Exit Fenton

A kind heart he hath. A woman would run through fire　　100
and water for such a kind heart. But yet I would my
master had Mistress Anne; or I would Master Slender
had her; or, in sooth, I would Master Fenton had her. I
will do what I can for them all three, for so I have

---

87 yourself, good] F (your selfe good); your self; good WARBURTON　　93.1] ROWE (*after* 92);
not in F　　95 and] F; or HANMER (*conj.* Johnson)　　98.1] *as* NCS; *not in* F　　99.1] F2 (*after*
98); *not in* F

87 **Come ... Fenton** Warburton's emendation makes Mistress Page address the first
four words to Anne, either duplicating
her previous reply to Anne or (assuming
that she hears Anne's expostulation
about Caius) telling Anne rather un-
kindly not to concern herself about her
suitor's unattractiveness. F's punctuation (followed here) makes Mistress Page,
more naturally, reply to Fenton's appeal
in a full line of verse, the following line
also being end-stopped and its sense
pointing forward to the next two lines.

90 **affected** inclined (i.e. what she 'affects' or
likes, I will like too). Mistress Page, who
persists in favouring Caius as a suitor,
must be speaking disingenuously in order
to end the interview.

93 **gentle mistress** i.e. Mistress Page

94 **This** i.e. this mollifying of Mistress Page
towards Fenton

95 **a fool and a physician** The proverbial
'Every man is either a fool or a physician
to himself' (Tilley M125) contrasts the
two: Mistress Quickly makes them synonymous with each other and with
Caius. She must be referring to him
alone, and not to him and Slender, for
Page's mind is made up in Slender's
favour.

97 **once tonight** some time tonight; compare *1 Henry IV* 5.2.72, 'once ere night'.

98 **There's ... pains** Q indicates what was
evidently thought a suitable amount:
'Here nurse, theres a brace of angels to
drink.'

101 **such a kind heart** such a kind-hearted
man

promised, and I'll be as good as my word—but speciously for Master Fenton. Well, I must of another errand to Sir John Falstaff from my two mistresses. What a beast am I to slack it!   *Exit*

3.5   *Enter Falstaff*
FALSTAFF Bardolph, I say!
    Enter Bardolph
BARDOLPH Here, sir.
FALSTAFF Go fetch me a quart of sack; put a toast in't.
                                                Exit Bardolph
Have I lived to be carried in a basket like a barrow of butcher's offal, and to be thrown in the Thames? Well, if I be served such another trick, I'll have my brains ta'en out and buttered, and give them to a dog for a new-year's gift. 'Sblood, the rogues slighted me into the river with as little remorse as they would have drowned a blind bitch's puppies, fifteen i'th' litter! And you may   10
know by my size that I have a kind of alacrity in sinking. If the bottom were as deep as hell, I should down. I had

3.5] F (*Scena Quinta.*)   o.1] Q1 (*Enter Sir Iohn Falstaffe.*); *Enter Falstaffe, Bardolfe, Quickly, Ford.* F; *Enter Sir Iohn Falstaffe and Bardolfe.* Q2   1.1] *as* NCS; *at* o.1 F   3.1] THEOBALD; *not in* F
8 'Sblood, the rogues Q; The rogues F   slighted] F; slided Q   10 a blind bitch's] F (a blind bitches), Q; a bitch's blind THEOBALD

105–6 **speciously** in error for 'specially' (as at 4.5.104)
106 **of** on
108 **slack it** neglect it
3.5.3 **toast** piece of hot toast, often put into beer or wine, when it became a 'sop'
4 **barrow** barrow-load
8 **'Sblood** An oath typical of Falstaff (e.g. *1 Henry IV* 1.2.73, 2.2.35, 2.5.248) and therefore probably authentic, though expurgated from F.
  slighted Not found elsewhere in Shakespeare except in the sense of 'contemptuously ignored' (*2 Henry IV* 5.2.93; *Caesar* 4.2.59); if it has that sense here the construction *slighted me into the river* is very free. Q's 'slided' is a recognized form of the past tense of 'slide', but Shakespeare has neither 'slid' nor 'slided' elsewhere. 'Slided' is not appropriate to the action of tipping someone out of a basket (contrast *thrown*, l. 5). It is therefore rejected, but its sound helps to reinforce F's reading; otherwise

'slinged', a recognised alternative to 'slung', and used of throwing a person in some direction (*OED sling v.*[1] 2), might have a stronger claim to consideration. The NCS editors' conjecture, '"sleighted"', i.e. "conveyed dexterously", with a quibble upon "slided"', requires the verb (not in *OED*) to be a Shakespearian coinage from the noun 'sleight' (*OED sb.*[1] 3).
10 **blind bitch's** Theobald's emendation gives the probable meaning, since there is a mention of drowning blind (i.e. very young) puppies in *Two Gentlemen* 4.4.3–5 and *Othello* 1.3.335–6, and there is no obvious reason why a litter should be destroyed because the bitch that has produced them is blind. But the fact that Q concurs with F suggests that Shakespeare wrote the phrase, and the actor delivered it, in this form.
  you An indication that this soliloquy is directly addressed to the audience.

been drowned but that the shore was shelvy and
shallow—a death that I abhor, for the water swells a
man, and what a thing should I have been when I had
been swelled! I should have been a mountain of
mummy.

Enter Bardolph with two goblets of sack

BARDOLPH Here's Mistress Quickly, sir, to speak with you.

FALSTAFF Come, let me pour in some sack to the Thames
water, for my belly's as cold as if I had swallowed   20
snowballs for pills to cool the reins. ⌈*He drinks*⌉ Call
her in.

BARDOLPH Come in, woman.

Enter Mistress Quickly.

⌈*Falstaff drinks*⌉

MISTRESS QUICKLY By your leave; I cry you mercy. Give
your worship good morrow.

FALSTAFF (*to Bardolph*) Take away these chalices. Go, brew
me a pottle of sack finely.

BARDOLPH With eggs, sir?

FALSTAFF Simple of itself. I'll no pullet-sperm in my
brewage.   *Exit Bardolph* ⌈*with the goblets*⌉   30
How now?

MISTRESS QUICKLY Marry, sir, I come to your worship from

16 I should have been] F; By the Lord Q   17 mummy] F; money. Now is the Sacke brewed?
Q   17.1] *as* NCS; *not in* F   21 He drinks] *as* NCS; *not in* F   23.1] Q; *not in* F   23.2] *as* NCS
(*after* 25); *not in* F   29 no pullet-sperm] F (no Pullet-Spersme); none of these pullets sperme
Q; no pullet-sperms OXFORD   30 Exit ... goblets] *as* CAPELL; *not in* F

13–14 **the shore was shelvy and shallow** i.e.
the bank was sloping and the river therefore shallow. *Shelvy*, being applied to the
shore in this passage, cannot mean 'having sandbanks' (*OED*'s only definition,
citing this passage first, though it does
add 'perhaps used by some writers' in the
sense of 'shelving', from *shelve v.*³, i.e.
sloping).

17 **mummy** dead flesh (*OED sb.*¹ 1b)

17.1 **two goblets** Falstaff refers to *these chalices* at l. 26. No doubt he drinks each off
at a draught. As he has called for a quart of
sack each goblet must contain one pint.

21 **reins** literally kidneys, but the idea is the
quenching of lust: compare 5.5.11,
'When gods have hot backs'.

24 **By . . . mercy** Mistress Quickly apologizes
for interrupting Falstaff while he is drinking.

26 **chalices** goblets. In its literal sense the
word was not limited, as now, to the cup
of the Eucharist. Shakespeare's other two
uses of it (*Hamlet*, 4.7.132, *Macbeth*
1.7.11) are both in connection with
poison.

26–7 **brew ... finely** Falstaff has not found
two pints of sack with hot toast suffici-
ently thirst-quenching or warming, so he
now calls for a *pottle* (four pints) to be
brewed *finely* (i.e. probably heated and
enriched with spices, e.g. ginger: *OED*
defines *brewage* (l. 30) as 'a concocted
beverage').

29 **Simple of itself** unmixed (*viz.* with eggs).
Shakespeare may mean Falstaff's rejection of *pullet-sperm* to refer to the use of
eggs as an aid to sexual potency: compare *reins* (l. 21 and n.).

Mistress Ford.

FALSTAFF Mistress Ford? I have had ford enough. I was thrown into the ford. I have my belly full of ford.

MISTRESS QUICKLY Alas the day, good heart, that was not her fault. She does so take on with her men; they mistook their erection.

FALSTAFF So did I mine, to build upon a foolish woman's promise.   40

MISTRESS QUICKLY Well, she laments, sir, for it, that it would yearn your heart to see it. Her husband goes this morning a-birding. She desires you once more to come to her, between eight and nine. I must carry her word quickly. She'll make you amends, I warrant you.

FALSTAFF Well, I will visit her; tell her so. And bid her think what a man is. Let her consider his frailty, and then judge of my merit.

MISTRESS QUICKLY I will tell her.

FALSTAFF Do so. Between nine and ten, sayst thou?   50

MISTRESS QUICKLY Eight and nine, sir.

FALSTAFF Well, be gone. I will not miss her.

MISTRESS QUICKLY Peace be with you, sir.   *Exit*

FALSTAFF I marvel I hear not of Master Brook. He sent me word to stay within. I like his money well.

                    Enter Ford disguised as Brook

  · O, here he comes.·

FORD Bless you, sir.

FALSTAFF Now, Master Brook, you come to know what hath passed between me and Ford's wife?

FORD That, indeed, Sir John, is my business.   60

FALSTAFF Master Brook, I will not lie to you. I was at her

42 yearn] F (yern)   53 Exit] Q; not in F   55.1] as Q (Enter Brooke.); not in F   57 Bless you] F; God saue you Q

---

35 **I have my belly full** (a) (literally) my belly is full of 'Thames water'; (b) (colloquially) I have had quite enough (OED *belly full*: compare *Cymbeline* 2.1.20, 'Every jack-slave hath his bellyful of fighting')

36 **good heart** poor thing (i.e. Mistress Ford)

37 **take on with** rage at

38 **erection** in error for 'direction' (instruction)

39 **mine** i.e. my erection. Falstaff proceeds to explain the word figuratively, but his

reply always gets a laugh in the theatre, and legitimately, for OED *sb*. 4 cites an instance dated 1594 of 'erection' in the physiological sexual sense.

42 **yearn** move to compassion (OED *v*.¹ 7)

47 **frailty** In Shakespeare, always moral frailty (compare 2.1.214). Falstaff here represents his own resolution (to keep an appointment with adulterous intent) as a sign of moral *merit* (l. 48).

52 **miss** fail

house the hour she appointed me.

FORD And how sped you, sir?

FALSTAFF Very ill-favouredly, Master Brook.

FORD How so, sir? Did she change her determination?

FALSTAFF No, Master Brook, but the peaking cornuto her
husband, Master Brook, dwelling in a continual 'larum
of jealousy, comes me in the instant of our encounter,
after we had embraced, kissed, protested, and, as it
were, spoke the prologue of our comedy; and at his   70
heels a rabble of his companions, thither provoked and
instigated by his distemper, and, forsooth, to search his
house for his wife's love.

FORD What, while you were there?

FALSTAFF While I was there.

FORD And did he search for you, and could not find you?

FALSTAFF You shall hear. As good luck would have it,
comes in one Mistress Page, gives intelligence of Ford's
approach, and, in her invention and Ford's wife's
distraction, they conveyed me into a buck-basket.   80

FORD A buck-basket!

FALSTAFF By the Lord, a buck-basket! Rammed me in

63 And how sped] Q; And sped F   77 good luck] F; God Q   78 gives] F; Giues her Q
Ford's] F; her husbands Q   79 in] F; by Q   81 A buck-basket!] F (A Buck-basket?)   82
By the Lord] Q; Yes F

63 **how sped you** Q's reading (= how did you
get on?) is preferable to F's (= did you
succeed?) because of Falstaff's reply. If
Ford had asked his question in F's form
the answer would be 'No'. F several times
omits the word and may have done so here.
Compare ll. 123–4, 'you shall know how
I speed'.

64 **ill-favouredly** badly

66 **peaking** mean-spirited (*OED a.* 1)
cornuto cuckold (Italian: literally,
'horned one')

67 **'larum** alarum (alarm), in the sense
either of a call to arms (*OED* 4) or a
warning of danger, especially by ringing
a bell (*OED* 5)

68 **comes me in** comes in. The ethic dative,
here with the force 'to my undoing'.
the instant at the instant
encounter meeting (with a strong sexual
implication: compare *Much Ado*,
3.3.145, 4.1.94)

69 **protested** sworn (our love)

72 **distemper** disease (i.e. jealous madness)

77 **good luck** good fortune (*OED*, *good luck*),
here personified. There is no need to
regard this expression as an expurgation
of 'God' (Q).

78 **gives intelligence** There is no need to
introduce 'her' from Q ('You shall heare
sir, as God would haue it, | A little before
comes me one *Pages* wife, | Giues her
intelligence of her husbands | Approach:
and by her inuention, and *Fords* wiues
| Distraction, conueyd me into a buck-
basket.'), since F's expression may mean
that intelligence was given both to Mistress Ford and to Falstaff.

79 **in** Neither F's 'in' nor Q's 'by' is strictly
appropriate to both *invention* and *distraction*. Q's 'by' relates to the nearer noun.
F's 'in' relates (loosely) to the whole
phrase, and has the sense 'what with'.

82 **By the Lord** F's 'Yes', which is particularly weak, probably marks an expurgation. Q's 'By the Lord' is characteristic of
Falstaff.

82–3 **Rammed me in with** In 3.3.123 and

with foul shirts and smocks, socks, foul stockings, greasy napkins, that, Master Brook, there was the rankest compound of villainous smell that ever offended nostril.

FORD And how long lay you there?

FALSTAFF Nay, you shall hear, Master Brook, what I have suffered to bring this woman to evil for your good. Being thus crammed in the basket, a couple of Ford's knaves,   90
his hinds, were called forth by their mistress to carry me in the name of foul clothes to Datchet Lane. They took me on their shoulders, met the jealous knave their master in the door, who asked them once or twice what they had in their basket. I quaked for fear lest the lunatic knave would have searched it; but Fate, ordaining he should be a cuckold, held his hand. Well, on went he for a search, and away went I for foul clothes. But mark the sequel, Master Brook. I suffered the pangs of three several deaths: first, an intolerable fright to be   100
detected with a jealous rotten bell-wether; next, to be compassed like a good bilbo in the circumference of a peck, hilt to point, heel to head; and then, to be stopped in like a strong distillation with stinking clothes that

84 greasy] F, Q; and greasy ROWE   85 smell] F, Q; smells HANMER   100 several]
F; egregious Q

1 37 it was made clear that the dirty linen was put in the basket after Falstaff was inside it, so the sense is 'fixed me firmly in with' (*OED v.*[1] 1c); compare *stopped in*, l. 103, where the clothes acted as stopper.

84 **that** so that

85 **rankest compound of villainous smell** Q's version of the phrase ('a compound of the most | Villanous smel') shows that F's 'of villainous smell' is adjectival (= stinking), so the different sense of F's 'rankest' is 'most pestilential' (compare 'rank diseases', *2 Henry IV* 3.1.38). A *compound* is a substance composed of several elements (as itemized by Falstaff).

90 **knaves** servants; synonymous with *hinds*

96-7 **Fate ... cuckold** 'Cuckolds come by destiny' was proverbial (Tilley C 889); compare *All's Well* 1.3.62–3, where this proverb and the more familiar one 'Marriage and hanging go by destiny' (Tilley M682) are both alluded to.

101 **with** by
rotten diseased. In a general pejorative sense (sheep-rot is suggested by the metaphorical *bell-wether*) rather than referring to Ford's disease of jealousy.
bell-wether literally a ram (sometimes, though not necessarily, castrated) with a bell tied around its neck, which led the flock (*OED* 1), and applied metaphorically to Ford as leader of the *rabble* (l. 71); also, figuratively, one who makes much noise (*OED* 3a, citing this passage).

102 **compassed** curved (*OED v.*[1] 14)
bilbo See 1.1.146. The sword was of good quality if it could be flexed without snapping.

103 **peck** a shallow cylindrical measure that holds the equivalent of two gallons of dry goods (e.g. oats), about the size of a modern washing-up bowl

104 **distillation** product of distilling, *strong* alluding to the smell of Falstaff's own sweat

fretted in their own grease. Think of that, a man of my
kidney—think of that—that am as subject to heat as
butter; a man of continual dissolution and thaw. It was
a miracle to 'scape suffocation. And in the height of this
bath, when I was more than half stewed in grease, like a
Dutch dish, to be thrown into the Thames, and cooled,   110
glowing hot, in that surge, like a horseshoe. Think of
that—hissing hot—think of that, Master Brook!

FORD In good sadness, sir, I am sorry that for my sake you
have suffered all this. My suit, then, is desperate? You'll
undertake her no more?

FALSTAFF Master Brook, I will be thrown into Etna, as I
have been into Thames, ere I will leave her thus. Her
husband is this morning gone a-birding. I have received
from her another embassy of meeting. 'Twixt eight and
nine is the hour, Master Brook.   120

FORD 'Tis past eight already, sir.

FALSTAFF Is it? I will then address me to my appointment.
Come to me at your convenient leisure, and you shall
know how I speed; and the conclusion shall be crowned
with your enjoying her. Adieu. You shall have her,
Master Brook; Master Brook, you shall cuckold Ford.

                                                      Exit

FORD Hum! Ha! Is this a vision? Is this a dream? Do I
sleep? Master Ford, awake; awake, Master Ford!

---

111 surge] F (serge); forge CAPELL *conj.*   126.1 *Exit*] Q; *not in* F

105 **fretted** The sense here seems to be
'dissolved'. *OED*'s most relevant definition of *fret* (v.¹ 7) is 'to waste or wear
away; to decay, become corrupt'.
Shakespeare's only other use of *fret* with
reference to clothes is 'he frets like a
gummed velvet' (*1 Henry IV* 2.2.2–3),
i.e. 'chafes himself away'.
105–6 **of my kidney** of my nature. *OED sb.* 2
cites an instance from *c.*1555.
107 **dissolution** dissolving
109 **bath** the technical term for a piece of
equipment used in chemistry for producing a steady heat at high temperature
(*OED sb.*¹ 14, 15)
110 **Dutch dish** The Dutch were
proverbially fond of butter: in Dekker's
Shoemaker's Holiday (1599) Sc.4.57, a
supposed Dutchman is called 'butter-box'.

111 **surge** Though explained by some editors (Hart, NCS) as Falstaff's perspiration,
this word seems rather to refer to the
Thames. The sense is debatable: the F
spelling 'serge' for 'surge' is not elsewhere
found in Shakespeare, nor recognized by
OED, and when Shakespeare has 'surge'
elsewhere he means the sea and its waves.
If 'surge' *is* the word, it may be used with
Falstaffian exaggeration. Capell's 'forge'
(= smithy) works only if the Thames is
seen specifically as the pail of water for
cooling hot iron; but in Shakespeare
'forge' is associated with the forge proper
and with shaping hot metal (as in
4.2.207).
113 **good sadness** true seriousness
116 **Etna** the Sicilian volcano
119 **embassy** message (cf. *Henry V* 1.1.96)

There's a hole made in your best coat, Master Ford. This
'tis to be married; this 'tis to have linen and buck- 130
baskets! Well, I will proclaim myself what I am. I will
now take the lecher. He is at my house. He cannot
'scape me. 'Tis impossible he should. He cannot creep
into a halfpenny purse, nor into a pepperbox. But lest
the devil that guides him should aid him, I will search
impossible places. Though what I am I cannot avoid, yet
to be what I would not shall not make me tame. If I have
horns to make me mad, let the proverb go with me—I'll
be horn-mad. *Exit*

4.1 *Enter Mistress Page, Mistress Quickly, and William*
MISTRESS PAGE Is he at Mistress Ford's already, think'st
thou?
MISTRESS QUICKLY Sure he is by this, or will be presently.
But truly he is very courageous mad about his throwing
into the water. Mistress Ford desires you to come
suddenly.
MISTRESS PAGE I'll be with her by and by. I'll but bring my
young man here to school.
Enter Evans

138 me] HALLIWELL (*conj.* Dyce (*Remarks*)); one F   139 *Exit*] F (*Exeunt.*)
  4.1] F (*Actus Quartus. Scœna Prima.*)   0.1] ROWE; *Enter Mistris Page, Quickly, William,
Euans.* F   1 Mistress] F (M.)   8.1] ROWE (*after* 10); *after* F (4.1.0.1)

129 **There's . . . coat** 'To pick a hole in a
  man's coat' (Tilley H522) is proverbial
  for finding a hidden fault in somebody;
  compare Fluellen's version of the expression in *Henry V* 3.6.85. Ford does not use
  it quite in this sense, and there may be
  sexual innuendo (in the sense 'someone
  is seducing your wife').
134 **halfpenny purse** a small purse made to
  hold small coins; compare *LLL* 5.1.70.
  Ford's unconsciously comic seriousness
  is well displayed by this sentence: that
  Falstaff, of all men, could hide in such
  places is a hilarious notion. In 5.5, as
  Falstaff, Oscar Asche invented the gag
  'I'll creep into an acorn cup' (Crosse,
  Shakespearean Playgoing, p. 28), perhaps
  remembering this passage, 4.2.148–50,
  and *Dream* 2.1.30–1.
136 **what I am** i.e. to be what I am, *viz.* a
  cuckold; compare *what I would not*. After
  having reiterated the word 'cuckold'
  three times in 2.2.295, Ford now twice

avoids it.
138 **me** F's 'one' is an easy misreading:
  compare *Shrew* 1.2.171 and perhaps
  Twelfth Night 3.3.7.
4.1 Q omits this scene and substitutes a
  version of 3.4.
  1 **Mistress** F's 'M.' is used as an abbreviation of both 'Master' and 'Mistress' (e.g.
  at 3.5.32). Though Ford is the house-
  holder, the fact that Falstaff's visit is to
  Ford's wife makes 'Mistress' the preferable expansion.
  3 **presently** in a moment
  4 **courageous** Other indefinite uses of this
  word are in *Dream* 4.2.24 ('O most
  courageous day!') and *Merchant* 2.2.9
  ('the most courageous fiend').
  6 **suddenly** at once
  7 **by and by** in a moment
7–8 **my young man** William's age is probably seven or eight, at which boys usually
  began their grammar-school education.

Look where his master comes. 'Tis a playing day, I see.
How now, Sir Hugh, no school today?   10
EVANS No. Master Slender is let the boys leave to play.
MISTRESS QUICKLY Blessing of his heart!
MISTRESS PAGE Sir Hugh, my husband says my son profits
    nothing in the world at his book. I pray you, ask him
    some questions in his accidence.
EVANS Come hither, William. Hold up your head. Come.
MISTRESS PAGE Come on, sirrah. Hold up your head.
    Answer your master, be not afraid.
EVANS William, how many numbers is in nouns?
WILLIAM Two.   20
MISTRESS QUICKLY Truly, I thought there had been one
    number more, because they say "Od's nouns'.
EVANS Peace your tattlings.—What is 'fair', William?
WILLIAM *Pulcher.*
MISTRESS QUICKLY Polecats! There are fairer things than
    polecats, sure.
EVANS You are a very simplicity 'oman. I pray you
    peace.—What is *lapis*, William?
WILLIAM A stone.
EVANS And what is 'a stone', William?   30
WILLIAM A pebble.
EVANS No, it is *lapis*. I pray you remember in your prain.
WILLIAM *Lapis.*
EVANS That is a good William. What is he, William, that
    does lend articles?

11 let] F; get COLLIER 1853

11 **is let ... play** has had the boys given a
holiday. Evans's usage elsewhere, and
Fluellen's, do not reinforce this expression's authenticity; nor, on the other
hand, do they support Collier's emendation. Evans's words in F are perhaps
meant to be comically awkward, having
the unintended sense 'has allowed the
boys to leave off playing'.

15 **accidence** Latin grammar. The *book* is, in
the general sense, 'learning', and in the
particular sense the standard primary
textbook, William Lilly and John Colet's
A Short Introduction of Grammar (1549;
Shakespeare probably alludes to the edition of 1577).

20 **Two** i.e. singular and plural

22 **'Od's nouns** a corruption of the oath
'God's (i.e. Christ's) wounds'

23 **tattlings** prattle (with Evans's plural)

24 *Pulcher* This word, like *lapis*, is given as
an example in Lilly's grammar.

25 **Polecats** The word is used abusively by
Ford in 4.2.171, but the incongruity here
is more amusing if the word simply
means the animal. Polecats were regarded as vermin.

31 **A pebble** William's common-sense reply
draws attention to Evans's mechanical
application of Lilly's advice (in his
preface) to test the pupil's ability to
translate both out of Latin and into it.
There is no quibble on *stone* (testicle)
here.

WILLIAM Articles are borrowed of the pronoun, and be
  thus declined: *Singulariter, nominativo, hic, haec, hoc.*

EVANS *Nominativo, hig, haeg, hog.* Pray you mark: *genitivo,
  huius.* Well, what is your accusative case?

WILLIAM *Accusativo, hinc.*   40

EVANS I pray you have your remembrance, child. *Accusativo, hung, hang, hog.*

MISTRESS QUICKLY 'Hang-hog' is Latin for bacon, I warrant
  you.

EVANS Leave your prabbles, 'oman.—What is the focative
  case, William?

WILLIAM *O—vocativo—O—*

EVANS Remember, William. Focative is *caret.*

MISTRESS QUICKLY And that's a good root.

EVANS 'Oman, forbear.   50

MISTRESS PAGE (*to Mistress Quickly*) Peace!

EVANS What is your genitive case plural, William?

WILLIAM Genitive case?

EVANS Ay.

WILLIAM *Genitivo, horum, harum, horum.*

MISTRESS QUICKLY Vengeance of Jenny's case! Fie on her!
  Never name her, child, if she be a whore.

---

38 *haeg*] This edition; *hag* F   40 *hinc*] F; *hunc* HALLIWELL   42 *hung*] POPE; *hing* F
55 *Genitivo*] SINGER; *Genitiue* F   56 Jenny's] F (Ginyes)

36–7 **Articles . . . hoc** A direct quotation
from Lilly's grammar.

37 ***Singulariter, nominativo*** singly (i.e. the
singular number), in the nominative case

40 ***hinc*** William's mistake for '*hunc*'. He has
transferred the vowel of *hic* to the accusative, accidentally producing the Latin for
'hence'. Halliwell, emending to '*hunc*',
implies that William can remember the
masculine form but not the feminine or
neuter ones.

42 ***hung*** Pope's emendation must be right: it
is incredible that Evans should repeat
William's error in the act of pointing it
out to him. F's error was probably due to
concentration by scribe or compositor
on Evans's substitution of 'g' for 'c'.

45 **prabbles** disturbance. In Shakespeare
'brabble' (*sb.* and *v.*) is 'brawl'. Compare
I.1.50, 'pribbles and prabbles'.
focative vocative. Evans's pronunciation,
suggesting 'fuck', introduces a series of
innuendos.

47 **O—*vocativo*—O** William says 'O' while
he tries to remember the answer (which
does not exist, the question being a trick
one). 'O' is also the usual interjection
when using the vocative. In addition, 'O'
suggests the female genital organ: compare *Romeo* 3.3.88–90, where the
quibble is clear. For the quibble in *case*
(not present in l. 39, 'accusative case',
but introduced here by 'focative') compare l. 56.

48 **is *caret*** Lilly regularly has *caret* (Lat. 'is
wanting'): *is* is the English verb, not, as
has been suggested by J. W. Binns
(*Shakespeare Survey* 35 (Cambridge,
1982), p. 127), the Latin pronoun *is*,
meaning 'he': Binns is more rigorous
than Evans in avoiding redundancy.

49 **that's** i.e. carrot is. Mistress Quickly is
unconsciously carrying on the innuendo,
a carrot by its shape suggesting the penis.

56 **Vengeance of** a plague on
Jenny's case *case* is frequently found in

EVANS For shame, 'oman!

MISTRESS QUICKLY You do ill to teach the child such words.
(*To Mistress Page*) He teaches him to hick and to hack,   60
which they'll do fast enough of themselves, and to call
'horum'. (*To Evans*) Fie upon you!

EVANS 'Oman, art thou lunatics? Hast thou no under-
standings for thy cases, and the numbers of the gen-
ders? Thou art as foolish a Christian creatures as I
would desires.

MISTRESS PAGE (*to Mistress Quickly*) Prithee hold thy peace.

EVANS Show me now, William, some declensions of your
pronouns.

WILLIAM Forsooth, I have forgot.   70

EVANS It is *qui, quae, quod*. If you forget your *quis*, your
quaes, and your *quods*, you must be preeches. Go your
ways and play, go.

MISTRESS PAGE He is a better scholar than I thought he
was.

EVANS He is a good sprag memory. Farewell, Mistress
Page.

---

60 *To Mistress Page*] This edition; *not in* F   62 'horum'] F (*horum*); 'whorum' OXFORD   *To
Evans*] This edition; *not in* F   63 lunatics] CAPELL; Lunaties F; lunacies ROWE   64 of]
F; and COLLIER 1853   the] F; thy WHITE *conj.*   65 foolish a] This edition; foolish F   66
desires] F; desire POPE   71 *quae*] POPE; *que* F   72 *quaes*] POPE; *Ques* F   preeches]
F; preeched WHITE *conj.*

Shakespeare in the sense of the female
genital organ (e.g. *Romeo* 3.3.84–5, the
same speech cited in l. 47 n.). By *Jenny*
Mistress Quickly means 'this woman
Jenny, whoever she may be'; compare
LLL 3.1.117–8, where Costard takes 'en-
franchise thee' to mean 'marry me to one
Frances'.

60 **to hick and to hack** At 2.1.47 *hack* seems
to be used with sexual innuendo, and the
context here also suggests it. *Hick* (sometimes conjecturally explained as hiccup)
is probably no more than an extension of
hack, as the word 'hick-hack' might be
coined by analogy with 'tick-tack',
'hanky-panky' etc. *Hack* alone would not
carry the mind back to *hic, haec, hoc*.

62 **to call 'horum'** Mistress Quickly, having
concluded that *hang-hog* is Latin for bacon, now concludes that *horum* is Latin

for whore.

63 **lunatics** Capell's emendation is probably
right (compare 4.2.113); though F's
'Lunaties' could be even more easily read
(in secretary hand) as 'lunacies', Evans
does not make a noun plural when using
it as an adjective (e.g. 'a very simplicity
'oman').

71–2 **your quis … quods** Oliver seeks further innuendo here, with quibbles on
'keys', 'case', and 'cods' (testicles), but
this is strained.

72 **preeches** breeched (i.e. whipped)

76 **is** i.e. has. Compare Fluellen's 'He is not
. . . any hurt in the world', *Henry V*
3.6.9–10.
       sprag Evans's pronunciation of *sprack*
(*OED a.* = smart). OED notes (*sprag a.*)
that this passage is the source of later
uses of 'sprag' and has led to its inclusion
in dialect glossaries.

MISTRESS PAGE Adieu, good Sir Hugh.   *Exit Evans*
  Get you home, boy.   *Exit William*
  (*To Mistress Quickly*) Come, we stay too long.   *Exeunt*

4.2   *The buck-basket brought out.*
       Enter Falstaff and Mistress Ford

FALSTAFF Mistress Ford, your sorrow hath eaten up my
  sufferance. I see you are obsequious in your love, and I
  profess requital to a hair's breadth, not only, Mistress
  Ford, in the simple office of love, but in all the accoutrement, complement, and ceremony of it. But are you sure
  of your husband now?
MISTRESS FORD He's a-birding, sweet Sir John.
MISTRESS PAGE (*within*) What ho, gossip Ford! What ho!
MISTRESS FORD Step into th' chamber, Sir John.
                                         Exit Falstaff

       Enter Mistress Page

MISTRESS PAGE How now, sweetheart, who's at home   10
  besides yourself?
MISTRESS FORD Why, none but mine own people.

78 *Exit Evans*] STEEVENS 1793; *not in* F   79 *Exit William*] OXFORD; *not in* F   80 *To Mistress*
Quickly] OXFORD; *not in* F
    4.2] F (*Scena Secunda.*)   0.1] This edition; *not in* F   0.2] ROWE; *Enter Falstoffe, Mist. Ford,*
Mist. Page, Seruants, Ford, Page, Caius, Euans, Shallow. F; *Enter misteris Ford and her two men.* Q
8 *within*] ROWE; *not in* F   9 Step ... Sir John] F; Step behind the arras good sir Iohn Q
9.1 *Exit Falstaff*] ROWE; *He steps behind the arras.* Q; *not in* F   9.2] *as* F2; Q *places after a*
version of 7; *not in* F   10 sweetheart] F (sweete heart)

4.2.0.1 Before this scene begins it is necessary for the buck-basket to be set out on
  stage, where it will be wanted later, for
  John and Robert do not bring it in with
  them. In Q the scene begins with Mistress
  Ford instructing them: 'Do you heare?
  when your M. comes take vp this basket
  as you did before, and if your M. bid you
  set it downe, obey him' (compare
  ll. 97–9), after which Falstaff enters.
1–2 **your sorrow ... sufferance** i.e. your
  sorrow has made me forget my suffering
2 **obsequious** compliant to my wishes (*OED*
  a. 1), i.e. reciprocating my love
3 **to a hair's breadth** exactly. Proverbial
  (Tilley H29).
3–5 **not only ... of it** The exact sense of this
  florid speech is doubtful. It may mean
  either 'not only in the physical act of love
  but in all love's formal courtesies' or 'not

only in simply feeling love but in giving it
  full expression'. In either case there
  seems to be an undercurrent of sexual
  suggestion beneath a surface of
  gallantry. *Accoutrement* is apparel or
  equipment, *complement* accompaniment
  or consummation (*OED*).
8 **gossip** friend (a term used between
  women: *OED sb.* 2)
9 **chamber** inner room. They are at present
  supposed to be in the hall, or main room,
  of the house. In Q Falstaff hides behind
  the arras again, but F's 'the chamber'
  suggests that he leaves by one stage door
  just before Mistress Page enters by the
  other. The aside 'Speak louder' (wrongly
  placed by Q in its equivalent of 3.3
  instead of in this scene) is appropriate to
  Falstaff's greater distance from the conversation.

MISTRESS PAGE Indeed?

MISTRESS FORD No, certainly. (*Aside to her*) Speak louder.

MISTRESS PAGE Truly, I am so glad you have nobody here.

MISTRESS FORD Why?

MISTRESS PAGE Why, woman, your husband is in his old
lunes again. He so takes on yonder with my husband, so
rails against all married mankind, so curses all Eve's
daughters of what complexion soever, and so buffets   20
himself on the forehead, crying 'Peer out, peer out!',
that any madness I ever yet beheld seemed but tame-
ness, civility, and patience to this distemper he is in
now. I am glad the fat knight is not here.

MISTRESS FORD Why, does he talk of him?

MISTRESS PAGE Of none but him, and swears he was
carried out, the last time he searched for him, in a
basket; protests to my husband he is now here, and
hath drawn him and the rest of their company from
their sport to make another experiment of his suspicion.   30

---

15 I am so glad] F; I am glad This edition *conj.*   17 lunes] THEOBALD; lines F; vaine Q
23 this] This edition (*conj.* Collier); this his F

---

13 **Indeed?** really and truly? (not expressing
incredulity but relief)

14 **No, certainly** 'Positively no one else.'

15 **I am so glad** Shakespeare has over 120
instances of 'I am glad', 'I am right glad',
'I am very glad', etc., but no other
instance of 'I am so glad', which is to be
contrasted with F's phrases at ll. 24 and
31, and with Q's 'but I am glad he is not
here'. F's reading may have been affected
by the phrase 'he so takes on' (l. 18) and
the two parallel phrases which immediately follow it. But in view of the expression 'so loud and so melancholy' at
1.4.86 I do not emend.

18 **lunes** fits of madness. Theobald's emendation is supported, in the speech, by
madness (l. 22) and *this distemper he is in
now* (ll. 111–13). Compare *Winter's Tale*
2.2.33: 'These dangerous, unsafe lunes
i'th' King, beshrew them!' OED does not
record 'lune' outside Shakespeare's
works till the 18th c. (an allusion to the
present passage in its emended form); it
gives the present passage under 'line',
sb.² 29, in the plural, defined as 'goings-

on, fits of temper', compared with 'on a
line' (= in a rage: Warwickshire dialect),
and noted as peculiar to Shakespeare;
one other example is cited, *Troilus*
2.3.129 ('watch | His pettish lines, his
ebs, his flowes' in F). In this *Troilus*
passage 'lines' is also commonly
emended to 'lunes' (which is consistent
with the imagery in 'ebbs' and 'flows').
Hibbard takes 'lines' to mean role or part,
but OED gives no instance of this (*sb.¹*
23g) before 1882; Hamlet's references to
'lines' (2.2.542, 3.2.4) are to lines of text
in a whole play or in a particular speech.
Q's 'in his old vaine', far from confirming
F's 'lines' (as Oliver maintains), is a
substitution for whichever word was authentic and can confirm neither of them.

21 **Peer out** peep out (OED *peer v.²* 2).
Addressed by Ford to his horns.

23 **this distemper** In F's 'this his distemper',
'his' duplicates 'he is in now', makes a
less satisfactory antithesis with 'any
madness', and (as Jowett notes) may
easily have been interpolated under the
influence of the adjacent 'this', or 'dis-',
or 'he is'.

But I am glad the knight is not here. Now he shall see
his own foolery.

MISTRESS FORD How near is he, Mistress Page?

MISTRESS PAGE Hard by, at street end. He will be here
anon.

MISTRESS FORD I am undone. The knight is here.

MISTRESS PAGE Why then you are utterly shamed, and
he's but a dead man. What a woman are you! Away
with him, away with him! Better shame than murder.

MISTRESS FORD Which way should he go? How should I   40
bestow him? Shall I put him into the basket again?

    Enter Falstaff

FALSTAFF No, I'll come no more i'th' basket. May I not go
out ere he come?

MISTRESS PAGE Alas, three of Master Ford's brothers watch
the door with pistols, that none shall issue out; otherwise you might slip away ere he came. (*Aside to him*) But
what make you here?

FALSTAFF What shall I do? I'll creep up into the chimney.

MISTRESS FORD There they always use to discharge their
birding-pieces.   50

⌈MISTRESS PAGE⌉ Creep into the kiln-hole.

FALSTAFF Where is it?

MISTRESS FORD He will seek there, on my word. Neither
press, coffer, chest, trunk, well, vault, but he hath an
abstract for the remembrance of such places, and goes
to them by his note. There is no hiding you in the house.

FALSTAFF I'll go out, then.

41.1] ROWE; *not in* F   46 *Aside to him*] This edition; *not in* F   49–51] DYCE (*conj.*
Malone); *Mist. Ford.* There they alwaies vse to discharge their Birding-peeces; creepe into the
Kill-hole. F; *Mistress Page.* There ... kiln-hole. NCS   51 kiln-hole] F (Kill-hole)

---

35 **anon** directly

47 **what make you here?** what are you
doing here? (as in 2.1.216). Compare
Mistress Page's indignation at 3.3.129.

49–50 **use ... birding-pieces** are accus-
tomed to fire off their guns, because 'it
was a safe way to discharge the fire-arms
or to dislodge the soot (or both)' (Oliver).
In Glen Byam Shaw's production (Stratford-upon-Avon, 1955) 'Ford discharged
his birding-piece up the chimney and

emerged black with soot' (Shattuck,
p. 37).

51 ⌈MISTRESS PAGE⌉ The insertion of this
speech-prefix is necessary. Mistress Ford
is so categorical about her husband's list
of hiding-places (ll. 53–6) that this suggestion must come from Mistress Page.
into the kiln-hole in at the oven door

54 **press** cupboard

55 **abstract** list

MISTRESS ⌈PAGE⌉ If you go out in your own semblance,
you die, Sir John—unless you go out disguised.

MISTRESS FORD How might we disguise him?   60

MISTRESS PAGE Alas the day, I know not. There is no
woman's gown big enough for him; otherwise he might
put on a hat, a muffler, and a kerchief, and so escape.

FALSTAFF Good hearts, devise something; any extremity
rather than a mischief.

MISTRESS FORD My maid's aunt, the fat woman of Brentford, has a gown above.

MISTRESS PAGE On my word, it will serve him. She's as big
as he is; and there's her thrummed hat and her muffler
too.—Run up, Sir John.   70

MISTRESS FORD Go, go, sweet Sir John. Mistress Page and I
will look some linen for your head.

MISTRESS PAGE Quick, quick! We'll come dress you
straight. Put on the gown the while.   *Exit Falstaff*

MISTRESS FORD I would my husband would meet him in
this shape. He cannot abide the old woman of Brentford.
He swears she's a witch, forbade her my house, and
hath threatened to beat her.

MISTRESS PAGE Heaven guide him to thy husband's cudgel,
and the devil guide his cudgel afterwards!   80

MISTRESS FORD But is my husband coming?

MISTRESS PAGE Ay, in good sadness is he, and talks of the
basket too, howsoever he hath had intelligence.

---

58 PAGE] MALONE; *Ford* F   60 MISTRESS FORD] F1; *not in* F2   64 Good ... extremity] F; *For
Gods sake deuise any extremitie* Q   66 the fat woman] F; *Gillian* Q   66–7 Brentford] F
(*Brainford*), *and so thereafter*   74] F2 (*Exit*); *Exit Mis. Page, & Sir Iohn. Enter M. Ford, Page,
Priest, Shallow, the two men carries the basket, and Ford meets it.* Q; *not in* F

58 MISTRESS ⌈PAGE⌉ This speech properly
belongs to her, because she can report on
the situation outside the house (compare
ll. 44–6). F wrongly has two consecutive
speech-prefixes for Mistress Ford.

63 **muffler** a scarf to cover part of the face
and the neck (*OED* 1a)
kerchief a piece of linen about the head
(under the hat)

66–7 **the fat woman of Brentford** Brentford
is about twelve miles to the east of
Windsor. Q's '*Gillian of Brainford*' is an
obvious piece of associative invention by
its compiler: a humorous poem, *Jyl of*

braintfords Testament (Robert Copland,
c.1560), had made the name proverbial:
'What can be made of Summer's last will
and testament? Such another thing as
Gillian of Brentford's will, where she
bequeathed a score of farts among her
friends' (Nashe, *Summer's Last Will and
Testament*' (1600), *Works*, iii.235).

69 **thrummed** fringed

72 **look** look for (*OED* v. 6d)

76 **shape** dress (here with the sense of disguise)

82 **sadness** seriousness, i.e. truth

MISTRESS FORD We'll try that; for I'll appoint my men to
carry the basket again, to meet him at the door with it
as they did last time.

MISTRESS PAGE Nay, but he'll be here presently. Let's go
dress him like the witch of Brentford.

MISTRESS FORD I'll first direct my men what they shall do
with the basket. Go up; I'll bring linen for him straight.   90

MISTRESS PAGE Hang him, dishonest varlet! We cannot
misuse him enough.   ⌜*Exit Mistress Ford*⌝
We'll leave a proof, by that which we will do,
Wives may be merry and yet honest too.
We do not act that often jest and laugh;
'Tis old but true: 'Still swine eats all the draff.'   *Exit*
          Enter ⌜*Mistress Ford,*⌝ *John and Robert*

MISTRESS FORD Go, sirs, take the basket again on your
shoulders. Your master is hard at door. If he bid you set
it down, obey him. Quickly, dispatch!   *Exit*

⌜JOHN⌝ Come, come, take it up.   100

⌜ROBERT⌝ Pray heaven it be not full of knight again!

⌜JOHN⌝ I hope not. I had as lief bear so much lead.
          They lift the basket.
          Enter Ford, Page, Shallow, Caius, and Evans

FORD Ay, but if it prove true, Master Page, have you any

---

92 misuse him] F2; misuse F1   *Exit ... Ford*] *as* CAPELL (*after* 90); *not in* F   96 *Exit*]
CAPELL; *not in* F   96.1] *as* CAPELL; *Enter Ser.* F2 (*after* 99); *not in* F1   99 *Exit*] CAPELL;
Exeunt Mrs. Page and Mrs. Ford. THEOBALD; *not in* F   100, 102 JOHN] OLIVER; *1 Ser⟨uant⟩.* F
101 ROBERT] OLIVER; *2 Ser⟨uant⟩.* F   102 as lief] F2; liefe *as* F1   102.1] NCS; *not in* F
102.2] ROWE; *not in* F

---

84 **try** 'make an experiment on' (Hibbard)

91 **dishonest varlet** immoral rogue

92 *Exit Mistress Ford* Mistress Ford goes out
to fetch Falstaff's head-linen and to summon John and Robert. Mistress Page's
couplets, addressed directly to the audience, bridge the gap to Mistress Ford's
return, which coincides with her own
exit.

94 **Wives may be merry** Shakespeare makes
similar allusion to the play's title in other
comedies (*Shrew, Measure, All's Well*).

95 **act** i.e. commit misconduct

96 **'Still swine eats all the draff'** Proverbial
(Tilley S681): 'It is the silent pigs that eat
all the pigswill'.

98 **hard at door** just at the door

102.2 *Caius* Oliver notes that though Caius
does not speak he seems to be required
on stage because he took part in the
corresponding scene (3.3) and because
he was to be one of the birding party, all
of whom Ford has brought with him
(ll. 28–30). F includes him in the opening 'massed entry' (4.2.0.1).

103–4 **Ay, but ... again?** Retorting to an
expostulation uttered by Page before
their entry, to the effect that if Ford's
suspicion proves false he will appear a
fool, Ford says that if it proves true (and,
through his negligence, his wife commits
adultery) he will be irremediably a fool.

way then to unfool me again? *(To John)* Set down the
basket, villain.

John and Robert set down the basket

Somebody call my wife. Youth in a basket! O you
panderly rascals! There's a knot, a gang, a pack, a
conspiracy against me. Now shall the devil be
shamed.—What, wife, I say! Come, come forth! Behold
what honest clothes you send forth to bleaching!   110

PAGE Why, this passes, Master Ford. You are not to go
loose any longer; you must be pinioned.

EVANS Why, this is lunatics. This is mad as a mad dog.

SHALLOW Indeed, Master Ford, this is not well, indeed.

FORD So say I too, sir.

Enter Mistress Ford

Come hither, Mistress Ford, Mistress Ford the honest
woman, the modest wife, the virtuous creature, that
hath the jealous fool to her husband! I suspect without
cause, mistress, do I?

MISTRESS FORD Heaven be my witness you do, if you   120
suspect me in any dishonesty.

FORD Well said, brazen-face, hold it out.—Come forth,
sirrah!

He opens the basket and begins lifting up clothes

104 *To John*] This edition; *not in* F   104–5 Set ... villain.] F; Set ... villains. COLLIER
1853; Set downe the basket you ssaue, | You panderly rogue set it downe. Q   105.1]
OXFORD; *not in* F   107 gang] F2 (ging); gin FI   115.1] HANMER; *not in* F   120–1] F; I
Gods my record do you. And if you mistrust me in any ill sort. Q   123.1] *as* ROWE; *not in* F

104–5 **Set down the basket, villain**
   Shakespeare may have remembered, and
   expected his audience to remember,
   Gloucester's command 'Villains, set
   down the corpse' when he intercepts the
   funeral procession of Henry VI (*Richard
   III* 1.2.36).
105 **villain** If F is correct, Ford addresses the
   servant who is holding the front end of
   the staff on which the basket is slung. On
   the other hand, 'rascals' (l. 107) may
   support Collier's emendation.
106 **Somebody call my wife** Nobody moves
   to obey him, and at l. 109 he calls to her
   himself.
   Youth in a basket Hart cites 'Speak,
   sweet mistress, am I the youth in a
   basket?' (Rowley, *A New Wonder, a
   Woman Never Vexed, c.*1625) in support
   of his interpretation 'fortunate lover';

this may be the meaning, though a
   second example cited by him does not
   obviously bear this sense. The present
   passage is the first recorded appearance
   (Tilley Y51, Dent) of the expression,
   whose origin is not known. 'Youth' may
   mean the character Youth, a prodigal
   gallant in the early 16th-c. moral inter-
   ludes *Youth* and *Lusty Juventus*, referred
   to in Marlowe's *Jew of Malta* 2.3.117–19.
107 **gang** F2's 'ging' is an early form of the
   word.
108–9 **Now ... shamed** Now the truth shall
   be told: alluding to the proverb (Tilley
   T566) 'Speak the truth and shame the
   devil'. Compare *1 Henry IV* 3.1.55–6.
111 **passes** is beyond anything
122 **hold it out** persist (hold out) in your
   pretence: ironical

PAGE This passes!

MISTRESS FORD Are you not ashamed? Let the clothes alone.

FORD I shall find you anon.

EVANS 'Tis unreasonable. Will you take up your wife's clothes? Come, away.

FORD (*to John and Robert*) Empty the basket, I say.   130

⌈PAGE⌉ Why, man, why?

FORD Master Page, as I am a man, there was one conveyed out of my house yesterday in this basket. Why may not he be there again? In my house I am sure he is. My intelligence is true, my jealousy is reasonable. (*To John and Robert*) Pluck me out all the linen.

MISTRESS FORD If you find a man there, he shall die a flea's death.

> *John and Robert empty the basket*

PAGE Here's no man.

SHALLOW By my fidelity, this is not well, Master Ford. This   140
wrongs you.

EVANS Master Ford, you must pray, and not follow the imaginations of your own heart. This is jealousies.

FORD Well, he's not here I seek for.

PAGE No, nor nowhere else but in your brain.

FORD Help to search my house this one time. If I find not what I seek, show no colour for my extremity. Let me

---

129 Come, away] F; Come away ROWE; (*to the others*) Come, away! NCS   130 *to John and Robert*] *as* NCS; *not in* F   131 PAGE] OXFORD (*conj.* Lambrechts); *M. Ford.* F   135–6 *To John and Robert*] OXFORD; *not in* F   138.1] This edition; *Page assists him* NCS; *He takes out clothes* OXFORD; *not in* F

---

127 **I shall find you anon** Addressed to Falstaff, supposedly in the basket.

128–9 **take up your wife's clothes** The same unconscious indecency is exploited in *Shrew* 4.3.160 ('Take up my mistress' gown to his master's use!').

131 ⌈PAGE⌉ 'Why, man, why?' is in Page's style and not in Mistress Ford's, and Ford, in reply, speaks to Page.

135 **intelligence** information

137–8 **he shall die a flea's death** i.e. I'll undertake to kill him by crushing him with my finger-nails (for he will be small enough). A humorous variation on 'die a dog's death', i.e. die wretchedly (*OED dog*

sb. 15d; Tilley D509).

140 **By my fidelity** by my faith. 'Even the oaths uttered by Shallow can sound precious' (Oliver).

142–3 **follow ... heart** Evans's conflation of two phrases from evening prayer: 'We have followed too much the devices and desires of our own hearts' (the General Confession), and 'he hath scattered the proud in the imagination of their hearts' (Magnificat). Typically, he makes 'imagination' plural.

144 **here** in the basket

147 **show ... extremity** offer no excuse for my extravagant behaviour

for ever be your table-sport. Let them say of me, 'As
jealous as Ford, that searched a hollow walnut for his
wife's leman'. Satisfy me once more. Once more search   150
with me.

John and Robert refill the basket and carry it out

MISTRESS FORD What ho, Mistress Page! Come you and the
old woman down. My husband will come into the
chamber.

FORD Old woman? What old woman's that?

MISTRESS FORD Why, it is my maid's aunt of Brentford.

FORD A witch, a quean, an old cozening quean! Have I
not forbid her my house? She comes of errands, does
she? We are simple men; we do not know what's
brought to pass under the profession of fortune-telling.   160
She works by charms, by spells, by th' figure, and such
daubery as this is, beyond our element; we know
nothing. ⌜*He takes up a cudgel*⌝ Come down, you witch,
you hag, you! Come down, I say!

MISTRESS FORD Nay, good sweet husband!—Good gentlemen, let him not strike the old woman.

MISTRESS PAGE ⌜*within*⌝ Come, Mother Pratt; come, give
me your hand.

151.1] This edition; *Exeunt John and Robert with the basket* OLIVER; *not in* F   156 my maid's
aunt of] F; my maidens Ant, *Gillian of* Q   162 daubery] F (dawbry)   is, beyond] F; is
beyond WHEATLEY   163 He ... cudgel] *as* NCS; *not in* F   166 let him not] Q3; let him F
167 within] This edition; *not in* F   Pratt] F (*Prat*)

148 **table-sport** 'the subject of your dinner-
 table jokes' (Oliver)
149 **a hollow walnut** Compare *Hamlet*
 2.2.255, 'bounded in a nutshell'.
150 **leman** lover
157 **quean** a general derogatory term for a
 woman, perhaps here with the specific
 implication of 'bawd'
158 **of errands** i.e. on a go-between's business
159 **simple men** i.e. men, and therefore, in
 the eyes of women, simple
160 **under the profession of** in the name of
161 **by th' figure** i.e. by astrology. To draw
 up a horoscope was called casting, setting, or erecting a 'figure' (*OED sb.* 14).
162 **daubery** pretence (*OED*). This sense is
 derived from the craft of plastering: compare *Richard III* 3.5.28, 'So smooth he
 daubed his vice with show of virtue'.

162 **beyond our element** beyond the range of
 our understanding (ironical). The literal
 sense of *element*, here used figuratively, is
 the particular element (earth, water, air,
 or fire) in which a creature naturally lives.
167 ⌜*within*⌝ By taking the hand of
 'Mother Pratt' Mistress Page implies that
 they are coming down the stairs, which
 are to be imagined as just outside the
 door. In some modern productions the
 stairs are visible, but it is more dramatic
 and amusing if Ford is waiting for
 'Mother Pratt' to come in sight at this
 moment.
 Mother Pratt Pratt is an established English surname, perhaps derived from
 'prat', *a*., astute (*OED*). 'Neighbour Pratt'
 is a character in John Heywood's early
 16th-c. interlude *The Pardoner and the
 Friar*.

FORD I'll pratt her.

Enter Mistress Page leading Falstaff disguised as an old woman.

Ford beats Falstaff

Out of my door, you witch, you rag, you baggage, you   170
polecat, you runnion! Out, out! I'll conjure you, I'll
fortune-tell you!   *Exit Falstaff*

MISTRESS PAGE Are you not ashamed? I think you have
killed the poor woman.

MISTRESS FORD Nay, he will do it.—'Tis a goodly credit for
you.

FORD Hang her, witch!

EVANS By yea and no, I think the 'oman is a witch indeed.
I like not when a 'oman has a great peard. I spied a
great peard under her muffler.   180

FORD Will you follow, gentlemen? I beseech you, follow.
See but the issue of my jealousy. If I cry out thus upon
no trail, never trust me when I open again.

PAGE Let's obey his humour a little further. Come, gentlemen.

Exeunt Ford, Page, Shallow, Caius, and Evans

MISTRESS PAGE Trust me, he beat him most pitifully.

---

169 pratt her] F (*Prat-*her)   169.1–2, 169.3, 172.1] Q (*Enter Falstaffe disguised like an old woman, and misteris Page with him, Ford beates him, and hee runnes away.*); *not in* F   170 rag] F1 (Ragge); Hagge Q3; Rag F2; Hag F3   179 spied] This edition; spie F; espied Q   180 her] Q (vnder her mufler a great beard); his F   185.1] *as* Q (*Exit omnes.*); *not in* F   186 Trust me] F; By my troth Q

169 **I'll pratt her** Hart rightly compares *1 Henry IV* 2.2.88–9, 'You are grand-jurors, are ye? We'll jure, ye, faith.' Compare also Pistol's 'Master Fer? I'll fer him, and firk him, and ferret him', *Henry V* 4.4.27–8. The threatening verb is a nonce-word. This idiomatic usage is incompatible with editors' interpretations of 'prat' as 'buttock' (NCS: *OED sb.*², rogues' slang, usually in plural, first example 1567) or 'practise tricks' (Oliver: *OED v.*, Scottish).

170 **rag** a term of contempt (a rag being a type of worthlessness)

171 **runnion** another term of contempt, of obscure origin (*OED*)

175–6 **'Tis ... you** Ironical.

179 **spied** The past tense (as in Q's 'espied') is required because Falstaff is no longer in sight. F's 'spie' is close against the right-hand margin.

180 **her** Q's reading is correct. F's 'his' is a simple mistake arising from the scribe's or compositor's knowledge that the person was Falstaff. Compare 3.3.169, 'what [F who] was in the basket'.

181 **follow** i.e. follow me

182–3 **cry out ... open again** Imagery and terms from hunting with hounds: to *cry out* and *open* are to bark, and a *trail* is a quarry's scent.

184 **obey his humour** comply with his eccentric behaviour

186–8 Q completely spoils this exchange, substituting 'By my troth he beat him most extreamly' and the reply 'I am glad of it, what shall we proceed any further?'

MISTRESS FORD Nay, by th' mass, that he did not: he beat
him most unpitifully, methought.

MISTRESS PAGE I'll have the cudgel hallowed and hung
o'er the altar. It hath done meritorious service.   190

MISTRESS FORD What think you? May we, with the warrant of womanhood and the witness of a good conscience, pursue him with any further revenge?

MISTRESS PAGE The spirit of wantonness is sure scared out
of him. If the devil have him not in fee-simple, with fine
and recovery, he will never, I think, in the way of waste
attempt us again.

MISTRESS FORD Shall we tell our husbands how we have
served him?

MISTRESS PAGE Yes, by all means, if it be but to scrape the   200
figures out of your husband's brains. If they can find
in their hearts the poor unvirtuous fat knight shall be
any further afflicted, we two will still be the ministers.

MISTRESS FORD I'll warrant they'll have him publicly
shamed, and methinks there would be no period to the
jest should he not be publicly shamed.

MISTRESS PAGE Come, to the forge with it, then shape it. I
would not have things cool.   *Exeunt*

4.3   *Enter Host and Bardolph*

BARDOLPH Sir, the Germans desire to have three of your
horses. The Duke himself will be tomorrow at court, and
they are going to meet him.

HOST What duke should that be comes so secretly? I hear

207 it, then shape] F; it then, shape HANMER   208 *Exeunt*] F; *Exit both.* Q
4.3] F (*Scena Tertia.*)   1 Germans desire] CAPELL; Germane desires F

189–90 **I'll have . . . altar** Compare Iden's
words after slaying Cade, *2 Henry VI*
4.9.67–8: 'Sword, I will hallow thee for
this thy deed, | And hang thee o'er my
tomb when I am dead.'
194 **spirit** devil (compare 3.3.203)
195–6 **in fee-simple . . . recovery** in absolute
possession (legal terms)
196 **waste** act of damage. Another legal
term (*OED sb.* 7), strictly applicable to
damage by a tenant, but here used with a
general sense more like 'trespass'.
201 **figures** fantasies (compare *Caesar*
2.1.230, where the words are synony-

mous). The image in *scrape* is of erasing
writing with a knife.
203 **ministers** agents
205 **period** See 3.3.42 n.
207 **Come . . . shape it** F's punctuation suits
the implied sense ('Let us bring it to the
forge', etc.) better than Hanmer's, which
makes *shape it* sound like an imperative
addressed to Mistress Ford.
4.3.1 **Germans desire** Capell's emendation is
required by *the gentlemen* and *They* in the
Host's reply.
4 **comes** that comes (Abbott 244)

not of him in the court. Let me speak with the gentlemen. They speak English?

BARDOLPH Ay, sir. I'll call them to you.

HOST They shall have my horses, but I'll make them pay:
I'll sauce them. They have had my house a week at
command; I have turned away my other guests. They   10
must come off: I'll sauce them. Come.   *Exeunt*

4.4   *Enter Page, Ford, Mistress Page, Mistress Ford, and
Evans*

EVANS 'Tis one of the best discretions of a 'oman as ever I
did look upon.

PAGE And did he send you both these letters at an instant?

MISTRESS PAGE Within a quarter of an hour.

FORD

Pardon me, wife. Henceforth do what thou wilt.

I rather will suspect the sun with cold

Than thee with wantonness. Now doth thy honour
stand

In him that was of late an heretic,

As firm as faith.

PAGE   'Tis well, 'tis well. No more.

Be not as extreme in submission as in offence.   10

But let our plot go forward. Let our wives

Yet once again, to make us public sport,

Appoint a meeting with this old fat fellow,

Where we may take him and disgrace him for it.

---

7 them] Q; him F   9 house] Q; houses F

4.4] F (*Scena Quarta.*)   0.1–2] F; *Enter Ford, Page, their wiues, Shallow, and Slender. Syr Hu.* Q
5 FORD] F; *Ford (kneeling)* NCS   6 cold] ROWE; gold F   10] F; *two lines, breaking after*
'submission' CAPELL

---

9 **I'll sauce them** Since this repeated phrase
immediately follows the phrases *I'll make
them pay* and *They must come off* (i.e. pay
up, *OED*) it seems to be simply the Host's
synonym for them. The implied imagery
is not clear: Hart glosses *sauce them* as
'pepper them' and NCS as 'make it hot for
them'; Hilda M. Hulme's explanation
(pp. 45–6), 'make them pay more for the
sauce than for the meat', seems doubtful.

9–10 **at command** at their disposal (*OED sb.*
4b). Exactly what this means is not clear,
nor in what sense the Host has *turned
away* his *other guests*. Falstaff, at any rate,
is evidently still lodging at the Garter.
Perhaps the Host means that he has kept
one or more rooms empty and reserved
for the coming Germans, and has refused
bookings from intending guests.

4.4.1 **discretions of a 'oman** examples of
feminine discretion. Evans's expression
is, as usual, eccentric, particularly in *look
upon*, which suggests an indecent idea
without itself being indecent.

FORD

There is no better way than that they spoke of.

PAGE How, to send him word they'll meet him in the Park
at midnight? Fie, fie, he'll never come.

EVANS You say he has been thrown in the rivers, and has
been grievously peaten as an old 'oman. Methinks there
should be terrors in him, that he should not come.   20
Methinks his flesh is punished; he shall have no desires.

PAGE So think I too.

MISTRESS FORD

Devise but how you'll use him when he comes,
And let us two devise to bring him thither.

MISTRESS PAGE

There is an old tale goes that Herne the Hunter,
Sometime a keeper here in Windsor Forest,
Doth all the winter-time, at still midnight,
Walk round about an oak, with great ragg'd horns;
And there he blasts the trees, and takes the cattle,
And makes milch-kine yield blood, and shakes a chain   30
In a most hideous and dreadful manner.
You have heard of such a spirit, and well you know
The superstitious idle-headed eld
Received and did deliver to our age
This tale of Herne the Hunter for a truth.

PAGE

Why, yet there want not many that do fear
In deep of night to walk by this Herne's Oak.
But what of this?

29 trees] HANMER; tree F   30 makes] F2; make F1

16 **they'll** The pronoun is appropriate to the
fact that both wives are sending the
message, and Mistress Quickly comes to
Falstaff 'from the two parties' (4.5.98),
but when Falstaff confides in 'Brook'
(5.1.8–27) and meets Mistress Ford
(5.5.14–21) he does not seem to be
expecting Mistress Page.

25 **Herne the Hunter** known only in this
play, and so probably Shakespeare's invention: see Introduction, p. 23 n. 1.

26 **Sometime** formerly

27 **midnight** accented on the second syllable

28 **ragg'd** of irregular shape

29 **blasts** blights

29 **trees** F's 'tree' is perhaps influenced by
oak in the previous line (Jowett). The
plurals *cattle* and *milch-kine* invite emendation here for consistency.
takes bewitches

30 **milch-kine** dairy cows
shakes a chain Compare the 'strange and
several noises | Of roaring, shrieking,
howling, jingling chains' listed in *Tempest*
5.1.231–2, and Milton's phrase 'Each
fettered ghost' ('On the Morning of
Christ's Nativity', l. 234).

33 **eld** people in the old days

36 **want not** are not lacking

MISTRESS FORD   Marry, this is our device:
　　That Falstaff at that oak shall meet with us,
　　Disguised like Herne, with huge horns on his head.   40
PAGE
　　Well, let it not be doubted but he'll come;
　　And in this shape when you have brought him thither,
　　What shall be done with him? What is your plot?
MISTRESS PAGE
　　That likewise have we thought upon, and thus:
　　Nan Page my daughter, and my little son,
　　And three or four more of their growth we'll dress
　　Like urchins, oafs, and fairies, green and white,
　　With rounds of waxen tapers on their heads,
　　And rattles in their hands. Upon a sudden,
　　As Falstaff, she, and I are newly met,   50
　　Let them from forth a sawpit rush at once
　　With some diffusèd song. Upon their sight,
　　We two in great amazèdness will fly.
　　Then let them all encircle him about,
　　And fairy-like to pinch the unclean knight,
　　And ask him why, that hour of fairy revel,
　　In their so sacred paths he dares to tread
　　In shape profane.

40] Q; *not in* F   Herne] F (*and throughout*); *Horne* Q (*and throughout*)   41 come;] *as* F
(come,); come, CAPELL   42 shape when] F2; shape, when F; shape; when CAPELL   47
oafs] F (Ouphes)   55 to pinch] F; to-pinch STEEVENS 1778 (*conj.* Tyrwhitt)

40 **Disguised . . . head** Page's previous speech
is not that of a man who will guess the
wives' device without being told it. His
phrase *in this shape* (l. 42) makes it certain
that Falstaff's disguise as Herne was
mentioned in Mistress Ford's speech and
that a line or more has been accidentally
omitted from F. A line from Q has been
inserted to fill the gap, though it is most
unlikely that it was accurately remembered from the original text, because the
whole scene is rewritten in Q, which here
reads 'Now for that *Falstaffe* hath bene so
deceiued, | As that he dares not venture
to the house, | Weele send him word to
meet vs in the field, | Disguised like *Horne*,
with huge horns on his head'.

47 **urchins, oafs, and fairies** Since they are
all to be similarly equipped with tapers
and rattles, these supernatural beings are
practically synonymous (so also in 5.5);

urchins may be defined as 'elves' (it clearly
does not mean 'hedgehogs' here) and *oafs*
as 'children of elves' (*OED*, which notes
that F's spelling 'ouphes' is apparently
the first occurrence of the word in that
form). The modern senses of *oaf* (dolt,
lout), derived from the derogatory sense
of 'changeling', are not applicable.

51 **sawpit** pit across which timber was laid to
be sawn

52 **diffusèd** confused, wild; compare *Henry V*
5.2.61, 'diffused attire'

55 **to pinch** The *to* here is to complete the
metre: its redundancy can be seen if one
imagines *to* before *encircle* and *ask*, which
are syntactically parallel to *pinch*. Oliver
compares *John* 4.2.238–42, but 'thou . . .
didst let' is there indicative, whereas here
let is subjunctive. For the traditional idea
that fairies pinched mortals for their
faults see 5.5.44.

⌈MISTRESS⌉ FORD   And till he tell the truth,
  Let the supposèd fairies pinch him sound
  And burn him with their tapers.
MISTRESS PAGE   The truth being known,   60
  We'll all present ourselves, dis-horn the spirit,
  And mock him home to Windsor.
FORD   The children must
  Be practised well to this, or they'll ne'er do't.
EVANS I will teach the children their behaviours, and I will
  be like a jackanapes also, to burn the knight with my
  taber.
FORD
  That will be excellent. I'll go buy them visors.
MISTRESS PAGE
  My Nan shall be the Queen of all the Fairies,
  Finely attirèd in a robe of white.
PAGE
  That silk will I go buy. (*Aside*) And in that time   70
  Shall Master Slender steal my Nan away
  And marry her at Eton. (*To Mistress Page and Mistress
      Ford*) Go, send to Falstaff straight.
FORD
  Nay, I'll to him again in name of Brook.
  He'll tell me all his purpose. Sure he'll come.

58 MISTRESS FORD] ROWE; *Ford.* F   67 visors] F (vizards)   70 time] F; tire THEOBALD   72
To . . . Ford] *as* HIBBARD; *To Mistress Page* OXFORD; *not in* F

60 **with their tapers** Not, presumably, the
  ones encircling their heads but additional
  ones (not mentioned by Mistress Page)
  carried in their hands. See 5.5.100,
  'Pinch him, and burn him, and turn him
  about.'
61 **dis-horn the spirit** For *spirit* as 'devil'
  compare 3.3.203 and 4.2.194, and for
  the association of the devil and horns
  5.2.13.
65 **jackanapes** alluding to the monkey's
  mischievous playfulness, not to Evans's
  intended costume.
66 **taber** i.e. taper. Evans's pronunciation
  allows the word to be mistaken for 'tabor'
  (drum), but not much humour can be got
  out of this, and probably none is intended.
67 **visors** masks

69 **robe** The Fairy Queen is, of course, to be
  dressed as a woman, and from the action
  involving Anne, Slender, Caius, and Fenton it appears that several of the subordinate fairies are also female. In *Dream* all
  the fairies who attend on Bottom are
  male, but the one who speaks to Puck is
  female.
70 **time** Theobald's emendation is unneccess-
  ary (and might mean that Slender would
  be wearing the 'tire'). The preposition *in*
  with *time* is not unusual in Shakespeare
  (e.g. *Richard II* 4.1.9, *Coriolanus*
  2.1.113).
72 **Eton** a village on the opposite (north) side
  of the Thames
73 **Nay** The sense is 'And not only that':
  Ford is not contradicting Page's suggestion or proposing an alternative.

MISTRESS PAGE
  Fear not you that. (*To Page, Ford, and Evans*) Go get us
    properties
  And tricking for our fairies.
EVANS Let us about it. It is admirable pleasures and fery
  honest knaveries.   *Exeunt Page, Ford, and Evans*
MISTRESS PAGE Go, Mistress Ford,
  Send quickly to Sir John, to know his mind.   80
                       Exit Mistress Ford
  I'll to the Doctor. He hath my good will,
  And none but he, to marry with Nan Page.
  That Slender, though well landed, is an idiot;
  And he my husband best of all affects.
  The Doctor is well moneyed, and his friends
  Potent at court. He, none but he, shall have her,
  Though twenty thousand worthier come to crave her.
                                 Exit

4.5   *Enter Host and Simple*
HOST What wouldst thou have, boor? What, thick-skin?
  Speak, breathe, discuss; brief, short, quick, snap.
SIMPLE Marry, sir, I come to speak with Sir John Falstaff
  from Master Slender.
HOST There's his chamber, his house, his castle, his

---

78 *Exeunt ... Evans*] ROWE; *not in* F   80 quickly] F; Quickly THEOBALD   80.1 *Exit ... Ford*]
ROWE; *not in* F   82 he, to] POPE; he to F   87.1 *Exit*] F2; *not in* F1
    4.5] F (*Scena Quinta.*)   0.1] Q; *Enter Host, Simple, Falstaffe, Bardolfe, Euans, Caius, Quickly.* F

75-6 **properties | And tricking** equipment
(i.e. tapers and rattles) and finery. The
theatrical sense of *properties* also occurs
in *Dream* 1.2.98.

77-8 **fery honest knaveries** Evans's unconscious paradox (with his characteristic
plural). For the idea, compare 2.1.90-2
and 4.2.191-3.

84 **he** Abbott (207) gives this example and
one other (not exactly comparable, since
in it 'he' is the subject of a subordinate
clause) in illustration of 'he' used for
'him'. F's comma after 'he' seems to
imply the elliptical sense 'And he [is the
suitor whom] my husband most affects
(i.e. likes)', or to mark off 'he' as the
theme or logical subject of the sentence.

87 **worthier** more deserving (rather than
better-endowed with money or land)

4.5.1 **thick-skin** i.e. insensitive fellow, dul-
lard; compare *Dream* 3.2.13

2 **breathe** use your breath; synonymous
with *speak* and *discuss* (for which compare 1.3.88)
snap Evidently synonymous with *brief,
short, quick*; compare *LLL* 5.1.56-7, 'a
quick venue of wit; snip, snap, quick and
home'. Q confirms that F is correct and
that 'snip' has not been omitted. The Host
uses *two* nouns, *three* verbs, and *four*
adverbs, and his following speech begins
with a series of *five* nouns.

5 **There's** The Host perhaps opens one of
the doors and indicates to Simple that
there is a staircase outside it. Compare
4.2, in which similar staging is implied
for Ford's house.
castle This improves on *house* as *house*

standing-bed and truckle-bed. 'Tis painted about with
the story of the Prodigal, fresh and new. Go, knock and
call. He'll speak like an Anthropophaginian unto thee.
Knock, I say.

SIMPLE There's an old woman, a fat woman, gone up into   10
his chamber. I'll be so bold as stay, sir, till she come
down. I come to speak with her, indeed.

HOST Ha? A fat woman? The knight may be robbed. I'll
call.—Bully knight! Bully Sir John! Speak from thy
lungs military. Art thou there? It is thine host, thine
Ephesian, calls.

FALSTAFF (*within*) How now, mine host?

HOST Here's a Bohemian Tartar tarries the coming down
of thy fat woman. Let her descend, bully, let her
descend. My chambers are honourable. Fie! Privacy?   20
Fie!

        Enter Falstaff

17 within] OXFORD; *he speakes aboue* Q2; *above* THEOBALD; *Enter Falstaff* ROWE; *not in* F
21.1] Q (*Enter Sir Iohn*), *after* 23; *not in* F

improves on *chamber* (the literally accurate word). *OED* gives an instance from 1588 of the familiar phrase: 'our law calleth a man's house his castle' (*castle sb.* 3e).

6 truckle-bed Bedrooms often had a low extra bed on 'truckles' (castors) which could be stored under the four-poster bed (the *standing-bed*).
   'Tis painted about This refers to pictorial wall-painting (*it* being the bedchamber). Such decoration was common. When Shakespeare means 'painted cloth' (e.g. *1 Henry IV* 4.2.26) he uses the whole expression.

7 the Prodigal Luke 15 was a favourite subject of 16th-c. artists and the inspiration of several 16th-c. plays about prodigals (e.g. Anon., *Misogonus*). Its use as the decoration of Falstaff's room is an appropriate reflection on his improvident and dissolute life.

8 Anthropophaginian cannibal (derived from Greek for man-eater). Here used principally for a grandiose simile, though possibly also with irony to mean that Falstaff will 'bite his head off', i.e. treat him fiercely (Oliver).

11 so bold as Simple's cliché would be appropriate if he were going to knock.
    stay wait
14–15 thy lungs military An example of 'the inversion portentous' (Vickers, p. 144).
16 Ephesian In *2 Henry IV* 2.2.141 'Ephesians . . . of the old church' probably refers to the unregenerate Ephesians whom St Paul warned against wine-drinking (Ephesians 5 : 18). Shakespeare may have conflated this idea with Romans 16 : 23: 'Gaius mine host, and of the whole church, saluteth you.' In the present context the word simply expresses the Host's grandiloquence.
18 Bohemian Tartar Tartar from Bohemia. Pure grandiloquent nonsense. There is a precedent for such joking in Medwall, *Fulgens and Lucrece* (c.1497), Part Two, l. 394, 'wild Irish Portingales'.
20 Privacy here in the special sense of 'goings-on in private' (*OED* 3: 'a condition approaching to secrecy or concealment'; this is the first example). The Host's implied accusation (which would require Falstaff to be having sexual relations with his other self) humorously draws attention to his ignorance of Falstaff's disguise.

FALSTAFF There was, mine host, an old fat woman even now with me, but she's gone.

SIMPLE Pray you, sir, was't not the wise woman of Brentford?

FALSTAFF Ay, marry was it, mussel-shell. What would you with her?

SIMPLE My master, sir, Master Slender, sent to her, seeing her go through the streets, to know, sir, whether one Nim, sir, that beguiled him of a chain, had the chain or   30
no.

FALSTAFF I spake with the old woman about it.

SIMPLE And what says she, I pray, sir?

FALSTAFF Marry, she says that the very same man that beguiled Master Slender of his chain cozened him of it.

SIMPLE I would I could have spoken with the woman herself. I had other things to have spoken with her too, from him.

FALSTAFF What are they? Let us know.

HOST Ay, come. Quick!   40

⌈SIMPLE⌉ I may not conceal them, sir.

28] My master ... Slender] STEEVENS 1778; My Master (Sir) my master *Slender* F; Marry sir my maister *Slender* Q   37 spoken with her] F; spoke of with her This edition *conj.*   41 SIMPLE] ROWE; Fal⟨*staff*⟩. F

24 **wise woman** woman skilled in magic
26 **mussel-shell** Either because Simple is gaping in expectation (Johnson) or because he is insignificant (Hart). An egg-shell (e.g. *Hamlet* 4.4, Additional Passage J44) is a more frequent type of worthlessness (Tilley E95).
28 **Master Slender** Steevens's emendation, despite Q's apparent confirmation of F's reading, is necessary: Simple cannot mean either 'my Master Slender' (i.e. the Master Slender belonging to me) or 'my master, Slender' (i.e. the surname without the title). The sequence 'master sir master Slender' in the copy might easily unsettle F's scribe or compositor and lead him to interpolate 'my' in an attempt to make it clearer. Q's reading might arise from the reporter's inaccurate recollection of the speech as 'Marry, sir, my master Master Slender sent me to her' and from the compositor's omission of one 'master'; Q makes the same error in its version of 1.4 (see Introduction, p. 49).

29–31 **whether ... or no** Compare the question put by Old Gobbo to his son, *Merchant* 2.2.41–3: 'Can you tell me whether one Lancelot that dwells with him dwell with him or no?'
29–30 **one Nim ... chain** The origin of this reported incident, introduced in order to give Simple something to enquire about, is probably Nashe's comment on Gabriel Harvey's friend Barnabe Barnes: 'What his soldiership is I cannot judge, but if you have ever a chain for him to run away with, as he did with a nobleman's steward's chain at his lord's installing at Windsor, ... he is for you' (*Have with you to Saffron-Walden*, 1596, *Works*, iii. 103).
37 **to have spoken** F's phrase may be influenced by *spoken* in the preceding line. In making *other things* the direct object of *to have spoken* it does not seem idiomatic: one would expect 'to have spoke of'. Q has no corresponding passage.
41 **conceal** In error for 'reveal', and thus giving the opening for Shakespeare's characteristic humour in the Host's reply.

HOST Conceal them, or thou diest.

SIMPLE Why, sir, they were nothing but about Mistress
  Anne Page: to know if it were my master's fortune to
  have her or no.

FALSTAFF 'Tis; 'tis his fortune.

SIMPLE What, sir?

FALSTAFF To have her or no. Go, say the woman told me
  so.

SIMPLE May I be bold to say so, sir?   50

FALSTAFF Ay, sir; like who more bold.

SIMPLE I thank your worship. I shall make my master glad
  with these tidings.   *Exit*

HOST Thou art clerkly, thou art clerkly, Sir John. Was
  there a wise woman with thee?

FALSTAFF Ay, that there was, mine host, one that hath
  taught me more wit than ever I learned before in my life.
  And I paid nothing for it neither, but was paid for my
  learning.

  Enter Bardolph ⌈muddy⌉

BARDOLPH Out, alas, sir, cozenage, mere cozenage!   60

HOST Where be my horses? Speak well of them, varletto.

BARDOLPH Run away with the cozeners. For so soon as I
  came beyond Eton, they threw me off from behind one

51 Ay, sir; like] F (I Sir: like); *I* tike, Q; Ay, sir Tike; like STEEVENS 1778 (*conj.* Farmer); Ay,
sir Tike; REED   53 *Exit*] ROWE; *not in* F   54 Thou art] Q; Thou are F   59.1 muddy]
OXFORD; *not in* F   60 Out, alas] F; O Lord Q   62 with] F; with by COLLIER 1853

46 **'Tis; 'tis his fortune.** This speech is best
   delivered as a one-word reply, followed
   by a three-word amplification as Simple
   looks uncomprehendingly at Falstaff.
   This prepares the audience for the joke in
   Falstaff's next speech.
51 **like who more bold** i.e. 'as bold as the
   boldest' (Sisson). Several editors have
   incorporated Q's 'tike', probably because
   the insult 'base tike' occurs in *Henry V*
   2.1.28 (F 'Tyke', Oxford 'tick'). Q may
   show the influence of the *Henry V* passage, since the comma (unless merely
   misplaced) suggests that 'tike' is not
   merely a misprint.
54 **clerkly** learned
54–5 **Was there** The Host is inquisitive, not
   incredulous. Falstaff's reply is humorous
   because the Host has no suspicion that
   Falstaff was himself the old woman. Bardolph's arrival prevents further questions.

58 **was paid** i.e. in blows, as Fluellen proposes to pay the supposed traitor Williams (*Henry V* 4.8.15). In the active sense
   of the verb Falstaff did pay for his learning
   by being beaten. 'Bought wit is best' was
   proverbial (Tilley W545).
60 **mere** absolute
61 **varletto** The Host's Italianized coinage
   from 'varlet' (i.e. servant: not here derogatory), not the Italian word *valletto*.
62 **Run away with the cozeners** Literally
   true, but there is unconscious humour
   here because the cozeners have run away
   with the horses, i.e. stolen them. Collier's
   emendation spoils this humour. Q's
   corresponding speech, in reply to the
   Host's 'Why man, where be my horses?
   where be the Germanes?' is 'Rid away
   with your horses.'
63–4 **from behind one of them** Bardolph was
   evidently riding pillion on the outward

of them in a slough of mire, and set spurs and away, like three German devils, three Doctor Faustuses.

HOST They are gone but to meet the Duke, villain. Do not say they be fled. Germans are honest men.

Enter Evans

EVANS Where is mine host?

HOST What is the matter, sir?

EVANS Have a care of your entertainments. There is a   70
friend of mine come to town tells me there is three cozen-Germans that has cozened all the hosts of Readings, of Maidenhead, of Colnbrook, of horses and money. I tell you for good will, look you. You are wise, and full of gibes and vlouting-stocks, and 'tis not convenient you should be cozened. Fare you well.

Exit

Enter Caius

CAIUS Vere is mine host de Jarteer?

HOST Here, Master Doctor, in perplexity and doubtful dilemma.

67.1] Q (*which transposes the arrival of Evans and that of Caius*); *not in* F   71–2 three cozen-Germans] F (three Cozen-Iermans); three sorts of cosen garmombles Q; three cozen Garmombles OXFORD   72–3 Readings] F (*Readins*), Q (Readings)   76.1 *Exit*] Q; *not in* F   76.2] Q (*see* 67.1); *not in* F

journey in order to be able to bring the horses back to Windsor once the Germans had met their Duke.

64–5 like ... Faustuses i.e. as if the devil were in them. The allusion springs from Faustus's being a German (the words 'German' and 'Germany' occur frequently in Marlowe's play). It also suggests that the event happened with magical suddenness. Particular incidents in *Doctor Faustus* involve mud and dirt (Sc.14: one of Faustus's enemies is dragged by devils through a lake of it) and a horse (Sc.15: sold by Faustus to a horse-dealer, it turns into a bundle of hay when he rides it into the water); these may have helped to suggest the allusion but are not necessary to its interpretation.

66 They ... Duke i.e. they will bring the horses back and will pay their bill

70 your entertainments i.e. the entertainment (hospitality) that you give to strangers

72 cozen-Germans A nonce-word (i.e. cozening Germans) quibbling on 'cousin-german' (first cousin, i.e. child of one's uncle or aunt). Q's reading 'cosen garmombles' seems to play upon the name Mömpelgard (see Introduction, pp. 5–6), but whether it was in the original text is debatable. It would be unlike Shakespeare's usual practice to use a word that made no sense except as an anagram. The word 'geremumble', used by Nashe as an abusive noun and as a verb (= ? to gut fish), seems to have had the 'g' pronounced soft (*OED*); if so, Q's 'garmombles' (with the 'g' hard) would be more evidently a play on 'Mömpelgard'.

72–3 Readings Reading (with Evans's characteristic plural)

75 vlouting-stocks Evans means 'flouts', but the word he uses recalls his grievance against the Host (compare 3.1.109–12).

78–9 perplexity and doubtful dilemma Triply synonymous, for emphasis, and in the Host's characteristic style.

CAIUS I cannot tell vat is dat; but it is tell-a me dat you   80
  make grand preparation for a duke de Jarmany. By my
  trot', dere is no duke that the court is know to come. I
  tell you for good will. Adieu.   *Exit*
HOST (*to Bardolph*) Hue and cry, villain, go! (*To Falstaff*)
  Assist me, knight.—I am undone! (*To Bardolph*) Fly,
  run, hue and cry, villain!—I am undone!

          Exeunt Host and Bardolph ⌜severally⌝
FALSTAFF I would all the world might be cozened, for I
  have been cozened and beaten too. If it should come to
  the ear of the court how I have been transformed, and
  how my transformation hath been washed and cud-   90
  gelled, they would melt me out of my fat drop by drop,
  and liquor fishermen's boots with me. I warrant they
  would whip me with their fine wits till I were as
  crestfallen as a dried pear. I never prospered since I
  forswore myself at primero. Well, if my wind were but
  long enough, I would repent.

          Enter Mistress Quickly ⌜with a letter⌝
  Now, whence come you?
MISTRESS QUICKLY From the two parties, forsooth.
FALSTAFF The devil take one party, and his dam the other,
  and so they shall be both bestowed. I have suffered more   100

81 Jarmany] F (*Iamanie*)   83 Exit] Q; *not in* F   84–5 to Bardolph/To Falstaff/To Bardolph]
OXFORD; *not in* F   84 Hue] ROWE; Huy F   86 hue] ROWE; huy F   86.1] OXFORD; *Exit.*
Q; *Exeunt Host and Bardolph* CAPELL; *He runs forth with Bardolph after* NCS; *not in* F   96 long
enough] F; long enough to say my prayers Q   96.1] This edition; *Enter Mistresse Quickly.* Q
(*after* 97); *not in* F

81 **grand** (Fr.) great
82 **that the court is know to come** that the
    court knows to have come (or to be
    coming)
84 **Hue ... go!** i.e. Go and raise the alarm,
    Bardolph! A *hue and cry* is a call for the
    general pursuit of those who have just
    committed a crime.
90 **my transformation** that into which I
    was transformed (i.e. firstly dirty wash-
    ing and secondly an old woman).
    In *Troilus* 5.1.50 Thersites refers to
    Menelaus as 'the goodly transformation
    of Jupiter' (i.e. the bull, i.e. the cuck-
    old).
92 **liquor** grease (to make waterproof)
94 **dried pear** Falstaff is compared to a
    shrivelled apple in *2 Henry IV* 2.4.1–9. In
    All's Well 1.1.157–60 Paroles compares

virginity to a withered pear. *Crestfallen* is
in this context imaginatively figurative
(as Oliver notes, though it need not refer
to a defeated fighting-cock, being used of
exhausted horses in *Caesar* 4.2.26: 'They
fall their crests').
95 **forswore myself at primero** cheated at a
    card game and swore that I had not. The
    game is described in David Parlett, *The
    Penguin Book of Card Games* (1979),
    p. 401.
96 **long enough** Q's additional words are less
    probably an accidental omission from F
    than an interpolation.
98 **parties** Shakespeare's use of 'party' for
    person, except in a legal context, is
    usually comic, e.g. *LLL* 4.2.133,
    5.2.665, *Antony* 5.2.240.
100 **bestowed** lodged; compare *Hamlet*

for their sakes, more than the villainous inconstancy of
man's disposition is able to bear.

MISTRESS QUICKLY And have not they suffered? Yes, I
warrant; speciously one of them. Mistress Ford, good
heart, is beaten black and blue, that you cannot see a
white spot about her.

FALSTAFF What tell'st thou me of black and blue? I was
beaten myself into all the colours of the rainbow; and I
was like to be apprehended for the witch of Brentford.
But that my admirable dexterity of wit, my counterfeit-   110
ing the action of an old woman, delivered me, the knave
constable had set me i'th' stocks, i'th' common stocks,
for a witch.

MISTRESS QUICKLY Sir, let me speak with you in your
chamber, you shall hear how things go, and, I warrant,
to your content. Here is a letter will say somewhat.
Good hearts, what ado here is to bring you together!
Sure, one of you does not serve heaven well, that you
are so crossed.

FALSTAFF Come up into my chamber.   *Exeunt*   120

4.6   *Enter Fenton, ⌈with a letter,⌉ and Host*

HOST Master Fenton, talk not to me. My mind is heavy. I
will give over all.

FENTON

Yet hear me speak. Assist me in my purpose,
And, as I am a gentleman, I'll give thee
A hundred pound in gold more than your loss.

109–10 Brentford. But] *as* THEOBALD; *Braineford*, but F   117 here is] F; is here This edition
conj.

    4.6] F (*Scena Sexta.*)   0.1 *with a letter*] This edition; *not in* F

2.2.524–5: 'will you see the players well
bestowed?'

101–2 **the villainous … disposition** the
cursed instability of man's natural con-
stitution, i.e. the disadvantage of not
being invulnerable

104 **speciously** in error for 'specially' (as at
3.4.105–6)

110–11 **But that … delivered me** Falstaff, as
at Gadshill and at Shrewsbury in *1 Henry
IV*, speciously boasts of his resourceful-
ness after having exhibited fear. No dis-

tinction can be drawn between the *action*
of an *old woman* and that of a *witch*.

114 **let me** i.e. only let me, if you will let me

117 **Good hearts** poor things

    here is This does not seem idiomatic and
may be an error for 'there is' (by misreading) or for 'is here' (by transposition).

4.6.2 **give over all** i.e. give up my efforts on
your behalf. The Host spoke in support of
Fenton's suit in 3.2.59–63. Compare
Troilus 1.1.87–8 (Pandarus to Troilus):
'Pray you, speak no more to me. I will
leave all as I found it. And there an end.'

HOST I will hear you, Master Fenton, and I will, at the
least, keep your counsel.

FENTON

From time to time I have acquainted you
With the dear love I bear to fair Anne Page,
Who mutually hath answered my affection,   10
So far forth as herself might be her chooser,
Even to my wish. I have a letter from her
Of such contents as you will wonder at,
The mirth whereof so larded with my matter
That neither singly can be manifested
Without the show of both. Fat Falstaff
Hath a great scene. The image of the jest
I'll show you here at large. Hark, good mine host:
Tonight at Herne's Oak, just 'twixt twelve and one,
Must my sweet Nan present the Fairy Queen—   20
The purpose why is here—in which disguise,
While other jests are something rank on foot,
Her father hath commanded her to slip
Away with Slender, and with him at Eton
Immediately to marry. She hath consented. Now, sir,
Her mother, ever strong against that match,

16 Fat Falstaff] F; fat Sir *Iohn Falstaffe* F2; wherein fat Falstaff MALONE; Fat Falstaff in't
IRVING/MARSHALL   25] F; *as two lines, breaking after* 'consented' MALONE   26 ever strong
against] POPE; euen strong against F; still against Q

13 **contents** The stress is on the second
syllable.
14 **so larded with my matter** is so inter-
mingled with my present subject (i.e. my
plan to steal Anne away). For the ellipsis
of 'is' see Abbott 403.
16 **the show** the showing
16–18 **Fat Falstaff ... large** These lines may
have been added by Shakespeare, after
writing the rest of the speech, in order to
let Fenton give the Host at least a hint of
why Anne is to act the Fairy Queen. The
defective metre in l. 16 has been taken as
evidence that Falstaff may originally
have been called Oldcastle here (J. M.
Robertson, *The Problem of 'The Merry
Wives'*, 1917, p. 29), but more probably
something has been accidentally omitted.
Q's quite different version of the two half-
lines 16–17 occurs in the following
wholly rewritten passage: 'And in a robe

of white this night disguised, | Wherein
fat *Falstaffe* had a mightie scare [for
scene?], | Must *Slender* take her and carrie
her to *Catlen* [for *Eaton*, i.e. Eton], | And
there vnknowne to any, marrie her.'
This, while not helping to restore the F
version, does show that *fat Falstaff* was
probably part of it.
17 **scene** The word is used, as often by
Shakespeare, in the sense of a part of a
play.
18 **here** in the letter; so too at l. 21, which
may reinforce the suggestion that the
passage *Fat Falstaff ... large* is an addition.
22 **something rank on foot** somewhat abun-
dantly in progress. *Rank* is used adverbially in *Troilus* 1.3.196.
26 **ever** F's 'even' gives no satisfactory sense
in the context, and Q's 'still' confirms the
emendation.

And firm for Doctor Caius, hath appointed
That he shall likewise shuffle her away,
While other sports are tasking of their minds,
And at the dean'ry, where a priest attends,   30
Straight marry her. To this her mother's plot
She, seemingly obedient, likewise hath
Made promise to the Doctor. Now thus it rests:
Her father means she shall be all in white,
And in that habit, when Slender sees his time
To take her by the hand and bid her go,
She shall go with him. Her mother hath intended,
The better to denote her to the Doctor—
For they must all be masked and vizarded—
That quaint in green she shall be loose enrobed,   40
With ribbons pendent flaring 'bout her head;
And when the Doctor spies his vantage ripe,
To pinch her by the hand, and, on that token,
The maid hath given consent to go with him.

HOST

Which means she to deceive, father or mother?

FENTON

Both, my good host, to go along with me.
And here it rests, that you'll procure the vicar
To stay for me at church 'twixt twelve and one,
And, in the lawful name of marriage,
To give our hearts united ceremony.   50

---

38 denote] CAPELL (*conj.* Steevens); deuote F   41 ribbons pendent] F (Ribonds-pendant)
49 marriage] This edition (*conj.* Walker); marrying F

28 **shuffle her away** hastily and secretly take
   her away (*OED v.* 5b)
29 **tasking of** keeping busy
30 **dean'ry** dean's house. Shakespeare has
   no references to deaneries other than
   here and at 5.3.3 and 5.5.198, so it can
   be taken that this is the deanery attached
   to St George's Chapel in Windsor Castle
   (Hart) rather than some parsonage.
40 **quaint** handsomely (as in Shakespeare's
   other uses of the word with reference to
   dress)
41 **flaring** streaming in the wind
43 **To pinch** i.e. he is to pinch
45 The Host, here and in his next speech,
   has his only verse lines, being subdued to
   the style of the scene.
47 **here it rests** here lies the point (i.e. of my

request)
49 **marriage** Walker's conjecture is probable, because F's *marrying* here denotes
   the marriage-state or the marriage-
   ceremony, while elsewhere in Shakespeare it denotes the action of the verb 'to
   marry' (as also in *OED marrying vbl. sb.*). If
   Crane's copy read 'marryage' he may
   have misread it as 'marryinge', especially
   if he thought of *marriage* as a word of two
   syllables. Compare the usage and the
   metrical value of the word in *Much Ado*
   5.4.30, 'In the state of honourable marriage', and in *Lucrece* 221, 'This siege that
   hath engirt his marriage'.
50 **give ... ceremony** 'unite ι.. with the full
   sanction of religious rites' (Oliver)

HOST

Well, husband your device. I'll to the vicar.

Bring you the maid, you shall not lack a priest.

FENTON

So shall I evermore be bound to thee;

Besides, I'll make a present recompense.

Exeunt ⌈severally⌉

5.1 *Enter Falstaff and Mistress Quickly*

FALSTAFF Prithee, no more prattling; go; I'll hold. This is the third time; I hope good luck lies in odd numbers. Away, go! They say there is divinity in odd numbers, either in nativity, chance, or death. Away!

MISTRESS QUICKLY I'll provide you a chain, and I'll do what   5
I can to get you a pair of horns.

FALSTAFF

Away, I say; time wears. Hold up your head, and

mince.   *Exit Mistress Quickly*

Enter Ford disguised as Brook

54.1] OXFORD; *Exeunt.* F; *Exit omnes.* Q
  5.1] F (*Actus Quintus. Scœna Prima.*)   0.1] ROWE; *Enter Falstoffe, Quickly, and Ford.* F   7
Exit ... Quickly] ROWE (*after* 6); *not in* F   7.1] *as* ROWE; *not in* F

51 **husband your device** nurture your plan
52 **Bring you** This could be either conditional ('if you bring') or imperative; both interpretations would equally suit the sense.
54 **make a present recompense** give you an immediate reward
5.1 This scene is omitted by Q.
  1 **hold** keep the appointment
1–2 **This is the third time** 'The third time pays for all' is proverbial (Tilley T319). Compare *Twelfth Night* 5.1.34, 'The third pays for all.'
  2 **good ... numbers** 'There is luck in odd numbers' is proverbial (Tilley L582).
  3 **divinity** divine power (*OED sb.* 3)
  4 **either ... death** This seems to mean that to be born, or to die, on an odd-numbered day is lucky, and that lucky events of fortune also occur on odd-numbered days. On the Pythagorean tradition that odd numbers were superior to even ones see Alastair Fowler, *Spenser and the Numbers of Time* (1964), pp. 5–6.
  5 **chain** See 4.4.30. No dramatic use is

made of this chain, nor is it referred to in 5.5, and it is hardly ever carried by Falstaff in performance, though it is represented e.g. in Smirke's well-known painting (ill. 5). Since it is mentioned twice, and Mistress Quickly undertakes to provide it, it had better be part of Falstaff's equipment in 5.5. It can easily be removed from view by one of the fairies after they cease to pinch Falstaff.
  7 **Away ... mince** An iambic hexameter line. Compare *Henry V* 2.1.122, 'Let us condole the knight—for, lambkins, we will live', which likewise ends a prose dialogue.
    wears wears away, runs on (*OED v.*[1] 19)
    Hold ... mince The general sense seems to be 'make haste', but there is no parallel passage in Shakespeare. Slender is said to 'hold up his head' but to 'strut in his gait' (1.4.27–8). According to Portia, *Merchant* 3.4.67–8, 'two mincing steps' equal one 'manly stride'. Falstaff probably means 'Go as fast as your mincing pace will let you.'

How now, Master Brook! Master Brook, the matter will
be known tonight or never. Be you in the Park about
midnight, at Herne's Oak, and you shall see wonders.   10
FORD Went you not to her yesterday, sir, as you told me
you had appointed?
FALSTAFF I went to her, Master Brook, as you see, like a
poor old man, but I came from her, Master Brook, like a
poor old woman. That same knave Ford, her husband,
hath the finest mad devil of jealousy in him, Master
Brook, that ever governed frenzy. I will tell you: he beat
me grievously, in the shape of a woman; for in the
shape of man, Master Brook, I fear not Goliath with a
weaver's beam, because I know also life is a shuttle. I   20
am in haste. Go along with me. I'll tell you all, Master
Brook. Since I plucked geese, played truant, and
whipped top, I knew not what 'twas to be beaten till
lately. Follow me. I'll tell you strange things of this
knave Ford, on whom tonight I will be revenged, and I
will deliver his wife into your hand. Follow. Strange
things in hand, Master Brook! Follow.   *Exeunt*

5.2   *Enter Page, Shallow, and Slender*
PAGE Come, come, we'll couch i'th' Castle ditch till we see
the lights of our fairies. Remember, son Slender, my
daughter—

17 tell you: he] STEEVENS 1778; tell you, he F; tell you he OLIVER   19 Goliath] F (Goliah)
   5.2] F (*Scena Secunda.*)   2 lights] This edition; light F   2–3 my daughter—] This
edition; my daughter. F2; my ⌄ F

19–20 **Goliath ... beam** 1 Samuel 17: 7:
   'And the shaft of his spear was like a
   weaver's beam' (one of the two wooden
   rollers on which the warp is wound and
   the cloth rolled).
20 **life ... shuttle** Job 7: 6: 'My days pass
   over more speedily than a weaver's shuttle.'
22 **plucked geese** 'Apparently plucking
   feathers from a living goose, to use the
   feathers for some game, was a schoolboy
   prank' (Oliver); or it may have been done
   as an act of daring, geese being aggres-
   sive when roused.
23 **whipped top** used a whip to make a top
   spin.

26–7 **Strange things in hand** remarkable
   doings are afoot. The phrase is curious in
   drawing together *strange things* and *into
   your hand* from earlier in the speech and
   giving them a different sense.
5.2 This scene is omitted in Q.
1 **couch** lie hidden
2 **lights** Here and in l. 11 the plural seems
   necessary because each fairy will have a
   light; compare 5.3.14, 'with obscured
   lights'.
2–3 **my daughter—** Page is about to remind
   Slender that Anne will be dressed in
   white. Slender thereupon interrupts. In F
   a full stop is often used when a sentence is
   incomplete.

SLENDER Ay, forsooth. I have spoke with her, and we have
a nay-word how to know one another. I come to her in
white, and cry 'mum'; she cries 'budget'; and by that
we know one another.

SHALLOW That's good too. But what needs either your
'mum' or her 'budget'? The white will decipher her well
enough.—It hath struck ten o'clock.   10

PAGE The night is dark. Lights and spirits will become it
well. Heaven prosper our sport! No man means evil but
the devil, and we shall know him by his horns. Let's
away. Follow me.   *Exeunt*

5.3   *Enter Mistress Page, Mistress Ford, and Caius*

MISTRESS PAGE Master Doctor, my daughter is in green.
When you see your time, take her by the hand, away
with her to the deanery, and dispatch it quickly. Go
before into the Park. We two must go together.

CAIUS I know vat I have to do. Adieu.

MISTRESS PAGE Fare you well, sir.   *Exit Caius*
My husband will not rejoice so much at the abuse of
Falstaff as he will chafe at the Doctor's marrying my
daughter. But 'tis no matter. Better a little chiding than
a great deal of heart-break.   10

MISTRESS FORD Where is Nan now, and her troop of fairies,
and the Welsh devil Hugh?

MISTRESS PAGE They are all couched in a pit hard by
Herne's Oak, with obscured lights, which, at the very

11 Lights] OXFORD; Light F
5.3] F (*Scena Tertia.*)   6 *Exit Caius*] F2 (*after* 5); *not in* F1   12 Welsh devil Hugh]
CAPELL; Welch-deuill Herne F

5 **nay-word** pass-word (as in 2.2.119)
6 **mum** 'mumbudget' (*OED*) is a children's
  game in which silence is required; *mum*
  = silent, *budget* = a purse (perhaps used
  in this context figuratively for the mouth;
  hence there may be unconscious innuendo in Shallow's *her budget*).
11 **Lights and spirits** NCS, conjecturing this
  emendation, compares *Troilus* 5.1.62–3:
  'Hey-day, sprites and fires.'
13 **know ... horns** Proverbial: 'The devil is
  known by his horns' (Tilley D252). A

humorously literal application of a figurative expression.
5.3 This scene is omitted in Q.
7 **abuse** ill-usage
10 **heart-break** *OED*'s first example is dated
  1583. Mistress Page's observation,
  though it sounds like a proverb, is not
  recorded as one.
12 **Hugh** Oliver cites Ford's 'Well said, fairy
  Hugh' (5.5.130) in support of Capell's
  emendation. Apart from these two instances Evans is always 'Sir Hugh'.

instant of Falstaff's and our meeting, they will at once
display to the night.

MISTRESS FORD That cannot choose but amaze him.

MISTRESS PAGE If he be not amazed, he will be mocked. If
he be amazed, he will every way be mocked.

MISTRESS FORD We'll betray him finely.   20

MISTRESS PAGE

Against such lewdsters and their lechery,
Those that betray them do no treachery.

MISTRESS FORD The hour draws on. To the Oak, to the
Oak!   *Exeunt*

5.4   *Enter Evans ⌈disguised⌉, and William Page and
other children disguised as Fairies, ⌈with rattles in
their hands⌉*

EVANS Trib, trib, fairies! Come, and remember your parts.
Be pold, I pray you. Follow me into the pit, and when I
give the watch-'ords, do as I pid you. Come, come; trib,
trib!   *Exeunt*

5.4] F (*Scena Quarta.*)   0.1–3] This edition; *Enter Sir Hugh Evans, disguised as a satyr, and
William Page and other children, disguised as fairies* OXFORD; *Enter Euans and Fairies.* F

17 **cannot choose but amaze him** cannot fail
to terrify him

18–19 **If he ... every way be mocked** Even if
he is not terrified, he will be mocked (for
his misbehaviour); and if he is terrified he
will be mocked for his credulity as well as
for his misbehaviour.

21 **lewdsters** lewd persons (*OED*'s first recorded use of the word)

5.4 This scene is omitted in Q.

0.1 **Evans disguised** Q's stage direction, at
the point corresponding to 5.5.35.1,
states that he is '*like a Satyre*', but there is
nothing in the text of F or Q to confirm
this. In F he is referred to as 'the Welsh
devil' (5.3.12) and laughingly addressed
as 'fairy Hugh' (5.5.130). In Q, explaining to Falstaff that the fairies were boys,
he adds 'and I was | Also a Fairie that did
helpe to pinch you.' *OED* recognizes two
meanings of 'satyr' which might be appropriate: a goat-footed wood-god (the
usual sense in Elizabethan literature) and

a kind of ape (illustrated in Edward
Topsell's *History of Four-footed Beasts*,
1607). Neither of these could be represented in an easily discarded costume,
and it is unlikely that Evans presents a
highly incongruous appearance after the
fairy episode when he resumes his own
character. If he disguises himself in a
cloak of shaggy material he may pass, for
the purposes of the stage direction, as a
'satyr'.

2 **Follow me into the pit** Literally, into the
sawpit where they will lie hidden; but a
frequent sense of *pit* is hell (*OED sb.*[1] 4:
Hamlet 4.5.130, 'the profoundest pit';
Lear 4.5.125, 'the sulphurous pit'),
which makes the parson's instruction
humorously incongruous. The joke has
been prepared by the phrase 'the Welsh
devil', 5.3.12.

3 **watch-'ords** Evans's plural. Of course
there is only one (unspecified) watch-
word to be given.

5.5   *Enter Falstaff disguised as Herne,* ⌈*with a buck's*
horns upon his head, and with a chain in his hand⌉

FALSTAFF The Windsor bell hath struck twelve; the
minute draws on. Now, the hot-blooded gods assist me!
Remember, Jove, thou wast a bull for thy Europa. Love
set on thy horns. O powerful love, that in some respects
makes a beast a man, in some other a man a beast!
You were also, Jupiter, a swan for the love of Leda.
O omnipotent love, how near the god drew to the
complexion of a goose! A fault done first in the form of a
beast—O Jove, a beastly fault!—and then another fault
in the semblance of a fowl—think on't, Jove, a foul   10
fault! When gods have hot backs, what shall poor men
do? For me, I am here a Windsor stag, and the fattest, I
think, i'th' forest. Send me a cool rut-time, Jove, or who

5.5] F (*Scena Quinta.*)   0.1–2] *as* OXFORD; *Enter sir Iohn with a Bucks head vpon him.* Q;
Enter Falstaffe, Mistris Page, Mistris Ford, Euans, Anne Page, Fairies, Page, Ford, Quickly,
Slender, Fenton, Caius, Pistoll. F   2 hot-blooded gods] F1 (hot-bloodied-Gods); hot-bloodied
god F4

5.5.0.1–2 The form of Falstaff's disguise as
Herne the Hunter is debatable. See Appendix C.

1–2 The minute draws on the appointed
moment (*OED* 1c: first example) is near

2 the hot-blooded gods Though only Jupiter's exploits are referred to in the rest of
the speech, there is no need to emend
with F4. The plural is acceptable as an
opening invocation, and was doubtless
suggested by the passage in Lyly's *Euphues* which is here parodied: 'Love
knoweth no laws. Did not Jupiter transform himself into the shape of Amphi-
tryon to embrace Alcmena, into the form
of a swan to enjoy Leda, into a bull to
beguile Io, into a shower of gold to win
Danae? Did not Neptune change himself
into a heifer, a ram, a flood, a dolphin,
only for the love of those he lusted after?
Did not Apollo convert himself into a
shepherd, into a bird, into a lion, for the
desire he had to heal his disease? If the
gods thought no scorn to become beasts
to obtain their best beloved, shall Euphues be so nice in changing his copy to
gain his lady?' (Lyly, i. 236).

3 Europa Europa, daughter of Agenor the
king of Phoenicia, was carried off to Crete
by Jupiter, who appeared to her in the
form of a white bull and swam away with
her on his back.

3–4 Love set on thy horns the love that you
felt placed horns on your head

5 makes a beast a man transforms a dull
man into a witty one
a man a beast transforms a wise man into
a fool

6 Leda Leda, daughter of Thestius, king of
Aetolia, was seduced by Jupiter in the
form of a swan.

8 complexion appearance. The goose is a
type of stupidity.

9 beastly filthy (the most frequent sense in
Shakespeare). The quibble again recalls
Euphues: 'And in that you bring in the
example of a beast to confirm your folly,
you show therein your beastly disposition, which is ready to follow such beast-
liness' (Lyly, i. 240).

10 foul with a quibble on 'fowl'

11 hot backs lustful loins

13 rut-time mating season

can blame me to piss my tallow? Who comes here? My
doe?

Enter Mistress Ford ⌈followed by⌉ Mistress Page

MISTRESS FORD Sir John! Art thou there, my deer, my male
deer?

FALSTAFF My doe with the black scut! Let the sky rain
potatoes, let it thunder to the tune of 'Greensleeves',
hail kissing-comfits, and snow eryngoes; let there come   20
a tempest of provocation, I will shelter me here.

⌈*He embraces her*⌉

MISTRESS FORD Mistress Page is come with me, sweetheart.

FALSTAFF Divide me like a bribed buck, each a haunch. I
will keep my sides to myself, my shoulders for the fellow
of this walk, and my horns I bequeath your husbands.

15.1] as NCS; *Enter mistris Page, and mistris Ford.* Q; *not in* F   21.1] as CAPELL; *not in* F   22
sweetheart] F (sweet hart)   23 bribed] F (brib'd-); bribe- THEOBALD

14 **to piss my tallow** 'if I urinate my fat
away' (Hibbard). Bucks, having become
lean at the end of rutting-time, were said
to have pissed their tallow.

15.1 Falstaff is at first aware only of Mistress
Ford because 'the night is dark' (5.2.11).

16 **deer** The *deer/dear* quibble (again at
l. 117) is also applied to Falstaff in *1
Henry IV* 5.4.106–7. The imagery of
ll. 16–21 recalls that of *Venus* 229–40,
where Venus, embracing Adonis, says
'I'll be a park, and thou shalt be my deer'
and offers him 'brakes obscure and
rough, | To shelter thee from tempest and
from rain'.

18 **scut** short tail. As applied to Mistress Ford
it must have an additional meaning,
presumably the pubic hair (*OED tail sb.*[1]
5c, the penis, or (often) the female puden-
dum). There is no indication elsewhere in
the play that Mistress Ford is dark-haired.

18, 19, 20 **Let** The sense is not 'though the
sky should rain potatoes', etc., but 'now
let the sky rain potatoes', etc., because
the *tempest of provocation* will encourage
Falstaff to *shelter* himself in Mistress
Ford's arms (or in her body).

19 **potatoes** Here (as in *Troilus* 5.2.56, 'potato finger') the Spanish or sweet potato
(*Batatas edulis*) is meant. It was thought
to have aphrodisiac qualities.

Greensleeves the popular love song of
2.1.58

20 **kissing-comfits** perfumed *comfits* (sweet-

meats) for sweetening the breath

20 **eryngoes** sweetmeats made from the can-
died root of *Eryngium maritimum*, the sea-
holly, another aphrodisiac: *OED*'s first
instance.

21 **provocation** sexual stimulation

22 **sweetheart** Oliver points out that F's
spelling 'sweet hart' may indicate a quibble on *heart/hart*.

23 **Divide...buck** A reference to 'cutting up
a "bribed" or stolen buck quickly, so as to
get it out of the way before the keepers
could come up' (*Shakespeare's England*, ii.
345); *OED bribe v.* 1.

haunch buttock (with an allusion to the
thrusting motion of the sexual act)

24 **sides** Shakespeare often refers to the sides
as strained by the passions, e.g. *Twelfth
Night* 2.4.92, *Antony* 4.15.39, *Lear*
2.2.370.

shoulders Traditionally part of the keeper's fee (Hart quotes William Harrison,
Description of England (1587), ii. 19). This
leads on to Falstaff's bestowing of his
horns. There is no need to suppose, with
NCS and Hibbard, that he is quibbling
about fighting the keeper or shouldering
him off, neither of which ideas occurs
elsewhere in Shakespeare in association
with shoulders.

24–5 **the fellow of this walk** the keeper
responsible for this part of the forest

25 **my horns I bequeath your husbands**
With the usual allusion to cuckoldry.

Am I a woodman, ha? Speak I like Herne the Hunter?
Why, now is Cupid a child of conscience: he makes
restitution. As I am a true spirit, welcome!
      ⌈*A noise of rattles within*⌉
MISTRESS PAGE Alas, what noise?
MISTRESS FORD Heaven forgive our sins!   30
FALSTAFF What should this be?
MISTRESS FORD *and* MISTRESS PAGE Away, away!
                                        They run off
FALSTAFF I think the devil will not have me damned, lest
the oil that's in me should set hell on fire. He would
never else cross me thus.

      Enter Evans, William Page, and children, disguised as
      before, with lighted tapers ; 'Mistress Quickly'
      disguised as the Queen of Fairies, 'Pistol' disguised as
      Hobgoblin, and Anne Page disguised as a fairy

28.1] This edition; *A noise within* OXFORD; *There is a noise of hornes, the two women run away.*
Q; *not in* F   30 Heaven] F; God Q (*Mis⟨tress⟩. Pa⟨ge⟩.* God forgiue me, what noise is
this?)   32.1] *as* Q (*see* 28.1); *not in* F   35.1–4] This edition, *as* OXFORD (which has no inverted
commas, and which has 'one' instead of 'Pistol'); *Enter Fairies.* F; *Enter sir Hugh like a Satyre, and*
boyes drest like Fayries, mistresse Quickly, like the Queene of Fayries : they sing a song about him, and
afterward speake. Q

26 **woodman** (*a*) huntsman (*OED* 1); (*b*)
    woman-hunter (*OED* 1b)
27 **child of conscience** a conscientious child,
    i.e. one who obeys his sense of right
27–8 **makes restitution** restores what he
    wrongfully withheld
28 **a true spirit** 'As I am a true man' was a
    common asseveration, e.g. *1 Henry IV*
    2.1.92, where the retort plays a humor-
    ous variation, as does the present expres-
    sion.
28.1 *A noise of rattles within* See 4.4.49.
    Q's '*noise of hornes*' anticipates its '*noyse*
    of hunting' at 101.1. Since the fairies have
    to carry tapers and also pinch Falstaff,
    they had better not bring their rattles on
    stage.
29 This may be either a question or an
    exclamation (to signify which a mark of
    interrogation is often used in F): 'What
    dreadful noise is this?' or 'What a dread-
    ful noise!'
34 **set hell on fire** burn hell out; humorous,
    since hell is traditionally imagined as a
    place of unquenchable fire.
35.2, 3 '*Mistress Quickly*', '*Pistol*' This
    edition interprets F's speech-prefixes for
    Mistress Quickly and Pistol as meaning

that the actors formerly playing these
parts now play whoever impersonate the
Queen of Fairies and Hobgoblin. It is
significant that (*a*) neither Mistress
Quickly nor Pistol takes part in the final
mocking of Falstaff, whereas Evans does;
(*b*) Evans's part in the masquerade has
been emphasized in advance, whereas
nothing has hinted that the other two
will take part; (*c*) Evans has one characteristic expression, 'Pray you' (l. 76;
compare 1.2.11; 3.1.1, 33, 75, 78, 115;
3.3.225; 4.1.27, 32, 38, 41; 5.5.132),
which is extra-metrical and therefore
conspicuous, in the speech immediately
before Falstaff mentions 'that Welsh
fairy', whereas Pistol has none ('vile',
which he also uses at 1.3.90 and on five
other occasions in the two other plays
where he appears, is a common word in
Shakespeare), and Mistress Quickly's departure from her usual style is notorious.
In Q, where the speeches are quite different, only Mistress Quickly and Evans are
the speakers, and some attempt has been
made to catch Evans's pronunciation
throughout, though only his one prose
speech is in anything like his idiom ('It is

'MISTRESS QUICKLY' *as Queen of Fairies*

Fairies black, grey, green, and white,
You moonshine revellers, and shades of night,
You orphan heirs of fixèd destiny,
Attend your office and your quality.
Crier Hobgoblin, make the fairy oyes.   40

'PISTOL' *as Hobgoblin*

Elves, list your names; silence, you airy toys.
Cricket, to Windsor chimneys shalt thou lep.
Where fires thou find'st unraked and hearths unswept,
There pinch the maids as blue as bilberry.
Our radiant Queen hates sluts and sluttery.

36, 54, 83, 89 'MISTRESS QUICKLY' *as Queen of Fairies*] This edition; *Qui.* (36, 89), *Qu.* (54, 83)
F; *Quic.* (*five speech-prefixes*) Q; *Queen* COLLIER (*conj.* Harness); *Anne* HALLIWELL (*conj.*
Harness)   38 orphan heirs] F (Orphan heires); ouphen heires THEOBALD (*conj.* Warburton);
ouphs, and heirs KEIGHTLEY   41 'PISTOL' *as Hobgoblin*] This edition; *Pist.* F; *Evans.* THEO-
BALD   42 lep] This edition; leape F

right indeed, he is full of lecheries and
iniquitie'), while Mistress Quickly speaks
as unlike herself as she does in F. See
Introduction, pp. 38–40.

36 The first line of the speech is a tetrameter,
the rest are pentameters.

37 **shades** spirits. In *Dream* 3.2.348 Oberon
is called 'king of shadows', i.e. of the
fairies.

38 **You orphan . . . destiny** Not definitely
explained. The line 'Unfathered heirs and
loathly births of nature' (2 *Henry IV*
4.3.122), though it refers to prodigious
malformed offspring (i.e. offspring nothing like their parents in appearance) and
not to fairies, at least suggests that *orphan
heirs* is a unit equivalent to a noun and
that *of fixed destiny* stands in adjectival
relation to it, rather than that *orphan* is
adjectival and *heirs of fixed destiny* a
noun-phrase. The probable sense, then,
is 'you creatures, not of mortal birth,
whose lot (e.g. to appear only at night;
compare *Dream* 3.2.379–96) is fixed'.

39 **Attend** listen to
   office business, employment; here virtually synonymous with *quality*. Compare
   Henry V 3.6.136–9, where a distinction
   is drawn between Montjoy's 'office' (i.e.
   his present business) and his 'quality' (i.e.
   his employment, that of a herald).

40 **Crier ... oyes** Hobgoblin (Puck, Robin
   Goodfellow) is the fairies' *crier* (as in
   'town crier') who makes announcements
   after calling 'oyes' (*oyez*, Old Fr. for

'hear'). The rhyme *toys* shows that *oyes* is
monosyllabic.

41 **list your names** listen for your names
   (and for what each of you is to do)
   airy toys insubstantial beings. In *Dream*
   3.1.152–3 Bottom's 'mortal grossness' is
   to be 'purged' to make him 'like an airy
   spirit'. *Toys* are 'trifles'. *Dream* 5.1.2–3
   'suggests that "fairy" and "toy" were
   associated in Shakespeare's mind'
   (Oliver). The rhyme *fairy oyes/airy toys* is
   notable.

42 **Cricket** An appropriate name for a fairy
   who inspects *chimneys* (i.e. fireplaces),
   since the house-cricket (*Acheta domestica*)
   is 'an insect that squeaks or chirps about
   ovens and fireplaces' (Johnson's *Dictionary*).
   lep leap. The variant pronunciation of the
   verb is required for the (near-) rhyme
   with *unswept*. In Marlowe, *Hero and Lean-
   der* ii. 57–8, 'step' rhymes with 'lep' (the
   spelling of the first edition, 1598). The
   verb is appropriate to the *cricket*, which
   resembles a grasshopper.

43 **unraked** not banked up (with ashes or
   small coal) in order to keep them alight
   without active burning (*OED rake v.*[1] 5)

44 **pinch** Fairies traditionally punished slut-
   tishness in this way. Hart gives illustrative quotations, including one from
   Nashe, *Terrors of the Night* (1594).
   bilberry a plant with edible berries of deep
   blue colour

45 **Our radiant Queen** the Queen of Fairies
   rather than Elizabeth I. The *Windsor*

FALSTAFF *(aside)*

> They are fairies; he that speaks to them shall die.
> I'll wink and couch; no man their works must eye.
>> *He lies down and hides his face*

EVANS

> Where's Bead? Go you, and where you find a maid
> That ere she sleep has thrice her prayers said,
> Raise up the organs of her fantasy;   50
> Sleep she as sound as careless infancy.
> But those as sleep and think not on their sins,
> Pinch them, arms, legs, backs, shoulders, sides, and shins.

'MISTRESS QUICKLY' *as Queen of Fairies*

> About, about!
> Search Windsor Castle, elves, within and out.
> Strew good luck, oafs, on every sacred room,
> That it may stand till the perpetual doom
> In state as wholesome as in state 'tis fit,
> Worthy the owner and the owner it.
> The several chairs of order look you scour   60
> With juice of balm and every precious flower.
> Each fair instalment, coat, and several crest,

46 *aside*] OXFORD; *not in* F   47.1] OXFORD; *Lies down upon his face.* ROWE; *not in* F   48 Bead]
F (Bede); *Pead* Q   50 Raise] F; Rein HANMER (*conj.* Warburton); Rouse COLLIER 1853
fantasy;] THEOBALD; fantasie, F   56 oafs] F (Ouphes)

chimneys are those of the whole town,
not just of the Castle.

47 **wink and couch** close my eyes and lie
down.

48 **Bead** A *bead* is both a type of smallness
(*Dream* 3.2.331: 'you bead, you acorn')
and, as a bead in a rosary, associated
with prayers (*Errors* 2.2.191, *Richard II*
3.4.146). As NCS (glossary) notes, 'It is
Parson Hugh, albeit disguised, who gives
him his holy commission.'

50 **Raise ... fantasy** arouse the faculties of
her imagination, i.e. cause her to dream
pleasant dreams

51 **Sleep she** may she sleep. Theobald's
punctuation is necessary, since that in F
gives the sense 'though she is sleeping',
and the point is not to draw a contrast but
to draw a comparison between *careless*
(i.e. carefree) *infancy* and a sleep filled
with sweet dreams.

52 **those as** those who (*OED as, adv.* (*conj.*,
and rel. pron.) 24, citing Philemon Hol-

land, *Plutarch's Morals*, 1603, p. 222:
'To those as have no children')

54 **About, about** Go about your business. In
view of its special nature as a command,
this short line is not incomplete.

57 **perpetual doom** Day of Judgement

58 **In state ... fit** 'as "healthy" in state
(condition) as it is fitting in state (dignity)' (Oliver). The next line amplifies the
latter phrase: 'It is worthy of the owner
(Queen Elizabeth), and the owner is worthy of it.'

60 **The several chairs of order** each stall
assigned to a knight of the Order of the
Garter, in the choir of St George's Chapel
in Windsor Castle.

61 **balm** a fragrant garden herb, especially
'balm-gentle' (= balm-mint, *Melissa offic-
inalis*), though there are others (*OED* 9)

62 **instalment** place of instalment, i.e. stall
coat coat of arms. That of each knight
was blazoned on the stall-plate nailed to
the back of the stall.
crest device borne on top of a helmet.

With loyal blazon, evermore be blest!
And nightly meadow-fairies, look you sing,
Like to the Garter's compass, in a ring.
Th'expressure that it bears, green let it be,
More fertile-fresh than all the field to see;
And *Honi soit qui mal y pense* write
In em'rald tufts, flowers purple, blue, and white,
Like sapphire, pearl, and rich embroidery,   70
Buckled below fair knighthood's bending knee.
Fairies use flowers for their charactery.
Away, disperse!—But till 'tis one o'clock,
Our dance of custom round about the oak
Of Herne the Hunter let us not forget.

EVANS

Pray you, lock hand in hand; yourselves in order set;
And twenty glow-worms shall our lanterns be,
To guide our measure round about the tree.—
But stay! I smell a man of middle earth!

FALSTAFF (*aside*) Heavens defend me from that Welsh fairy,   80
lest he transform me to a piece of cheese!

64 nightly meadow-fairies] F (Nightly-meadow-Fairies); nightly, meadow-fairies CAPELL   69
em'rald tufts] F (Emrold-tuffes)   80 *aside*] OXFORD; *not in* F   Heavens] F; God Q (God blesse
me from that wealch Fairie.)

Each knight's crested helmet was set
above his stall.

63 **With** together with
   blazon banner bearing the coat of arms.
   That of each knight was hung (on a staff
   projecting from the wall) above his helmet.

64 **nightly meadow-fairies** Crane, the scribe,
   who hyphenated the three words together for F, evidently understood *nightly*
   adjectivally (*OED a.* 2: belonging to the
   night; compare *Titus* 2.3.97, 'the nightly
   owl or fatal raven'). If *nightly* is understood adverbially, the sense is more probably 'during the night' (*OED adv.* 2;
   compare *Romeo* 4.1.81) than 'every
   night' (*OED adv.* 1; compare *Twelfth
   Night* 1.3.34), because the fairies are
   being given orders for this particular
   night even if they do the same things
   every night.

65 **compass** circle. These fairies are those
   who, in their nocturnal dancing, form
   the 'green sour ringlets' (*Tempest*

5.1.37), or fairy rings, in fields.

66 **expressure** expression. Rare in Shakespeare, and, in this sense (i.e. impression?), unique: *OED* c (this passage only)
   defines it as 'picture'.

68 *Honi ... pense* (Fr.) 'shamed be he who
   thinks evil of it': the motto of the Order of
   the Garter, as embroidered in gold on the
   blue ribbon.

72 This line completes a rhyming triplet.
   charactery writing (i.e. they write not in
   ink but in flowers). The stress is on the
   second syllable (compare *Caesar* 2.1.307,
   'All the charactery of my sad brows').

74 **dance of custom** customary dance

76 **Pray you** See l. 35.2, 3 n.

79 **man of middle earth** mortal (as distinct
   from fairy). *Middle earth* (from ME *middel-
   erd*), referring to the earth as midway
   between heaven and hell, was not quite
   archaic (*OED* gives an example dated
   1600). Not found elsewhere in
   Shakespeare.

80 **Welsh fairy** See l. 35.2, 3 n.

81 **cheese** See 1.2.12–13.

'PISTOL.' *as Hobgoblin (to Falstaff)*
     Vile worm, thou wast o'erlooked even in thy birth.
'MISTRESS QUICKLY' *as Queen of Fairies (to Evans)*
     With trial-fire touch me his finger-end.
     If he be chaste, the flame will back descend
     And turn him to no pain; but if he start,
     It is the flesh of a corrupted heart.
'PISTOL.' *as Hobgoblin*
     A trial, come!
EVANS   Come, will this wood take fire?
          Evans burns Falstaff's finger with his taper
FALSTAFF O, O, O!
'MISTRESS QUICKLY' *as Queen of Fairies*
     Corrupt, corrupt, and tainted in desire!
     About him, fairies, sing a scornful rhyme,   90
     And, as you trip, still pinch him to your time.
          Fairies dance around Falstaff, pinching him
FAIRIES *(sing)*
          Fie on sinful fantasy!
          Fie on lust and luxury!
          Lust is but a bloody fire,
          Kindled with unchaste desire,
          Fed in heart, whose flames aspire,
          As thoughts do blow them, higher and higher.
          Pinch him, fairies, mutually,
          Pinch him for his villainy.

82 *to Falstaff*] OXFORD; *not in* F   83 *to Evans*] This edition; *to fairies* OXFORD; *not in* F   87.1]
This edition; *They burn Sir John with tapers* OXFORD; *not in* F   91.1] *as* OXFORD; *not in* F   92
FAIRIES *(sing)*] This edition; *The Song.* F

82 **worm** any animal that creeps or crawls;
    a reptile, an insect (*OED sb.* 2)
    o'erlooked looked upon with the evil eye
    (*OED overlook v.* 7), i.e. bewitched. Here
    the sense seems to be extended to 'ac-
    cursed'.
83 **trial-fire** 'testing fire (as in the trial by
    ordeal)' (Hibbard)
84 **descend** Here used without any sense of
    downward motion, and equivalent to
    'turn'; a usage not found elsewhere in
    Shakespeare, nor recorded in *OED*, and
    probably resulting from the need for a
    rhyme.
85 **turn him to** put him to (*OED turn v.* 43b)

87 **this wood** i.e. Falstaff, who is called
    kindling-wood in a jocular metaphor
90 **About him** circle around him
92 **fantasy** desire (*OED* 7)
93 **luxury** lechery (Church Lat. *luxuria*).
    Synonymous with *sinful fantasy* and *lust*.
94-7 **Lust . . . and higher** The quadruple
    rhyme reflects the coherence of the state-
    ments and the development of the idea.
94 **a bloody fire** 'a fire whose origin is in the
    blood' (Walker)
96 **aspire** rise (*OED* 5)
97 **blow** i.e. like bellows
98 **mutually** together (*OED* 2)

Pinch him, and burn him, and turn him about,   100
Till candles and starlight and moonshine be out.

> *While the Fairies sing, enter Caius at one door and*
> *exit stealing away a Fairy in green; enter Slender at*
> *another door and exit stealing away a Fairy in white;*
> *enter Fenton and exit stealing away Anne Page. After*
> *the song a noise of hunting horns within. The Fairies*
> *hastily retire. Falstaff rises and begins to run away.*

> *Enter Page and Mistress Page, and Ford and Mistress*
> *Ford*

PAGE

Nay, do not fly; I think we have watched you now.
Will none but Herne the Hunter serve your turn?

MISTRESS PAGE

I pray you, come, hold up the jest no higher.—
Now, good Sir John, how like you Windsor wives?

> *She points to the horns*

See you these, husband? Do not these fair yokes
Become the forest better than the town?

101.1–6] This edition; *Here they pinch him, and sing about him, & the Doctor comes one way &*
steales away a boy in red. And Slender another way he takes a boy in greene: And Fenton steales
misteris Anne, being in white. And a noyse of hunting is made within: and all the Fairies runne away.
Falstaffe pulles of his bucks head, and rises vp. Q; *not in* F   101.7–8] This edition; *And enters M.*
Page, M. Ford, and their wiues, M. Shallow, Sir Hugh. Q; *Enter Page, Ford, Mistress Page, and*
Mistress Ford. CAPELL; *not in* F   105.1] HANMER; *not in* F

101.2, 3 *a Fairy* The boys taken away by
Caius and Slender are dressed as female
fairies. Probably Slender should take the
Queen of Fairies, who is Anne Page's
substitute and should therefore be
dressed in white. See Introduction,
p. 40 n.

101.5–6 *The Fairies hastily retire* See
l. 121n.

101.6 *Falstaff ... away* Q's stage direction
includes '*Falstaffe pulles of his bucks head,*
and rises vp', and its subsequent dialogue
includes Page's 'Why how now sir *Iohn,*
what a pair of horns in your hand?' and
Ford's 'Those hornes he ment to place
vpon my head.' F's dialogue, which is
different, implies that Falstaff is still wearing the horns. See Appendix C.

101.7–8 That only the two married couples
should enter (F) is more appropriate to
the denouement than that they should be
accompanied by Shallow (Q, which gives
him a line of greeting to Falstaff), who

has nothing to do with the wives' plot,
and who makes no comment on his
nephew Slender's discomfiture. If the
couples enter as couples this also emphasizes the final harmony that is approaching.

102 **watched you** kept you in view in order
to catch you (*OED watch v.* 11a)

104 **hold up the jest no higher** continue the
jest no longer. Compare *Dream* 3.2.240
('hold the sweet jest up'), *Much Ado*
2.3.120 ('He hath ta'en th'infection.
Hold it up.'). The use of *higher* in this
passage is exceptional.

106–7 **See you ... town?** Since Ford, not
Page, has been the jealous husband, it
might be conjectured that these lines
belong to Mistress Ford; but it is better
that she does not taunt her husband with
the fault which she has forgiven; and she
has her speech (completing the quartet)
at ll. 115–17.

106 **yokes** i.e. crescent-shaped antlers: *OED*

FORD Now, sir, who's a cuckold now? Master Brook,
Falstaff's a knave, a cuckoldly knave. Here are his
horns, Master Brook. ⌈*He removes the horns from Fal-*   110
staff's head⌉ And, Master Brook, he hath enjoyed
nothing of Ford's but his buck-basket, his cudgel, and
twenty pounds of money, which must be paid to Master
Brook. His horses are arrested for it, Master Brook.

MISTRESS FORD Sir John, we have had ill luck; we could
never meet. I will never take you for my love again, but
I will always count you my deer.

FALSTAFF I do begin to perceive that I am made an ass—

FORD ⌈*holding up the horns*⌉ Ay, and an ox too. Both the
proofs are extant.   120

110–11 *He ... head*] This edition; *not in* F   116 meet] F; mate NCS   118 ass—] This
edition; Asse. F; ass. *He takes off the horns* OXFORD   119 *holding up the horns*] This
edition; *not in* F

yoke sb. 4: 'applied to various objects
resembling the yoke of a plough'.
Shakespeare nowhere else uses *yokes* in
this sense, but he several times refers to
the 'horned' moon (e.g. *Dream* 5.1.235,
where the next line makes an allusion to
cuckoldry).

108 **who's a cuckold now?** This implies that
Falstaff is still wearing the horns.
Master Brook This parodies Falstaff's
speeches to 'Brook' in 2.2, 3.5, and 5.1.

114 **arrested** seized by legal warrant (the
legal term: *OED v.* 11), i.e. by officers
acting for Ford. The idea was probably
suggested to Shakespeare by his earlier,
different, idea (expressed by Mistress
Page, 2.1.89) that Falstaff would court
himself into debt and have to pawn his
horses.

116 **meet** i.e. get together (with an indirect
sexual allusion). NCS's emendation
'mate' makes the remark crudely literal,
and rests on a crudely literal distinction
('they had "met" three times, but never
"mated"'). Shakespeare has the verb
'mate' in the NCS sense only in *All's Well*
1.1.90–1 ('The hind that would be
mated by the lion | Must die for love'), and
nowhere quibbles on *meet/mate* (as Oliver
hesitantly suggests that he may be doing
here).

117 **deer** With a quibble on 'dear'. *Deer* leads
on to *ass*, and *ass* to *ox*.

118 **ass—** The punctuation is emended here
so that 'And these are not fairies' is the
end of the sentence instead of an isolated
interrogative or exclamatory phrase.
Compare the punctuation at 5.2.3.
Ford's interjected remark (perhaps holding up the horns in his hands) is short
enough not to disrupt the sense of Falstaff's; and Falstaff's completion of his
own sentence helps to re-establish his
psychological authority.

119 **ox** The type of cuckoldry, as the ass is
the type of stupidity: compare *Troilus*
5.1.55–7, where Thersites, descanting
on Menelaus' cuckoldry and stupidity,
says that he is 'both ass and ox' and 'both
ox and ass'. There is also 'a reference to
the diction of the tenth commandment'
(Hart): Exodus 20: 17.

119–20 **Both the proofs are extant** Ambiguous. It may mean (*a*) these two horns
prove you to be an ox, or (*b*) this pair of
horns proves you to be both an ox
(literally) and an ass (figuratively, for
wearing them). Roberts, p. 113, believes
that 'asslike ears' should also be worn as
part of Falstaff's disguise because of this
passage: this is to take Ford's words
much too literally.
extant in existence. Oliver states that
there is a quibble on a literal sense, i.e.
'standing up', 'protuberant' (*OED a.* 1),
but this is unlikely.

FALSTAFF And these are not fairies. I was three or four times in the thought they were not fairies; and yet the guiltiness of my mind, the sudden surprise of my powers, drove the grossness of the foppery into a received belief, in despite of the teeth of all rhyme and reason, that they were fairies. See now how wit may be made a Jack-a-Lent when 'tis upon ill employment!

EVANS Sir John Falstaff, serve Got, and leave your desires, and fairies will not pinse you.   .

FORD Well said, fairy Hugh.   130

EVANS (*to Ford*) And leave you your jealousies too, I pray you.

FORD I will never mistrust my wife again till thou art able to woo her in good English.

FALSTAFF Have I laid my brain in the sun and dried it, that   . it wants matter to prevent so gross o'erreaching as this? Am I ridden with a Welsh goat too? Shall I have a coxcomb of frieze? 'Tis time I were choked with a piece of toasted cheese.

121 are] F; were Q (Why then these were not *Fairies?*);   fairies.] F (fairies:); fairies? THEOBALD   I was] F; By the Lord I was Q   128 EVANS] F; *Evans* (*returns, without his satyr-mask*) NCS

121 **these are** The verb ('are', not 'were') is theatrically significant. The fairies, though they ceased pinching Falstaff when they were interrupted, have not left the stage, merely withdrawn to the rear of it. In the following line *were* refers to the time when they were intimidating him. In Q, where Falstaff uses 'were', he is asking a question, to which Mistress Page replies 'No sir *Iohn* but boyes'; but in F, since nobody replies, he is not asking a question.

124 **powers** understanding
  foppery foolery. As recorded in *OED*, and as used by Shakespeare elsewhere (*Merchant* 2.5.35, *Measure* 1.2.125, *Lear* 1.2.116), the word refers to people's playing the fool, and this meaning is acceptable here as applied to the impersonators of the fairies. *OED* also, however, compares Ger. *Fopperei*, Du. *fopperij*, 'hoaxing', and modern editors from Hart onwards have interpreted the present passage in this sense, which is acceptable as applied to the intention to deceive Falstaff; compare 'so gross o'erreaching', l. 136.

125 **received belief** 'article of faith, absolute conviction' (Hibbard). *OED received, ppl. a.* 'generally accepted ... as true'.

125–6 **in despite ... reason** in direct opposition to common sense. Both 'in spite of one's teeth' and 'neither rhyme nor reason' were proverbial phrases (Tilley S764, R98).

126 **wit** intelligence.

127 **Jack-a-Lent** 'a butt for every one to throw at' (Onions). See 3.3.23.

128 **desires** Like *jealousies* (l. 131), this word is meant in the singular sense by Evans.

137 **ridden ... goat** harassed (*OED ride v.* 17b) by a Welshman. Compare *Henry V* 5.1.27, 'Not for Cadwallader and all his goats' (Pistol, to Fluellen).

138 **coxcomb of frieze** fool's cap made of *frieze* (a coarse woollen cloth with a nap on it, which Falstaff contemptuously associates with rustic Welshmen; compare *flannel*, l. 162).

139 **toasted cheese** Here taken to be the typical food of the Welsh (compare 1.2.12, 5.5.81), though not peculiar to them in Shakespeare (e.g. Cade in *2 Henry VI* 4.7.11, Nim in *Henry V* 2.1.7–8).

EVANS Seese is not good to give putter. Your belly is all   140
putter.

FALSTAFF 'Seese' and 'putter'? Have I lived to stand at the
taunt of one that makes fritters of English? This is
enough to be the decay of lust and late-walking through
the realm.

MISTRESS PAGE Why, Sir John, do you think, though we
would have thrust virtue out of our hearts by the
head and shoulders, and have given ourselves without
scruple to hell, that ever the devil could have made you
our delight?   150

FORD What, a hodge-pudding? A bag of flax?

MISTRESS PAGE A puffed man?

PAGE Old, cold, withered, and of intolerable entrails?

FORD And one that is as slanderous as Satan?

PAGE And as poor as Job?

FORD And as wicked as his wife?

EVANS And given to fornications, and to taverns, and
sack, and wine, and metheglins, and to drinkings, and
swearings and starings, pribbles and prabbles?

140 **give** add to

143 **makes fritters** (figuratively) chops up
the English language into fragments and
fries them in batter

144 **late-walking** In conjunction with *lust*
this implies disreputable errands late at
night. Here only in Shakespeare, but
compare 'night-walking heralds',
Richard III 1.1.72.

149 **you** i.e. you, of all people (emphatic)

151 **hodge-pudding** a pudding (see 2.1.29)
made of a medley of ingredients (*OED*)
bag of flax a sack into which flax is
gathered. Prince Hal calls Falstaff 'wool-
sack' in *1 Henry IV* 2.5.135.

152 **puffed** inflated; compare *2 Henry IV*
5.3.90–1, 'goodman Puff of Barson'

153 **Old, cold, withered** These epithets correspond to the presentation of Falstaff in
2 Henry IV 2.4.
intolerable excessive (*OED* 1c); compare
1 Henry IV 2.5.544, 'this intolerable deal
of sack'. Oliver sees a quibble on 'impossible to bear or carry (literally)', but to
quibble is not in Page's style.

154–6 **And one ... wife?** In Job 1 and 2,
Satan urges God to test Job's piety by
reducing him to poverty, and Job's wife
urges him to 'curse God, and die'. Noble

(p. 272) draws attention to the marginal
gloss in the Bishops' Bible (1568, 1572)
at Job 2 : 9 : 'A cruel temptation of an evil
and ungodly wife.' Falstaff describes himself in *2 Henry IV*, 1.2.128, as 'as poor as
Job, ... but not so patient'.

154 **slanderous** Commentators (e.g. Oliver,
Hibbard) apply this word to Satan's pre-
diction that in adversity Job will curse
God (Job 1 : 11 ; 2 : 5). This does not seem
quite satisfactory: without the following
mention of Job no spectator would recognize the allusion, and even with it the
relevance to Falstaff's misconduct (his
abuse of Ford in 2.2 and 3.5?) is not clear.
Perhaps the reference to Satan is merely
derogatory in a general way (he is called
the father of lies in John 8: 44), and not
specifically to the Satan of the Book of Job.
In *1 Henry IV* 2.5.468 Falstaff is called
'that old white-bearded Satan'.

158 **metheglins** a spiced mead of Welsh
origin (with Evans's plural)

159 **swearings and starings** An established
phrase (here with Evans's plural): *OED*'s
earliest instance is dated 1548 (*stare v.*
3a). 'Staring' implies the arrogant look
that accompanies the 'swearing'.
pribbles and prabbles See 1.1.50 and n.

FALSTAFF Well, I am your theme. You have the start of   160
me. I am dejected. I am not able to answer the Welsh
flannel. Ignorance itself is a plummet o'er me. Use me as
you will.

FORD Marry, sir, we'll bring you to Windsor, to one
Master Brook, that you have cozened of money, to
whom you should have been a pander. Over and above
that you have suffered, I think to repay that money will
be a biting affliction.

PAGE Yet be cheerful, knight. Thou shalt eat a posset
tonight at my house, where I will desire thee to laugh at   170
my wife that now laughs at thee. Tell her Master
Slender hath married her daughter.

MISTRESS PAGE (*aside*) Doctors doubt that. If Anne Page be
my daughter, she is, by this, Doctor Caius's wife.

Enter Slender

SLENDER Whoa, ho, ho, father Page!

PAGE Son, how now! How now, son! Have you dispatched?

SLENDER Dispatched? I'll make the best in Gloucestershire
know on't. Would I were hanged, la, else!

PAGE Of what, son?   180

SLENDER I came yonder at Eton to marry Mistress Anne
Page, and she's a great lubberly boy. If it had not been
i'th' church, I would have swinged him, or he should

174.1] Q (*which transposes the arrival of Slender and that of Caius*); *not in* F

160 **theme** subject, i.e. of your derision
have the start of i.e. have the advantage
over. A common figurative expression
(Tilley S828) derived from holding the
advantage in a race.
161 **dejected** cast down, humiliated
162 **flannel** See l. 138 and n.
Ignorance ... o'er me i.e. I am sunk twice
deeper than the utmost depth of ignorance. Shakespeare uses the image of the
plummet literally in *Tempest* 3.3.101,
5.1.56–7. It is the lead weight (therefore
an appropriate metaphor to use in connection with ignorance) at the end of a
line for sounding the depth of the sea.
NCS superfluously postulates a quibble
on 'plumbet' (= plunket, a woollen
fabric; *OED*).
169 **posset** See 1.4.7 and n.
173 **Doctors doubt that** Proverbial (Tilley

D426: 'That is but one doctor's opinion').
Dent cites Greene, *A Quip for an Upstart
Courtier* (1592): ' "The doctors doubt of
that," quoth Cloth Breeches, "for I am of
a different opinion".' There is also a
quibble on Caius's title.
174.1 **Enter Slender** In Q his entry follows
that of Caius. In modern productions he
and Caius often bring the boys on stage
with them.
175 **father Page** Slender's unthinking use of
the phrase he has used before (3.2.54),
and Page's reply, draw attention to Slender's failure to *dispatch* (settle the business, *OED v.* 10).
180 **Of what** i.e. know of what? (picking up
know on't, l. 179)
182 **lubberly** loutish
183 **swinged** thrashed; the 'g' is pronounced like 'j'

have swinged me. If I did not think it had been Anne
Page, would I might never stir! And 'tis a postmaster's
boy.

PAGE Upon my life, then, you took the wrong.

SLENDER What need you tell me that? I think so, when I
took a boy for a girl. If I had been married to him, for all
he was in woman's apparel, I would not have had him.   190

PAGE Why, this is your own folly. Did not I tell you how
you should know my daughter by her garments?

SLENDER I went to her in white, and cried 'mum', and she
cried 'budget', as Anne and I had appointed. And yet it
was not Anne, but a postmaster's boy.   *Exit*

MISTRESS PAGE Good George, be not angry. I knew of your
purpose, turned my daughter into green, and indeed she
is now with the Doctor at the deanery, and there
married.

    Enter Caius

CAIUS Vere is Mistress Page? By gar, I am cozened. I ha'   200
married *un garçon*, a boy: *un paysan*, by gar, a boy. It is
not Anne Page. By gar, I am cozened.

MISTRESS PAGE Why? Did you take her in green?

---

193 white] ROWE 1714; greene F; red Q   195 *Exit*] This edition; *not in* F   197 green]
ROWE 1714; white F   199.1] Q (*see* 174.1); *not in* F   201 *un garçon*] CAPELL; oon Garsoon F
un paysan] CAPELL; oon pesant F   203 take] F; not take POPE   green] POPE; white F

185 **would ... stir** A frequent asseveration
  (Tilley S861).
185-6 **postmaster's boy** stable-boy working
  for the supplier of posting horses, i.e.
  horses hired out (originally to messengers carrying letters) to cover a stage of
  the road rapidly
187 **you took the wrong** Page means 'you
  failed to follow your instructions'. Slender, who had followed them to the letter,
  misunderstands Page and makes a
  literal-minded retort in a tone of 'confused bravado' (Vickers, p. 146).
189 **for a girl** instead of a girl
190 **had him** accepted him as a wife (with an
  unintended suggestion of 'consummated
  the marriage physically')
193 **her in white** the woman wearing white.
  F's transposition of the colours white and
  green (here and at ll. 197 and 203;
  contrast 4.4.69, 4.6.34, 4.6.40) is difficult to account for. See Introduction,

pp. 55-6.
195 *Exit* The stage direction is desirable, to
  correspond with the evident exit of Caius,
  thus eliminating Anne's two unwelcome
  suitors from the final tableau which
  Anne and Fenton complete. In Q all this is
  managed quite differently: Shallow enters with the Pages and the Fords, though
  he never speaks; Caius returns to complain before Slender does, and both re-
  main to be addressed in Ford's final
  speech ('He [i.e. Fenton] hath got the
  maiden, each of you a boy | To waite vpon
  you, so God giue you ioy').
201 **married** Thus going one better than
  Slender. In Q Slender twice declares that
  he has married the boy he stole away,
  and Evans cries 'Ieshu M. *Slender*, cannot
  you see but marrie boyes?'
  un paysan (Fr.) a peasant; perhaps therefore a farmer's boy

CAIUS Ay, by gar, and 'tis a boy. By gar, I'll raise all
　Windsor.   *Exit*
FORD This is strange. Who hath got the right Anne?
　　　Enter Fenton and Anne Page
PAGE
　My heart misgives me. Here comes Master Fenton.
　How now, Master Fenton!
ANNE
　Pardon, good father. Good my mother, pardon.
PAGE
　Now, mistress, how chance you went not with Master
　　　Slender?   210
MISTRESS PAGE
　Why went you not with Master Doctor, maid?
FENTON
　You do amaze her. Hear the truth of it.
　You would have married her most shamefully
　Where there was no proportion held in love.
　The truth is, she and I, long since contracted,
　Are now so sure that nothing can dissolve us.
　Th'offence is holy that she hath committed,
　And this deceit loses the name of craft,
　Of disobedience, or unduteous title,
　Since therein she doth evitate and shun   220
　A thousand irreligious cursèd hours
　Which forcèd marriage would have brought upon her.
FORD (*to Page and Mistress Page*)
　Stand not amazed. Here is no remedy.
　In love the heavens themselves do guide the state.
　Money buys lands, and wives are sold by fate.

205 *Exit*] CAPELL; *not in* F   206.1] Q; *not in* F   223 *to Page and Mistress Page*] OXFORD; *not in* F   amazed. Here] F (amaz'd, here); amazed. There This edition *conj.*

210 **Now, mistress . . . Slender?** A line of verse (albeit rather free) to correspond with the following line of Mistress Page's.
212 **amaze** 'bewilder (here by asking two questions simultaneously)' (Oliver)
214 **proportion ... love** proper loving relationship between the parties
215 **contracted** betrothed (i.e. by our own secret agreement)
216 **sure** firmly united (i.e. by our marriage)
219 **unduteous title** undutifulness (*title* is synonymous with *name*, l. 218)

220 **evitate** Synonymous with *shun*: Shakespeare's only use of the word, which is a rare one.
223 **Here** One would expect 'there'. If *here* is correct, it must have the sense 'in these present circumstances'.
224 **guide the state** rule
225 **Money buys lands** i.e. and does not buy wives
　wives are sold by fate Alluding to the proverb 'Marriage and hanging go by destiny' (Tilley M682).

FALSTAFF (*to Page and Mistress Page*) I am glad, though you
　　have ta'en a special stand to strike at me, that your
　　arrow hath glanced.
PAGE
　　Well, what remedy? Fenton, heaven give thee joy!
　　What cannot be eschewed must be embraced.   230
FALSTAFF
　　When night-dogs run, all sorts of deer are chased.
MISTRESS PAGE
　　Well, I will muse no further.—Master Fenton,
　　Heaven give you many, many merry days!—
　　Good husband, let us every one go home,
　　And laugh this sport o'er by a country fire,
　　Sir John and all.
FORD　　　　　　　　Let it be so, Sir John.
　　To Master Brook you yet shall hold your word,
　　For he tonight shall lie with Mistress Ford.   *Exeunt*

226 *to Page and Mistress Page*] This edition; *not in* F   236 so, Sir John.] F (so (Sir *Iohn*:)); so.—
Sir John, THEOBALD

227 **stand** huntsman's position from which
　to shoot. Falstaff keeps up the allusion to
　himself as a buck.
228 **glanced** struck obliquely and turned
　aside
230 **What . . . embraced** What cannot be
　avoided must be accepted. A sententious
　remark in proverbial style: compare
　'What cannot be cured must be endured'
　(Tilley C922).
231 **When . . . chased** A similar remark, in
　jesting tone, without any proverbial
　counterpart. *OED* does not record *night-
　dogs*, but Hart quotes Abraham Fleming's
　Of English Dogs (1576): 'The farmers . . .
　call this kind of dog [i.e. the thievish dog]
　a night cur, because he hunteth in the

dark.' Falstaff's jest is that there is no
controlling the intrigues of a night.
232 **muse** grumble (*OED v.* 6)
236 **Let it be so, Sir John** F's punctuation, by
　which Ford addresses all six words to
　Falstaff, is preferable to Theobald's. It is
　not Ford's place, but Page's, to agree to
　Mistress Page's proposal (and Page's si-
　lence implies consent). Ford thereupon,
　as the person hitherto most aggrieved by
　Falstaff's misdeeds and his most exultant
　derider, warmly presses the invitation
　upon him.
237–8 **To Master . . . Mistress Ford** The play
　resembles *Merchant* in ending with a jest
　in couplet form.

THE TEXTUAL CRUX AT 1.1.19–20

'SALT fish' can mean either 'salted fish' (*OED salt a.*[1] 2) or 'salt-water fish' (*OED salt a.*[1] 3a). On the only other occasion when Shakespeare uses the expression it is in the former sense: in *Antony* 2.5.15–18 Cleopatra is remembered to have had a diver hang a salt fish on Antony's hook when he was angling (in North's Plutarch it is 'some old salt fish ... like unto those which are brought out of the country of Pont', which puts the sense beyond doubt).

Hart, who recognizes only this sense of 'salt fish', says 'Shallow seems to mean that an "old coat" should have a salted fish, not a freshwater fish like the luce.' This is open to at least three objections: (*a*) it does not fit F's phrase 'the salt-fish, is an old Coate', which would need to be something like 'the salt fish is meet for an old coat'; (*b*) it would be a strange flight of fancy for Shallow; (*c*) Shallow seems too well pleased with his old coat of arms to wish it different.

Hotson sees in the passage 'an allusion to the combined arms of the great Fishmongers' Company. The Fresh or Stockfishmongers' coat displayed luces, and that of the Saltfishmongers' bore dolphins. Of the two, the Saltfishmongers' coat was the more ancient' (Hotson, p. 95). But to make F's 'the salt-fish' mean either 'the coat of the Saltfishmongers' or 'the dolphin' is to strain the sense, and few members of the original audience would be likely to know which coat was the older, or to find any humour in the allusion even if they did. And why should Shallow be interested in the matter?

The NCS editors emend Shallow's final phrase to 'the salt fish is an old cod', arguing that 'as Evans made no difference between *d* and *t*, Shallow apparently imagined that the parson was speaking of "cod" and perhaps even suspected him of a "salt" jest (cf. "codpiece")'. The supposed innuendo, without anything in Evans's character or in the context to provoke it, can be immediately rejected. The mispronunciation theory is equally implausible. It requires Shallow to think that Evans means 'cod' when he says 'coat' and when his conversation is about old coats and the lice on them. It also fails to explain why F prints 'Coate' in Shallow's speech.

The NCS editors also assert that '"cod" makes excellent sense in Shallow's speech, since "luce" was a term applied not only to the fresh-water pike but also, though according to Shallow incorrectly, to the salt-water cod or hake (v. *NED*)'. Reference to *OED*, however, under 'luce', reveals that there are only two kinds of luce, (1) the pike and (2) 'Luce of the sea, sea-luce: the hake, *Merlucius vulgaris*'; and reference to the entries under 'hake' and 'cod' reveals that though the hake resembles the cod they belong to different genera (the cod being *Gadus morrhua*) and their names were never synonymous nor even colloquially interchangeable. This argument for emending to 'cod' accordingly also fails.

Sisson (*New Readings* pp. 62–3) argues for retaining F's reading, with slight repunctuation, because 'the common colloquial omission of *it*, or *and it*, and this use of *the*, are well within Shallow's, and Elizabethan, idiom'. His reading may be paraphrased as 'The luce is a fresh-water fish, and also a salt-water fish—it is an old coat.' Abbott, in his discussion of ellipses, confirms that where the nominative is in no doubt it is sometimes omitted, particularly when the verb is 'has', 'is', 'was', etc. (382, 400), but he does not give any example that is closely comparable to Sisson's reading. The chief weakness of this reading, however, lies in Shallow's declaring that the luce, i.e. the heraldic pike, is both a fresh-water fish and a salt-water fish (which it is not)—or, alternatively, that it is eaten both fresh and salted (which it is not).

EVANS'S SONG IN ACT 3, SCENE 1

The following transcription of the setting of Marlowe's 'Come live with me and be my love' is based on that published by Edward W. Naylor, *Shakespeare and Music* (1931), p. 182. The setting was originally published in William Corkine's *The Second Book of Airs* (1612).

Come live with me and be my love,

And we will all___ the plea-sures prove That
[And a thou - sand va - grom posies] [By

hills and val - leys,_ dales and fields,
shal - low ri - vers,_ to whose falls

And all the crag - gy moun-tains yields
Me - lo - dious birds sing mad - ri - gals]

FALSTAFF'S DISGUISE AS HERNE THE HUNTER

F AND Q differ significantly in their accounts of Falstaff's disguise as Herne
the Hunter, both in the hatching of the plot (F's 4.4) and in later scenes.

In F's 4.4 Herne the Hunter is said to 'Walk round about an oak with
great ragg'd horns' and to shake a chain. After Falstaff shall have
assumed that disguise and been exposed, the plotters will 'dis-horn' him.
In 5.1 Mistress Quickly says to Falstaff, 'I'll provide you a chain, and I'll
do what I can to get you a pair of horns.' This is the last that we hear of
the chain, but when Falstaff appears in 5.5 he alludes to his disguise as
making him 'a Windsor stag, and the fattest, I think, i'th' forest'; in his
triumph he resolves to bequeath his horns to Ford and Page. When the
fairies discover him they make no mention of his appearance, only of his
identity as a mortal and his licentious moral character. But when the
Fords and Pages arrive, they refer several times to his horns: they are
'fair yokes' which 'become the forest better than the town'; they are the
proof that Falstaff is 'a cuckoldly knave'; they are 'both the proofs' that
he is an ox as well as an ass.

In the plotting scene in Q Mistress Page says

> Oft haue you heard since *Horne* the hunter dyed,
> That women to affright their little children,
> Ses that he walkes in shape of a great stagge.

The wives resolve to invite Falstaff to meet them

> Disguised like *Horne*, with huge horns on his head.

Mistress Quickly is not involved in procuring his disguise, and the next
reference to it is the stage direction '*Enter sir Iohn with a Bucks head vpon
him.*' Falstaff has the equivalent of his two remarks in F:

> And I am here a Stag, and I thinke the fattest
> In all *Windsor* forrest

and

> For my horns Ile bequeath the[m] to your husbands.

When Evans has smelt a man of middle earth all the fairies search for the
intruder, and Evans finds him:

> See I haue spied one by good luck,
> His bodie man, his head a buck.

The Fairy Queen calls him 'this same metamorphised youth'. After they have pinched him and run away, '*Falstaffe pulles of his bucks head, and rises vp.*' Consistently with this stage action Page greets him with

Why how now sir *Iohn*, what a pair of horns in your hand?

and Ford explains,

Those hornes he ment to place vpon my head,
And M. *Brooke* and he should be the men.

The question is whether Falstaff simply puts on a pair of buck's horns (the antlers of a fallow deer) or assumes a closer resemblance to an animal by wearing a property head. Jeanne Addison Roberts, who inclines to the latter view, has found two illustrations, dated 1798 and 1812, showing Falstaff 'with the face of a deer as well as the horns—a bit like Bottom in his ass's head' (p. 113), and reproduces the earlier of them as the frontispiece to her book. This engraving shows Falstaff in soliloquy wearing a mask like a buck's face with antlers. He might be saying, 'It doth make some obstruction in the speech, this buck's head', for it covers his whole face, which makes it unlikely that the artist, William Gardiner, was accurately representing an actual performance. In any case, so late an illustration can be no guide to what was done by the original actors. Q has more claim to be regarded as a guide, but since many of its other stage directions as well as much of its text are inconsistent with F its evidence is open to doubt. The ass's head of *A Midsummer Night's Dream* may have influenced Q's stage directions and dialogue. It must also be remembered that a buck's 'head' is a technical term for its antlers (*OED head sb.* 6), as Roberts recognizes (p. 112), and as the phrase 'what a pair of horns in your hand?' may imply, even though the rest of Q's references to the buck's head and to Horne's being in a stag's shape rather point the other way. F at least gives no support to the idea that Falstaff is wearing a property head, and so it seems most appropriate to equip him simply with a pair of antlers, attached to his head by some means that will allow for their rapid removal.

ALTERATIONS TO LINEATION OF THE FOLIO

THIS list records only changes of verse to prose, of prose to verse, and of line-arrangement within verse. It does not record variant punctuation, variant spelling, or variant diction within the passages cited. For example, the prose of 1.3.85 is attributed to Q, though its diction ('I haue operations in my head, which are humors of reuenge') differs from F's ('I haue opperations, | Which be humors of reuenge').

In most of the play's scenes prose predominates, a fact undoubtedly recognized by the printers both of Q and of F. In Q many passages of prose are arbitrarily chopped into lengths of a line or less, each new line beginning with a capital letter. This can never have been intended to be verse, merely to look like verse. In F the prose is usually printed as such. The deviations, though numerous enough to require their removal from the textual collations to this appendix, form a small proportion of the whole, and are of small importance. Sometimes, as when the end of a short prose speech is turned up or down to save a line of type, they seem to result from purely technical considerations. At other times, as when the first few words of a speech are printed as a short line separate from what follows, they may mark the fact that the speaker is moving from address into aside, or vice versa (examples are at 1.4.62–3 and 3.5.3), but more often than not there is no such change of direction within the speech. Compositor B seems to have been more given to dividing speeches in this way than Compositors A and C, to judge from their relative frequency in the parts of the text that he is believed to have set: this suggests that such division was not a feature of the scribal copy nor of the authorial foul papers. Though such passages are described in this appendix as verse, they are verse only in the negative sense that they are not set as normal prose, not in the positive sense that they have pretensions to metrical form.

The true verse is mostly printed as such in F, but Pistol's is often printed as prose (as it often is in *2 Henry IV* and *Henry V*), and there are a few other failures to recognize verse lines.

1.1.4–5	In ... coram] F4; *one line with last word turned up* F
106–7	I will ... answered] POPE; *verse, divided after* this FQ
145–8	Ha ... liest] POPE; *prose* F
218–19	That ... her] POPE; *verse, divided after* must F
1.3.81–2	Let ... poor] POPE; *prose* F
85	I ... revenge] Q; *verse, divided after* operations F
96	Thou ... on] HIBBARD; *prose* F

1.4.43	Ay ... you] CAPELL; *verse* F
49–50	*Oui ... Rugby*] POPE; *verse, divided after* quickly F
62–3	*O ... Larron*] POPE; *verse, divided after* closet F
2.1.12–18	By me ... Falstaff] CAPELL; *divided after* night, might F
20–2	One ... with] POPE; *verse, divided after* age, unweighed F
105–7	He woos ... perpend] POPE; *prose* F
109–11	With ... name] CAPELL; *divided after* prevent, with F
139–40	I ... go] POPE; *verse, divided after* not melancholy FQ
141–2	Faith ... Page] POPE; *verse, divided after* head F
164–5	I ... Garter] POPE; *verse, divided after* that F
2.2.2–3	Why ... open] STEEVENS 1793; *prose* F
13	Didst ... pence] Q; *prose* F
88–9	Ten ... fail her] POPE; *verse, divided after* eleven F
3.1.16–20	To shallow ... To shallow] POPE; *prose* F
22–5	Melodious ... To shallow (*etc.*)] POPE; *prose* F
28	To ... falls] POPE; *prose* F
41–2	What ... Parson] POPE; *verse, divided after* word F
92–3	Peace ... Machiavel] POPE; *verse, divided after* Garter FQ
3.2.7–8	O ... courtier] F4; *one line with last word turned up* F
48–50	And ... of] POPE; *verse, divided after* sir, Anne, money F
55–6	You ... altogether] F3; *verse, divided after* wholly for you F
75–6	Well ... Page's] POPE; *verse, divided after* you well F
3.3.16–17	I ... direction] POPE; *one line with last word turned up* F
19–20	How ... you] F4; *one line with last two words turned up* F
21–2	My ... company] F3; *verse, divided after* door F
55–6	A ... neither] POPE; *verse, divided after* John F
76–7	Well ... it] F3; *verse, divided after* love you F
79–80	Nay ... mind] F3; *verse, divided after* do F
89–91	O ... ever] POPE; *verse, divided after* done F
97–8	What ... in you] ROWE; *verse, divided after* upon you F
127–8	Let ... counsel. I'll in] POPE; *verse, divided between* see't *and* I'll F
141–4	Pray ... this] POPE; *verse, divided after* cause, jest F
148–50	Buck ... appear] F3; *verse, divided after* the buck, you buck F
156–7	Good ... much] POPE; *verse, divided after* contented F
158–9	True ... me, gentlemen] F3; *verse, divided after* up gentle-men, anon F
161–2	By ... in France] F3; *verse, divided after* of France F
166–7	I ... John] F3; *verse, divided after* better F
3.4.22–3	Break ... himself] POPE; *verse, divided after* Quickly F
24–5	I'll ... venturing] F4; *one line with last four letters of* venturing *turned down* F
27–8	No ... afeard] POPE; *verse, divided after* me F

34–5	And ... you] POPE; *verse, divided after* Fenton F
36–7	She's ... father] POPE; *verse, divided after* coz F
82	I mean ... husband] ROWE; *prose* F
87–8	Come ... enemy] ROWE 1714; *divided after* Master F
96	Look ... doing] POPE; *verse* F
3.5.3	Go ... in't] F3; *verse* F
24–5	By ... morrow] POPE; *verse, divided after* mercy F
26–7	Take ... finely] POPE; *verse, divided after* chalices F
39–40	So ... promise] ROWE; *one line with last word turned up* F
56	O ... comes] POPE; *verse* F
58–9	Now ... wife] F3; *verse, divided after* know F
61–2	Master ... me] POPE; *verse, divided after* you F
113–15	In ... more] F3; *prose, the second sentence beginning on a new line* F
4.1.78–80	Adieu ... long] POPE; *verse, divided after* Hugh F
4.2.42–3	No ... he come] POPE; *verse, divided after* basket F
91–2	Hang ... enough] POPE; *verse, divided after* varlet F
173–4	Are ... women] POPE; *verse, divided after* ashamed F
184–5	Let's ... gentlemen] POPE; *verse, divided after* further F
4.4.25–6	There ... forest] POPE; *divided after* the F
67	That ... visors] POPE; *verse, divided after* excellent F
68–9	My ... white] ROWE 1714; *divided after* the F
77–8	Let ... knaveries] POPE; *verse, divided after* about it F
4.6.45	Which ... mother] ROWE; *prose* F
5.5.16–17	Sir ... male deer] POPE; *verse, divided after* my deer F
33–5	I ... thus] POPE; *verse, divided after* damned, fire F
80–1	Heaven ... cheese] POPE; *verse, divided after* fairy F
82	Vile ... birth] ROWE 1714; *prose* F
92–5	Fie ... desire] POPE; *two lines, divided after* luxury F
98–9	Pinch ... villainy] POPE; *one line* F
102–3	Nay ... turn] ROWE; *prose* F
108–10	Now ... horns, Master Brook] POPE; *verse, divided after* cuckold now, cuckoldly knave F
121	And ... fairies] POPE; *verse* F
173	Doctors doubt that] POPE; *verse* F
176–7	Son ... dispatched] POPE; *verse, divided after* now son F
191–2	Why ... garments] POPE; *verse, divided after* folly, daughter F
210	Now ... Slender] POPE; *divided after* mistress F
229–30	Well ... embraced] ROWE 1714; *prose* F

INDEX

An asterisk indicates that the note supplements information given in *OED*.

Index

upon good dowry, 1.1.218
upon my necessity, 2.1.122
urchins, 4.4.47
urinals, 3.1.13, 81
*use, 3.3.37

vagrom, 3.1.24
varletto, 4.5.61
Vaughan Williams, Ralph,
   p. 26n.
vengeance of, 4.1.56
Verdi, Giuseppe, p. 25n.
very note, 1.1.152
via, 2.2.145
Vickers, Brian, pp. 27n., 35n.
vile, 1.3.90
villainy, 1.4.62; 2.3.15
'visaments, 1.1.35
visors, 4.4.67
vlouting-stog, 3.1.109
voice, 1.3.42
vouchsafe, 2.2.38
voyage, 2.1.166
vultures, 1.3.81

wag, 1.3.6; 2.1.210; 2.3.64
waist, 1.3.37
wait upon, 1.1.249
walk, 2.2.287; 5.5.25
want, 4.4.36
warrener, 1.4.25
wart, 1.4.139
Warton, Thomas, p. 35n.
waste, 1.3.38; 4.2.196
watched, 5.5.102
Wayte, Frances, p. 8
Wayte, William, pp. 7–8
weapon, 1.4.112
weathercock, 3.2.15
weaver's beam, 5.1.20
Webster, Benjamin, p. 38n.
wee, 1.4.20
welkin, 1.3.86
well, 1.1.246
well-willers, 1.1.65

Wells, Stanley, pp. 58n., 65n.
Welsh goat, 5.5.137
what the dickens, 3.2.16
what the good-year, 1.4.115–16
what though, 1.1.253
what's your will, 2.2.150
whelm, 2.2.130
which is more, 2.2.73
which is pretty virginity, 1.1.41–2
White, R. S., p. 28n.
Whitehall, p. 4.
whiting-time, 3.3.124
whitsters, 3.3.13
wight, 1.3.20
will, 1.1.211; 1.3.45–6
Willard, Edmund, p. 36
Windsor Castle, pp. 1, 4, 5, 10, 23,
   52
Windsor Park, pp. 2, 23, 24
wink, 5.5.47
wise woman, 4.5.24
wit, 5.5.126
with the devil's name, 2.1.22–3
wittolly, 2.2.257
woodman, 5.5.26
word, 3.1.41
worm, 5.5.82
worthier, 4.4.87
worts, 1.1.111
would I might never stir, 5.5.185
would I were young for your sake,
   1.1.237–8
writes, 1.1.8
Württemberg, Frederick, Duke of,
   and Count Mömpelgard, pp. 5–6

yearn, 3.5.42
Yed Miller, 1.1.142
yellowness, 1.3.94
yoke, 2.1.160
yokes, 5.5.106
you do yourself wrong, 1.1.288–9
young ravens, 1.3.32
your friend, 1.4.133
youth in a basket, 4.2.106

242